Terminology and Phraseology in Research Papers in the Domains of New Technologies

ŁÓDŹ STUDIES IN LANGUAGE

Edited by Barbara Lewandowska-Tomaszczyk and Łukasz Bogucki

VOLUME 73

Aleksandra Beata Makowska

Terminology and Phraseology in Research Papers in the Domains of New Technologies

PETER LANG

Berlin - Bruxelles - Chennai - Lausanne - New York - Oxford

Bibliographic Information published by the Deutsche Nationalbibliothek
The Deutsche Nationalbibliothek lists this publication in the Deutsche Nationalbibliografie; detailed bibliographic data is available online at http://dnb.d-nb.de.

Library of Congress Cataloging-in-Publication Data
A CIP catalog record for this book has been applied for at the Library of Congress.

This publication was financially supported by the University of Lodz, Poland.

ISSN 1437-5281
ISBN 978-3-631-87320-5 (Print)
E-ISBN 978-3-631-91066-5 (E-PDF)
E-ISBN 978-3-631-91067-2 (E-PUB)
DOI 10.3726/b21321

Published by Peter Lang GmbH, Berlin, Deutschland

info@peterlang.com - www.peterlang.com

Table of Contents

Introduction 9

Chapter 1 Scientists as a community 13

1.1. Knowledge, science and technology in the modern world ... 13

1.2. Scientists as a community and the role of their language 18

1.2.1. Scientists as a community of practice 18

1.2.2. Scientists as a community of interests 21

1.2.3. Scientists as a speech community 24

1.2.4. Scientists as a discourse community 29

1.3. Concluding remarks to Chapter 1 31

Chapter 2 Scientific language and writing 33

2.1. Language as an instrument of knowledge transfer 33

2.1.1. The status of English in scientific writing 37

2.1.2. Drawing a borderline between a general and specialised language 43

2.1.3. Distinctive features of the scientific language 48

2.2. Scientific writing as specialised texts 55

2.2.1. The characteristics of scientific and technical texts 55

2.2.2. Hybridisation in the world of science 62

2.2.3. Pragmatic aspects of scientific writing 65

2.3. Research article as a text and genre 68

2.4. Concluding remarks to Chapter 2 74

Chapter 3 Terminology and phraseology in scientific writing 75

3.1. The status of terminology 75

3.2. Classifications of terms 78

3.3. Types of definitions and their implications for terminology 81

3.4. Polarisation between two approaches to terminology 86
3.4.1. The traditional approach to terminology 86
The onomasiological approach to terminology description 86
The clear-cut character of concepts 87
The synchrony principle 88
Definitions in the traditional approach 88
Monosemy 89
Standardisation of terminology 89
3.4.2. Cognitive approaches to terminology 93
Metaphorisation of terminology 93
Terminological synonymy 96
Terminological polysemy 100
3.4.3. Terminological prototypes and peripheries 103
3.4.4. Terminology in the frame-based approach 107
3.5. The connection between the interdisciplinarity of science and the project-specific terminology 111
3.6. Migration of terminology as a manifestation of interdisciplinarity 113
3.7. Multimodality in research papers 114
3.8. Manifestations of scientific terminology 116
3.8.1. Neologisms 117
3.8.2. Borrowings 121
3.8.3. Compression 123
3.9. Phraseology in scientific texts 125
3.9.1. Collocations in scientific writing 129
3.9.2. Multiword terms 131
3.10. Concluding remarks to Chapter 3 134
Chapter 4 Corpora in analyses of scientific writing 135
4.1. Corpora in analyses of specialised languages 135

4.2. Building specialised corpora for terminological and phraseological analyses 137

4.3. Terminological and phraseological data retrieval and analysis 141

4.4. Corpus linguistics in defining characteristic features of the scientific language 145

4.5. Building ontologies from terms extracted from a corpus 151

4.6. Concluding remarks to Chapter 4 155

Chapter 5 The MTCS corpus, its design, tools and methodology 157

5.1. Research material: the MTCS corpus of research articles 157

5.2. The MTCS corpus design 158

5.3. The tools used for the scrutiny 170

5.4. Text upload and MTCS corpus compilation 172

5.5. The aim of studies of the language of new technologies 174

5.6. Methodology 175

5.7. Concluding remarks to Chapter 5 182

Chapter 6 Macrostructure and multimodality of the MTCS research articles 183

6.1. The macrostructure of the MTCS research papers 183

6.2. Multimodality in the MTCS research papers 188

6.3. Concluding remarks to Chapter 6 201

Chapter 7 The scrutiny of MTCS terminology 203

7.1. The MTCS terminology: an overview 203

Overlaps of keyword terminology: 203

Syntactic characteristics 205

7.2. The interdisciplinary character of the MTCS research papers 205

7.3. Neologisms 207

7.4. Borrowings 213
7.5. Compression 215
7.6. Metaphorisation of MTCS terminology 220
7.7. Terminological synonymy 228
7.8. Polysemy 238
7.9. Standardisation of MTCS terminology 243
7.10. Definitions 248
7.11. The ontology of MTCS terminology 255
7.12. Concluding remarks to Chapter 7 258

Chapter 8 Phraseology in the MTCS research articles 261
8.1. Collocations in the MTCS research papers 261
8.2. Drawing a borderline between a collocation and a multiword term 265
8.3. Multiword terms 271
8.4. Lexical bundles in the MTCS research articles 277
8.5. Concluding remarks to Chapter 8 286

Chapter 9 Supplementary analysis of the MTCS research articles 289
9.1. Presence of the author in the MTCS scientific texts 289
9.2. Concluding remarks to Chapter 9 302

Final remarks 303

Bibliography 311

Appendix 1 337

Appendix 2 341

Introduction

Knowledge, science and technology and their transfer constitute factors which determine development in the modern world. Transfer of knowledge, referred to as transfer of powers, has transformed various spheres of human activity (Baumann, 1997: 728; Montgomery, 2000: 2–3). Moreover, language is a tool or an instrument, in the communication process, which enables the knowledge expansion (Olszewska, 2010; Grucza, 2015; Gajda, 1982). The emergence of new concepts and pushing the boundaries of the unknown bring about the development of specialised vocabulary (Temmerman, 2000). Due to its high level of abstraction, scientific writing is considered to be the most prestigious and complex.

Research results necessitate their validation in the permanent written form in carefully elaborated research articles, tailored to the needs of target readers published in peer-reviewed journals (Biber, 2006; Gajda, 1982; Rowland, 1999A, 1999B; Fathalla, 2004; Belt, Mottonen & Harkonen, 2011). Therefore, scientific writing is considered one of the formal stages in the completion of scientific work (Branson, 2004). By publishing results, scientists inform the public about their studies, pave the way for their research on the global scientific arena, and strengthen the position of their scientific institution (Todorović, 2003). As a result, scientific writing has taken the role of the scientists' spokesperson that communicates research results to the target audience which nowadays has become diversified due to easy Internet access to scientific texts (Pearson, 1998).

A scientific paper constitutes a report of all the stages of the conducted studies or even a product for sale (Branson, 2004; Belt et al., 2011). Yet, despite the accepted and widely-used IMRAD format, there are domain-specific modifications of the genre. There are differences with respects to the reasons of creating scientific texts, their language, symbols, graphics, and the constitution of the body of text, the expectations of the target audience, and the changing characteristics of readers since nowadays scientific texts are at their fingertips.

Moreover, the language of science is a reflection of the specificity of the subject field and the characteristics of its users. It also exerts influence on the general variety because scientists do not work in isolation from the society, but they are deeply involved in the education process of future professionals (Gajda, 1990). However, there is no agreement as to its place in the classification of natural language varieties as well as the status of scientific writing as specialised texts (Klemensiewicz, 1953; Wilkoń, 2000; Cabré, 1998). Language researchers cannot agree whether to treat scientific and technical communication as well as scientific and technical discourse as joint concepts or separate entities (Pérez-Llantada Aurìa, 2001; Iljinska & Smirnova, 2014).

Each scientific discipline develops its own, peculiar or domain-specific means of communication. However, disciplines have been evolving, becoming more interdisciplinary and detailed, and as a result hybridised (Dury, 2005; Iljinska & Smirnova, 2014). These trends pertain also to scientific texts and terminology, the latter being the most salient feature of the specialised language which acts as a vehicle in knowledge transfer (Sager et al., 1980; Mohammadi, 2013; Gajda, 1990; Montgomery, 2000). In addition, scientific communities communicate in linguistic patterns, using more or less fixed lexical units that are also specific to a given subject field which also perform important functions in meaning-making in texts (Postolea, 2014; Müldner-Nieckowski, 2016; Biber, 2006).

The current study attempts at providing a comprehensive analysis of the scientific variety in English in the empirical and practical disciplines of new technologies: microelectronics, telecommunication and computer science (MTCS). The main goal is to determine distinctive features of the language of new technologies used by researchers in the given disciplines. The major emphasis is placed on the characteristics af single and complex terms in a wide array of terminological aspects, such as borrowings, abbreviations, hybrids and neologisms used by international teams of scientists and engineers. The current study also aims at studying polysemy and synonymy in terminology as functional linguistic phenomena in specialised communication (Peason, 1998; Temmerman, 2000). Oh the other hand, the scrutiny also tries to establish the degree to which terminology is standardised. Another study's objective is to determine the terminological status of collocations and show the differences in the constitution and functions of phraseological units between the MTCS domains and other disciplines. This monograph also tries to verify whether the relatively young age of the MTCS domains and interdisciplinarity affect domain-specific terminology and phraseology. Finally, it investigates whether authors are present in these highly technical and empirical domains, which belong to hard sciences, and compares the results with soft sciences and how the authors maintain clarity, precision and conciseness of expression in order to communicate science within publishers' constraints.

The methodology adopted for the study is based on standard corpus linguistics techniques, such as keywords (keyword terminology), n-grams (lexical bundles), concordances and frequency lists which allow for providing a systematic and comprehensive description of the scientific language of technical and empirical disciplines of microelectronics, telecommunication and computer studies. The competitive advantage of corpus linguistics lies in the unique possibility of studying text corpora that are comprised of authentic texts collected according to a set of requirements. These analyses are conducted via dedicated computer programmes which enable the scrutiny of large amounts of textual data, which results in maintaining greater representativeness and reliability of obtained results. The generated keywords, concordances and frequency lists constitute excellent input data for further linguistic analyses. Quantitative analyses with the use of the corpus methodology and tools help reveal the hidden aspects of a given language which otherwise would remain unveiled. The study also entails the qualitative scrutiny which is performed on the basis of keyword terminology, concordances and n-grams generated from the MTCS corpus (compiled by the author) along with methods of analysing terminology and phraseology in order to expose typical tendencies in the terminology creation and use, as well as the terminological status of collocations and textual functions of phraseological units, all of which contribute to the successful transfer of knowledge in science.

The monograph is divided into nine chapters, four theoretical and five practical ones.

Chapter 1 discusses the importance of science and knowledge in the modern world and deals with scientists and engineers as an academic community analysed from different perspectives and relationships they form. These include the scientific community treated as a community of practice (CoP) which constitutes a point of departure for the notions of a sociorhetorical discourse community, speech community (SpCom), community of interests (CoI) and professional learning community (PLC).

Chapter 2 provides a general discussion on the scientific language and writing. The investigations begin with the patterns used in formal scientific communication. Then, the status of different languages in scientific publications is discussed. This chapter also attempts at contrasting scientific and technical communication, and delimiting the features of the language of new technologies. In addition, there is a comprehensive overview of text typologies in order to determine the place of technical scientific articles in the galaxy of functional texts. Finally, the characteristic features of the macrostructure of a research paper are explored.

Chapter 3 provides an overview of the concepts that constitute a framework for the scrutiny of terminology and phraseology in the language of new technologies. These include aspects of the two polarising approaches to terminology: the traditional and cognitive methods of studying terms. In addition, the chapter discusses manifestations of terminology and the issue of modality in scientific writing. Finally, it also concentrates on phraseology, from collocations via multiword terms up to non-idiomatic phraseological units.

Chapter 4 discusses corpora in studies of specialised languages, and terminological studies in particular. It also tackles the use of the corpus linguistics methodology in delimiting characteristic features of the scientific language as well as provides a theoretical framework for building ontologies from terminology generated via a dedicated computer programme.

Chapter 5 opens the practical part by discussing the details of collected and compiled scientific articles for the MTCS corpus, its design, and the upload stage. It also provides the aims of the study and the methodology applied to perform the analyses.

Chapter 6 presents details of the scrutiny of the macrostructure of the MTCS research articles. The chapter concentrates on the structure of the research paper as well as the use of multimodal elements.

Chapter 7 shows the details of empirical analyses of MTCS terminology. They are focused on the cognitive aspects of technical terminology contrasted with the problem of standardisation. It also presents the analysis of definitions which are compared with the corpus realisations and a dedicated terminological standard (IEC). Finally, the author developed an ontology for the MTCS terminological system on the basis of keyword terminology along with the corpus and dictionary definitions.

Chapter 8 contains the analysis of the MTCS phraseology which entails collocations and their terminological status, followed by multiword terms and ending with non-idiomatic phraseological units.

Chapter 9 is the supplementary analysis of the authorial presence in the research articles contrasted with other studies on the subject.

The last chapter is followed by Final Remarks which contain conclusions drawn from the conducted study and obtained results. The monograph ends with the bibliography and appendices. Figures, tables and examples have a separate numeration for each chapter. In addition, the author performed all translations from Polish and German into English in order to facilitate understanding of the text.

Chapter 1 Scientists as a community

The current chapter deals with scientific circles as a community communicating via specific language, and thus contributing to progress in science. The discussion starts with roles of knowledge, science and technology as factors determining developments in the modern world. Knowledge transfer, also called transfer of powers, has revolutionised various spheres of human activity (Baumann, 1997; Montgomery, 2000). Moreover, language is treated as a tool or an instrument in knowledge expansion. As new concepts emerge, they push the boundaries and bring about the creation of specialised vocabulary as well as unique linguistic patterns.

Additionally, the chapter concentrates on scientists and engineers as a community that has developed and uses unique means of communication which reflect the specific character of their work. The language they use in their writing reflects the individual aspects of a community. Since scientists and engineers work on novel solutions, they need new names for new concepts and new ways of explaining unfamiliar phenomena. The point of departure in the analysis of academia is the concept of a community of practice (CoP) (Wenger, 1998), which constitutes the base for other types of communities, i.e. speech community (SpCom) (Gumperz, 1968; Swales, 1990), sociorhetorical discourse community (Swales, 1990), community of interests (CoI) (Henri & Pudelko, 2003), or professional learning community(PLC) (Owen, 2014; Servage, 2009; Roberts & Pruit, 2003).

1.1. Knowledge, science and technology in the modern world

The development of the modern civilisation is the pursuit to self-cognition and the cognition of reality (Gajda, 1990: 8). Talking about the expansion of human cognitive boundaries necessitates the usage of three notions, i.e. knowledge, science and technology. These three interconnected ideas are the foundations of the modern civilisation which influence people's lives and bring invaluable profits, because countries' welfare is measured on the grounds of its scientific and technological advances.

Knowledge is an invaluable and powerful resource that scientists possess and constantly expand, which brings measurable benefits, defined as 'information, facts, data, know-how, and experience', or 'the result of the exploring subject's activities', containing three aspects: informational, methodological and axiological (Grucza, 2015; Simavi, Tangri & Grigorov, 2013: 7; Gajda, 2001: 184). Gajda (2001) also distinguishes ideal knowledge, the main goal of the scientific activity aimed at reaching 'factual or verifiable knowledge that reflects a certain state of affairs', which is hard to achieve (2001: 184)'. On the other hand, Simavi et al. (2013) divide knowledge into explicit and tacit. The first type 'can be codified and written down to be shared' in an unidirectional way via 'written knowledge materials', e.g. research papers or books', whereas the latter is defined as unsaid and not formalised knowledge. Grucza (2013) looks at the problem from the scientists' perspective as individuals and distinguishes idioknowledge and polyknowledge (terms being a hybrid, but giving insights into the problem). The first type is 'the specific individuals', or specialists', knowledge on the subject that is their own immanent feature' which is the creation or reconstruction of one's own expertise (Grucza, 2013: 114)', whereas the latter the author (2013) defines as the sum or the logical cross-section of a given set of specialist idioknowledges (2013: 115). In other words, the 'polyknowledges' are intersections of 'knowledges'[1] possessed by given individual specialists, but not the logical sums of specialist idioknowledges. However, Grucza's (2013) explanations of the terms are complex mathematical metaphors which might cause confusion.

Science in turn is 'knowledge about the world, especially based on examining, testing, and proving facts'[2], or as 'one of the most effective ways of acquiring new knowledge about the world (…) and its transfer to the society (Gajda, 2001: 183)', which is the result of the scientific intellectual aura (Gajda, 2013: 62). Moreover, Olohan (2016) states that the notion denotes practical and intellectual activities that embrace studies of a systematic nature concerning the way the physical and natural world is structured and how it behaves (2016: 6). According to Godin & Gingras (2000), science has two aspects: methods of investigating objects and knowledge deriving from these activities (2000: 44). For Gajda (1990) science is a specific human activity based on the 'cognition of reality, which results in scientific knowledge' and contains a few elements, i.e. 'people and institutions involved, the cognitive process itself, scientific knowledge and scientific literature that records it (Gajda, 1990: 8–9)'.

Science can be further divided into types, depending on their subjects and aims as well as it has different levels of idealisation, with empirical and natural

1 The ungrammatical use of plural with regard to the noun *knowledge* is a conscious translation of the ungrammatical Polish solution proposed by Grucza (2013: 114–115). The Polish noun *wiedza /knowledge/* does not have a plural form either.

2 https://www.ldoceonline.com/dictionary/science, 11.11.2018.

sciences occupying lowest levels. The division based on subjects, and objects being a part of the set of subjects may be misleading, because 'two or even more different sciences may be interested in the same set of objects, but having different features or functions (Grucza, 2017B: 21)'. The MTCS domains are interconnected, deal with the same objects from different perspectives, which is reflected in Grucza's (2017B) findings that sciences are elements mutually tied with intersecting interests. Moreover, science is linked with practice, and the notions which are mutually connected, which is illustrated by the author (2017B) in Figure 1.1. below:

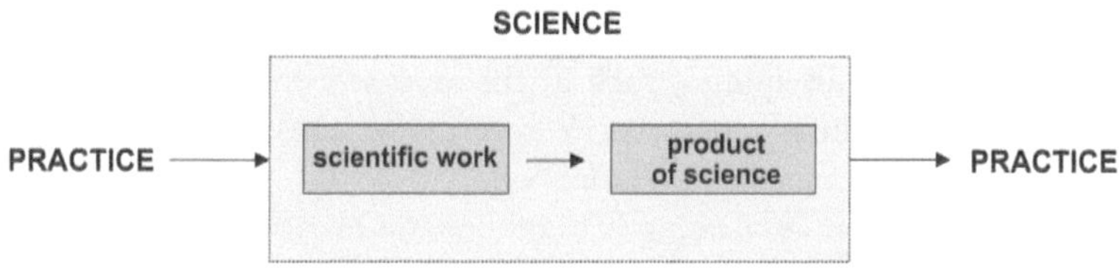

Figure 1.1.: Grucza's (2017B) illustration of the relationships between science and practice (2017B: 36)

Therefore, scientific work is creative and cognitive, which aims at the cognition of the subject of study, as well as transferential which concentrates on passing the knowledge to the public. On the other hand, there are practical aspects of science, but these refer to its products. This division is linked to two simple categories, i.e. the basic one that leads to the creation of new knowledge and the applied one that 'explores the unknown' and 'develops new technologies (Richter, 1995: 4)'. However, new technologies are developed either during fundamental or strategic research.

Finally, technology is for Olohan (2016) scientific knowledge in industrial applications. It is defined as 'a human activity which transforms the reality (natural and social) in a creative way (...) on the basis of the scientific knowledge as well as by the means of specific technological knowledge (Gonzalez, 2005: 9)'. The result of these intersubjective activities is a visible or tangible product. Godin & Gingras's definition (2000), however, is the most comprehensive and embraces all elements mentioned: machinery, artefacts and knowledge (2000: 44). In addition, Richter (1995) links technology to applied, fundamental and strategic research in which scientists 'explore the unknown and solve problems (1995: 4)'.

The three notions are interconnected, as each has an impact on the other, which is reflected in their definitions. However, the first two are abstract, whereas the latter is considered to be a real or tangible product of the two or the 'real artifact', which can take the form of a registered patent (Gonzalez, 2005: 11). Richter (1995) believes they are strictly connected, and it is useless to determine if 'science creates technology or technology creates science', because 'today's technology is based on yesterday's science and today's science is based on today's technology', which leads to a 'spiral of science', a spinning wheel driving the two notions (1995: 3). However, the subordinate position of science is emphasised, but questioned and technology is placed on leading position depending on the viewpoint (Olohan, 2016: 6–7; Gonzalez, 2005: 9–12). Therefore, the term technoscience prevails mainly in European literature, which emphasises the interaction between the notions and their interconnected character (Gonzalez, 2005: 8–10). Moreover, close relationships between science and technology create new scientific disciplines, such as the analysed domains, whose names reflect the interdisciplinary character (Wenger, 1998: 115), e.g. *microelectronics*, *telecommunication*, or *information technology*.

Knowledge transfer, i.e. passing it to others and broadening one's horizons, is seen as 'the transfer of certain powers', which are in fact the 'powers of imagination and practice' bringing benefits from its exchange (Simavi et al., 2013: 8–10; Montgomery, 2000: 2). Benefits for knowledge providers include creating new relationships with other countries, which facilitate economic and political cooperation. Moreover, donor countries improve their global image, and 'present themselves as centers of development and innovation' who via the exchange 'receive valuable feedback' which allows for the validation of the results and looking at a given project from other perspectives (Simavi et al., 2013: 9). As a result, knowledge sharing helps to expand the existing knowledge stock and to adapt technology to local conditions at a modest expense.

Moreover, science improves country's competitiveness and gives it economic security measured in terms of 'the deficit, technology policy, competitiveness, supporting high-tech industry due to the scientific revolution (Suchodolski, 1979: 32; Richter, 1995: 2; Reinbothe, 2011). As a result, scientific institutions are strongly encouraged to cooperate with the industry and civil society organisations, which becomes one of the key objectives (Richter, 1995: 6; European Commission, 2007: 7). The European Union promotes such activities since they allow them to remain ahead of the key players on the global market. Close collaboration with business and other international institutions brings benefits, such as new students, acclaimed researchers, additional income and prestige, which 'may well give an important boost to both quantity and quality of the research undertaken (European Commission, 2007: 7)'. Many innovations are currently being developed at the companies' R&D departments, often in cooperation with academia. Therefore, scientific institutions need to establish active relationships with the industry 'in order to maximize the use of the research results (European Commission, 2007: 7)'. Thus, the emphasis is placed on practical aspects of scientific research, which the analysed domains of new technologies fully fulfil.

However, the role of knowledge, science and technology should not be reduced only to the country- or the institution-level, as they also affect average people's lives (Suchodolski, 1979). Without scientific advances and technological solutions all spheres of human lives would be poorer (Richter, 1995). Therefore, the OECD countries treat creating a scientific and technological culture as an objective in their scientific and technological policies, because social misunderstanding of science, or scientific illiteracy, can bring detrimental results (Godin & Gingras, 2000: 43–44; Gajda, 1999). Hence, the role of the popular-scientific discourse has become increasingly socially important. The way the society perceives science will determine modernity, because its social support depends only on its understanding (Gajda, 1999: 14; Wyroba, 2005: 211). 'The public understanding of science' is built on two levels: individual and social (Godin & Gingras, 2000). In terms of the first, every individual contributes to the popularisation of science: managers by investing in research and providing training for their subordinates, workers by knowing how to use the technology, teachers who pass knowledge and develop students' abilities, parents who awaken their children's interests for science and technology, and finally average people who are up-to-date with the latest technology (Godin & Gingras, 2000). On the other hand, scientific and technological awareness is built at the social level, where different institutions have their share in the creation of the scientific and technological culture, such as universities, state laboratories or companies dealing with new technologies, 'other educational institutions, research funding agencies, risk-capital companies, scientific and engineering associations, consulting firms, technical repair and maintenance shops', but also 'ministries, consulting organizations, teaching establishments at all levels, the media, museums, public libraries, scientific leisure clubs, and organizations devoted to the promotion and diffusion of science and technology' (Godin & Gingras, 2000; Reinbothe, 2011). As a result, science has become 'people's common experience', because scientific education is a important part of people's professional career (Suchodolski, 1979: 32–33). Science and technology are not only means, but precious values that shape lifestyles that have led to the emergence of the new intellectual community (Moles, 1962in Suchodolski, 1979: 34).

In conclusion, knowledge, science and technology are notions that are mutually connected and interdependent. The first two concentrate on more theoretical aspects and the third deals with practical applications of the two. The importance of the three can be measured at different levels: global, national and individual. Therefore, a lot of emphasis is put on knowledge expansion, scientific development and technological advances. As a result, countries strive to create a scientific and technological culture (Godin & Gingras, 2000) in the society so that the group of people who work in these fields, i.e. scientists and engineers, are provided with favourable circumstances or working conditions in order to contribute the overall success of the country and society. Moreover, analysing different aspects of the scientific community allows for a better understanding of their work, the relationships inside the group, and more importantly the language they communicate in as well as their contribution to progress.

1.2. Scientists as a community and the role of their language

Scientists constitute a group of people who share a passion for exploring unexplored areas in different fields and gain the utmost degree of expertise. They either work individually or in research groups on novel solutions which facilitate technological advances, and they contribute to the increase in the country's welfare, which in the end improves the quality of people's lives (Fathalla, 2004: 13). The other branch of their activities involves teaching university students and coaching PhD students who are to become future professionals and scientific staff. The fact that they deal with highly specialised domains and state-of-the-art technology determine their interests, goals and language.

Scientists form a community of specialists that can be labelled with a number of names: community of practice (CoP), sociorhetorical discourse community, speech community (SpCom), or community of interests (CoI), depending on the aspect of the group that is emphasised: the characteristics of the community, professional activities, professional development as teachers or the language they develop and use.

1.2.1. Scientists as a community of practice

The whole community of scientists share a set of characteristics and form one unit to be able to be analysed as a community of practice (CoP). Scientists and researchers 'share a concern, a set of problems, or a passion about the topic, and deepen their knowledge and expertise in this area on an ongoing basis (Wenger, McDermott & Snyder, 2002: 4 in Agrifoglio, 2015: 26)', which contributes to 'knowledge creation, knowledge sharing and identification (Katzy & Ma in Agrifoglio, 2015: 26)', and as a result, to the 'development of social capital (Lesser & Storck, 2001: 833)'. It is Wenger (1998) who provides scientists communicating with colleagues in laboratories as an example of a community of practice, but he does not provide a clear division within the internal structure of the scientific community. Therefore, the whole scientific community can be either treated as one big community of practice, or each research group and scientists specialising in a given field can be analysed separately as sub-communities of practice, because 'this universe of discourse is far from being monolithic or uniform in form (Livnat, 2012: 21)'.

Membership in this work-related or interest-related group is voluntary, as academic circles gather around a selected field of study (domain) in order to broaden their knowledge on the subject, by collaborating and interacting with themselves, which is referred to as 'social participation (Lesser & Storck, 2001: 832; Agrifoglio, 2015: 27)'. Wenger (1998) defines it as the 'embodied, delicate, active, social, negotiated, complex process of participation (1998: 49)'. Moreover, unlike teams and task forces which are established only to accomplish a certain assignment, communities of practice, 'do not have launching and dismissal dates' (1998: 96). The authority arises by the interaction between members and communities are 'only responsible to their members (Lesser & Storck, 2001: 832)'.

In order to form a community of practice, scientists need to share defined characteristics, i.e. the domain, the community and the practice (Wenger-Trayner & Wenger-Trayner, 2015). Members of the community of practice must be committed to the domain, as the 'shared competence' is the distinguishing feature of the community (Wenger-Trayner & Wenger-Trayner, 2015: 2), for example scientists specialising in mastering a given field of study and mastering a set of indispensable skills.

The second characteristic is the community which can be defined as the relationships between the members that facilitate the expansion of knowledge, for instance the distinction within the group into more, less experienced and versed scientists. Competencies may be complementary and overlapping, which means that researchers share domain knowledge and specialise in narrow areas within the domain. Moreover, the idea of community does not entail homogeneity, but rather diversity, in which members need to learn how to deal with conflicts and difficult situations (Wenger, 1998: 76–77). As a consequence, heterogeneity of the group is a frequent phenomenon since scientists in the fields of new technologies work in multinational groups on international projects. The common goal or the joint enterprise in a scientific community, which in this case is the result of research, is the bond that ties the group together.

The third feature is the concept of practice which Wenger-Trayner & Wenger-Trayner (2015) define as 'a shared repertoire of resources: experiences, stories, tools, ways of addressing recurring problems (2015: 2)', but for Wenger (1998) it comprises 'the implicit and the tacit', i.e. 'what is said and what is left unsaid; what is represented and what is assumed (1998: 47)'. The notion 'includes the language, the tools, the documents, images, symbols, well-defined roles, specified criteria, codified procedures, regulations and contracts (1998: 47)' which can be interpreted as scientists' expertise, research tools and materials, documentation, reports, contracts, the scientists' roles in a group or ways of conducting research. In addition, Wenger (1998) defines the tacit elements, i.e. 'implicit relations, tacit conventions, subtle cues, untold rules of thumb, recognizable intuitions, specific perceptions, well-tuned sensitivities, embodied understandings, underlying assumptions and shared world-views', i.e. all the elements that are known subconsciously, instinctively or are taken for granted or something that 'comes naturally (1998: 47)'. These can be understood in the world of science as knowledge, unwritten rules, or elements which the scientists are somehow aware of, but are left unsaid, which are, however, limited in number as the discussed group's role is to explain the inexplicable and explore the unexplored.

Practice is characterised by three dimensions: 'mutual engagement, a joint enterprise and a shared repertoire (Wenger, 1998: 73)'. The first dimension defines the characteristics of practice which 'exists because people are engaged in actions whose meanings they negotiate with one another (1998: 73)', which entails work of the whole scientific community and 'involves not only our competence, but also the competence of others' as well as 'the contributions and knowledge of others (1998: 76)'. In the case of the scientific community, mutual engagement can be understood as research to which all members contribute in terms of their competencies, knowledge and expertise and negotiate, cooperate and interact with each other in order to make further developments or achieve their goals. The second characteristics feature – joint enterprise – constitutes a bond that joins the community which in the case of scientists can be understood as research results that are being expected and finally achieved (1998: 80). However, communities operate in 'historical, cultural institutional' contexts containing 'specific resources and constraints (1998: 79)'. The results of conducted research are a part of a broader system and their academic institutions keep control over their work. The third feature is the shared repertoire and 'includes routines, words, tools, ways of doing things, stories, gestures, symbols, genres, actions or concepts that the community has produced or adopted in the course of its existence, and which have become part of its practice (1998: 83)'. Every scientific community has developed its own 'set of shared resources' – elements typical for each sub-community (1998: 83).

Meaning plays a vital role in CoPs as it is a part of practice and it is understood as 'an experience of everyday life (1998: 53)', which in the hard sciences can be understood as the reflection of phenomena occurring in the world in the scientific work. In science, negotiation of meaning, one of the processes connected with meaning, might entail creating new solutions as it involves the production of 'a new situation, an impression, an experience'.

Membership in a community of practice is not fixed (Wenger, 1998: 99): new members are admitted, the less experienced are 'integrated into the community' and old members leave the structures, which is a reflection of the professional life cycle in any academic institution. In terms of the internal structure of the scientific sub-communities of practice, members can be divided into two types, i.e. old-timers and newcomers. The first group is comprised of experienced scientists, well-established and renowned worldwide, being an authority in a given field of studies who are 'more experienced members', i.e. acknowledged scientists who are 'involved in increasingly complicated tasks (Agrifoglio, 2015: 27)' who perform reproductive transferential work as teachers and creative cognitive and transferential work as scientists (Grucza, 2017: 30). The latter group consists of novice researchers, PhD students or university students who want to improve their skills and expand their knowledge on the subject, and as such perform cognitive absorptive work as learners (Grucza, 2017 A: 30).

All in all, the scientific community taken as a whole or analysed individually as sub-communities meet criteria required to be assigned to communities of practice. Scientists' work revolves around expanding knowledge, participating in group work and conducting research, which can be broadly understood as practice. However, the research itself can be the focal point in the analysis of every scientific sub-community, and the project group in particular.

1.2.2. Scientists as a community of interests

The concept of a community of interest (CoI) derives from the notion community of practice, as members from various CoPs or representatives of other communities are 'assembled around a topic of common interest (Henri & Pudelko, 2003: 478)'. Fischer (2001A) considers a community of interests to be a group gathered 'to solve a particular (design) problem of common concern', and pertains to interdisciplinary heterogeneous teams formed to complete a project, research or design. According to Henri & Pudelko (2003), it pertains to a group of individuals possessing unique knowledge who share it with other participants, which is the case of members of interdisciplinary scientific project or research groups. Even in the monodisciplinary teams there are individuals who specialise in specific sub-domains, but members do not necessarily 'share their individually appropriate knowledge' on a regular basis (Henri & Pudelko,

2003: 478). Such knowledge gained through participation is 'more personal than collective', and participation in the community's activities is closer to peripheral in the CoPs (Henri & Pudelko, 2003: 478). Learning takes place on an individual basis: the knowledgeable pass directly their unique knowledge and ideas that has not been accessible elsewhere to those in want of broadening their horizons (Fischer, 2000: 528).

Depending on the type of activity the community is engaged in, there are three forms of exchanges (Henri & Pudelko, 2003). The first type, the most common among scientists and engineers, is action centred which emerges to perform the project. The second type is project oriented topic which is devoted to 'topic definition and elaboration (Henri & Pudelko, 2003: 479)'. This type occurs in the initial stage of forming a scientific CoI. Finally, group procedures management can be observed when the group defines the formal organisation of its functioning after the group's emergence.

Communication in such a community may be distorted, as the community is built from diverse individuals, who have different perspectives and vocabulary, but 'shared understanding', and compromise is reached as the project progresses. As a result, the community 'has great potential to be more innovative and more transforming than a single CoP', on the condition that they can use the 'symmetry of ignorance' as an 'opportunity for creativity' by taking advantage of the diversity, 'because stakeholders belonging to different cultures use different cultures, different norms, symbols and representations, which leads to the creation of new boundary objects, or the extensions of existing human knowledge in different domains. (Fischer, 2000: 527–528; Fischer, 2001A: 4)'.

Creativity is an indispensable feature of analysed scientific communities, understood as the psychological creativity (opposed to historical) – 'personally novel and meaningful to stakeholders', because 'knowledge workers and designers have to engage in creative activities to cope with the unforeseen complexities of everyday, real-world tasks (Fischer, 2000: 527)'. For example, in R&D teams in the domains of new technologies, members often apply knowledge from well-established and traditional domains, like mathematics, science and engineering on the one hand, but also 'create new knowledge in the course of understanding the unique aspects of their problems (Fischer, 2000: 527)'.

While working on a project, scientists, engineers and designers often refer to other professionals' expertise, because the majority of projects they are involved in are 'complex systemic problems', which are characterised by a set of features:

- problems for which *expertise and knowledge is widely distributed* (…)
- problems of a *magnitude* such that individuals and even large teams cannot solve (…)

- problems of a *systemic nature* requiring the collaboration of many different minds from a variety of background (…) (Fischer, 2014: 201).

As a result, the use of '*multiple* knowledge systems and multiple centers' results in members' meaningful participation in and contribution to the project, production of high-quality artefacts and contextualised thorough information about the project (Fischer, 2001A: 5–6; 2000: 528–529).

The community is also characterised by 'a variable lifespan', either are ephemeral or more permanent in terms of existence (Henri & Pudelko, 2003: 478). For example, scientists may be engaged to conduct only a short-term project or sign perennial contracts to perform complex studies. Moreover, community emerges when the problem or the project arises and its existence depends on the completion of the research or project, or can be described as fixed (Fischer, 2001B; Henri & Pudelko, 2003: 479). Nevertheless, some projects prove to be long lasting or are designed to be in operation for a long time, such as the ones created at CERN, DESY or ITER research centres (some of which being at first large-scale research projects), where one can distinguish examples of communities of interest gathered in these large R&D institutes. International research centres, like ITER, DESY or CERN, have emerged to facilitate research and technological advances in hard sciences. Design workers, either from academic or industrial circles, form international design groups that work on a given task. Team members of various origins and diverse cultures collaborate on projects, e.g. build devices and appliances, develop dedicated software, and perform experiments and measurements in order to verify their ideas or implement invented software or appliances. ITER in France is the largest fusion reactor in the world, built in collaboration of 35 nations and thousands engineers and scientists engaged in designing and building the only energy project of its kind in the world[3] (Claessens, 2020). Another research centre – DESY in Hamburg – is the place where 3000 guest researchers from 40 countries conduct research in its accelerators and professionals are trained. Here, academia also have the opportunity to cooperate with business and industry on state-of-the-art technologies that will be beneficial for the society.[4] Finally, CERN is the centre for nuclear research where 'the world's largest and most complex scientific instruments' are available to researchers and professionals to conduct their studies and experiments. According to the report from 31 December 2017, there were 1229 scientists and engineers

3 https://www.iter.org/, 10.09.2018.
4 http://www.desy.de/about_desy/desy/index_eng.html, 10.09.2018.

and 890 technical workers from 27 countries engaged in scientific activities at CERN[5].

To sum up, members of research groups, forming hybrid communities of interest, are of different nationalities, backgrounds, languages, culture, knowledge, experience. Collaborating on an interdisciplinary task or project, they develop common knowledge and find a compromise. By participating in the community's activities, they create common understanding by benefiting from community's diversity, which provides spaces for broadening horizons and expanding human knowledge. Another manifestation of their collaboration is the language that they use, which is a basis for further studies, e.g. scientists forming a discourse or a speech community, both of which will be discussed in the forthcoming sections of the chapter.

1.2.3. Scientists as a speech community

The analysis of the scientific community can also be focused on the linguistic rules or 'patterned regularities in the *use* of language' that the scientists employ, and as such they can be treated as a speech community (Bloomfield, 1933; Fishman, 1971 in Swales, 1990: 23). The term is defined by Bloomfield (1933) as 'a group of people who interact by means of speech (1933: 42)'. However, this definition is very general, and it has been considered insufficient, unsatisfactory and limited by other specialists on the subject (Patrick, 2004: 578–579; Hymes, 1972: 54; Morgan, 2004: 3; Wardhaugh, 2006: 122). Moreover, Hymes (1972) emphasises confusion caused by reducing 'the notion of a speech community to that of a language' and proposes the functionalist approach, which focuses on the contextualised use of language (Johnstone & Marcellino, 2010), and reflects the way scientists use the language to communicate science (Hymes, (1972: 47).

The key features of a speech community are linguistic norms and a social structure of the community (Gumperz, 1968; Hymes, 1972; Wardhaugh, 2006; Patrick, 2004). Patrick (2004) also mentions a 'persistent link between community and language form' discussed in Sapir and Whorf's findings (2004: 577), which is noticeable in the way scientists communicate. It also includes 'a shared set of norms, local knowledge, beliefs and values (Morgan, 2004; Wardhaugh, 2006: 124)'. As a result, scientist share and expand knowledge in their domain, believe in scientific methods, conduct research and share some of the views.

---

5 https://cds.cern.ch/record/2317058/files/CERN-HR-STAFF-STAT-2017-RESTR.pdf, 10.09.2018.

Hymes (1972) provides two necessary conditions that a community needs to meet in order to be considered a speech community, i.e. it is 'a community sharing rules for the conduct and interpretation of speech, and rules for the interpretation of at least one linguistic variety (1972: 54)'. Thus, on the one hand, the definition restricts the use of language, but it allows the existence of linguistic differences on the other. Scientific communities meet both of these criteria as scientists develop their own verbal communicative means and linguistic varieties are common since the community consists of members of various nationalities and cultures. Moreover, Gumperz (1968) compares speech community to a 'socially defined universe' and concentrates his definition on the linguistic aspects, and the referential function in particular. Therefore, a speech community is 'any human aggregate characterized by regular and frequent interaction by a means of shared body of verbal signs and set off from similar aggregates by significant differences in language usage (1968: 43)'. This definition allows for identifying the language scientific communities develop and use as a distinct body of verbal and non-verbal means of communication. Language is of the utmost importance not only in communication, but also in 'meaningful participation in society and culture (Gumperz, 1968; Morgan, 2004: 1)'. Thus, speech communities 'are groups that share values and attitudes about language use, varieties and practices' who 'develop through prolonged interaction among these who operate within these shared and recognised beliefs and value systems regarding forms and styles of communication (Morgan, 2004: 1)'. As a result, Morgan's definition best describes scientists as a speech community.

However, Wardhaugh (2006) points out definition problems, because the concept of speech community revolves around 'groups of speakers' who are difficult to determine and define, because people gather for a variety of reasons, groups' existence may be varied, so is the geographical proximity (2006: 119). As a result, scientific communities are diversified in terms of age, sex, gender, nationality or culture, and group together mainly for vocational reasons. Moreover, groups' existence may either be permanent or temporary and members meet either face-to-face, or via modern means of communication. On the other hand, Morgan (2004) provides a list of criteria by which communities can be defined and classified, i.e. 'space, place, affiliation, practices', as well as different combinations of these factors (2004: 2). Therefore, the author (2004) allows for including national, international and online groups to the community with 'no physical, visual or auditory contact', but emphasises that members must share some characteristics in order to be a part of the community. In the case of scientific circles, scientists gather around conducting research and expanding knowledge. The inclusion into the research group depends more on one's expertise than on the geographical proximity, therefore meetings are frequently held online. Moreover, Morgan (2004) emphasises people's increased mobility which results in social changes as people's 'relationships and interactions continue and change, and are sustained through the use of evolving technology and media', which 'enhances, recognises and re-creates communities (2004: 1–2)'. This goes in alliance with Martín-Martín's (2003) study which provides a criterion to distinguish a speech community from the discourse community which is the 'physical proximity (2003: 154)'. Moreover, Swales (1990) sees a speech community as centripetal, which means that it integrates its members into one big group (Swales, 1990: 24; Martín-Martín, 2003: 154). As a result, modern scientific communities gather around both expertise and the subject of research, and members from distant scientific institutions are invited to collaborate. As group members specialise in a given field, they tend to develop a specific 'language, discourse and verbal styles (Morgan, 2004: 2)'.

Increased mobility of scientific communities may be linked to Hymes' ideas of language field and speech field (Hymes, 1972: 55). Scientists using English (in the case of the domains of new technologies) as a lingua franca travel to distant places in order to conduct research, and they are able to communicate effectively. Speech network is a subordinate term for the speech field and embraces 'the specific linkages of persons through shared varieties and speaking rules across communities (Hymes, 1972: 55)'. Therefore, scientists form an international community with different first languages and have contacts with other people, members of other communities sharing the same language or variety.

Moreover, Hymes (1972) distinguishes very general categories and subcategories, like speech situations, speech events, speech acts, speech styles, ways of speaking and components of speech that are common phenomena. Speech situations are 'situations associated with (or marked by the absence of speech, such as ceremonies and meals, or others, like conferences) (Hymes, 1972: 56)'. Speech events refer to 'activities, or aspects of activities, that are directly governed by rules or norms for the use of speech (Hymes, 1972: 56)', which may be narrowed to conversations, lectures or conference presentations in the academic circles. A speech act 'represents a level distinct from the sentence, and not identifiable with any single portion of other levels of grammar, nor segments of any particular size defined in terms of other levels of grammar' which 'implicates both linguistic form and social norms (Hymes, 1972: 56–57)', e.g. greetings, commands, or oaths. The status of the utterance may depend on the 'conventional formula' or social relationships between the interlocutors. Speech styles are understood as a 'statistical frequency of elements already given in the linguistic description or as a deviation from some norm given by such description'e.g. scientific language is characterised by the extensive use of the Passive Voice in English in order to achieve objectivity of the message (Hymes, 1972: 57; Hyland, 2009 A; Gajda, 1982, 2001; Maćkiewicz, 1996; Wytrębowicz, 2009). On the other hand, scientific texts in both languages contain nouns with very complex attributives, which is rather uncommon in the general language. Ways of speaking is the most 'primitive term' which is 'the communicative behaviour' or 'the communicative competence of persons (Hymes, 1972: 58)'. Since scientists' work depends on the written language, they possess extensive vocabulary and a wide range of forms of expression.

Gumperz (1968) assumes the existence of linguistic varieties within one community which the author calls a verbal repertoire. Narrowing the term to the scientific language/register, scientists form 'a linguistically heterogeneous group speaking regionally differentiated varieties (Kerswill, 1994: 37 in Patrick, 2004: 592)'. Moreover, it can be observed that it consists of specialised idiolects (actual languages of every individual scientist) (Grucza, 2009, 2013) as every scientist perceives the world in their own peculiar/idiosyncratic way (academia are comprised of great individuals/minds), which is reflected in their writing (thus providing the proof for the connection with the Sapir and Whorf's theory). This individual linguistic variety within the community can be connected with the linguistic range, i.e. 'the total amount of purely linguistic differentiation that exists in a community (Gumperz, 1968)'. Moreover, scientists being a part of a research team within the scientific institution, they develop a language specific only to this organisation, or more broadly taken, scientists of one nationality create a scientific polylect – a sum of all scientific idiolects (Grucza, 2009, 2013) (which will be discussed in section 2.1 in the next chapter). As a result, the whole scientific speech community is characterised by the 'heterogeneity of production and homogeneity of norms (Labov, 1982: 50 in Patrick, 2004: 591)'.

On the other hand, later studies on the subject allow the existence of multilingual and/or international speech communities. As a result, certain languages have been considered 'contact languages'. Treating a scientific community as an international speech community, one can draw parallelisms to multilingual communities, such as immigrants: a lingua franca (English) can be understood as a contact language and the language choice depends more on the prestige and urge to reach wider audience (to promote research, improve a citation index, etc.). Moreover, Gumperz (1968) claims that certain languages take precedence over others (called by the author language loyalty). This phenomenon can be traced in the analysed scientific speech community, where the language most often chosen for the international communication is English, gaining a status of a new Latin in scientific texts in the analysed domains (which will be discussed in section 2.1.1. in the next chapter). In a multinational community, there are varieties in the way the lingua franca is used, and scientists' mother tongues exert an influence on English, giving way to a variety called International English (Gumperz, 1968; Wardhaugh, 2006). These aberrations or varieties are copied and merge by spreading worldwide via scientific writing. This mixing and blending, which does not allow to draw clear borderlines, is referred by Gumperz (1968) as compartmentalization. However, Hymes finds this 'diversity of speech' within the community problematic in certain areas of life, such as 'education, national development, transcultural communication (1972: 38)'.

Furthermore, dealing with unexplored areas and new concepts that require new names leads to a 'transitional polysemy', as individual researchers give different names to the same new concepts until one finally becomes an established term, which is another source of variations (Dury, 2005). In addition, code-switching is also a common phenomenon in scientific writing. Terms that appear in the majority language are often borrowed into the minority language, e.g. (Example (1.3.) below)

(1.3.) *CMOS (complementary metal-oxide semiconductor*) – abbreviation that stands for the full name of the technology of producing integrated circuits.

However, code-switching is used because the minority language has not developed the equivalent of a new term yet. On the other hand, in some bilingual communities it serves as a manifestation of shared identity or distinction from other speakers (Wardhaugh, 2006: 123).

Another feature of a specialised language, including the scientific language is the restriction of topics and types of interactions. According to Gumperz (1968), social appropriateness is not as important as their function. Research papers are written to communicate research results to the public and to serve as textbooks in the process of educating professionals, so its primary functions are informative and/or referential.

In conclusion, language is one of the distinctive features of scientists and engineers specialising in domains of new technologies. Therefore, this professional group can be treated as a speech community since their unique linguistic means meet the criteria set by specialists on the subject. Their language within their professional environment should be subject to further scrutiny, which will be described in the following chapters of the monograph.

1.2.4. Scientists as a discourse community

Language, one of the disctinctive features of a scientific community, 'is a form of social behaviour' and the 'discourse is a means of maintaining and extending the group's knowledge and of initiating the new members into the group' as well as it is 'epistemic or constitutive of the group's knowledge (Herzberg, 1986: 1 in Swales, 1990: 21)'. In this sense, the notion of discourse community is similar to community of practice as it revolves around knowledge and knowledge sharing between researchers, as well as inciting the involvement of new members in the group (Swales, 1990). However, in the case of the discourse community, it is the discourse that determines the community, whereas in the latter (community of practice), it is the community that shapes the discourse (Swales, 1988: 212). As a result, scientific language the key feature that allows for treating a scientific community as a discourse community and at the same time the scientists create and use a language that makes them a speech community. The notions differ with respects to their character, 'speech communities are centripetal (they pull people in) whilst discourse communities are centrifugal (they set people, or parts of people, apart) (Swales, 1988: 212)'. The first notion accepts all people to form one big scientific community, whereas the latter divides the whole group into subgroups which are 'occupational or speciality-interest (Martín-Martín, 2003: 154)'.

Another distinction introduced by Swales (1990) is the sociolinguistic and sociorhetorical character of the communities. A speech community is sociolinguistic, i.e. 'the development and maintenance of its discoursal characteristics' of the group are determined by its needs, such as socialisation and group solidarity, whereas a discourse community is sociorhetorical, i.e. its linguistic behaviour is function-driven as its members 'link up in order to pursue objectives that are prior to those of socialization and solidarity' and the '*goals* tend to predominate in the development and maintenance of its discoursal characteristics (Swales, 1990: 24)'. Therefore, the scientific community as a whole can be characterised as sociorhetorical, since their main aim is to conduct research and produce expected results.

Moreover, there is no agreement between the researchers on the matter of the character of the two notions. Due to definition problems connected with the notion, the author of the monograph decided to adopt Bizzell's (1992) tentative solution who defines a discourse community as 'a group of people who share certain language-using practices' that can be analysed from two perspectives: that in which 'stylistic conventions regulate social interactions both within the group and in its dealings with outsiders' and that in which 'canonical knowledge regulates the world views of group members, how they interpret experience (Bizzell, 1992: 222)'. The first perspective has been taken from the notion of the community, and the latter has been borrowed from the concept of interpretive community. However, the room for various interpretations in the case of fields of new technologies is limited, as research results in the fields of new technologies are based on experiments and numerical data that allow to draw conclusions assumed by the authors, and research papers are functional objective texts that are written to reflect stages in research, irrespective of the nationality or culture of the authors. In addition, the term 'discourse' provides room for a broader definition in which the community is 'bound together primarily by its uses of language' (in this sense similar to a speech community) but also 'by other ties as well, geographical, socioeconomic, ethnic, professional, and so on (Bizzell, 1992: 222)', which allows for labelling the academic community the discourse community. However, in opposition to Swales (1990), the membership in a discourse community entails some acceptance of 'its world view (Bizzell, 1992: 228)'.

Swales (1988), proposes a set of features that define discourse communities which can be applied to the scientific community:

1. Members of the scientific discourse community 'share common public goals (Swales, 1988: 212)'.
2. The community has developed 'specific means of intercommunication within the group either in the spoken or the written form with the same participants (Swales, 1990: 25)'.
3. The community's survival depends on the provision of information and feedback used for different purposes.
4. The community 'has developed and continues to develop discoursal expectations (Swales, 1988: 212)'.
5. Members of the discourse community 'possess an inbuilt dynamic towards an increasingly shared and specialized terminology (Swales, 1988: 212)'.
6. The community maintains a 'critical mass of members with a suitable degree of relevant discoursal and content expertise (Swales, 1988: 213)'.

Swales (1988) provides limitations to his criteria as not all groups of people that share these characteristic features and can be considered a discourse community. Moreover, each member can be a part of several discourse communities and the number of communities they participate in may be different (Swales, 1988: 213). Finally, the involvement in the participants may vary as 'the discourse community can operate successfully even when the level of personal relationship remains low (Swales, 1988: 213)' because it can function even if the activities are not central for its members' lives. However, Swales' (1988) definition of the discourse community has been subject of criticism 'for being very narrow' as well as 'for the very restrictive role' the author assigns to it (Martín-Martín, 2003: 155).

To sum up, discourse community is a notion very close to the speech community, but the main difference is the direction of influence, in the first it is the community that actually shapes their language. Moreover, the community develops its own terminology and genres in order to communicate effectively as well as create a common goal that drives the group. Finally, the community's existence depends on expert members that will guide novice incomers.

1.3. Concluding remarks to Chapter 1

Knowledge expansion is the key determinant in the creation and development of modern societies. Therefore, scientific work is considered of the utmost importance in the strengthening of the country's position in the world. Moreover, specific working conditions, i.e. constant development, exploring the unknown, sharing knowledge with other experts, learning from each other, teaching novices, determine the language scientists employ and the type of the community they form. Depending on the set of criteria, academia meet the requirements to be considered a community of practice, community of interest, speech community or adiscourse community. The notions of communities are more or less thoroughly and explicitly defined; they overlap, or stem one from another. Various aspects are in the centre of their attention, such as scientists' expertise, language, social roles, etc. which along with the dual nature of modern scientific disciplines, such as the analysed domains of new technologies. On the one hand, modern scientific disciplines narrow the scope of interest, but tend to acquire an interdisciplinary character on the other, which affects the language employed, which pertains both to terminology and phraseology. Moreover, the structure of the scientific community, its distinctive features, and the specificity of the subject field they specialise have implications on scientists' language and types of texts they create, which will be discussed in Chapter 2.

Chapter 2 Scientific language and writing

The current chapter discusses the position of the scientific language and scientific texts. The investigations begin with the role of language in science as an instrument or tool in the expansion of knowledge. Language of science is a reflection of the specificity of the subject field and the characteristics of its users. It also exerts influence on the general variety because scientists do not work in isolation from the society, and are also involved in the education process of future professionals, as mentioned in the previous chapter. However, there is no agreement regarding its place in the classification of natural language varieties as well as the status of scientific writing as specialised texts. Language researchers cannot agree whether to treat scientific and technical communication as one concept or separate entities either. Therefore, the author attempts at delimiting the position of the scientific and technical language of new technologies among the language varieties as well as scientific communication.

The chapter is also focused on scientific texts, because research is communicated and validated in the permanent written form via research articles which perform various functions. Despite the accepted and widely-used IMRAD format, there are domain-specific modifications of the genre, i.e. differences with respects to the reasons for creating scientific texts, their language, symbols, graphics, and the constitution of the body of text in order to live up to expectations of the target audience, and the changing characteristics of readers since nowadays scientific texts are easily accessible. For these reasons, the author attempts to establish the factors that govern the structure of the scientific article in the domains of new technologies.

2.1. Language as an instrument of knowledge transfer

Academia cannot exist without communication both in terms of communicating the research results and in educational situations as teachers and learners (Hyland, 2009B). It is the language that allows people's cognition and knowledge expansion as well as an important factor in the understanding of science worldwide (Gajda, 1982; Grucza, 2015; Montgomery, 2000: 189). Therefore, languages are compared to instruments of cognition and knowledge creation and constitute basic communicative tools (Olszewska, 2010: 170; Grucza, 2015: 67; Gajda, 1982: 24). Languages have two basic functions, i.e. they either describe and create the reality, which in this case is creating knowledge, or they transfer knowledge. Thus, without a language, knowledge of the future cannot be created. On the other hand, language as a tool of human cognition, 'connected with creation and expression of thought' consists of mental images and objects that enable cognitive processes needed to describe reality (Gajda, 1990: 12, 1982; Grucza, 2015: 70). Moreover, language embodies and records new knowledge and acts as a means of knowledge transfer. This process takes place at an individual level, since every individual creates their own knowledge by reconstructing the meaning from texts (Grucza, 2015: 63, 65). It is the language that allows to express, create, transfer and reorganise knowledge on both sides: in the sender's and the recipient's minds. Therefore, language functions as an instrument; it performs both a communicative and epistemic function. Moreover, language and thought are related in an epistemic relationship, i.e. the language allows for expressing the social achievements in texts (Gajda, 1982: 27).

In scientific circles, written communication is indispensable as one of its function is recording the findings and spreading them worldwide (Gajda, 1982). It is a complex process, which is stretched in time as written texts are carefully elaborated on by the authors, edited and re-edited after the reviewer's comments, and finally are published and to reach the possibly largest group of people to be read by target audience (Biber, 2006: 3; Gajda, 1982). Thus, scientific communication has a mass character as well as the form of the monologue and communicates a special scientific message that tends to be abstract, generally valid and socially and geographically uniform (Gajda, 1982: 36–37; Sager, Dungworth & McDonald, 1980: 50–51). Therefore, it is possible to develop a model of communication. Grucza (2015) proposes a simple communication model in science which illustrates the process of expressing and reconstructing knowledge from scientific texts.

Figure 2.1. The model of expressing and reconstructing knowledge proposed by Grucza (2015: 66)

Grucza's (2015) communication model depicted in Figure 2.1. above is related to the model of expressing and reconstructing knowledge (Figure 2.2. below) proposed by Makowska (2018). It does not cover all aspects of scientific communication, because it concentrates on the creation of a person's individual language, and knowledge as a result of the received stimuli.

Makowska (2018) has developed a communication model of the written language in science based on the Losee's (1999) model of human communication which is depicted in Figure 2.2. below. The author of the message codifies it into thoughts, based on their knowledge and experience, then expresses it in words (a language), and encodes the thoughts in writing in research papers. Then, the addressee decodes the written text using visual processes (Losee, 1999: 9; Makowska, 2018). The message is then transformed into recipient's thoughts, but undergoes the process of evaluation: agreement, disagreement, comparisons with the addressee's experience and knowledge or other already existing literature and knowledge on the subject. The scrutiny of the written material contributes to the re-evaluation and reformulation of the recipients' knowledge and experience. In a perfect or idealised communication situation, the processes of encoding and decoding of the research paper are reverse (Losee, 1999; Sager et al., 1980: 46). However, real-life situations are affected by negative influences – noise or errors, such as the incompatibility of lexical and knowledge structure, interference from grammar or the distortion of sound or script, in the process of communication, called a noise modified communication or imperfectly inverted communication (Losee, 1999: 14; Sager et al., 1980: 46). The misunderstanding of concepts or misinterpretations – disruptions that stem from an individual different understanding of the written message, different personal experience and individual conceptualisation of reality – disturb the decoding process of the written text in the receiver's thoughts (Sager et al., 1980: 46; Lewandowska-Tomaszczyk, 2010: 108; Makowska, 2018). The evaluation of the message, i.e. agreeing, disagreeing and comparing is the essence of the reverse process of decoding, and ends in knowledge broadening in the addressee's mind. As a result, the resulting thoughts in the receivers' mind are not equal to the author's thoughts, the addressee's knowledge does not equal the author's, and finally the receiver may not be affected by the message in the way the sender intended it (Makowska, 2018).

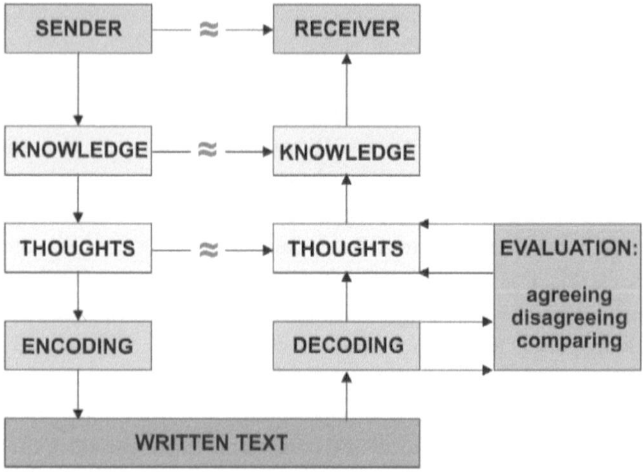

Figure 2.2. Communication model of the written language developed on the basis of Losee's model of human communication (Losee, 1999: 9) in Makowska (2018)

After comparing the two models, it can be concluded that knowledge encoding in a language by means of scientific writing by the authors and its reconstruction, evaluation and updating in the reader's mind are the convergent elements. On the other hand, text decoding and evaluation is parallel to Gajda's (1990) findings, however he states that the discrepancy between the sender's scientific knowledge and the recipient's colloquial knowledge depends on the jargonism (the degree to which the language is difficult to comprehend) of the scientific language and may not be easy to overcome (1990: 27).

However, according to Rus (2014), applying general communication schemes to the needs of specialised communication may be incomplete. It is not only the message that should remain in the centre of attention. Other factors, like the interlocutors, their professional characteristics, the specificity of their community, or the contexts should also be taken into account (Collier & Toomey, 2013 in Rus, 2014: 655). Moreover, the analysis should also include the purposes which technical communication serve apart from the 'transmission of information', i.e. 'to propose, to argue, to persuade, to defend, to coerce, to instruct, etc. (Rus: 2014: 655)'.

In conclusion, written communication in science is one of the stages in conducting research. It functions as a means of validating the obtained results, passing information, but also serves other purposes. Language functions as a communicative tool or an instrument in this process. Moreover, the participants should also be taken into account, when scrutinising scientific communication. In addition, the authors' decision where to publish and which language to choose is also dictated by the need to reach the widest audience and gain higher prestige.

2.1.1. The status of English in scientific writing

Knowledge cannot expand without the linguistic means as the language is 'the carrier of culture' and 'an important means of maintaining and developing countries (Jiao & Wenjing, 2013: 2262)'. Moreover, science should 'be universal among the world's languages', therefore there should not be any differences in terms of standards of expression across languages (Montgomery, 2000: 255; Seweryn, 2010; Gajda, 1990). As a result, science should find one international language, also referred to as Gemeinsprache /*common language*/, as multilingualism is viewed as an obstacle in order to maintain its universal character and enable efficient knowledge transfer (Montgomery, 2000: 255; Gnutzmann & Rabe, 2014: 33; Seweryn, 2010; Gajda, 1990). There is a 'need for a global language' in academic and business circles as scientists from different countries can communicate via a common, global language, i.e. a lingua franca which stimulates intellectual development and scientific advances, as well as popularises scientists as a community (Crystal, 2003: 13). Furthermore, technosphere, science and technology are among areas where dominating languages are favoured which facilitate international communication and access to information for wider audience (Seweryn, 2010: 3).

The language of the international communication and the language of technology and media is now English (Borowiak, 2008) and is considered now to be a global language (Crystal, 2003), world language (Eckert, Johann, Känzig, Küng, Müller, Schwald & Walder, 2014: 106), a world's lingua franca (Borowiak, 2008) or the 'hypercentral' language of the world (de Swaan, 2001), having 'the unique characteristics of the universal language' (Jiao & Wenjing, 2013: 2264; Crystal, 2003; Drubin & Kellogg 2012) and is also referred to as 'a "new Latin" for the world's scientific output (Montgomery, 2000: 256)' or even 'the international lingua franca of research and scholarship (Hyland, 2009A: 4)'. According to Drubin & Kellogg (2012), English 'is now used almost exclusively as the language of science' which is also described as 'the international currency of science and technology (Graddol, 2000: 9)'. Its dominance and expansion might be linked to the 'economic, technological, and cultural power (Crystal, 2003: 7)' throughout the history, which is referred to as 'economic, technological and cultural influence' (Graddol, 2000: 4). Moreover, its global status derives from a very specific role that is acknowledged across countries, which is called the increasing *globalization of science* (Crystal, 2003: 3; Seweryn, 2010). As a result, English plays the role of 'the academic gate-keeper' because it spreads as fast as 'computer-mediated developments', such as the World Wide Web (Swales, 1997: 376).

The dominant position of English in international academic circles is facilitated by the 'increasing use of the Internet (Montgomery, 2000: 262)'. At the end of the 20th century 'online journals, preprint archives, conference proceedings, major databases of all types, educational resources' were published online (Montgomery, 2000: 262). As the Internet was an American invention, English-speaking scientists benefited by using the medium to a great extent and sites in other languages provided in the English version, too. Therefore, the Internet is perceived as 'a powerful agent in the globalization of scientific English (Montgomery, 2000: 263)'. As a result English works as a 'wider window on the world' that 'has paved the way for the enormous resources (Swales, 1997: 377)'.

One can observe, however, a certain hierarchisation of languages in which English is placed on top positions. De Swaan (2001) and Graddol (2000) divide world languages into the galaxy or a pyramid of languages, which are depicted in Figure 2.3. below.

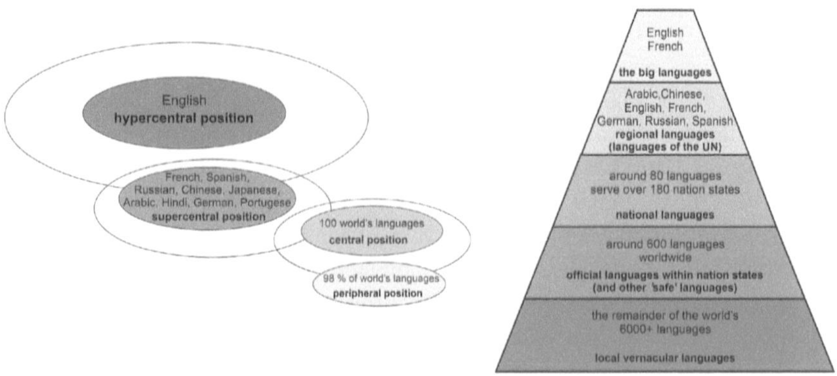

Figure 2.3. De Swaan's galaxy of world languages or constellation of languages (2001: 4–6) and Graddol's (2000) hierarchy of world languages

The categorisations are similar as they divide the global system of languages into four or five groups. De Swaan's constellation consists of 4 positions: peripheral, central, supercentral and hypercentral, whereas Graddol (2000) provides a pyramid of 5 language groups. The highest are De Swaan's hypercentral language and Graddol's big languages, i.e. English and English with French respectively. The second level occupy supercentral, 12 'solar' languages and regional languages, i.e. 'UN, like Arabic, Chinese, also referred to as international languages (Brutt-Grieffler, 2006)'. The next group is comprised of De Swaan's central or 'planetary' languages which account for about 100 in number and often have the status of national or official languages and Graddol's national languages that cover about 80 languages. Peripheral languages are the lowest in De Swaan's hierarchy and include 'the languages of memory' spoken 'by less than 10 percent of humankind (De Swaan, 2001: 4)'. Graddol's fourth group constitute official languages within nation states which account for about 600 languages and the last group consists of local vernacular languages with the remaining over 6000 languages. Graddol's (2000) division concentrates more on the geographical coverage of each group, not the influence they exert as it is in the case of De Swaan (2001). All in all, both hierarchies place English on the top position. However, Hamel (2007) argues that the division into hypercentral, supercentral, central, and peripheral languages is only partially correct, and that the dominance of English in science is exaggerated as the studies to prove its position are biased (Hamel, 2007: 61).

As English is the most expansive language, and dominates in different aspects of communication, anglophony, 'monopoly of English' or even the 'hegemony of English' has turned out to be 'the communicative norm in almost all scientific disciplines (Seweryn, 2010: 3; Gnutzman & Rabe, 2014: 31; Eckert et al., 2014: 106; Hamel, 2007: 53)'. Swales (1997) even compares it to the 'tyrannosaurus rex' – 'a powerful carnivore gobbling up the other denizens of the academic linguistic grazing grounds (1997: 374)'. Its dominance in scientific circles can be linked to the domain of language behaviour or language choice developed by Schmidt-Rohr (1933), and refreshed by Fishman (1972). Therefore, scientists discussing results of their research may choose to speak English in certain settings to certain recipients, i.e. their target audience is limited to the specialists on the subject (horizontal communication). Therefore, the predominant majority of scientists make a decision to publish in English to expand the number of readers and quotes and to 'gain access to the vast scientific literature', 'communicate with other scientists anywhere in the world', and to be recognised worldwide (Drubin & Kellog, 2012). As a result, the status of English as the international language of science has been measured

> 'by the sheer quantity of publications, by the use of English in technology and technology transfer, by the most favored foreign language studied by science and engineering students worldwide, by the most frequent source language for scientific translations, or by any number of other measures (Stevens, 1992 in Montgomery, 2000: 256)'.

The dominant position of English is also manifested by a wide array of its applications. It is a means of communication 'in various fields around the world, including politics, economy, trade, culture diplomacy, tourism, communication, natural science and academic research of humanities' (Jiao & Wenjing, 2013: 2263; Brutt-Griffler, 2006). Eckert et al. (2014), concentrate the influence of English on 'the language of technology, science and commerce (2014: 107)'. The areas in which English dominates internationally include the working language of organisations and conferences on the first position and the second position being occupied with scientific publications (Steiner, 1975 in Graddol, 2000: 8). English is also the language used in the tertiary education, placed on the fifth position in the ranking as well as the language of the technology transfer and the communication in the Internet (position number 11 and 12 respectively) (Graddol, 2000: 8). Moreover, the dominance of English stems from the fact that scientists work in teams on international projects in order to gain 'the access to modern laboratories or precise measuring equipment', both of which contribute to the increase in the scientific output in English (Seweryn, 2010: 10–11). According to Jiao & Wenjing (2013) and Gajda (1990), English is the language of publications and information in the Internet which amount to 80 % of all written materials. Hyland (2009) evaluates that by 2050 half of the world's population will speak English, which changes its status in academic circles from a foreign language to an academic skill. Moreover, specialised literature is written in English and scientists who gain access to it often decide to publish in English themselves (Borowiak, 2008). Hamel (2007) estimates that English as the language of publication tends to be more likely chosen in natural, social sciences and humanities, but in hard sciences, like mathematics and physics, English is the most dominating language. Moreover, its dominance accounts for the '95 % of 925,000 scientific papers written in English' both by native speakers and non-native speakers of English proportionally by half (Jiao & Wenjing, 2013: 2263). It leads, however, to 'an asymmetric relation between the Anglophone native speakers and their non native counterparts in the international communication' since non-natives may be faced with discrimination on the grounds of their command of English (Hamel, 2007: 66; Gnutzman & Rabe, 2014: 34). In other words, it is their level of English that is subject to criticism, not the level of their scientific achievements (Drubin & Kellog, 2012). On the other hand, native speakers of English gain the competitive edge over non-native speakers in terms of the 'subtle nuances, linguistic intuition, rich and precise vocabulary, and conscious knowledge of the norms of the scientific discourse (Gajda, 1990; Gnutzman & Rabe, 2014: 34; Drubin & Kellog, 2012)'. Non-native authors are faced with higher opportunity costs of publishing in English, because they spend about 4–5 thousand hours learning a foreign language along with the constant improvement of their scientific writing skills, as well as laborious pre-publishing editing (Gajda, 1990; Swales, 1997; Gnutzman & Rabe, 2014: 34). As a result, the time and effort devoted to language learning might affect a scientist's scientific work negatively (Gajda, 1990). Scientists, being non-native speakers of English, spend more time assimilating reports to the writing conventions in English than native-speakers, and therefore devote less time to their research (Crystal, 2003: 16).

As mentioned above, publications in international journals provide wider audience for the validation of the results of research, and serve as an indicator of the assessment of the researchers' advances. Moreover, international journals with high impact factors gain higher prestige and their authors will be 'acknowledged by the top scientific community' if they publish in English (Gnutzman & Rabe, 2014: 33; Hamel, 2007: 6; Reinbothe: 2011). Therefore, scientists publish the results of their studies in English in journals that are noted in the Science Citation Index (SCI) in order to gain a higher recognition for their work (Gnutzman & Rabe, 2014: 33; Reinbothe, 2011). English-speaking scientific communities are also perceived as more prestigious and leading in the development of science, so are the international conferences (Seweryn, 2010: 8). For example, in American journals, 98 % of citations referred to papers in English and the remaining 2 % to publications in other languages (Wellish in Seweryn, 2010: 9). However, data based on the SCI, proving 'the English monopoly in the international communication', are 'biased towards English', and the analyses are not objective (Hamel, 2007: 61).

Transfer languages in science should 'certainly display little or no important variation in any single language' as science has a universal character (Montgomery, 2000: 255; Seweryn, 2010: 5). However, since there are varieties of English around the world, so there are differences in the scientific writing conventions which are manifested in terms of the language used, the cognitive content, or the organisation of the text itself even though the papers are written in English (Montgomery, 2000; Gnutzmann & Rabe, 2014). Although the British and American varieties of English have been considered a standard, the way the scientists, with English being their second or foreign language, communicate and write in English or in LFE (localised form of English) differ significantly (Montgomery, 2000). '"Errors", "misuse" and "deviations"' of the standard are not linguistic, but cultural problems which have become standards in some communities. Moreover, the nativisation is the "fate of any living international form of speech' because the conventions of writing in English in terms of grammar, syntax and lexis differ significantly across LFEs and 'these apparent slips constitute proper usage (Montgomery, 2000: 257–258)'. However, Steiner (1975) calls this process internationalisation or modulation of English, and claims that it has a detrimental effect on proper English. Different norms of scientific writing in English across countries reflect the 'conventions of each particular linguistic community', and may not follow the rules of the 'standardized scientific discourse' but be more of 'a series of technical dialects (Montgomery, 2000: 257)'. As a result, there are different writing conventions and requirements placed on the researcher. Moreover, one cannot escape taking account of the cultural influence, as research areas and positions on the theory and knowledge differ greatly (Gnutzmann & Rabe, 2014). As a result, different cultural and religious connotations play an important role in the scientific writing. On the other hand, Swales (1997) raises the question whether foreign scholars should conform to the English writing conventions or whether they should introduce more diversity into the Anglophone scientific writing.

Multilingualism in scientific writing is, however, on the decline, because there is 'a pronounced trend toward English as the medium for the publication of scientific research (Brutt-Grieffler, 2006: 695)'. Studies show that English still is considered the world language as it has the status of the official language in 63 countries, which places the language on the first position (Ammon, 1998 in Brutt-Griffler, 2006; Crystal, 1997: 359 in Brutt-Grieffler, 2006: 693). Moreover, the number of speakers that use the language on different levels varies between 500 million and 1 billion (Brutt-Grieffler, 2006: 691). The most important data concern, however, the languages of scientific publications. For instance, in the articles indexed by Chemical Abstracts, English was placed in the first position, with a marked increase from 62.3 to 82.5% over the years 1978–1998. German, French and Polish as languages of publications occupy the 6th, 7th and 8th position with the downward trend (Jean Laponce, 2003: 60 in Brutt-Griffler, 2006: 694). When it comes to languages of publications in natural sciences, English established its leading position with an increase from 74.6% to 90.7% from 1980 to 1996. Again, French and German are placed in the 4th and 5th positions but their number dwindled almost threefold (Ammon, 1998: 167 in Brutt-Griffler, 2006: 694). Humanities also confirm the hegemony of English as the language of scientific communication since the number of articles published in the language rose from 69.1 to 82.5 over the years 1978–1995 (Ammon, 1998: 167 in Brutt-Griffler, 2006: 695). Seweryn (2010) gathered data on the languages of publications in maths, medicine, linguistics and literature in which English has been dominating with a continuing upward trend. Moreover, the "MEDILINE" database indicates that English is well-established as the leading language of publications whose number more than doubled from 1963 to 2003.

Again, German, French and Polish are placed on the subsequent positions, with a declining tendency (Seweryn, 2010: 16). Surprisingly, data in the "MLA International Bibliography" shows that the strong position of English in linguistics and literature in 1920s was deeply undermined, and dropped by a half in 1950s. However, the numbers started to improve, and by 2006, 69.6% of publications were in English. Other languages fluctuated over the period but their importance is rather marginal (Seweryn, 2010: 18). Yet, Seweryn (2010) finds the results inconclusive as the data present the American perspective.

All things considered, English has won the position of the world language in a number of spheres, among which there is scientific communication. Publishing in English is indispensable to gain wider recognition and secure a sufficient level of quotations. Nevertheless, non-native speakers of English pay a higher price for publishing in English in terms of costs of learning the language, terminology and writing conventions in English which, however differ across countries. Moreover, English hegemony may lead to the increasing number of Anglicisms in specialised communication, or even to the death of minority languages as speakers tend to choose more prestigious languages. On the other hand, bilingual professionals have also affected English, and produced a simplified variety in the international communication in specialised fields.

2.1.2. Drawing a borderline between a general and specialised language

Language is a distinctive feature of a group of people, a nation that use it to communicate in 'its economic, social, political and cultural development differentiated by the grammatical system and vocabulary (Klemensiewicz, 1953: 6)'. The general variety is taught at school, is used in public life and the written form acts as artistic creation and a means of information transfer in science and education nationwide. It is characterised by rich lexicon as well as rather stable codified ortoephic and ortophonic norms which are varied depending on the functional types of verbal communication. The user of the general language is, according to Klemensiewicz (1956), an educated person. The written variety of the general language records the life of national culture, i.e. the results of the scientific thought among others. It is reflected both by the vocabulary that is broadened and modified because it describes abstract objects, features or activities and carefully elaborated and logical complex sentences. Yet, despite the fact that these views on the language might constitute a point in departure in the discussion on the place of the specialised language, they have become obsolete.

Other language researchers classify scientific language among the varieties of the general language, indicating its function, i.e. the functional variety of the general language. Wilkoń (2000) includes the language of science among the written varieties with some influences from languages of the past, which is depicted in Figure 2.4. below. The author's classification is very general, does not allow for placing the language of engineering in its exact place.

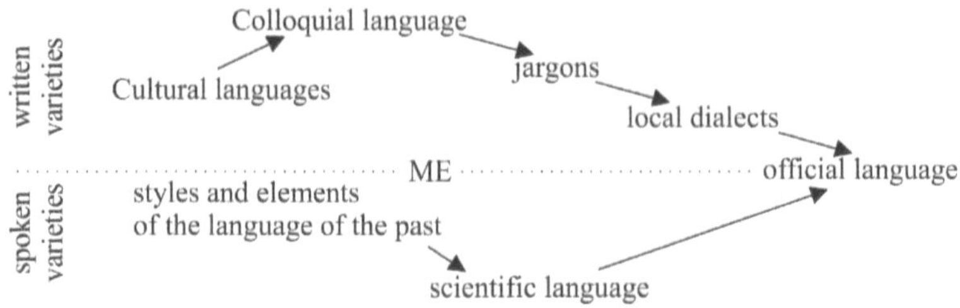

Figure 2.4. Wilkoń's (2000) classification of language varieties (2000: 74).

According to Cabré (1998), general language and its specialised varieties overlap. Both varieties are 'based on a common system': there is an intersection between them. The features that are shared by both types of languages include:

a. The same graphic system of expression, the same alphabet.
b. The same phonological system; if we read the texts aloud, the phonetic units are the same in both cases.
c. The same morphological system.
d. The same syntactic rules for the construction of phrases and sentences.
e. The same sentence types (1998: 73).

On the other hand, there are three features that separate the two: 'linguistic (lexical, morphological, and syntactic) pragmatic (situation, originators and recipients of the message) and functional (the communicative intention) (1998: 72)'. The biggest difference lies in the vocabulary. Cabré (1998) distinguishes three groups of lexemes found in specialised texts:

a. General language lexical items, e.g. *brain, medicine, slice, pressure, rock, temperature*
b. Specific lexical items that can be attributed to a borderline area between general language and special language: *imaging, invasive, scanner, chemical composition, metamorphic, recrystallization*
c. Lexical items specific to special texts: *adenosine triphosphate, lactic acid, spectroscopy, basaltic, diagenesis, protolith* (1998: 73).

However, specialised texts are characterised by a more frequent use of certain structures and categories in comparison to the general language texts, i.e.

a. Morphological structures based on Greek or Latin formatives: *diagenesis*, *igneous*, *pathological*
b. Abbreviations and symbols: *MRI*, *C*
c. Nominalizations based on verbs: *accumulation*, *identification*, *recrystallization*
d. Straightforward sentence structure with little complex subordination (1998: 73).

The last category, however, stays in contradiction to other researchers' findings who state that subordinate clauses and complex sentence structures are the most frequently used in specialised texts, and scientific writing in particular (Biber, 2006).

In terms of pragmatic features, Cabré's (1998) claims that topics should be restricted to the domain-specific issues. Otherwise, they cannot be included in the range of specialised communication, which contradicts the practical and applicative character of the MTCS domains: the devices are used in other fields, not necessarily considered specialised. Moreover, topics are strictly connected with the purpose of the text: academic, educational or popular scientific (Gajda, 1999).

Specialised languages are also differentiated from the general one in terms of their function – they are created to 'exchange objective information on a specialised topic' in an impersonal way (Cabré, 1998: 75)'. Therefore, the majority of specialised texts include 'description, definition, classification, enumeration, calculations, reasoning, argumentation, citation, reference' and serve referential purposes (Cabré, 1998: 75). The text elements that are to enhance impersonalisation and objectivity include:

- first person plural as a means of expressing modesty
- the present tense
- absence of exclamations
- short sentences
- avoidance of unnecessary redundancy
- frequent use of impersonal formulae
- noun phrases
- other systems of representation, e.g. drawings, tables, in the body of the text (1998: 75).

However, objectivity in scientific writing is considered to be a myth (Hyland, 2009A). According to Hyland (2011), the persuasive character of scientific writing is not a new phenomenon.

Cabré (1998) also distinguishes a set of other features that differentiate specialised texts from the general language by means of:

1. an implicit dialogue between the author and the reader;
2. the personal position in the texts hidden behind phrases, like *according to the author, in our opinion,* etc.;
3. indirect persuasion of the reader 'by providing arguments, citing data, providing examples, explaining, etc. (1998: 75)';
4. metalinguistic elements, such as 'explanations, definitions, parenthetical material, synonyms, etc. (1998: 75)', which Varantola (1987) refers to as the information density;
5. carefully written text with attention to language appropriateness, text format and layout.

Cabré's findings (1998) are partially parallel to earlier, Klemensiewicz's study (1953).

Specialised texts are also characterised by varying levels of abstraction and 'several varieties of special languages (Cabré, 1998: 76)'. The variations observed in specialised languages are akin to those found in the general language, i.e. dialect, register and style, but their range is limited due to the horizontal character of expert-to-expert specialised communication, as well as objectivity, precision and unambiguity of the information exchange. However, discourse differs when comparing a conference paper and a spontaneous conversation on the same topic. Yet, there might arise problems of understanding and communication disturbances between experts in different domains due to the proliferation of new vocabulary as new devices, machines, processes, facts or relationships (Mentrup, 1976: 432). Therefore, the drive for precision, unambiguity or objectivity which might prove to be an unattainable goal.

In addition, terms differ from words with respects to the way they describe specialised reality, are used for referential purposes and as such enhance the referential function of specialised texts (Klemensiewicz, 1953; Cabré, 1998; Kontutyté; 2017; Rincke, 2010). Moreover, there are five pragmatic factors between the general language and terminology:

a. the basic purpose
b. the subject dealt with
c. the users
d. the communicative situations in which both codes are found
e. the types of discourse in which terms or general language words appear (1998: 112–113).

However, there are no clearly established, sharp barriers between the varieties; they are penetrable through 'transitional areas (Klemensiewicz, 1953: 10–11)'. It is hard to draw a clear borderline between the general and domain-specific languages, because of the growing importance of science and technology, popularisation of scientific knowledge and the shift in the perception of scientific domains due to the emergence of new inter- or multidisciplinary fields of science (Cabré, 1998: 71; Campos & Torner Castells, 2010; Gajda, 1990: 31; Rincke, 2010). Moreover, it is difficult to determine whether the language use is general or specialised as there are specialised texts aimed at non-experts which might be unintelligible (Kontutytė, 2017: 2017). For example, advertising, fiction and popular science literature contain elements of the specialised languages. For this reason, communication disturbances may also occur between specialists within a given field.

Specialised languages exert the influence on the general language, and vice versa in terms of lexis and syntax, among others languages of science and technology (Kontutytė, 2017). For example, in German, there is a trend towards nominalisation in the general language, the use of empty verb constructions, compounds or prepositional attributives, or an increase in the use of the feminine forms of nouns, ad hoc word formations and the frequent use of prefixation. Specialised languages also affect the general language by the use of metaphors or idiomatic expressions that have their origins in specialised communication. Moreover, terms in a general language and specialised language become not antonymous, but complementary (Dörr, 2014: 30–31). Both varieties influence each other, with terms becoming de-specialised due to its frequent use in the general language. On the other hand, the general language helps to explain abstract concepts, models or descriptions with the use of common expressions. New terms are built by 'borrowings, calques, metaphorical extensions, metonymy, definition development, or in rare cases by creating new words.'

Specialised languages are also distinguished from general ones in terms of the target audience of written texts. In the past, it were mainly engineers, technicians and scientists with a sufficient level of subject knowledge that were the recipients of technical texts (Byrne, 2012: 30). However, nowadays the professional audiences have become more heterogeneous due to easy access to specialised or technical texts. As a result, both experts and non-experts can be equally interested in scientific and technical texts (Collier & Toomey, 1997). For instance, experts in one field might want to expand their knowledge in other domains, or are on the lookout for new information, and as such they can be considered both experts and non-experts at the same time (Collier & Toomey, 1997). Due to such diversified audiences and their diverse needs; there emerged various documents and document types. As a result, deep understanding of the target readership is crucial in technical/scientific writing. On the other hand, recipients of a scientific text are capable of receiving its content because they are specialists or practitioners (students, apprentices, or early-stage researchers) possessing knowledge on the subject, but also laypersons are interested in popular and scientific texts (Gajda, 2001: 183). After publishing the text, the authors are out of control as for the target audience (Collier & Toomey, 1997).

In conclusion, drawing a clear borderline between general and specialised texts can prove to be a challenging task. Nowadays, texts have become hybrydised, specific terminology appears in different types of texts, and target readership has become diversified due to the popularisation of science and easy access to information thanks to the Internet. For this reason, the borderlines between the general and specialised languages have become blurred.

2.1.3. Distinctive features of the scientific language

The language the scientists use has been the subject of constant dispute. There is no agreement between language researchers regarding its status, as well as the position of the scientific language in the typology among the varieties of the national language. Neither is there a consensus regarding its name, because the names which are given to denote scientific means of communication include a scientific language, scientific register, scientific jargon or a scientific style. For the purpose of the study, the author decided to use the term scientific language on the basis of frequency of occurrence resulting from a corpus analysis. It is present at every stage of research, but it comes to the fore at the moment of publication of results (Gajda, 1982: 100). It also serves as a means of message transfer as well as 'materialisation of scientific information (1982: 99–100)'. Hence, a scientist needs to master scientific writing norms, because general writing skills are not sufficient to produce successful scientific texts.

Klemensiewicz (1953) classifies scientific language among varieties of the literary language. Its main function is the truthful description of reality in an objective way. The authors reflect and explain facts that they have observed which 'constitute a search, statement or verification of an assumption (Klemensiewicz, 1953: 28)'. As a result, a hypothesis may become a proved law or may lead to building connections between facts that were previously considered unrelated. Moreover, the way the scientists express themselves should be unambiguous and precise (Gajda, 1982: 108). But there is no agreement concerning the place of the scientific language within the linguistic varieties. Zdunkiewicz-Jedynak (2008) classifies it among varieties of the general language, and assigns it three functions: cognitive, informational and cumulative. The first is the drive for new knowledge, the second is the tool for passing it to other members of the scientific community, whereas the third describes the need to accumulate and gather knowledge for future generations.

Kołupajło (2014) proposes a "global" approach to the scientific language, i.e. moving away from the syntactic or terminological perspective, and moving towards a synthesis of humanities and hard sciences. The language of science should be perceived from the functional perspective, because scientific languages are no longer limited to one domain. In communicating science, there are two polarising extremities, called the double process of exchange (Ehlich, 2006: 23 in Kołupajło, 2014: 178). On the one hand, there is communicativeness, i.e. the drive or need to make science approachable and comprehensible, but on the other, the asceticism of communication sets the boundaries on the grounds that the innovative character of scientific output is beyond the comprehension.

Scientific language possesses four basic characteristic features of a scientific language: abstractness, accuracy, objectivity and internationality (Zdunkiewicz-Jedynak, 2008: 128). The first is manifested with the use of abstract concepts, unnatural and iconic codes, intertextuality, metaphors and interpretation. The use of the impersonal sentences, modal phrases expressing doubts or wariness and the lack of expressive elements constitute the elements of objectivity. Finally, the international character of scientific writing is connected with the use of internationalisms, foreign words or loan words that account for 30 % of the academic text.

The key factor determining scientific language is its vocabulary (Kontutytė, 2017; Klemensiewicz, 1953; Lemke, 1990A; Cabré, 1998; Kurkowska & Skorupka, 2001; Rincke, 2010). On average, terminology accounts for 20–30 % of all words in a scientific text and includes mainly nouns, verbs and adjectives (Gajda, 2001: 185–188; Cabré, 2006 in Campos & Torner Castells, 2010). Moreover, terms that appear are clear cut, unclear cut, polysemous and even may look like general lexicon vocabulary, but in specialised contexts acquire a special meaning (Zdunkiewicz-Jedynak, 2008: 129). Moreover, scientific texts contain nouns that express mental concepts, abstract adjectives and verbs denoting conceptual activities, concrete verbs have metaphorical meanings that emphasise the abstract character of scientific style (Kurkowska & Skorupka, 2001: 271, 278). There is also a high frequency of words indicating features and relationships, such as adverbs, adverbial phrases, pronouns and conjunctions. Scientific articles contain modal phrases which express author's doubts, suppositions or certainty. Apart from lexical units, scientific texts also include ancillary non-linguistic signs that function as signs of specialised, scientific and technical concepts which are called scientific codes (Gajda, 1982: 102; Gajda, 2001: 185). One of these are formalised languages that are developed in order to 'purify' the natural language irregularities, and include mathematical, physical or chemical formulae. The main advantage of using symbols is their clear-cut and idealised character, as well as effectiveness. However, they are still ancillary communicative systems, and they are limited in terms of the type of users. The other are iconic codes, such as graphs, maps, diagrams, schematic or technical drawings, which either complement, or duplicate the verbal message and as a result facilitate the reader's decoding of the message.

Biber (2006) finds certain linguistic features and specific grammatical structures the most characteristic of the scientific writing. Word classes, like nouns, adjectives and prepositions, are more frequent in academic texts than others, but nouns and prepositional phrases cannot be thought of as typical in academic texts since they are common in every register. There are also tendencies towards specific features, like nominalisations, noun phrases with multiple modifiers, stance noun + *of* –phrases. On the other hand, there are structures which appear less often, such as the copula *be*, existence verbs, derived verbs, and passive voice verbs. Moreover, relative clauses with the relative pronoun *which* and non-finite relative clauses (*-ing* clauses and *-ed* clauses) are most frequently found. With regards to other clauses, extraposed complement clauses 'controlled by adjectives (e.g. *It is possible that. . ., It is important to. .*)' and concessive sub-adverbial clauses are often used by researchers in their writing.

Scientific language also develops its own terminology (discussed in detail in Chapters 3 and 7) which should be precise, sharply defined and limited, i.e. restricted only to sci/tech areas and form a whole theoretical concept system (Bartmiński & Niebrzegowska-Bartmińska, 2009; Klemensiewicz, 1953; Gajda, 2001: 185–186). This view, however, reflects the traditional approach to terminology. Gajda (2001) opposes Klemensiewicz's (1953) view on monosemy, by stating that treating all scientific concepts as artificially clearly defined is an oversimplification because not all terms are based on a limited number of qualities and clearly defined. Moreover, terms exhibit a higher level of polymorphism than colloquial lexical units, because older and newer meanings coexist, terms denote various intersecting concepts and scientific concepts are not clearly defined and unidimensional. As a result, due to its deficiencies connected with natural proliferation of terminology and its polymorphic character, there is a drive towards creation of a system of concepts and terms, and finally towards normalisation which refers mainly to the technical terminology, but it has to be performed carefully (Gajda, 1982: 109, 2001: 188).

With regards to syntax, phonetic and inflectional rules are consistent with the norms of the general language, which also pertains to new term creation (Klemensiewicz, 1953; Gajda, 2001). However, the overall purpose of syntactic means is to facilitate monosemy, clarity and precision (Klemensiewicz, 1953: 31). Therefore, scientific writing lacks in emotional load, and it is highly abstract – scientific texts are almost devoid of emotionally loaded expressions, such as elliptical sentences, exclamations, parentheses, apostrophes (Klemensiewicz, 1953: 31; Kurkowska & Skorupka, 2001; Zdunkiewicz-Jedynak, 2008: 129). Moreover, the language of scientific texts is the reflection of the complicated line of argumentation (Klemensiewicz, 1953: 31–32). As a result, compound-complex sentences appear quite frequently that mirror the cause and effect relationship, condition and result (Klemensiewicz, 1953: 32; Kurkowska & Skorupka, 2001). Thus, the whole text is one internally closely bound entity of the line of thinking that is to convince the reader about the content. Furthermore, sentences are longer than in artistic texts, with the predominant majority of subordinate clauses. In English, grammatical structures that are the most frequently used include passive voice, abstract nouns, verbs denoting abstract relation, such as *be, have* or *represent*, instead of active verbs (Lemke, 1990A: 21).

Scientific language is also characterised by the use of natural language together with other signs, e.g. iconic such as the code of the technical drawing (Gajda, 1990: 28). In mathematics, chemistry or logic, the emergence of symbols and symbolic languages is connected with the increase in the abstractness of cognition – of concepts and theories – all of which lead to the formalisation (Gajda, 1990: 28; Kurkowska & Skorupka, 2001). The substitution of vast amounts of texts with formulae is the result of maximising the information density in the minimal space, precision and purity of presenting the abstract content, which is referred to as the CIO principle, i.e. Crucial Information Only (Gajda, 1990: 28; Gajda, 2001; Varantola, 1987).

Factors determining the scientific language include lexical, grammatical and textual elements (Gajda, 2001: 188). When it comes to word choice, scientists choose abstract lexemes along with borrowings (Gajda, 2001: 188; Kurkowska & Skorupka, 2001). Scientific language in hard sciences also contains formulae and algorithms (Kurkowska & Skorupka, 2001). Another characteristic feature of scientific texts is the use of quotations, footnotes and links to references (Kurkowska & Skorupka, 2001). They are also characterised by a high degree of schematisation because terms, phrases and expressions are often replaced by symbols, but the process refers to the whole text (Gajda, 1982: 109). Moreover, elements, such as graphs, tables, or schematic drawings, accelerate the reading process, and make the text easier to comprehend. In terms of the form, conventionalisation and stabilisation are desired qualities of scientific texts. However, the individual usage of the scientific language, as research is performed by individual scientists, or borrowing some elements from other language varieties may disturb the stereotypical character of scientific writing. The norm of the scientific language is manifested at different levels: international, national, temporal, or by norms of the natural language and other semiotic systems. Therefore, it should acknowledge all its complexity.

Wilkoń (2000) gathers the summary of the characteristics of the scientific language, based on previous research on the subject. Scientific language is characterised by the following set of features:

1. its own domain-specific semantic systems
    a) development of the subordination relation between semantic fields of signs
    b) regular hierarchisation of concepts, avoiding synonymy
    c) tendency to adopt foreign vocabulary to avoid synonymy
    d) creating neologisms and neosemantisms
    e) frequency of two- or multiword signs
    f) restriction of semantic fields of signs
    g) pursuit for monosemy and transparency.
2. low frequency of expressive words/formations/expressions
3. tendency to abstractness
4. reverse tendency to specification and accurateness of descriptions and analyses, especially in empirical writing
5. specific syntactic features:
    a) use of complex hypotactic relations
    b) lack of ellipses, nominal sentences, apostrophes, or exclamations
    c) emphasising the relations of thought continuity and dependence between sentences constituting the whole line of scientific thinking (...)
6. frequent use of symbols and formulae, schemas, graphs, tables, ideograms as well as formal languages (2000: 63–65).

The analysed domains of new technologies, however, combine the elements of the scientific language with the technical one, due to their multidisciplinary and the practical-technical character. Technical language is a different variety which Klemensiewicz (1953) classifies as normative-didactic, but these fairly practical and applicative domains gather around professionals. As a result, their language can also be classified as a professional variety that develops among an isolated social group gathered around common interests and professional activities (Communities of Practice). However, professional language is rather marginal, facultative and subordinate towards varieties, such as a scientific language, since members use it only for the communication within the group (Klemensiewicz, 1953). Therefore, the MTCS language can be classified as a profilect, i.e. a purely professional variety that is characterised with the use of the colloquial language and specialised vocabulary (Wiltoń, 2000: 99). The definition is, however, imprecise since the analysed research papers are written in a formal language, meeting the requirements of formal scientific writing. Wiltoń (2000) is inconsistent with the description, since he later claims that profilects function in the scientific language, official varieties and even dialects (2000: 99). Moreover, sociolects characteristic for intellectuals, among which there are academic circles do not diverge from the linguistic norm. On the other hand, Klemensiewicz (1953) contradicts his findings by the claim that some professional languages are closely connected with the scientific language (1953: 41). As a result, the MTCS domains use a mixture of the scientific, technical and professional languages on the academic level, which is partially consistent with the horizontal structure of specialised languages (depicted in Table 2.1. below). The structure encompasses languages of various professions as parallel entities, and is based on the search for factors of (inner) domain-specific communicative means (Möhn & Pelka, 2007). The structure also classifies technical languages as theoretical languages that are mainly scientific languages. Yet, on the one hand the analysed MTCS domains have developed their own communicative means, the multidisciplinary and practical character of these new fields of studies results in the mixing or sharing of common terminology, on the other. Thus, they cannot be assigned to any of these categories as they constitute a hybrid.

Table 2.1. Horizontal structure of specialised languages (Möhn & Pelka, 2007: 31)

specialised language							
theoretical language			**practical language**				
scientific language		**technical language**		**institutional language**	**language of the economy**		**language of consumption**
language of natural sciences	language of humanities	language of the production	language of manufacture	language of the service sector			(…)

Variations in the scientific language stem from different sources. Scientific languages may vary according to the subject of research. In this case one can distinguish the scientific language of humanities and of technology (Mikołajczak, 1990). On the other hand the distinction may be based on the relation between the sender and the receiver, resulting in the ambiguous division into proper scientific language with subvarieties: specialised and popularising, as well as the popular scientific. The third method of differentiating scientific languages is the genological categorisation in which genres are classified depending 'on the structural fields of the sender, receiver, the sender-receiver relation, the sending and receiving situation, and sending-receiving situation (Mikołajczak, 1990: 14; Gajda, 1982)'.

Another way of analysing specialised languages is based on the vertical stratification and the assumption that there are layers of abstraction across specialised languages (Hoffmann, 1985: 64–70 in Möhn & Pelka, 2007: 34–36). There are four layers, from the highest, most abstract to the lowest – dealing with the production matters (depicted in Figure 2.5.).

	... law	science	technics	mathematics ...
A. The language of theoretical basic science		x		x
B. The language of experimental science	x	x	x	x
C. The language of applied sciences and technics	x	x	x	x
D. The language of the material production	x	x	x	
E. The language of consumption	x	x	x	

Figure 2.5. Hoffmann's vertical stratification of selected specialised languages (1985: 66 in Möhn & Pelka, 2007)

On the other hand, Varantola (1987) claims that generalisations concerning the scientific/technical style are controversial, which this leads to producing the following theses about the sci/tech language:

- the most common tense in sci/tech discourse is the present/past/present progressive
- there is no unified scientific style
- there is a unified scientific style
- there is a style of physics and the style of chemistry but no common style for the two
- it depends on writers' individual styles whether they resemble each other or not (1987: 33).

The conclusions that are drawn include the influence of 'the topic, its treatment, the publication in question, subject-, culture-, or country specific conventions, individual style and idiosyncrasies or mannerisms' on the scientific style (Varantola, 1987: 33).

In conclusion, the language of science is characterised by a number of domain-specific features. Borderlines across domains are fuzzy as they have become interdisciplinary and hybrydised. The domains of new technologies are at the crossroads of categories, or in other words, the categories they fall into overlap. The theoretical assumptions are taken from well-established, traditional hard sciences, like maths, physics, or chemistry, and as such can be classified partially as the language of the theoretical science. On the other hand, the domains are fairly practical and develop devices and applications that are widely used, so they fall into the categories of applied sciences, because research is based on tests and experiments in order to provide practical solutions, often employing mass-scale production.

2.2. Scientific writing as specialised texts

Texts written by 'epistemological communities' are a valuable and abundant source for analyses, because of the language and its communicative purpose. However, texts are not all the same but have a heterogeneous character – 'consist of sections with different communicative functions (Trosborg, 1997; Göpferich, 2000: 232)'. Therefore, specialised texts are aimed at expert audience in order to share the level of knowledge and comprehend what is being communicated (via vertical communication) (Santos & Costa, 2015: 158). As a result, the authors are able to decide what to communicate explicitly and what to leave unsaid.

Scientific writing is a salient example of a specialised text in terms of its purpose. Scientists publish articles not only to inform about their research and the obtained results, but also create space for discussion, to express uncertainties, and provoke polemic (Santos & Costa, 2015). In addition, research papers are 'the place of proposals and counterproposals, of provocation, replies, defences, discussions' as well as 'exploration, of risk and judgement (Santos & Costa, 2015: 158)'. They act as reviews of established theories and replies to previous articles, defend one's point of view, or explore the unknown.

2.2.1. The characteristics of scientific and technical texts

Specialised texts, including technical and scientific texts, are diverse and omnipresent. They are created to serve various purposes or satisfy specific needs of specific audiences (Byrne, 2012). Collier & Toomey (1997) quantify the readers and specify the reasons for reading technical and scientific texts, i.e. 66 %

students and 78 % professionals read the texts in order to perform certain tasks. Moreover, information in science and technology is provided by experts and is needed by professionals or practitioners to 'gather information for practical application (Collier & Toomey, 1997)'.

Byrne (2012) raises the question of distinguishing technical and scientific texts. It is not an easy task to classify texts as 'purely technical, purely scientific, or something else (Byrne, 2012: 47)' and the distinction is possible on the basis of unique features or factors. Some apply to both types of texts, whereas some categories are characteristic only to scientific or technical ones. Technicality is the feature which is supposed to distinguish them, but its measures are subjective, and graded (Copek, Barker, Delisle, Szpakowicz & Delannoy, 1997). The authors (1997) also raise the question whether a technical text is a genre, text type or a number of genres (1997: 393–394).

Byrne (2012) also identifies a set of categories, by which one can distinguish technical and scientific texts, i.e. a language with metaphors and terminology, facts and specifications, references, graphics, formulae and finally equations and scientific notation.

1. language

In technical texts, language should be clear and simple to reduce the workload reading it or to avoid the risk of misunderstanding. Simple instructions should be given in a chronological order, or 'present a logical cause and effect structure (2012: 48)'. Scientific texts, on the other hand, are characterised by "a broader range of linguistic devices" apart from a limited use of a simple language, because their aim is not only to transfer information, but also to produce expected effects, and receive an expected response from the target audience or to 'understand the implications and associations of the information being conveyed (Byrne, 2012: 48–49)'.

Another linguistic feature, commonly used in scientific texts, are metaphors. Technical texts contain metaphorical language which explains new notions with familiar concepts, e.g. via metaphorical extensions common in the IT language, but their use is limited. In academic texts, metaphors and similes are incredibly useful and valuable, because they allow providing 'neat and tidy' terms for concepts and help the readers understand what the author means.

2. terminology

Terminology is the most obvious distinctive feature of technical and scientific texts. Terms are the easiest to notice in technical texts, because they are 'complex-looking and often scary words (Byrne, 2012: 51)'. Their frequency may vary from

5–10 % up to 50 % of the total word count of the text, depending on the text type (Newmark, 1988: 151; Byrne, 2012: 51; Źrałka, 2007). Moreover, acronyms and abbreviations with various domain-specific and institution-specific meanings are a common phenomenon in technical texts.

However, Byrne (2012) makes a distinction between specialised and general terms both of which might be a source of confusion for the addressees. Specialised terms behave like general terms and general terms might acquire special meanings in different contexts.

3. formulae, equations and scientific notations

The second most important feature of scientific and technical texts are formulae, equations and scientific notations which are considered to be 'fundamental components of how scientists and technicians communicate (Byrne, 2012: 56)'. The 'ancillary semiotic systems', i.e. the translation of 'the written substance into another notation' perform essential functions in such texts, i.e. allow to express abstract concepts and ideas in a clear and concise way (Sager et al., 1980: 15; Byrne, 2012: 56)'. Scientific notation, for presenting 'figures which are too large or small' in a standard decimal notation. Moreover, units of measure are mostly standardised symbols that are frequently used to describe certain physical quantities. Moreover, formulae allow for a concise and compact transfer of information, like 'chemical reactions, mathematical operations in a symbolic manner' or 'to express general relationships between quantities or variables (Byrne, 2012: 57)'. Their effectiveness lies in their universal intelligibility. In the MTCS research papers, a substantial number of formulae is used, such as the one depicted in Figure 2.6. below.

$$\Delta_{perp} = \frac{M_S \cdot \left(H_K^{perp} - 4\pi M_S\right) \cdot V}{2k_B T}.$$

Figure 2.6. An exemplary formula extracted from the English MTCS corpus

Finally, equations are clear for all mathematicians, but they are usually accompanied by explanations.

4. facts and specifications

In technical texts, facts and specifications are presented mainly bare, without further explanations, either as a part of text or in lists, tables or in bullet points. In contrast, scientific texts are also littered with hard facts, but they are incorporated in the text.

5. references

References constitute another characteristic feature of scientific and technical texts. In both types of texts, the authors make references to other documents, such as 'laws, directives and standards in the case of technical documents, or to books and journal papers in a scientific text. In the IT domains, the authors refer to 'diagrams, interface items, menus or accompanying documents (Byrne, 2012: 53)'. Furthermore, scientific texts contain more traditional references which are used to validate the provided information, to support their arguments and increase the authors' credibility. Scientists also make use of footnotes that provide additional, or incidental information, as well as other references.

6. graphics

Graphics and illustrations are also frequently used in specialised texts, especially those which carry the instructional function. Visual information may take the form of diagrams, graphs, schematics, photographs, or screenshots. The visuals have to be accurate and consistent with the written content, as well as properly labelled in order to form one coherent and cohesive multimodal text. The visual elements are used to improve readers' comprehension of the text, such as the ones presented in Figure 2.7. below.

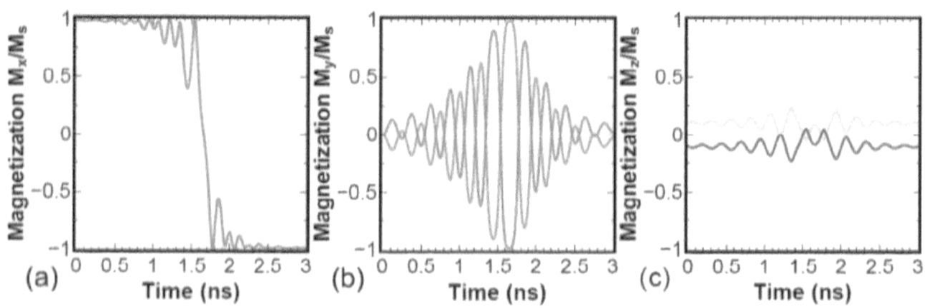

Figure 2.7. Exemplary graphics extracted from the English MTCS corpus

Moreover, Copek et al. (1997) prepare a list of 42 features that take into account lexical and syntactic elements as well as semantic, discursive, and pragmatic aspects of texts in order to assess their technicality (1997: 397). The criteria are listed below:

1	introduction or a summary setting out the content	22	colloquialisms
2	table of contents, index, appendices	23	vague terms
3	citations	24	meaning conveyed by denotation
4	quoted dialog	25	explicit analogs only
5	special fonts and punctuation	26	figurative language
6	title and headings follow a convention	27	examples
7	text clearly identifies its topic	28	ellipsis
8	text focused on its topic	29	text binders, general hedges
9	communicates a body of knowledge	30	discourse particles, general emphatics
10	serious and objective treatment	31	use of the third person
11	orderly and logical presentation of ideas	32	causative subordination
12	discussion becomes more complex as it proceeds	33	complex sentence structure
13	material organized hierarchically	34	domain-specific verbs with single senses
14	topics accessible at random	35	verbs in present tense
15	writing grammatical & sentences well-formed	36	stative sentences
16	terms defined in the text	37	passive constructions
17	non-textual elements	38	interrogative and imperative sentences
18	itemized lists	39	statements of opinion or belief
19	domain-specific terminology	40	generic reference
20	conventional expressions or formulae	41	unambiguous references
21	humor, sarcasm, invective	42	nominalizations (1997: 414).

According to Copek et al.'s (1997) definition, a technical text has to have an identified topic and transfer knowledge about it in a serious, objective and logical way. As a result, technical documents are organised hierarchically with titles and headings using special fonts or punctuation, which facilitates easy access to information and selective reading. The text is devoid of colloquial or offensive language and humour. Other characteristic features of technical texts include: same-sense domain verbs and generic and explicit references, citations, fixed structure (introductions, contents, tables, indexes, etc.), nominalisations, or lack of figurative language. Technicality is also emphasised by syntax, e.g. lack of imperatives and interrogatives, frequent use of the verb 'be', present tense and the third person, subordinated clauses, binders and hedges. Moreover, elements, such as terms defined in the text, non-textual elements (e.g. figures), and lists 'appear to be weak indicators' of technicality.

Budinsky (2001) understands technical writing as an all-embracing term that 'encompasses a wide variety of documents in science, engineering, and the skilled trades (2001: 1)'. There are four categories of technical documents listed by the author (2001) (also depicted in Figure 2.8. below).

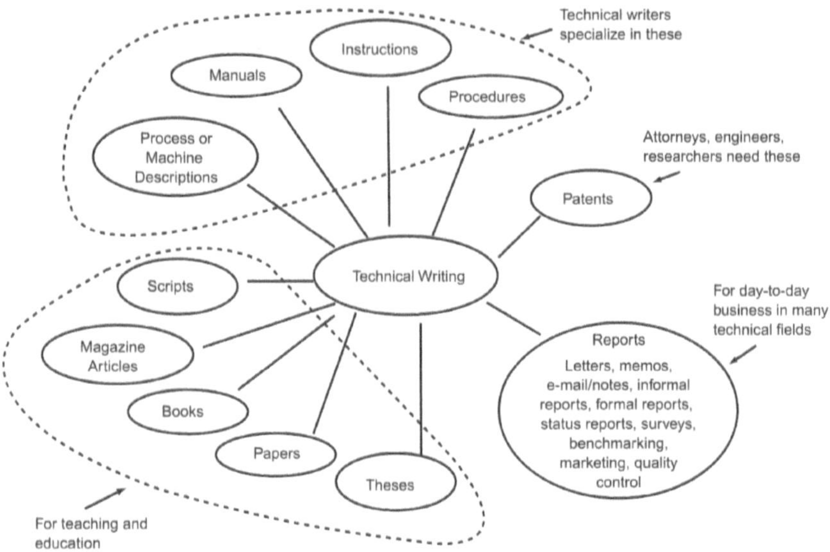

Figure 2.8. Budinsky's (2001) spectrum of technical writing with typical genres (2001: 2)

1. 'Reports and communications in day-to-day business' used to communicate the progress advanced in the application of technology,
2. 'Technical papers, magazine articles, books, and theses for purposes of education, teaching, and the sharing of information and knowledge' written by professionals,
3. Patents which require a close cooperation between lawyers and engineers or technicians,
4. 'Operational manuals, instructions, or procedures' that carry legal implications (Budinsky, 2001: 2–3).

Technical writing is characterised by a certain degree of formality and it is focused on a subject written with a view to transfer information or knowledge or incite an action. The full list of distinguishing features is as follows:

- It pertains to a technical subject.
- It has a purpose.
- It has an objective.
- It conveys information/facts/data.
- It is impersonal.
- It is concise.
- It is directed.
- It is performed with a particular style and in a particular format.
- It is archival.
- It cites contributions of others (Budinsky, 2001: 2).

The list is not as exhaustive as Copek's et al. (1997), but a number of attributives overlap. Moreover, Budinsky (2001) narrows the domains in which technical texts are used to discuss 'some aspect of engineering or the sciences in a given subject area':

- Philosophy, psychology, and religion
- History
- Geography and anthropology
- Social sciences
- Political science
- Law
- Education
- Fine arts
- Language and literature
- Science
- Agriculture (Budinsky, 2001: 3).

Collier & Toomey (1997) provide a general characteristics of technical literature. Each field and profession has its own writing standards. One can distinguish rough trends in the natural sciences, social sciences and humanities. Each domain has developed its own jargon and specialist language and the scientific writing is aimed at professional audience limited in number, and more likely to be similarly educated. Multiple authorship is more characteristic for natural sciences, such as physics, chemistry and biology than in social sciences and humanities. Articles in natural disciplines tend to be definitely shorter than the lattes. Visuals are mostly used by authors in natural and social sciences, whereas in humanities bibliographies are more expanded and footnotes appear more often. The authors also stick to the widely accepted format in natural and social sciences in comparison with the humanities (Collier & Toomey, 1997).

In conclusion, as mentioned above, technical and scientific writing has been evolving to adapt to the needs of the globalised world and more and more diversified audiences. Therefore, it is difficult determine clearly where the borderline lies between these two types of texts. The MTCS domains are a perfect example of such blends because they combine scientific writing with technical domains.

2.2.2. Hybridisation in the world of science

Hybridisation is 'a process whereby separate and disparate entities or processes generate another entity or process (the hybrid), which shares certain features with each of its sources but which is not purely compositional (Rowe & Schelling, 1991: 231 in Pieterse, 1994: 1; Sanchez-Stockhammer, 2012: 133)'. It is manifested in the world of science at different levels: from very global to very individual. It was Bakhtin (in Pieterse, 1994) who first used it in linguistics and it pertains to various aspects, such as: formal (e.g. blends), semantic (e.g. idioms), functional (e.g. syntax), etymological (e.g. languages) and communicative (e.g. double voice in the novel) (Sanchez-Stockhammer, 2012: 152).

At the very global level, hybridisation has been linked to globalisation (Pieterse, 1994). Even though globalisation is seen as the standardisation and uniformity of the world with the 'technological, commercial and cultural synchronisation emanating from the West', it allows for crossing the boundaries, a blend or a 'global melange', and finally creation of the new – a hybrid (Pieterse, 1994: 1). Technological exchange, enabled by the domains of new technologies, like microelectronics, telecommunication and information technology, leads to internationalisation. Thus, it is a well-established conceptualisation of globalisation and modernity as a ready-made package. However, globalisation understood as a hybrid allows for maintaining an individual identity and cultural diversity. For example, engineers and scientists specialising in the MTCS domains from different scientific institutions form new international teams that work on projects in international institutes. Such an approach to conducting research facilitates technological advances and knowledge transfer. It is the global melange of the scientific expertise and cultures, which results in an multidimensional and multidisciplinary approach.

Hybridisation is also manifested in the division of disciplines, which leads to creating specialised subdomains, and in the end to hybrid domains (Dogan, 1996). It is conducted by 'borrowing and lending concepts, methods, theories and praxes (Dogan, 1996: 296)'. The disciplines have become so fragmentary, that at present there are divisions of the subdomains. Moreover, a hybrid may consist of more than two disciplines with different proportions. However, the disciplines creating a hybrid do not have to meet halfway, but may create an enclave or a sector of the other. For this reason, the term hybridisation is more suitable or relevant in this context than interdisciplinarity. The interdisciplinary approach allows for seeing 'the problems caused by gaps between disciplines', but hybrids were created to fill in the gaps and the niches have dwindles. It is unrealistic and utopian to acquire knowledge of two disciplines. Although Dogan (1996) claims that the multidisciplinary approach divides the reality, and therefore is illusory, the MTCS domains are closely related, or interwoven, and successfully function in the world of science and technology.

Hybrids are also created at the linguistic level, starting with morphemes and sounds and ending with the communication level (Sanchez-Stockhammer, 2012). However, not all hybridisation phenomena appear in the analysed scientific writing. At the word level, new words are created threefold: either by creating new words, by borrowings, or by adding morphemes. The first method does not allow for hybrids, but the latter are common. In semantic hybrids, which involve an idiomatic component, new lexemes are created by adding morphemes from two sources. When it comes to the form, new lexemes are often created by blending (Sanchez-Stockhammer, 2012: 138). Changes in terminology also occur along with the evolution of text types (Iljinska & Smirnova, 2014: 96).

Hybridisation at the discourse level involves 'the layering of two or more cultural frames and it is the interleaving of scientific and non-scientific texts (Kamberelis & Wehunt, 2012: 510; Sanchez-Stockhammer, 2012: 145)'. Hybrid discourse practices, considered a creative and heterogeneous use of language, result in innovative solutions (Kamberelis & Wehunt, 2012). Scientists working in research groups form micro-communities while performing tasks, combine discourses and different fields of expertise, or knowledge and. Researchers often use 'verbal explanations, graphic representations, dramatic performances and theoretical equations to facilitate mutual understanding and gather knowledge (Kamberelis & Wehunt, 2012: 509). Hybridisation in scientific discourse is also manifested by the influences of non-scientific discourses, which appears in vertical expert-to-non-expert communication and vertical intertextuality[6], i.e. 'the way texts are built on prototypical texts that are paradigmatically related to them (Kristeva, 1986 in Kuhi, 2017: 61, 71)'. As a result, nowadays 'generic, stylistic and rhetorical conventions of non-scientific discourses' are borrowed in

6 Horizontal intertextuality refers to the sequential or syntagmatic relation of hybrid texts with source texts (Kristeva, 1986 in Kuhi, 2017: 73).

scientific discourses. As a result, the view of the 'faceless, objective, impersonal and asocial' discourse of science and knowledge has been challenged along with a strong desire to wipe scientific communication in general and written scientific communication in particular off any social and interpersonal character (Kuhi, 2017: 62–63)'. Moreover, the whole framework of dimensions of exploring hybridity of scientific discourses has been developed:

1. penetration of popularisation discourse in the discourse of science
2. penetration of instructional/pedagogical discourse
3. creating a balance between theoretical propositions and social possibilities
4. 'penetration of dialogic/cooperative discourse (2017: 69)',
5. scientific creativity and accountability to shared experience
6. penetration of competitive discourse
7. penetration of commodification discourse
8. traces of writer-responsible and reader-responsible cultures
9. penetration of ideological/political discourse (Kuhi, 2017).

Texts are subject to hybridisation, because they are constantly evolving. New text types appear as a mixture of the existing ones and in technical writing this phenomenon is considered to be one of the 'characteristic features of the changing nature of the technical text' (Sanchez-Stockhammer, 2012: 144; Iljinska & Smirnova, 2014: 96). Hybrids cross genre boundaries and contain elements and distinguishing features of other genres (Galster, 2005: 227 in Sanchez-Stockhammer, 2012: 144). This phenomenon also pertains to technical and scientific text which need to 'meet the needs of the present time and globalized science' due to the ongoing blurring of the boundaries between disciplines, styles, genres or functions (Iljinska & Smirnova, 2014: 95). Nowadays, texts belong to more than one genre and perform multiple functions (Iljinska & Smirnova, 2014: 95). The structure of a scientific text is a hybrid itself. Scientific writing is divided into chapters, sections and subsections, and the arguments in a paper are supported by references (Klimova, 2013: 53). Additionally, information is presented in a multimodal form, i.e. there are illustrations, graphs, or tables, as well as using different media to make it more legible and attractive to the target reader. Moreover, technical texts are hybrids with respects to the cultural diversity they are created, as well as to the translation process (Iljinska & Smirnova, 2014: 96). In this sense, both the source technical text, and the target text can be considered hybrids. The multifunctional and cross-disciplinary character of specialised, here: technical texts, also results from the use of the specific terminology from different disciplines in one texts. As a result, the etymology of the term, especially synonymous or polysemous, or its natural contexts might be difficult to trace, which might affect negatively the translation process of the text. Other factors, like cultural references or expressive linguistic means 'often determine context-dependent character of some terms (Iljinska & Smirnova, 2014: 96)'.

A blend of languages is also considered a hybrid (Sanchez-Stockhammer, 2012). Scientists make frequent use of this phenomenon, especially when using a minority language. New terms are created in English, since it is the language of new technologies and then 'migrate' to other languages. In this case code-switching is necessary because new terms, appearing rapidly in the world of technology, do not exist in minority languages. Moreover, non-native authors may produce an idiosyncratic hybrid language, an interlanguage while writing a paper when their foreign language skills are not sufficient (Selinker, 1972; Sanchez-Stockhammer, 2012).

To sum up, scientific and technical writing can be considered a hybrid which is manifested on various levels. The globalised world, cultures, languages, discourses, modes, genres, texts and terminology have been constantly evolving in order to adjust to the changing needs, which results in a mixture or mélange – a hybrid.

2.2.3. Pragmatic aspects of scientific writing

Scientific communication is specific with respects to lexical, syntactical and stylistic features as well as its primary function, i.e. to communicate and validate the obtained results. (Hyland, 1998: 439; Iljinska & Smirnova, 2010: 312; Gafiyatova, Korovina, Solnyshkina & Yarmakee 2017: 190). For this reason academic and technical texts as well as terminology are viewed to be relatively static and strictly organised and 'regulated by a set of norms and conventions that are not subject to considerable change (Iljinska & Smirnova, 2010: 312)'. In addition, such texts should be devoid of 'distracting inconsistencies' of the writing conventions and follow standards concerning punctuation, 'grammar, choice of vocabulary, application of rhetorical devices for crossreferencing and hypothesizing (Iljinska & Smirnova, 2010: 315)'. Valid as these norms may seem, scientific texts are created to convince the readers about research results via specialised rhetorical devices common in a given discourse community, which 'involves relating illocutionary acts to perlocutionary effects (Hyland, 1998: 440)'.

The results of Hyland' (1998) a study based on 28 research articles in 4 disciplines: microbiology, marketing, astrophysics and applied linguistics reveals that there are two types of of academic metadiscourse, i.e. textual and interpersonal with a set of categories assigned to each of them, which is summarised in Figure 2.9. below.

Category	Function	Examples
Textual metadiscourse		
Logical connectives	express semantic relation between main clauses	in addition / but / therefore / thus / and
Frame markers	explicitly refer to discourse acts or text stages	finally / to repeat / Our aim here / we try
Endophoric markers	refer to information in other parts of the text	noted above / see Fig 1 / table 2 / below
Evidentials	refer to source of information from other texts	according to X / Y, 1990 / Z states
Code glosses	help readers grasp meanings of ideational material	namely / eg / in other words / such as
Interpersonal metadiscourse		
Hedges	withhold writer's full commitment to statements	might / perhaps / it is possible / about
Emphatics	emphasise force or writer's certainty in message	in fact / definitely / It is clear / obvious
Attitude markers	express writer's attitude to propositional content	surprisingly / I agree / X claims
Relational markers	explicitly refer to or build relationship with reader	frankly / note that / you can see
Person markers	explicit reference to author(s)	I / we / my / mine / our

Figure 2.9. Functions of metadiscourse in academic texts (Hyland, 1998: 442)

Textual metadiscourse are the devices which permit to decipher the author's meanings and interpretations. Hyland (1998) identifies 5 categories, i.e. logical connectives, frame markers, endophoric makers, evidentials's role and code glosses. On the other hand, Hyland (1998) analyses interpersonal metadiscourse which reveals the writer's stance towards given information, i.e. hedges, emphatics, attitude markers, relational markers and person markers.

However, the reality is fuzzy, not clear-cut in terms of assigning functions to language units. Language use seems to be polypragmatic, because language units can perform more functions (Hyland 1998: 444). In order for a paper to be successful and convincing, the author needs to balance the subjectivity with logic as well as anticipate the audience's expectations. Textual forms are more frequent than interpersonal in scientific writing, which stems from the writer's guidance of the audience through the text and line of reasoning. Moreover, Hyland (1998) finds that 'there is no universal means of structuring knowledge above the social practices of the particular disciplinary communities (1998: 448)'. Research articles are a compromise among the members of the community regarding the discursive forms and their variations.

Scientific discourse is peculiar in terms of its lexical, syntactical and stylistic features, but some phenomena are similar to the general language use. Deictic elements differ in forms and functions are from other styles and genres (Gafiyatova et al., 2017: 190). There are two types of deictic elements in the academic discourse: conventional and endemic that 'function within fixed textual coordinates' responsible for text coherence and cohesion (Gafiyatova et al., 2017: 191). The first include typical deictic elements, like personal and demonstrative pronouns, whereas the latter are mainly characteristic for the academic writing, i.e. adjectives, adverbs and adverbials. Thus, scientific texts are restricted in use but not different from other types of prose in terms of 'the location, and identification of persons, objects, events, processes and activities being talked about, or referred to, in relation to the spatiotemporal context created and sustained by the act of utterance and the participation in it (Lyons, 1977: 637)'. However, scientific texts are devoid of temporal and 3-dimensional spatial coordinates that are characteristic for fiction and real life situations.

In scientific writing, one also can encounter contextual deixis, an umbrella term covering personal, spatial and temporal types. Moreover, academic texts need to contain a deictic centre, deictic vector and the antecedent and/or subsequent elements in order for the referential procedure to succeed. However, deictic elements are limited to the units of the text, i.e. either lexical units, sentences, paragraphs placed in the prior or following parts of the text or the whole scientific text, which are called intratextual deixis. Endemic deictic elements are of overriding importance as they appear primarily in scientific writing and include adjectives, adverbs and adverbials, such as *hereafter, in the previous chapter, above-mentioned aspects, the following reasons, in the last section*, etc. which can be treated as markers of the academic functional style (Gafiyatova et al., 2017: 194). Conventional deictic elements facilitate text cohesion as they concern smaller units, like sentences, but endemic deictic elements help build text coherence (in paragraphs or chapters). As a result, deictic elements in scientific texts prove to be essential for the textbuilding and to avoid tautology.

A view of scientific writing as objective, dehumanised, monosemic and strictly regulated has become a popular cliché. However, writers are actually present by using 'personal pronouns, third person with human reference (author, researcher, etc.), agentless and personified point of view constructions (Krapivkina, 2015: 1625)'. Furthermore, there are two opposing views on the topic, i.e. personal pronouns are either seen as distracters and should be omitted to maintain study's validity and objectivity, or should be used in order to emphasise human involvement in the study in order to avoid awkward-sounding formal syntactic structures.

Moreover, Krapivkina's study (2015) reveals that there are 3 writer's stances in scientific texts: as a researcher, as an opinion holder and as a representative (2015: 1626). These author's (2015) roles converge with Dontcheva-Navrátilová's (2013), but are not as exhaustive as the latter who identifies 5 major roles reflecting the degrees of authority which go in alliance with Hyland's study, (1998), and include a representative, discourse-organiser, recounter of the research process, opinion-holder, and originator.

Conventionally, academic novices are taught on academic writing courses to avoid personal pronouns, but the author's presence in the research article depends on internal factors, i.e. the writer's preparedness to act as a source of knowledge and external factors, like social and cultural background, epistemological and literacy tradition, and one's knowledge of genre and disciplinary conventions. Some writing styles, like Saxon, allow for the author's visibility and a higher degree of subjectivity, because Anglo-American scientific texts are aimed at initiating interaction with the audience. By being present, the author may persuade the readers, as well as encourage them to participate in the dialogue.

In conclusion, even though scientific texts, and research papers in particular, should be static, precise and objective, certain pragmatic elements are noticeable. The authors use metadiscourse devices to construct the meaning, and mark their presence to convince the reader about their theses, or interpretation of obtained results. Moreover, deictic elements affect text's cohesion and coherence, which has a positive effect on the reader's comprehension of the scientific text.

2.3. Research article as a text and genre

Scientific research is inseparably connected with communicating it to the wide audience via peer-reviewed journals (Rowland, 1999A, 1999B; Fathalla, 2004: 119–122; Belt, Mottonen & Harkonen, 2011: 7). For Belt et al. (2011), 'research can be seen as a product that must be sold to the target audience in the form of an article (2011: 7)'. Researchers who successfully publish their research are recognised and supported, which also brings benefits for their academic institution, such as 'giving credibility to the research, informing a broad audience of the achieved scientific results, adding credibility to one's own reputation, improving chances for personal promotion (Todorović, 2003: 203)'.

Nowadays, progress in telecommunication and new forms of communication have facilitated the process of exchange of scientific thought (Cabre, 1998: 4–5; Rowland, 1999A). Moreover, close cooperation between the industry and academic institutions is recommended by the institutions, like EU or the World Bank, since it is the innovative economy and technological advances that help the country remain competitive, strengthen its position in the global markets and improve the quality of its citizens' lives (European Commission, 2007; Simavi, 2013).

Research article, indispensable in the process of scientific communication, is 'a technical (or essayistic?) document that describes a significant experimental, theoretical or observational extension of current knowledge, or advances in the practical application of known principles' and it '(...) is the last step in the research process' and '(...) tells the story of the project from inception, through the data-collection process, statistical analysis, and discussion of the results (Medawar, 1999; O'Conner & Woodford, 1976 in Hengl & Gould 2002: 1; Branson, 2004)'. Thus, a research paper reports research findings that are have to be original, valid and previously unpublished, and also contribute to the expansion of knowledge by providing observations, proofs, or new data (Gordon, 1983 in Hengl & Gould, 2002: 1)'.

Research article is seen as the 'primary genre in science', and is created for the expert audience (Miller & Fahnestock, 2013: 2). Nowadays, however, along with the onset of online media readership has been widened from intended scientists, professionals, technicians, students, to practically anyone interested in the topic due to easy access to scientific writing in the electronic media, which gives rise to the 'interaction between scientific and public communities (Miller & Fahnestock, 2013: 3; Rowland, 1999A; Byrne, 2012;)'. Research papers are primarily written by professionals contain a highly specialised jargon, and are aimed mainly at experts (Pearson, 1998: 37). Therefore, writers and readers need to 'share a common language' in order to fully understand, and correctly interpret the content, because terminology in scientific articles might be acquire to a domain-specific meaning. Thus, both parties need to be able to communicate horizontally, i.e. to have a comparable level of expertise.

Gross et al., (2002) put forward a division of modern scientific articles into two categories: theoretical and experimental, which was summarised by Tehan (2009) which is provided in Table 2.2. below.

Table 2.2. Tehan's (2009) summary of Gross et al.'s (2002) division of modern research papers

Form 1: experimental, methodological or observational	**Form 2: theoretical**
abstract	abstract
introduction	introduction
materials and methods	theorem
results	proof of theorem
discussion	
conclusion (or summary)	conclusion (or summary)
acknowledgements	acknowledgements
references	references

In principle, scientific texts, and research papers in particular, are supposed to be rational, objective and impersonal, and provide information in a systematic way, because facts are presumed to speak for themselves (Gajda, 1982, 1990; Swales, 1990; Lindsay, 1995; Olszewska, 2009; Bartmiński & Niebrzegowska-Bartmińska, 2009). The authors should be hidden or invisible to ensure objectivity, which has its philosophical roots, i.e. to separate thoughts from feelings (Olszewska, 2009; Bartmiński & Niebrzegowska-Bartmińska, 2009). Moreover, the language should limited to the minimum and be like transparent glass which allows knowledge transfer to the addressee, or be like subtle and undisturbing music in the background (Olszewska, 2009; Day, 1999). At first glance, research articles are a carefully worded and re-edited written means of communication, monologues not intended to incite direct interaction, but the interactive character cannot be questioned (Gajda, 1982: 36–37; Sager et al., 1980; Olszewska, 2009; Bartmiński & Niebrzegowska-Bartmińska, 2009; Wytrębowicz, 2009). According to Olszewska (2009), a scientific paper, its parts or isolated sentences give rise to potential reactions from the reader's side. Since it is in the permanent, written form, the potential dialogue with the reader is anticipated by the authors (Wytrębowicz, 2009; Olszewska, 2009). Therefore, research papers are persuasive: to persuade the audience about the formulated hypotheses and reached via a choice of arguments to 'fit the community's assumptions, methods, and knowledge' because relying on presenting bare facts may not turn out to be satisfactory (Hyland, 1998; 2009B; Swales, 1990).

IMRAD is considered a standard of research paper writing, according to which the scientists should organise their articles (Lindsay, 1995; Branson, 2004; Nair & Nair, 2014). It acts as a prototype in terms of the structure and topics, around which peripheral combinations, or hybrids, roam like satellites (Tincheva, 2017). It contains 4 basic sections: Introduction, Methods, Results and Discussion. However, Branson (2004) and Nair & Nair (2014) provide more detailed lists of article sections (Table 2.3. below):

Table 2.3. The comparison of elements of modern research papers (Branson, 2014:1222; Nair&Nair, 2014:25).

Branson's (2004) list of sections	**Nair & Nair's (2014) list of sections & their purpose**	
The Abstract The Introduction Section The Methods Section Subjects Equipment Interventions or Study Procedures Data Analysis The Results Section The Discussion Section The Conclusions Section Acknowledgements Summary (Branson, 2004: 1222).	**Section**	**Purpose**
	Title	What the paper is about
	Authors	Names and affiliations of authors
	Keywords	Words other than those in title that best describe the paper
	Abstract	A stand-alone, short narrative of the paper
	Introduction	Why this paper? The problem, what is not known, the objective of the study
	Materials and methods	How was the study done?
	Results	What did you find?
	Discussion	What does it mean? What next? Interpretation of results and future directions
	Conclusion	Possible implications
	Acknowledgments	Who helped and how; what was the funding source?
	References	Details of papers cited
	Appendices	Supplementary materials

The modular structure of IMRAD brings advantages for different groups of interest. Firstly, it is helpful for the authors in the organisation of ideas, which makes the writing process easier (Lindsay, 1995; Wu, 2011). It also facilitates the editing and reviewing processes (Wu, 2011). And finally, clear division into units is more effective for the readers, searching particular information. Moreover, a well-defined structure and function serve like a cook-book, so the others can reproduce and repeat explained experiments. (Hengl & Gould, 2002: 6) As a result, 'a good paper is the one that is clear, coherent, focused, well argued and uses language that does not have ambiguous or equivoque meaning (Hengl & Gould, 2002: 6)'.

The IMRAD structure is, however, treated more as a guideline, a convention. Not all journals follow the style and may impose their own instructions (Nair & Nair, 2014). Moreover, Hyland's (2009B) studies reveal that the compliance with the format is domain-specific. His extensive study conducted on research articles in a wide array of scientific disciplines reveals differences in the structure of the analysed texts. Scientific papers in hard sciences, which are empirical and based on 'experimental proof', are more consistent with the IMRAD pattern. As a result, data are presented in the following way:

1. a gap in knowledge is highlighted, i.e. the purpose or reason for research,
2. hypothesis related to this gap is developed and presented,
3. finally, experimental findings are described to support the hypothesis.

On the other hand, research articles in humanities take the form of case studies or narratives. Thus, take the form of a more theoretical article (Gross et al., 2002).

Moreover, the difference in the structure between research articles might also come from the division of their elements into obligatory and non-obligatory. Figure 2.10. presents Wu's (2011) diagram of such elements which is a more elaborate version of Hill et al's (1982 in Swales, 1990) diagram. Key elements are presented in solid lines, whereas the voluntary ones in dotted lines. Therefore, the authors have a choice what to include in their writing. The main criterion is to arrange the elements in a logical order, because there is a certain degree of freedom in the arrangement of article sections (Lindsay, 1995).

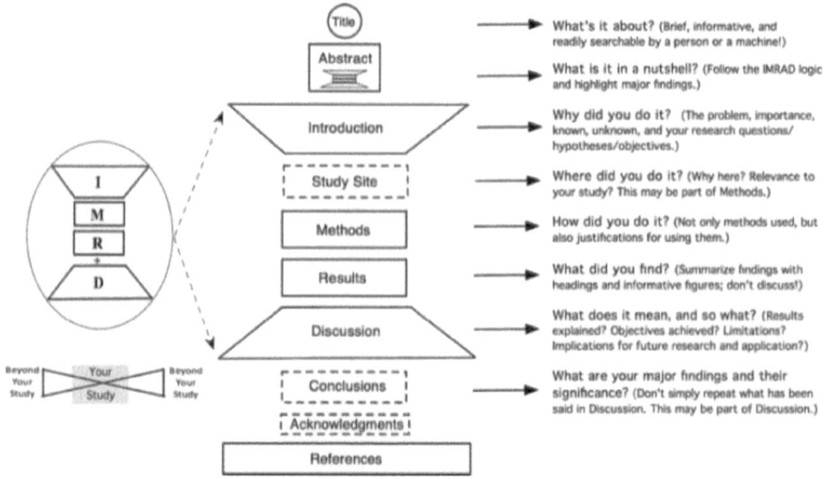

Figure 2.10. Wu's (2011) diagram of the IMRAD structure with obligatory and non-obligatory elements of the research article (2011: 1346)

The consistency with the standard structure of the research paper may also stem from different writing conventions among cultures (Galtung, 1981; Duszak, 1998). Various scientific communities develop specific forms of scientific writing which reflect 'the agreed view of the scientific community on what constitutes science (Meadows, 1998 in Wu, 2011: 1347)'. The differences might also be linked to researchers' nationality and the intellectual styles (Duszak, 1998; Galtung, 1981). The choice of linguistic strategies depends on models of the social structure (Duszak, 1998). Articles in English are treated as a commodity for sale, they are focused on the reader's capabilities, and reflect balanced social relationships, which is characteristic for the Saxonic style. The differences between intellectual styles are summarised by Galtung (1981), and depicted in Figure 2.11. below. However, easy access to international scientific texts allows for mixing the styles, especially in Polish there is a trend towards shifting more to the Saxonic way of writing (Duszak, 1998).

	Saxonic	**Teutonic**	**Gallic**	**Nipponic**
Paradigm-analysis	weak	strong	strong	weak
Descriptions: Proposition-production	very strong	weak	weak	strong
Explanations: Theory-formation	weak	very strong	very strong	weak
Commentary on other intellectuals: - paradigms - propositions - theories	strong	strong	strong	very strong

Figure 2.11. Galtung's guide to intellectual styles (1981: 823)

In conclusion, research articles are indispensable pieces of writing. Their structure has been evolving since its inception in the 17th century. The current standard, IMRAD, reflects stages in conducted research, yet the compliance level depends on the discipline and the described topic. Moreover, the differences also reflect a culture's writing tradition. The MTCS domains belong to hard sciences, and studies are based on experiments, therefore they score high in the IMRAD compliance, but there are still differences concerning the style, because the nationality of authors' of articles in English is heterogeneous, which might result in creating a hybrid.

2.4. Concluding remarks to Chapter 2

Chapter 2 concentrates on all aspects connected with the scientific language and texts. The investigations embraced the role of language in scientific communication, and its function of an instrument in knowledge transfer. Moreover, certain languages, like English, French or German, are considered modern languages of science, contributing to the expansion of knowledge worldwide, with the first as the most dominating in the world of science. Yet, it is not a straightforward task to locate the exact position of the specialised language with regard to the general language due to a number of shared features, because the boundaries overlap, especially for such disciplines, like the domains of new technologies, since they combine scientific and technical elements. On the one hand, the topics are strictly technical, but the approach is theoretical with a high level of abstraction. As a result, there emerge blends, or sci/tech communicative, textual and discursive hybrids.

Research articles, which serve referential and informative functions, act as reports in the research process, communicating its results to expert audience. The requirements for a successful scientific article pave the way for its structure and characteristic features. It should be written according to the scientific paradigm: it should be objective, rational and precise. Yet, the ways research papers are written reflect the specificity of the subject field, and there are cultural and stylistic differences, including subject specific terminology and phraseology, all of which lead to hybridity. However, it is not free from pragmatic aspects, because scientists need to convince the reader about their hypotheses and guide them through research to the interpretation of results.

The specificity of the scientific community, scientific work, writing and language determine specific terminology and phraseology which is discussed in the following chapter.

Chapter 3 Terminology and phraseology in scientific writing

The current chapter is focused on terminology and phraseology in scientific writing. The first is considered to be the most salient distinctive feature of specialised languages which allows free expansion of knowledge worldwide (Sager et al., 1980: 230; Zauberga, 2005: 107, in Mohammadi, 2013: 3; Gajda, 1990: 41; Montgomery, 2000: 189). In addition, the most recurrent and characteristic word combinations also facilitate scientific communication.

The investigations begin with the discussion on the status of terminology, classification of terms as well as types of definitions. Moreover, as the behaviour of terms is not static: terms tend to appear, disappear, change meaning or migrate among subject fields and to the general language, the study of the scientific language also embraces various aspects of terminology, such as neologisms, borrowings compression, interdisciplinarity and multimodality. In addition, the discussion tackles the polarising approaches to terminology, i.e. standardisation and the cognitive mechanisms.

Finally, the chapter includes deliberations on phraseological units as the most recurring word combinations in scientific texts. The rationale for the inclusion of the discussion on complex phrases is justified twofold. On the one hand, collocations in specialised languages form subject-field terminology, and non-idiomatic phraseological units perform important textual functions which contribute to meaning-making so vital in scientific texts on the other.

3.1. The status of terminology

The status of terminology as an independent scientific discipline is not well-established. The advocates of the traditional approach to terminology define it as an 'inter- and transdisciplinary field of knowledge dealing with concepts and their representations (terms, symbols, etc.) (Felber, 1984: 1)'. Its status as an independent discipline is based on the observation that 'an original theoretical framework has been developed to deal with phenomena of designation in special languages' as well as on the fact that 'in the field of communication terminology is considered a self-contained area of application (Sager, 1990: 1)'. On the other hand, Sager (1990) opposes it, and treats terminology as the 'number of practices that have evolved around the creation of terms, their collection and explication, and finally their presentation in various printed and electronic media (1990: 1)'.

Yet, terminology seen as an discipline in the traditional sense is also strongly criticised by Temmerman (2000), because the emergence of schools of terminology is not a determining factor, deciding on the scientific status of terminology. Its multiple definitions led to unclear and insufficient characteristics, which might be challenged (Felber, 1984; Sager, 1990; Temmerman, 2000). Even though domain-specific vocabulary constitutes its subject matter, and standardisation is its main objective, there are weaknesses in its theoretical framework. In the traditional approach, it is only specialised vocabulary taken into account as terminologists' main interest. The drive towards standardisation constitutes a restriction for objective terminological studies and limits the force towards the uncontrollable cognition and new knowledge (Gajda, 1990).

Temmerman (2000) is very strict in criticism of structuralism and its language description close to objectivism. It is not possible to describe meaning objectively and independently from 'human observation and experience', because meaning and categorisation are directly linked to the embodied understanding of the world (Johnson, 1987 in Temmerman, 2000: 3). Furthermore, the approach to terminology based on regulation, and

> 'the prescription of "good usage" reflected the era of the twentieth century progress and the needs of developing countries' as well as target users – scientists and engineers – who accepted the Greek and Latin origin of terms and the 'systemic patterns of terminology (Sager, 1990: 8)'.

This view, however, has been challenged due to the change in the approach to language description, the place of terminology in the classification of disciplines, influences from non-European language communities as well as language planning.

In addition, there are other views concerning terminology and its place in the galaxy of disciplines. Gajda (1990) proposes an equilibrium between standardisation and cognition, in order to facilitate progress and reduce chaos in specialised and technical communication. Pearson (1998) also takes a more balanced approach to the Traditional Approach to Terminology, and she explains the rationale behind standardisation as a way of reducing unnecessary confusion in communication due to the proliferation of terms, term migration, or modifications of their meanings across disciplines. Terminology is a discipline, which is even emphasised by the title of the section 'Emergence of terminology as a discipline', but does not agree with the traditional approach to studying terms in isolation, ignoring the context they appear in. The distinction between words and terms is futile without a context since words might be considered terms, occasional terms or non-terms. Therefore, the user's perspective is indispensable in terminological research.

In the past, linguistics and terminology were considered separate subject fields. Terminologists claimed that terms were not words and lexicologists treated specialised communication as a 'special case of general language (Faber, 2012: 15)'. Nowadays, terminology is treated as a part of linguistics, because according to its definition of the International Association of Terminology, it is 'the study of and the field of activity concerned with the collection, description, processing and presentation of terms, i.e. lexical items belonging to specialised areas of usage on one or more languages (Sager, 1990: 2)'.

Faber (2012) treats terminology as a young discipline, which 'has been for some time (…) in search of a theory (2012: 14)'. Terminologists have been wondering whether terminology should be a part of scientific domains, such as philosophy, sociology, cognitive science, or linguistics. Since terminology involves linguistic and cognitive activities, terminological studies should fall into linguistic analyses. As a discipline, it is mainly focused on practical applications, and concentrates on the 'elaboration of glossaries, specialized dictionaries and terminological and translation resources (Faber, 2012: 14)'. Moreover, as a young interdisciplinary field of study, it borrows elements and terminology from other fields (Sager, 1990). Philosophy and epistemology are a source of 'theories about the structure of knowledge, concept formation, the nature of definitions, etc.' psychology provides 'theories of perception, understanding and communication', and linguistics has lent terminology 'theories about the lexicon and its structure and formation (Sager, 1990: 4)'. Finally, terminology shares with lexicography 'methods of structuring and describing words' and 'experience about the presentation of information about words (Sager, 1990: 4)'. Thelen (2015) comes to the conclusion that terminology is 'an interdisciplinary and transdisciplinary discipline' 'linked to a range of (sub)disciplines, from Lexicology, Semantics, Cognitive Linguistics, Sociolinguistics, Communication, to Philosophy and Language Planning (2015 347)'.

In conclusion, terminology is a relatively young subdiscipline of linguistics with an interdisciplinary character. It is concerned with lexemes that are restricted to specialised communication. In scientific subject fields, like the dynamically developing MTCS domains, new concepts proliferate and standardisation does not keep pace with the changes. Therefore, cognitive forces, driving the progress, should not be limited in order not to hamper the scientific and technological development.

3.2. Classifications of terms

Specialised texts vary across disciplines, and they are aimed at different professional audiences. The degree of terminological complexity depends on the level of professionalism of target users, i.e. whether the texts are to be read by experts, professionals working in a given field, novices or trainees, as well as complete non-experts.

Terminology proliferates in research papers, because they tackle complex matters which are read and understood by highly professional audiences. Terms which are used by authors pertain to various subject fields and can be classified into categories. However, there are several typologies, from simpler to more complex, such as Newmark (1988); Gajda (1990) or Sager's (1983, 1990). According to Gajda (1990), terms are distinguished from the general lexicon and their position within the national language depends on their use, i.e. there are three basic spheres of functioning:

(a) internal (purely) scientific sphere (which is discussed in the monograph);
(b) external scientific sphere, i.e. didactics and popularisation of science;
(c) non-scientific sphere which leads to determinologisation of terms and terminologisation of the general lexicon (Gajda, 1990: 42).

Thus, Gajda (1990) divides the language into layers regarding lexical resources with the mutual relations between the general lexicon and terminology which is depicted in Figure 3.1. below:

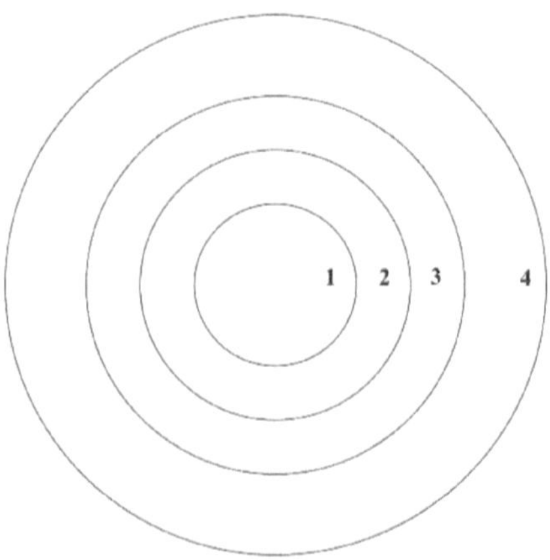

Figure 3.1. Gajda's (1990) layers in lexical resources – terminology in the lexical resource of the language (Gajda, 1990: 43)

Layer no 1 represents the general lexicon. The second layer contains the general lexicon with elements of professional vocabulary. The third layer consists of specialised vocabulary developed during the general education process, whereas the last, fourth layer depicts strictly professional vocabulary. This classification is based on the assumption that the general lexicon needed for everyday communication is limited to 1500 lexemes, whereas highly specialised lexicon is the richest in the lexical items, and terms account for 90 % of new vocabulary (Gajda, 1990: 42). However, the fourth layer is an oversimplification, as it does not allow to identify the place of the domain-specific terminology.

The spheres of use determine classifications of terminology. For this reason, one might identify varieties of technical language, or levels of technical vocabulary (Newmark, 1988). Early distinctions included 4 varieties: scientific, workshop, everyday usage and publicity/sales level. Currently, Newmark (1988) proposes a typology based on three levels:

(1) Academic. This includes transferred Latin and Greek words associated with academic papers (…),
(2) Professional. Formal terms used by experts (…)
(3) Popular. Layman vocabulary, which may include familiar alternative terms (…) (1988: 153).

All these typologies bear similarities, i.e. contain 3 to 4 categories, and are very general. Looking at the analysed technical texts, one can notice that the MTCS domains and texts exhibit scientific and professional/practical characteristics, which results in hybridised academic and professional terms. On the one hand, research and projects are purely scientific, but these technical disciplines have a practical/applicative character, and developed solutions are implemented, e.g. in banking, sports, medicine, high energy physics. Thus, the texts contain a mixture of academic and professional terms.

In scientific writing, the authors use fixed terms to identify the concepts they are discussing as well as provisionary terms – new term-alternatives that are created and have an ephemeral character. Moreover, authors use standardised, precise technical terms that are narrow in their semantic range and non-standardised, more general as well as generic descriptive terms whose motives of use in scientific writing include the situations in which:

'(1) the object is new, and has not yet got a name;
(2) the descriptive term is being used as a familiar alternative, to avoid repetition;
(3) the descriptive term is being used to make a contrast with another one (Newmark, 1988: 155)'.

Moreover, terminology is not chaotic, but it based on a system of categories and concepts and is a well-thought out process (Sager, 1983: 320). For this reason, scientific texts contain terms that can be classified into a general framework' which can act as 'points of reference necessary for fixing the reference of other terms':

a) Terms referring to observable **physical entities**. Chemical substances, plants, minerals, etc. do not require definitions as they are well-known and defined elsewhere; they do have different functions in different subject fields and may require a functional supplementary definition.
b) Terms referring to **scientific methods of analysis and description** do not require definition as they are well-known and rarely cause misunderstanding.
c) Terms referring to **properties relevant to established scientific and technological processes** are usually adequately defined, e.g. measurements.
d) Terms which are **standardized** are already defined and in most cases also classified to their position in a terminological structure, because standardized vocabularies are usually systematically structured (Sager, 1983, p. 320).

There is also the fifth category of 'terms designating other entities, concrete or abstract, manufactured products, industrial processes and perceived properties' which is considered to be unreliable, inconsistent and inaccessible (Sager, 1990: 50). As a result, the indication of contexts and disciplines is necessary because they are 'less rigidly fixed in the knowledge structure and (…) rely on a broad consensus among users for the confines of special reference associated with them (Sager, 1990: 50)'.

These categorisations of terms support the traditional approach to terminology, and the synchrony principle in particular (discussed in section *The synchrony principle*). However, the MTCS fields are relatively new and they are characterised by rapid developments in the linguistic means. Therefore, terminological complexity, borrowing terminology from traditional disciplines, proliferation of new terms and high frequency of internationalisms are among the challenges that linguists face when studying the scientific register in research papers. Sager et al. (1980) claim that terminological diversity may cause confusion and misunderstandings even among the users of specialised languages not only for linguists. Moreover, the approaches to terminology, i.e. Traditional Terminology and the Sociocognitive Approach do not agree on the description of terms, therefore corpus analysis will help discover domain-specific meaning of terms as well as context-dependent meaning nuances and shades.

In conclusion, the degree of terminological complexity is strictly connected with the level of professionalism of target users of specialised texts. The more expertise they possess, the more complex terminology is used, measured both by the level of terminological abstraction and building multiword terminological units which represent subordinate concepts. It is connected with the ideas of community of practice and discourse communities which develop specific vocabulary familiar to the inner circle of insiders. Moreover, along with the increase in the users' competency, the frequency of general language vocabulary drops.

3.3. Types of definitions and their implications for terminology

In rapidly changing globalised world, specialised vocabulary does not behave steadily, but tries to keep up with the changes. Terms are domain-specific, context-dependent and dynamic and their meanings evolve in time. Therefore, concepts behind terms need a name and a clear description in order to be understood and used properly in their natural contexts. There are three ways of describing them, i.e.

a) by definitions,
b) by their relationships to other concepts
c) by the linguistic forms, the terms, phrases, or expressions by which they are realized in any one language (Sager, 1983: 319).

Definitions constitute favoured and appropriate linguistic tools which allow for the portrayal of concepts in a consistent way with the use of the natural language (Löckinger, Kockaert & Budin, 2015: 60). They are the descriptions of meanings of verbal signs and contain a defined part (definiendum), and a defining part (definiens) (Lukszyn & Zmarzer, 2001: 116; Löckinger et al., 2015: 60). Their quality determines the quality of terminology work (Suonuuti, 2001: 19). Lukszyn & Zmarzer (2001) discuss various types of definitions and their functions which are summarised in Table 3.1. below:

Table 3.1. Lukszyn & Zmarzer's (2001) summary of different types of definitions (2001: 119)

type of definition	**function of the definition**
analytical definition	the determination of textual functions of a word
deictic (indicating) definition	evoking of the relevant image of the object
extensional definition	the determination of the range of applicable objects
intensional definition	the determination of the concept's structure
grammatical definition	the determination of the grammatical status of a word
constructive definition	the determination of constituent elements of an object
nominal (semantic) definition	the determination of a word's meaning in a dictionary
operational definition	the determination of the activities connected with a given object
pragmatic definition	the determination of the intended reaction of the addressee of the linguistic sign
predicative definition	the inclusion of the object into an appropriate collection
stipulative definition	the determination of the new content of the linguistic sign
real (factual) definition	the determination of the possibly widest range of characteristics of an object
structural definition	the indication of word-formative relations
synonymic definition	the determination of an appropriately wide range of synonyms

In terminology, however, there are two types of definitions which are the most widely used, i.e. intensional and extensional (Lukszyn & Zmarzer, 2001; Suonuuti, 2001; Lušicky & Wissik, 2015). The first type provides the description of a (specific) concept along with its superordinate (generic) concept and a set of delimiting features, and are characteristic for generic concept systems (Löckinger et al., 2015: 62; Suonuuti, 2001: 20–21; Lušicky & Wissik, 2015: 39). These useful tools have become a standard in the illustration of concepts, and are considered 'the most important type of definitions' in terminology science and management, such as DIN 2330 2013, 14; ISO 704 2009, 22; ISO 10241-1 2011, 26, but are not free from limitations (Löckinger et al., 2015: 66). Their creation requires systematic terminology work on the whole concept system, and they are more abstract in comparison to the extensional definitions.

By rule, intentional definitions should be explicit and clear, concise, precise, affirmative, non-circular, objective, give reference to a concept system and the domain, reliable to the source, suitable to the target audience, and linguistically correct (Lukszyn & Zmarzer, 2001; Suonuuti, 2001; Lušicky & Wissik, 2015; Löckinger et al., 2015). Moreover, deficient definitions should be avoided, among which there are incomplete, narrow, broad, negative, circular, or hidden ones. However, creating a bilingual terminological dictionary that facilitates a 'transfer of specialist knowledge' might be a challenging task at the macro-, medio- and microstructure level (Łukasik & Zych, 2014: 1).

On the other hand, extensional definitions contain basically a list, or enumeration of objects which a concept encompasses (Lukszyn & Zmarzer, 2001; Suonuuti, 2001; Lušicky & Wissik, 2015; Nilsson, 2015). Such definitions are not preferred in terminology and are considered improper or marginal in the terminology theory, because of a lack of real depth (Nilsson, 2015: 83). They contain the most important, subordinate concepts which are coordinate towards each other. In addition, listed elements might be mutually exclusive. Concepts might also be individual, or general as well as specific or partitive. However, intensional definitions also contain enumerations when a superordinate concept is provided; create a hybrid definition by the enumeration which can be treated as a definition which can complement intensional definitions in separated notes or explanations.

According to Nilsson (2015), extensional definitions are defined in the ISO 1087-1 (2000), but the way they are described lets them be interpreted as if they were not a proper definitions of terms. In addition, the ISO standard No 704 (2009) makes a distinction between the extensional definition, and the definition of extension. Moreover, there are a few subtypes of extensional definitions: partitive, calendaring, and headline definitions, concentrating on a specific aspect of enumeration.

Even though extensional definitions provide clear examples and are pedagogical, their usage contradicts the principles of ISO 1087-1 2000. Their usage is also constrained by a list of limitations as they do provide neither explicit characteristics of a concept nor a clear representation of the corresponding concept system. Their lifespan is rather limited, and they require previous knowledge of the elements provided.

Maintaining objectivity is one of the principles of writing a good definition, which is occasionally difficult to achieve (Löckinger et al., 2015). Ideally, it should be adequate, appropriate and credible, but should not reflect the interests of certain groups, e.g. the definition of cigarettes might be detrimental to the interests of their manufacturers. Persuasion techniques might be introduced in the definition, so that the definition is understood as the author intends, or so that the addressees take the author's position (Kublikowski, 2012: 273–274). Moreover, definitions are not stable and unchangeable, but the criteria of classification are modified depending on the social contexts, the pragmatic needs, and interests of social groups. Thus, the persuasive function might be manifested by the codifying function, i.e. in the way the authors want the users to understand and use a certain word, and therefore influence their behaviour. As a result, the concept of a real or factual definition is considered to be too strict, irrelevant and useless, because definitions are prone to change and are constantly updated depending on the needs and interests of specific social groups.

Temmerman (2000) on the other hand, questions definitions in the traditional sense and provides an alternative approach based on the prototype structure. The author (2000) also disagrees with the definition of concept, and puts forward a notion of units of understanding instead. These are prototypically structured and their definitions need to be reconsidered. The author (2000) also questions the objectivism paradigm, because understanding has a more complex structure than the ones based on logic and ontologies. Instead, understanding requires Idealised Cognitive Models (ICMs) and frames to categorise. Therefore, the encyclopaedic information will have to act as a source for 'information on different types of intracategorial structured understanding (facets) and on intercategorial understanding (2000: 67)'.

Concepts have a multidimensional character and are strongly dependent on the context which works as 'a dynamic construct that triggers or restricts part of knowledge associated with the context (León Araúz & San Martín, 2011: 175; Dash, 2008)'. Thus, term's meaning is verified by the contextual definition which acts as a form of fixation of the intension (Sager, 1983). It is not as rigorous as definitions in the 'close systems of reference of the taxonomies and other highly artificialized languages (…) (1983: 319)'. It is closer to 'the flexible definition in innovative technologies where functional characteristics are more often used than formal or material ones (1983: 319)'. Nevertheless, these external definitions might not meet target users' requirements due to their too specific or too broad to be suitable for the proposed subject classification. As a result, there might arise a need to 'construct a terminological definition in order to place the term in its appropriate knowledge structure (1983: 319)'. In order to do that, one needs to understand the intension of the term from 'existing definitions, from contexts, from consultation with specialists and through subject knowledge (1983: 319)'. In addition, Dash (2008) advises to consult language corpora as a useful source of information on context-based meanings. In order to obtain a satisfactory amount of information, one should refer to one of the four types of context: local, sentential, topical and global.

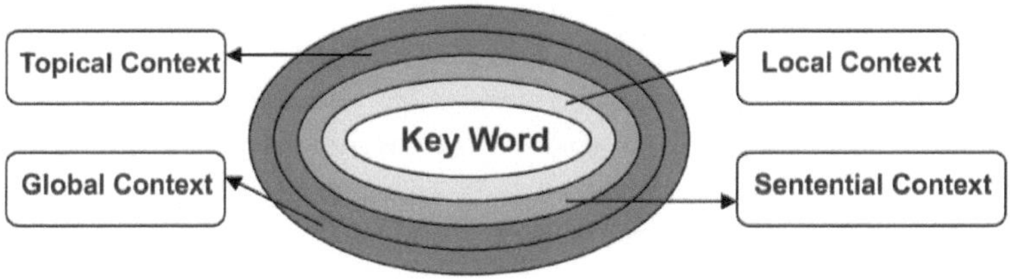

Figure 3.2. Dash's (2008) conceptual layering of a word's contexts within one text

The author (2008) develops a circular model (depicted in Figure 3.2. above) in which local context is the immediate linguistic environment of the word which acts as the most valuable source of information about the contextual meaning. Sentential context is the next one in line, when the immediate surroundings will not be satisfactory. Topical context, as the name suggests, gives details of the topic of the discussion, should the previous two fail to provide (Dash, 2008). Finally, global context is referred to when information from the extralinguistic world is needed to decipher the contextual meaning of the word (Dash, 2008: 23).

Pearson (1998) attempts to determine 'whether and how definitions are formulated in text' (1998: 89), and highlights gaps in previous research on the subject. The author (1998) summarises the discussion with an overall formula for a definition, i.e. '*an X is a Y + distinguishing characteristic* whereby *Y* is a class word or a subordinate term (1998: 104)'.

The shortcomings of previous research on the subject give room to Pearson's findings. The author (1998) refers to Austin's performatives, and claims that defining is a performative action. Didactic or informative texts written by experts for audiences with professional interests contain performative metalanguage elements. The circumstances are appropriate, i.e. the texts are written by competent persons, using a conventional procedure, and correct phraseology accepted by the addressees. Performatives can be divided into defining exercitives, and defining expositives. The first approach is used for definitions formulated for the first time, e.g. they are used in expert-to-expert communication in academic writing when the term is created, or a word is used in a new meaning, whereas the second is used when the definition is repeated, or rephrased. The second category, defining exposiveness, is used when the definition has already been coined, and is repeated, or rephrased for clarification, explanation, or reference. It is found mainly in textbooks, or where the terms are either polysemous, or acquire a domain-specific meaning different from the general language.

In conclusion, creating a clear, objective, precise and comprehensive definition is not an easy task due to their hybrid character, and the dynamic changes undergoing in the globalised world. Therefore, definitions have to reflect the dynamics of changes in the domains as well as the social contexts and interest of specific social group. Moreover, since the concept has to be well-defined, as one of the Wüsterian principles states, it is not possible to limit oneself only to one type of definition, emphasising only a few aspects of a notion, but create a hybrid instead.

3.4. Polarisation between two approaches to terminology

3.4.1. The traditional approach to terminology

The traditional approach to terminology or the General Theory of Terminology, developed by Wüster and the Vienna school of terminology, is based on five principles which, however, later have been questioned by the advocates of the cognitive approach (Temmerman, 1997; Temmerman, 2000: 4). It is based on the principle of objectivity and the Sausserian structuralist view of the language, and terminological work is aimed at language planning (Saussure, 1959).

The onomasiological approach to terminology description

The first principle, the onomasiological perspective to the description of terms assumes the precedence of the concept. Thus, in specialised communication, it is the concept that is the starting point in the 'terminology work', the basic and stable element in the terminology, the main focus, and 'should be considered in isolation from its label or term (Pearson, 1998: 10; Wüster, 1953: 12; Temmerman, 2000: 4–5; Felber, 1984: 102; Santos & Costa, 2015: 156)'. It is an 'element of thinking', a 'mental construct representing a material or immaterial object', 'which exists independently of a term (Felber, 1984: 103)'. Felber's (1984) definition was criticised by Temmerman (2000) as contradictory, because a concept is an integral part of the term, it is the meaning of the term. Felber (1984) lacks the consistency in the line of thinking, because he implies that there is a range of terms available for concepts and disregards the fact that 'meaning elements or even sound patterns can become terms when they are associated with the concept (Temmerman, 2000: 6)'. Terms without concepts are only words from the general lexicon.

Scientific activity is aimed at representation of knowledge, because 'what exists can be represented in a formal language (Stantos & Costa, 2015: 161)'. However, knowledge will always have an abstract character, and only conceptualisations are possible to be represented, or act as 'maps that describe territories (Clancey, 2007: 2 in Stantos & Costa, 2015: 162)'. Moreover, objective and exhaustive description of the world is not possible. Therefore, there is a contradiction with the traditional approach, since conceptualisation is viewed as a 'mental activity which can happen outside the language (Temmerman, 2000: 6)', and idealistically, the assignment of one term to one concept takes place at the end of the process. However, it is the language that allows conceiving and communicating concepts. On the other hand, there is a dilemma concerning 'what belongs to language and what belongs to concepts (Santos & Costa, 2015: 157)'. As a result, terminologists study texts, thus terms in context in particular, in order to gain knowledge indispensable to 'obtain information about concepts (Santos & Costa, 2015: 159)'.

The clear-cut character of concepts

According to the traditional approach to terminology, concepts are not isolated, but 'they have direct relationships to other concepts which have the same characteristics in their intensions (Felber, 1984)' which are understood as a sum of characteristics – intrinsic, of purpose and function and of origin (Felber, 1983: 4–5). A concept is a mental construction of a single object, which is represented by a symbol – a term in specialised communication (Felber, 1983; Pearson, 1998: 11). Only one concept, a mental construct – corresponds to one term – its label (Pearson, 1998: 11). Moreover, concepts can also be indirectly related to other concepts, e.g. are subsequent in time or space. A system of concepts, a structured conceptual field 'is only mentally accessible (Felber, 1984)'. The relationships between concepts are divided into several categories identified by Wüster (in Felber, 1984):

1. Logical relationships
2. Ontological relationships
    - 2.1. Partitive relationships
    - 2.2. Relationships of succession
    - 2.3. Relationships of material-product
3. Relationships of effect
    - 3.1. Causality
    - 3.2. Tooling
    - 3.3. Descent
        - 1.1.1. Genealogic descent
        - 1.1.2. Ontogenetic descent
        - 1.1.3. Descent between stages of substances (1984: 120–121).

Traditional Terminology strives to maintain objectivity and clarity (Temmerman, 2000). However, mental representations are based on the individual understanding of the world, and therefore subjective. There are some doubts concerning the objectivity. Is it a collective mental representation? Is it agreed upon? If so, on what grounds? Felber (1984) does not provide any explanation or proof. Moreover, clear delineation of concepts based on comparable characteristics, assumed by the traditional approach, is not always possible (Temmerman, 2000). Unambiguous and clear-cut concepts are an unattainable goal, and as a result, one should rely more on categories, since they contain a set of necessary and sufficient characteristics.

The synchrony principle

The traditional approach to terminology concentrates on concepts and the concept system rather than on vocabulary (Temmerman, 2000). The assignment of a pair concept-term is viewed as stable or permanent. Therefore, the process of evolution of concepts, their designations, and language development is ignored by the advocates of the Traditional Terminology.

Definitions in the traditional approach

A definition is a foundation for the scientific work and each concept should posses either a definition or at least an explanation (Felber, 1984: 160). The Vienna school of terminology identifies three types of definitions, i.e. intensional – a top-down approach to classifying concepts, extensional is the bottom-up classification and a part-whole description (Felber, 1983; Temmerman, 2000).

According to the tenets of Traditional Terminology, a definition should meet a set of requirements which are as follows:

1. The concepts used in definitions should be defined in the same or another reliable publication.
2. Tautology should be avoided.
3. When concepts are used with a restricted scope, this should be indicated by a note after the term (for instance: "for the present standard only").
4. A definition should be as concise as possible.
5. A definition should reflect the characteristics of the given concept.
6. A definition should reflect the position of the given concept in a definite system of concepts (Felber, 1983: 7).

The requirements can be applied to well-established terms, but for new designations they are exaggerated. The rules mentioned above do not take into account transition phases in the process of the establishing a term (Dury, 2005). Moreover, there is a contradiction in the line of thinking, because it is Felber himself who claims that it is not always possible to provide a definition.

Definitions are created to minimise the ambiguity, and ensure clarity and precision (Strehlow, 1983). In the case of technical terms, there are two challenges. Firstly, it is difficult to obtain precise definitions from various dependable sources. General language dictionaries do not include technical vocabulary, especially complex and highly specialised terms. Secondly, definitions are of other types, not only the three mentioned above. In addition, not all definitions contain the place of the concept in the concept system, and it is difficult to meet Felber's (1983) requirements in a concise way.

In Traditional Terminology, it is the intensional definition that takes precedence as 'it is more systematic than any other type of definition', it and reflects 'the position of a concept in a concept system (Temmerman, 2000: 9)'. However, the three types of definitions cannot be applied to all terms, and the explanations do not allow to indicate the concept's position in the concept system (Felber, 1984; Temmerman, 2000). Moreover, Temmerman (2000) believes that for the majority of terms it is not possible to 'create a meaningful intensional definition' which 'provides the information necessary to understand the term which designates the concept being defined (2000: 10)'.

Monosemy

Specialised communication is aimed at maintaining clarity and precision, and at the same time avoiding ambiguity (Felber, 1984: 179; Parysek, 2017: 176–177). Therefore, assuming idealistically, the term should be accurate, concise, correct, monosemous, easy to pronounce, spell and form derivatives, as well as be a constituent of the concept system. As a result, one term should be assigned to one concept and synonymy and polysemy are rejected (Temmerman, 2000). The assignment of a term to a concept is viewed as permanent and deliberate, leading to standardisation. Homonyms should be reduced and synonyms – eliminated, both of which, however, are necessary phenomena in term creation (Temmerman, 2000; Dury, 2005).

Standardisation of terminology

Standardisation of terminology derives from the need to achieve 'a higher level of precision than that required in general communication (Cabré & Sager, 1998: 194)'. However, Cabré & Sager (1998) point out a lack of agreement concerning terms normalisation and standardisation to be used in this context. The adherents of the first term emphasise the lack of the 'authoritarian connotation associated with words based on standard (1998: 194)'. The opponents opt for the latter term as the one which refers to 'decisions issued by authoritative bodies' and denotes 'the choosing of a specific term as a reference form (1998: 194)'.

Standardisation of terminology is a consensus reached by a 'representative commission (Cabré & Sager, 1998: 194)'. It is the reduction of existing varieties or alternatives to a single one, i.e. to produce 'one and only one designation for a well delimited concept (1998: 194)'. The process is the aftermath of a conflict concerning terminological alternatives (Sager, 1990: 115). Before establishing a standardised term, its suitability is verified by its usage in specialised contexts for a given period of time (Cabré & Sager, 1998: 197). Therefore, standardisation is a 'retrospective activity', but terminological alternatives may still be in use (Sager, 1990: 115). Moreover, the process might be preceded by the appearance of dictionaries, term banks or glossaries which might not influence it, but have a harmonising effect and serve as a reference.

Rapid scientific and economic progress results in the proliferation of new concepts and terms, which might lead to 'intolerable confusion (Felber, 1984: 15)'. Therefore, terminology commissions have been established to 'standardize concepts and terms (Felber, 1984: 15)'. As a result of their work, there are two types of standardisation of terminology:

1. standardization of terminological principles and of methods for terminography
2. standardization of vocabularies (terminology standards) (Felber, 1984: 15).

In order to perform the process of standardisation on the regional, national and international level, a number of standardising bodies have been established with a set of procedures, but there are no consistent methods of compilation (Cabré & Sager, 1998; Sager, 1990). At the national level there are several standards, such as DIN, BSI or ON (Sager, 1990). ISO has established a set of principles, and it is concerned with standardising technical vocabulary with the exception for electrical engineering and electronics (Cabré & Sager, 1998; Sager, 1990). The International Electrotechnical Commission (IEC) has been set up to deal with all matters concerning these domains, terminology included. Its committee for terminology has been working on the terminology, has published its dictionary, and developed an online terminology database http://www.electropedia.org/ with terms from "electrotechnology", i.e. the electrical engineering and electronics.

Standardisation of the relationship concept-term is seen as the main objective of terminology (Pearson, 1998: 12). It 'involves official recognition and acceptance of a term and its meaning (1998: 22)'. The rationale behind standardisation lies in the need to unify concepts and their system and definitions as well as to eliminate homonymy, synonymy and polysemy in order to facilitate precise and clear specialised communication (Felber, 1984; Cabré & Sager, 1998). The overall goal of standardisation is also the elimination of differences to facilitate exchange of thought (Cabré & Sager, 1998). The usefulness of standardisation also derives from the need to 'achieve compatibility of intention, knowledge and language' in specialised settings, especially in science, technology or economics (Sager, 1990: 123, 126).

There are two main purposes of standardisation. The first is either to select a term among existing alternatives to 'designate an already existing concept', and to select the best alternative among the suggestions to provide a name for a concept as well as to discard the linguistically unsatisfactory or grammatically incorrect ones (Nakos, 1983: 41). The second purpose is concerned with the promotion of the use of one, and only one name for a concept. Transparency of the term is an important factor in the promotion of the selected alternative, but it should not be the only criterion. Other criteria include adequacy, experts' acceptability, or the possibility to form derivatives. Moreover, methods of standardisation are parallel to the ways of making new words in a language (which is discussed in other sections of the current chapter), such as:

1. redefinition of words
2. redefinition of existing terms
3. derivation
4. composition
5. borrowing
6. compression (Sager, 1990: 120–122).

Their effectiveness and economy are varied, leading to the emergence and standardisation of more or less precise appropriate international terms.

Standardised terms in scientific and technical writing are supposed to maintain their monosemic, stable and static character. They designate concepts precisely, are emotionally neutral, and independent from the context (Iljinska & Smirnova, 2010). However, academic texts are complex and dynamically developing in order to cater to 'the needs of the present time, contemporary research, and globalized science (Iljinska & Smirnova, 2010: 312)'. Moreover, it is in science where the largest and the most intensive increase in concepts and technical vocabulary has been recorded.

On the other hand, standardisation of terminology poses a number of problems. The process hinders 'the natural creativity of language' and can be applicable to codified knowledge (Sager, 1990: 122–124). Moreover, the relation between the structure of knowledge and its clear-cut representation in the language is limited to specialised communication, and terms do not behave in a stable way, and might be polysemous in one discipline, or in various domains. Moreover, 'concept-words are notorious for their different meanings in various technologies', or might change their meaning when forming different collocations (Newmark 1988: 152). For this reason, standardisation will never cover all changes in the specialised language. Moreover, selected standards appear in the terminological publications along with the rejected alternatives. In addition, terminological recommendations do not reflect all subject-field terminology, but only the terms which have an agreed definition with others worth considering either not included or rejected. Moreover, standardised terminologies are not easily accessible due to their high costs, which leads to the situation that professionals are not aware of the official nomenclature and use the deprecated terms. Finally, target users might still use the rejected alternative as the one most natural in a given domain. For the above mentioned reasons, Pearson (1998), Cabré Castellví (2003) & Faber (2015) suggest that standardised terminology does not reflect real use of the language, and that standardisation is a wishful thinking, or an idealised vision of reality. Therefore, standardisation being a complex process, does not fully achieve its aims, and should be treated more as a 'device to facilitate the communication of information' rather than an aim to attain (Cabré & Sager, 1998; Sager, 1990).

Technical terminology has a cross-disciplinary, multi-functional and hybrid character, which might affect understanding of texts (Ijinska & Smirnova, 2014). The problem of hybridity in technical texts is also multiplied by the use of polysemous and synonymous terms from other domains. As a result, it is difficult to identify the exact meaning and the field the term belongs to. Moreover, terms nowadays do not behave ideally, but are context-dependent and culturally bound. However, certain technical domains, like civil engineering, 'display a tendency for standardization of terminology of professional vocabulary (Ijinska & Smirnova, 2014: 99)'. The tendency towards unifying cross-disciplinary terminology is also apparent, which is parallel with metaphorisation of terminology. For example, the trend towards the formalisation of computer design software terminology has improved the interoperability of different types of software. On the other hand, this subject field does not show consistency in the usage of standardised terms. All in all, standardisation is a retrospective process which does not keep pace with the changes in specialised languages, and as such should be limited to codified languages. However, it still 'remains a useful tool that organizes knowledge, registers new terms, and helps organize professional communication (…) (Ijinska & Smirnova, 2014: 106)'.

To sum up, standardisation of terminology presents a retrospective view on specialised languages. It is the preference of one term over a group of alternatives which is useful in technical and scientific communication agreed by official bodies, but at the same time might be a hindrance, an obstacle in the process of development of specialised languages. Therefore, natural processes, like metaphorisation, polysemy and synonymy should be acknowledged in specialised communication. As a result, there should be a twofold approach: on the one hand standardisation of well-established terms and recognition of newly coined terminology by means of new coinages, metaphorical extensions, or borrowings.

3.4.2. Cognitive approaches to terminology

Cognitive approaches to terminology form a counterbalance to the traditional approach. They acknowledge the phenomena which Traditional Terminology criticised and discarded as irrelevant in specialised communication. However, occurrences, such as terminological synonymy, polysemy or metaphorisation are present in specialised texts, and cannot be ignored in the rapidly developing specialised languages.

Metaphorisation of terminology

Metaphors are omnipresent in human understanding, language, thought and action and constitute means of 'structuring our experience' and provide projections of and mappings across different domains in the actual structuring of our experience (Lakoff & Johnsen, 2003: 4; Temmerman, 2000: 162, 164; Tabakowska, 2015: 43; Siqueira et al., 2009). They are not ornaments, a superficial linguistic phenomenon in the Aristotelian understanding, but cognitive mechanisms, and a specific way of thinking (Tabakowska, 2015: 39). They are even considered 'one of eight procedures of terminology creation', and a guidance in the 'construction of knowledge and the development of science' as well as a 'means of enriching terminology', and an unavoidable feature of the scientific language (Temmerman, 2000: 172; Pissolato de Oliveira, 2016: 151; Pułaczewska, 2010: 377; Ghajoyan, 2017: 28). However, in the traditional approach to terminology, the importance of metaphors was limited only to their naming capacity in the objective reality, because it was thought to be 'an impediment for unambiguous "scientific: naming and communication:" (Temmerman, 2000: 163, 170, 182)'.

According to Lakoff (1987 in Temmerman, 2000), our knowledge is organised in structures called idealised cognitive models (ICMs) with category structures and prototype effects as by-products. The process of metaphorisation involves a 'partial mapping of some ICM structure in a source domain onto a corresponding structure in a target domain (Temmerman, 2000: 165)'. Thus, a metaphor is a 'conceptual transfer based on resemblance' whose type determines the type of metaphor: material, functional and experiential (Temmerman, 2000: 167). A similar, but simplified description of mappings across the two domains provides Pissolato de Oliveira (2016), and identifies different types of similarities: partial, total, functional and visual, such as colours in particle physics..

Metaphors in scientific discourse differ from their use in the general language. There are two types of metaphors in scientific settings, i.e. conceptual and image metaphors (Tabakowska, 2015). In the technical contexts, anthropological metaphors 'reflect physical, moral and intellectual qualities' as well as humans' social activities, and non-anthropological ones depict 'the reality surrounding the human being (Ghajoyan, 2017: 29–33)'. The first are based on general conceptual schemas, and are considered to be regular elements of the scientific language and the latter are juxtapositions of two similar objects, and are used to name the unnamed (Tabakowska, 2015: 43–44). Moreover, there are five functions of metaphors in the scientific communication. The heuristic function directs the line of researcher's thought and paves the way for the line of research. The creative function constitutes a tool of broadening of human cognition and limiting the unknown, as well as of the creation and standardisation of terminology. Thus, a metaphor simplifies expert-to-expert communication, and clearly explains new notions via imagery to non-experts in the vertical communication. The explicative function, related to the didactic function, facilitates understanding in educational settings. Finally, the pragmatic or evaluative function, present mainly in the popular-scientific texts, allows the author to assess the message via a metaphor.

In the functional approach, metaphors act as cognitive tools in scientific writing. Yet, Tabakowska (2015) and Ijinska and Smirnova (2014) also discuss the dangers connected with the use of metaphors in scientific and technical texts. The choice of the source domain based on the similarity to the target domain might be subjective, culture-specific and not universal, which might lead to disturbances in intercultural communication. Moreover, the perception of metaphorical images may differ due to different national, historical, and individual aesthetic values. Additionally, juxtaposing two objects on the basis of one similar feature might lead to emphasising certain elements at the expense of others (Tabakowska, 2015: 45).

Even though ideal scientific terminology borrowed 'morphological and semantic resources' from classical languages: Latin and Greek, it was deprived of connotations in order to 'produce a non-ambiguous, one-to-one correspondence between a denotation and the object to be named (Pułaczewska, 2010: 379–380)'. However, the concept of 'scientific truth' has been replaced by knowable truth and independent facts by theory-laden, as nowadays one cannot speak of the absolute, and unconditional truth (Pułaczewska, 2010; Siqueira et al., 2009). As a result, scientific concepts are formed analogically to the ones of ordinary experience via metaphorical extensions, and as such scientific thought and language free from metaphors is an unattainable goal. Quite the opposite, metaphors are considered 'fundamental cognitive tools in the apprehension and formulation of concepts', and 'figurative expressions are part of terminological descriptions (Pissolato de Oliveira, 2016: 154; Siquiera et al., 2009: 161)'. Moreover, Ijinska & Smirnova (2014) find that metaphorical extensions of meaning are a frequent phenomenon in terminology creation in technical domains, like electricity, whose derivatives also function in information technology. There are specific tendencies in creation of terms via metaphorical extensions of meaning:

1. terms may be created on the basis of various field of reference (color symbolism, animal symbolism, etc.)
2. terms may be connotationally loaded (*killer bee, loan shark*)
3. terms may be created on the basis of allusions to cultural knowledge (*fallen angel*)
4. terms may be created on the basis of allusions to situational context (*baby Bills*) (2014: 104).

Moreover, metaphors in scientific texts are manifested in two ways:

(a) through new associations for pre-existing referents,
(b) through the revivals of metaphors that were taken as dead, or catachreses (Pissolato de Oliveira, 2016: 155–156).

Figurative elements in specialised texts play both a conceptual and aesthetic role (Siqueira et al., 2009). Metaphors help with the conceptualisation of the world, because 'human mind operates with concepts metaphorically that connect with other concepts of a similar structure (2009: 159)'. It is through the sensory perception and the interaction between language, the mind and the human body that we understand scientific and technical knowledge, because human 'reasoning has an embodied basis (2009: 159, 161)'.

On the other hand, some language researchers voice their objections to the pervasive role of metaphors in the scientific language and to the overuse of the metaphorical expressions in scientific texts. The opponents view figurative language in scientific contexts as a source of ambiguity and misunderstandings (Parysek, 2017). However, Parysek's (2017) critical view contains inconsistencies, because the author (2017) states that metaphors play specific roles in two areas of scientific language, i.e. in the creation of new theoretical concepts and in the theoretical modelling. Furthermore, the main feature of metaphors in science is their usability, not their sense. However, such an approach might lead to communication disturbances and the inhibition of the scientific development due to the restricted use of professional vocabulary, and abstract descriptions in scientific writing.

In conclusion, metaphors are a useful tool in general communication and in specialised contexts. They allow for an effective explanation of unfamiliar or new concepts via comparison with existing linguistic means and concepts. However, their presence and usage has still been considered undesirable for some researchers.

Terminological synonymy

Synonymy, 'equivalence of meaning' or 'sameness of meaning' allows to substitute linguistic units is considered undesirable in terminology, because it hinders specialised communication (Lipka, 1992; Cruse, 2004: 156; Pearson, 1998: 169; Polackova, 2001: 174; Čermák, 2010 in Cocca, Kendzora, Řeřicha & Martínez, 2016: 22). The notion is also defined as 'a horizontal paradigmatic relation of semantic similarity among lexemes (Čermák, 2010 in Cocca, et., 2016: 22)'. It stems from a rapid creation of new terms and leads to barriers and disturbances in communication (Jeż, 2014). Moreover, there are three factors that need to be taken into account in order to determine the degree of sameness or similarity between lexical units:

1. congruence between meanings (i.e. denotative and connotative contents and connotational and pragmatic elements)
2. congruence between distribution (i.e. the type of environment and texts in which a term may occur)
3. congruence between the extension of meaning denoting its collocability (Klégr, 2004 in Cocca et al., 2016: 22)

However, definitions are not always sufficient in determining the relations between terms, and other factors have often been neglected, such as the context which 'pragmatically has a decisive impact on determining the meaning of a lexical unit or units (Levická, 2009; Chromá, 2011: 40)'. Other aspects include granularity, and the grammatical congruence: lexical units need to belong to the same part of speech to be considered synonymous (Levická, 2009; Pearson, 1998: 170).

The degree of similarity or sameness might be linked to the tenets of the Periphery Theory (Lipka, 1992; Geeraerts, 1989; Cocca et al., 2016). Word classes do not have clear-cut boundaries, but are fuzzy (Lipka, 1992). As a result, they contain core or central members, prototypes and peripheries. Since prototypicality of categories is a complex notion, one cannot apply one set of criteria to define categories, their meanings overlap, family membership is not equally representative, and the category edges are blurred (Geeraerts, 1989). As a result, semantic categories of synonyms are scalar depending on the 'degree and intensity of variability of the differences in meaning (Cocca et al., 2016: 22)'. Some of them exhibit a higher family resemblance in terms of meaning than others, their meanings, and contexts of use overlap to a greater or lesser extent (Geeraerts, 1989; Lipka, 1992). These bigger or smaller differences, also called overlaps, determine the type of synonyms. Various language researchers identify at least two types of synonymy.

Lyons (1995) identifies four types of synonyms: absolute, near, partial and descriptive. Absolute synonyms occur extremely rarely in natural language, because they obligatorily need to meet the three criteria (which seems to be rather idealistic):

1. all their meanings are identical;
2. they are synonymous in all contexts;
3. they are semantically equivalent (i.e. their meaning or meanings are identical) on all dimensions of meaning, descriptive and non-descriptive (Lyons, 1995: 61)'.

However, the failure to fulfil one of the requirements above means the failure to satisfy the others. The second type of the phenomenon is near-synonymy, in which expressions need to be 'more or less similar, but not identical, in meaning (1995: 60)'. Near-synonymy should not be confused with partial synonyms, a category distinguished from the candidates for absolute synonyms that fail to meet all the criteria. However, this distinction is not clear. Moreover, the role of context should not be overlooked, and the collocational range in particular, because collocations form a part of a lexeme's meaning. The utterances might be grammatically correct, but still either 'collocationally unacceptable or unidiomatic (Lyons, 1995: 62)'. The nuances in lexical meaning revealed via collocational differences determine whether it is the case of synonymy, or near-synonymy. The last type of synonymy is descriptive, based on the descriptive meaning. However, it is the expressive meaning that shows whether an utterance is neutral, or implies approval or disapproval.

Lipka (1992) criticises Lyons' (1968) approach to synonymy with respects to a number of aspects. Firstly, Lyons (1968) narrows synonymy to cognitive synonymy and does not provide a thorough definition. Moreover, synonymy is a phenomenon that holds between lexical units, and not lexical items, contrary to Lyons' (1968) claim. Finally, Lipka (1992) undermines the irrelevance of synonymy for the structure of the language lexicon. On the other hand, the author (1992) concludes that for Lyons (1968) synonymy also includes groups of lexemes, not only equivalent lexical units.

Cruse (2004) proposes three degrees of synonymy, i.e. absolute, propositional and near, similar to Lyons (1968, 1995), but better justified and developed. Absolute synonymy is a 'complete identity of meaning' depending on the context which occurs rarely, because one incompatible context disqualifies a pair of words. The second type, propositional synonyms, can substitute each other 'in any expression with truth-conditional properties without effect on those properties', but differences in meaning need to include one or more of the following aspects:

1. differences in expressive meaning
2. differences of stylistic level (on the colloquial-formal dimension)
3. difference of presupposed field of discourse (Cruse, 2004: 158).

According to Cruse (2004), this type of synonyms is most often used in contexts involving emotions, placed on a different place on the euphemism-disphemism scale as well as in distant contexts with various implications and importance which, however, are not to be found in scientific writing. The third type, near-synonyms are not clearly defined by the author (2004), but are only contrasted with propositional and non-synonyms. Cruse (2004) provides two aspects that need to be considered when analysing near-synonyms. The first is the users' intuition which pairs are synonymous and which are not and the second is the relative closeness of meaning between words. Thus, the differences in meaning of near-synonyms 'must be either minor, or backgrounded, or both (2004: 159)'. There are three types of minor differences:

1. adjacent position on scale of 'degree' (…)
2. certain adverbial specializations of verbs (…)
3. aspectual distinctions (…)
4. difference of prototype centre (…)(Cruse, 2004: 159).

Cocca et al. (2016) discuss Dubuc's (1997) typology of terminological synonymy who identifies three types of synonyms: real, quasi and pseudo synonyms. Real synonyms can be used interchangeably, because they 'represent the same concept' (Cocca et al., 2016: 23)'. For this reason this type is similar to absolute synonyms discussed above. However, real synonyms, including syntactic variants, are interchangeable in contexts within one domain. The second type are quasi synonyms which are also used interchangeably, but under certain conditions, called labels, such as geographical, temporal, frequency and professional. The last type of synonyms are pseudo synonyms, not interchangeable due to 'specific diagnostic features' that 'narrow their semantic content (Cocca et al., 2016: 24)'.

Pearson (1998) adopts the ISO definition which states that synonymous terms are used interchangeably in all contexts within a subject field. When the contexts in which terms appear in the same meaning are limited, they are called quasi synonyms. Pearson (1998) finds the definition of the latter insufficient and rejects it. The author (1998) discusses Landheer (1989) and Trimble's (1985) types of synonymy: absolute in which 'two words have the same referent, and are in a two way replacement relation', and approximate, or quasi – 'when two words have the same referent but are not interchangeable (1998: 171)'. Finally, Pearson (1998) proposes a definition of terminological synonymy which stipulates that it is 'a term which means the same as another term used in the same communicative setting (1998: 172)'.

Nakos (1983), on the other hand, discusses synonymy in the context of standardisation and acknowledges three types of synonymy: real, near and false in specialised texts, and advises different approaches to standardisation. In the case of false synonymy, it might or might not be necessary, 'depending on how spread is the ill-use of two or more terms designating the same concept (Nakos, 1983: 41)'. Depending on the reference, they can have the same, or different meanings. Real synonyms have the same meanings, and are used interchangeably among experts, therefore standardisation is a necessity. Finally, near synonyms are context dependent, and standardisation is not imperative.

According to Nakos (1983), real and near synonymy occurs in scientific and technical writing. Therefore, contexts in which they occur should be analysed as well as dictionaries and other references should be consulted in order to verify their level of synonymy. In the case of false synonyms, such analyses are indispensable in order to standardise both the term and its definition. Real synonyms, which are a natural phenomenon appearing when specialists from different institutions independently work on the same idea, obligatorily need to be standardised in 'the fields that concern a great number of people', but in highly specialised domains accessible to few experts do not necessitate the normalisation process (1983: 43). On the other hand, near synonyms are not interchangeable, because they are used at different levels of speech, or registers, and do not appear in the same contexts. This phenomenon refers to the three levels of terminology proposed by Newmark: academic, professional and popular (1988: 155). In this case standardisation is not necessary.

Iljinska and Smirnova (2014) present a well-balanced standpoint on synonymy of terminology. On the one hand, the authors (2014) claim that synonyms are frequently used, but are not stylistically neutral, which might pose a challenge for specialised translators. Moreover, it is one of the phenomena that are problematic for terminology management, and the process of standardisation. On the other, synonymous terms are 'natural phenomena of scientific and technical language (2014: 106)'.

However, Temmerman (2000) treats synonymy in specialised communication as functional, which is overlooked by advocates of the univocity principle. The rationale behind its use lies in the need to emphasise a certain aspect, or element in a given context appropriate in very nuanced specialised communication. Language mechanisms allow for developing new designations, which reflect the 'creative process of growth of knowledge (2000: 153)'. Therefore, a diverse approach to terminography should be adopted. When the concept is clear-cut, the univocity principle should be applied, but in instances when categories exhibit a prototype structure, phenomena, like synonymy and polysemy, should be acknowledged.

In conclusion, synonymy in terminology was originally considered to be undesirable, bringing chaos to specialised communication. However, its existence in specialised contexts proves the development of the subject field and its terminology. Therefore, now it has been acknowledged, and is considered functional as it allows for expressing nuances of a term's meaning. The safest attitude is the dual approach to terminology with respects to synonymy. Following Temmerman (2000): the univocity principle should be applicable with clear-cut concepts, but in the case of terms with the prototypical structure the existence of synonymy and polysemy (discussed below) should be taken into account.

Terminological polysemy

Polysemy is a linguistic phenomenon deriving from 'human reflection of the world' and semasiologically from the evolution of meaning that poses a number of problems (Temmerman, 2000: 138; Grinev-Griniewicz, 2016). It is defined as 'a single word having two or more meanings', but they 'should be related to each other' in contrast to homonymy in which 'a word has two or more unrelated meanings (Pethő, 2001: 177–178)'. In specialised contexts, terms might have two or more meanings within one discourse community and can also be used in various fields (Chromá, 2006: 737).

In the traditional approach to terminology, polysemy is perceived as unwelcome, undesirable or controversial, because of the drive towards objectivity and precision, as well as 'due to strict definiteness of scientific and technical concepts (Grinev-Griniewicz, 2016: 23; Zolotukhin, 2016; Siqueira et al., 2009). As a result, terminological meanings which correspond to these concepts must be also strictly defined and separated. Moreover, there is a dilemma where the borderline between polysemy and homonymy lies, but these notions differ in terms of connections of meaning (Lyons, 1968; Zolotukhin, 2016). When the meanings are connected, then the lexemes are polysemous, whereas homonymy 'can be found only in a complete breakdown in relationship between meanings (Zolotukhin, 2016: 70)'. However, it is the users' intuition, or psychological criteria that are used in order to determine semantic relatedness, which might prove to be a challenging task (Lipka, 1992).

Polysemy is the result of borrowing, and the process of metaphorisation – extension of meaning – across domains and the general language (Temmerman, 2000; Bursina, 2014 in Zolotukhin, 2016; Iljinska & Smirnova, 2014). This process is called by Leitchik (2012 in Zolotukhin, 2016) inter-categorical polysemy which commonly appears in terminology. Some terms, like *cloning*, have become so extensively used that it has led to the meaning overload, and 'started suffering from ambiguity (Temmerman, 2000: 145)'. Confusion in specialised contexts is undesirable, therefore overloaded terms need to be replaced by a synonym, or a hyperonym.

According to the tenets of prototype semantics, the polysemic character of lexical units is increased, because it reflects shifts in their semantic structure (Temmerman, 2000). It is 'the synchronic result of diachronically increased informational density', being 'a consequence of the evolution of a unit of understanding, of the flexible adaptability of categories which have prototype structure and of the dynamics of structural stability in language (Temmerman, 2000: 153)'. Moreover, the character of terms is functional, because 'meanings of one word can refer to the same *object* but to different *concept areas*' they have a common linguistic reality but suggest its different conceptual features (Kosova, 2003: 66 in Zolotukhin, 2016: 69)'.

However, apart from polysemy, there is a conceptual heterogeneity of a terminological meaning, which is a consequence of 'different interpretations of the same denotative component (Kulikova & Salmina, 2002: 31 in Zolotukhin, 2016: 71)'. Thus, it might be the case of the modification of meaning or a new variant of the same meaning of the term. The same meaning might be described by different, coexisting definitions.

Zolotukhin (2016) also develops a content model of a lexical unit with multiple terminological meanings, which is depicted in Figure 3.3. below. This hypothetical lexical unit consists of two commonly used meanings in general language and three specialised or terminological meanings. Terminological meanings break down into terminological variants which then are divided into semes.

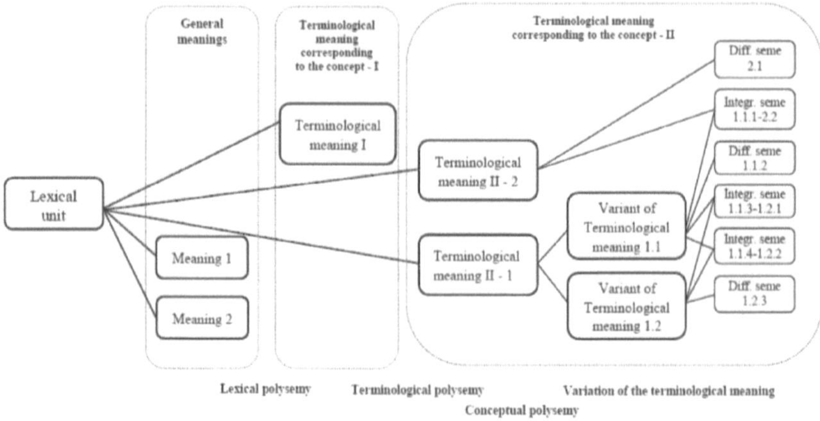

Figure 3.3. Zolotukhin's model of a lexical unit with multiple terminological meanings (2016: 73)

Literature on the subject discusses different typologies of polysemy, most of which are based on the polarisation relationship. Pethő (2001) finds that systematic and non-systematic types are the most often discussed, the first is referred to as polysemy, and the latter as homonymy. Moreover, the first is 'usually motivated metonymically, whereas non-systematic is motivated metaphorically (Pethő, 2001: 184)'. According to Grinev-Griniewicz (2016), traditional types of polysemy include radial and chain polysemy, but together with Dubieniec (2004) the author (2016) adds two new types, i.e. polysemy with a broadening of secondary meaning, and polysemy with narrowing meanings. Another typology, developed by Szajkiewicz (in Grinev-Griniewicz, 2016) includes monocentric polysemy which contains the original meaning, and polycentric polysemy with two or more semantic centres. Apresjan (1971 in Grinev-Griniewicz, 2016) proposes a division of the phenomenon based on the transfer of meaning into metonymically and metaphorically motivated polysemantism (which goes in alliance with Temmerman's studies, 2000) as well as regular – with the predictable relation between the senses and non-regular which are parallel to the systematic and non-systematic discussed by Pethő (2001). Regular polysemy is based on metonymy, and irregular – on metaphor presented by Vincente and Falkum (2017). However, the authors (2017) identify three types of polysemy: inherent (logical) which is understood as 'related senses of contradictory semantic types, regular, and irregular (idiosyncratic)'. The first two types derive from metonymy, and pertain mainly to nouns, whereas the latter is characteristic for all parts of speech, and stems from the metaphor.

However, polysemous terms might be problematic in specialised communication, especially in the process of translation of specialised texts (Iljinska & Smirnova, 2014: 104). Polysemous terms might be ambiguous, and their meaning might be determined by the context. As a result, the translator has to decide on the right meaning of the term in the right context. Even though polysemy is a natural linguistic phenomenon, it is a hindrance for terminology management and standardisation.

All things considered, polysemy is a phenomenon which proves the existence of creative forces and development of the language. Even though it was considered undesirable in specialised contexts, it is an economical way of expressing new concepts connected with the existing ones via metaphorical extensions or with the use of metonymy. However, the meaning of polysemous terms is strongly context-dependent which might be understood only by experts.

3.4.3. Terminological prototypes and peripheries

Categorisation is one of the most important cognitive abilities which facilitate understanding of entities, mental concepts, relations between them, and finally terms used to designate these entities (Temmerman, 2000; Faber, 2012). It is defined as the 'ability to see similarity in diversity' in order to understand the world (Taylor, 1995 in Faber, 2012: 52). Moreover, categorisation entails both motivation, i.e. a perceptual base of categories, as well as convention, i.e. learning, and it involves five types of activities in the cognitive process:

(i) forming a structural description of the entity
(ii) finding categories similar to the structural description
(iii) selecting the most similar representation
(iv) making inferences regarding the entity
(v) sorting information about the categorization in long-term memory (Faber, 2012: 52).

The Prototype Theory draws on other cognitive, philosophical and psychological theories, and opposes the Classical Theory of Meaning, assuming the all-or-nothing membership (Faber, 2012). It allows for the lack of necessary and sufficient conditions of category members, and it is based on a graded similarity to the ideal member (a prototype) (Faber, 2012; Adajian, 2005). Non-ideal members are gathered around the prototype, may or may not share a feature with it, but must be linked to other members. Thus, categories are characterised by the family resemblance. Moreover, conceptual categories possess a defining internal structure, and may be deprived of boundaries (Janda, 2000: 8 in Faber, 2012: 53; ten Hacken, 2008). Prototypes are more easily and accurately classified by language users as category members than peripheries. Therefore, understanding of meaning of words might be disturbed by category fuzziness (Faber, 2012).

According to Temmerman (2000), understanding constitutes a structured event with two aspects of units of understanding (proposed by Temmerman instead of concepts): intracategorial and intercategorial structures, as well as the prototype structure of the category (2000: 225). In contrast to the traditional approach to terminology, Sociogognitive Terminology treats category's existence as an integral part of the language. In terms of intracategorisation different information modules, such as 'features, core definition, historical information, procedural information', are distinguished which 'may have varying levels of prominence depending on the type of category (e.g. entity, activity, umbrella category) under consideration (2000: 225)'. However, in the cognitive model, perspective, domain and intention are yet to be revealed in terms of the intercategorial structures. Moreover, categories are prototypically structured. Very few categories possess necessary and sufficient features with the majority of blurred edges in terms of intensional definitions. On the other hand, analysing extensionally, category exemplars are more likely to show a structure of family resemblance, and their category membership is graded.

Adajian (2005) understands the term concept in the context of the Prototype Theory as a complex mental representation of categories, a membership based on similarity, possessing a sufficient level of properties to the prototypes. Yet, concepts are either referred to as internal mental representations – bodies of interest studied psychologically, or abstracta in a more philosophical sense, i.e. properties or universals.

Faber (2012) points out that both the Prototype Theory, and the classical approach to meaning are not free from limitations. It is unrealistic to 'assume that only prototype theory accounts for categorization (Faber, 2012: 53)'. Therefore, one should adopt a compromise solution, because both types of categories, i.e. classical and family resemblance, are considered psychologically real and natural. Language users instinctively explain, and identify concepts via family resemblance categories using rapid approximate reasoning. However, it is easier to explain certain categories by means of the Classical Theory. As a result, the core meaning of concepts should be determined with the classical approach.

The Prototype Theory also deals with the aspects of polysemy. Meanings of a polysemous lexeme revolve around a central sense, a prototype. Moreover, the distinction between synonyms, polysemes and homonyms in the traditional sense has been challenged, because they are hardly ever clear-cut (Faber, 2012). According to Lakoff (1987), composite prototypes or complex categories, which have a radial structure, i.e. form a network around the prototype meaning in the centre, pivot on the continuum from the centre to periphery meanings. This rule is also applicable to the morphology and syntax of polysemous lexical units. The radial aspect also accounts for the dynamicity of categories: the ideals travel from the centre to the periphery and back. Radiality is also linked to the notion of semantic network which is formed from the related senses, or lexical concepts of the word with prototypes and peripheries (Faber, 2012).

Knowledge is organised by means of the idealised cognitive models (ICMs) with category structures, and prototype effects as by-products of this process (Lakoff, 1987: 68). They are 'conventional conceptual representations of the way we perceive and organize reality (encyclopaedic knowledge)', and allow to judge instances as good examples of a category (Faber, 2012: 56). ICMs constitute a structured unity, or a gestalt, formed according to four principles:

- propositional structure (…)
- image-schematic structure (…)
- metaphoric mappings (…)
- metonymic mappings (…) (Lakoff, 1987: 68).

In principle, ICMs are abstract, because they 'do not represent specific instances'; simplified and schematic, as they 'partially represent what a particular culture knows about a concept within a culture', including myths and beliefs (Faber, 2012: 56). Moreover, an ICM is a cognitive phenomenon, since it allows for the explanation of the cognitive processes, such as categorisation and reasoning.

Category systems possess two dimensions: vertical and horizontal (Rosch, 1978 in Faber, 2012). The first shows how inclusive a particular category is: the higher the level a given category reaches, the more inclusive it is. One can distinguish three levels of specificity within categories at the vertical dimension: basic, superordinate and subordinate level. The basic level is considered the most cognitively and linguistically salient, which constitutes an 'image or a real-world referent', and results in the speakers' easiness to describe the items (Faber, 2012: 58). The basic-level terms occur more frequently, and show a monomorphemic structure. The other levels contain lexemes with more general, or more specific meaning which pose more difficulty in categorising and describing the superordinate and subordinate items. Moreover, in English superordinate level terms are uncountable, and subordinate level terms are mainly compounds formed of a basic-level term with a modifier.

On the other hand, the horizontal dimension demonstrates how distinct the category is within the same level of inclusiveness (Evans & Green, 2006: 256 in Faber, 2012: 57). Categories within one horizontal level display a certain level of similarity so that they are assigned to the same category, but at a different position: either towards the centre or periphery.

Ten Hacken (2008) applies the Periphery Theory to specialised contexts and claims that 'specialization is gradual (2008: 984)'. The author (2008) analyses terminology from selected domains: the technical, scientific, professional and legal field. The study reveals that in a scientific field definitions of terms refer to other terms and create a network, but concepts have clear and well-defined boundaries. In a legal field, definitions are constrained with some interaction between the constrains. In the professional field, the majority of terms are used to denote parts, tools or processes and their definitions do not have any boundary conditions. The author (2008) proposes a division of specialised language units into terms and specialised vocabulary. The first category is comprised of well-defined specialised units that do not exhibit prototype effects, and therefore are 'an absolute property (2008: 979)', whereas the second category is notions for 'concepts determined by necessary and sufficient conditions (2008: 984)'. Term is a combination of three elements, i.e. a form, a concept, and a domain. Terms are directly connected with particular domains. However, there are no clear-cut boundaries between words and terms in terms of specialisation, and therefore the determination 'what is as term makes the concept of *term* itself prototype-based (2008: 983)'. Moreover, it is not possible to draw fixed borderlines between specialised and other types of communication as well as between terms, the rest of vocabulary and phraseology.

Terms might be formed either onomasiologically, or semasiologically. In the first approach, the point of departure is the concept, with the name as a follow-up, which is characteristic for advanced sciences (ten Hacken, 2008). The second method of terminology formation, which is typical for legal terms, starts with the form, and it involves the determination of concept's boundaries. It 'occurs when an existing general language expression is transformed into a term by the specification of a set of necessary and sufficient conditions determining the boundaries of the concept (2008: 984)'.

To sum up, the Prototype Theory is a cognitivists' answer to the traditional approach. It allows for the categorisation of terminology from the most salient exemplars to peripheries, and treats linguistic phenomena, like polysemy or synonymy, as functional. The proponents of the theory adopt a realistic stance and propose a dual approach to terminology, either all-or-nothing, or based on the family-resemblance.

3.4.4. Terminology in the frame-based approach

Specialised knowledge can only be understood and acquired when concepts are organised in a system (Faber Benítez, Márquez Linares & Vega Expósito, 2005; L'Homme, 2018). The traditional conceptual model is taxonomical, it is a mere list of simple and complex nominal forms, devoid of settings and contexts of processes involved and it does not take psychological adequacy into account (Faber Benítez et al., 2005). Therefore, a new form of terminological representation should be dynamic and process-oriented, contain empirical evidence, and goal-driven categories that are mappings reflecting roles involved in the process with real-life examples. In other words, terminological analyses should concentrate on studies of behaviour of knowledge units in contexts (Faber Benítez et al., 2005; Faber, 2015).

Specialised texts follow text conventions or templates and are repetitive in terms of terms, phrases, sentences, or paragraphs (Faber & López Rodriguez, 2012). Moreover, scientific and technical texts are characterised by a high density of terms, and a distinctive use of syntactic constructions. Terminology, which activates domain-specific knowledge, is mainly comprised of compound nominal forms characteristic of the domain, with the domain-specific meaning and syntactic valence (Faber Benítez et al., 2005; Faber & López Rodriguez, 2012; Faber, 2015). As a result, proper understanding of the text necessitates 'knowledge of the domain, the concepts within it, the propositional relations within the text, as well as the conceptual relations between concepts within the domain (Faber & López Rodriguez, 2012: 26)'.

Drawing on cognitive psychological theories, a dynamic and situational conceptual system should contain four types of information:

1. contextually-relevant properties of the focal category
2. information about the background setting
3. likely actions that the agent could take to achieve an associated goal
4. likely introspective states that the agent might have while interacting with the category (Faber Benítez et al., 2005).

In the multidimensional approach to terminology, frames allow for the reflection of all dimensions of meaning with concepts not only defined, but also placed in a context of an action specific to a specialised domain (Faber Benítez et al., 2005; Faber & López Rodriguez, 2012). Multidimensionality is a 'difference in a perspective reflected in terminological definitions' and it 'occurs when a concept can be classified in more than one way (Faber, 2015: 18)'. Frame semantics is different in comparison to 'familiar theories of semantic fields' which assume paradigmatic and syntagmatic relationships between lexical units (Fillmore & Atkins, 1992: 76). It is based on cognitive frames, also referred to as knowledge schemata, and it posits that 'a word's meaning can be understood only with reference to a structured background of experience, beliefs, or practice, constituting a kind of conceptual prerequisite for understanding meaning (1992: 76–77)'. Moreover, every lexical unit can be linked to valence description, 'a description that specifies, in both semantic and syntactic terms, what the expression requires of its constituents and its context, and what contributes to the structures that contain it (1992: 78)'.

Frame-based terminology is the adaptation of frame semantics for analyses of specialised domains (Faber, 2015; Faber Benítez et al., 2005; Faber & López Rodriguez, 2012). Frame is grounded in meaning dependence on the context, and it is 'a cognitive structuring device based on experience that provides the background knowledge and motivation for the existence of words in a language (Faber & López Rodriguez, 2012: 27)'. It is also defined as 'a schematisation of experience, (a knowledge structure), which is represented at the conceptual level and held in long-term memory and which relates elements and entitles associated with a particular culturally embedded scene, situation or event from human experience (Evans, 2007: 85 in Faber, 2015: 15)'. They are a reflection of the lexical relations as well as components of meaning which are contained in terminographic definitions. These, in turn, are taken from specialised knowledge resources and specialised corpora and act as descriptions of a concept's properties. As a result, frames show explicitly the semantic and syntactic behaviour of a given lexical unit in its natural contexts (Faber Benítez et al., 2005; Faber & López Rodriguez, 2012). Frame network is in fact a classification: 'networks are divided into domains, the domains into frames, and the frames can go through several levels of specificity by using hierarchical inheritance (Faber Benítez et al., 2005: 3)'. However, Faber & López Rodriguez (2012) spot the problem with the concept of domain, both in terminological and linguistic terms. It can both refer to knowledge area and categories of domain-specific concepts. Moreover, conceptualisation and categorisation are important for the understanding of language and representation of meaning. Categories are organised either in a classical way, or as prototypes, in which categories are classified according to their similarity, because 'classical and family resemblance categories are psychologically real and natural (2012: 27)'.

Faber & López Rodriguez (2012) also make reference to Langacker's (1987) foregrounding and frame which allow for profiling of one concept in different domains, creating a domain matrix. Moreover, one concept might be looked at from different aspects of knowledge which activate an active zone, or Cruse's (2004) facet. The concepts of domain matrix and active zone are related to multidimensionality mentioned above. Key concepts in multidimensionality include figure, ground, profile and base. Profile is placed at the beginning, whereas base provides background information, but Faber & López Rodriguez (2012) do not explain the remaining concepts. As a result, the theory concentrates on three issues:

1. conceptual organization
2. the multidimensional nature of terminological units
3. the extraction of semantic and syntactic information through the use of multilingual corpora. (2012: 28).

Specialised domains are a sequence of events, and for each one can develop an event template which constitutes a frame for concept organisation. Domain-specific concepts are organised in a network with vertical, or hierarchical, and horizontal, non-hierarchical relations. As a result, a general frame-based event template can be developed and adapted for specific domains, which is depicted in Figure 3.4. below. According to Faber & López Rodriguez (2012), a 'template with a prototypical set of conceptual relations' characterises each subdomain (2012: 28). Thus, terminological definitions, obtained via corpus extraction and data analyses, are seen as frames or mini-knowledge representations. Corpus data are an invaluable source of information about a concept and its relations to others within the same domain.

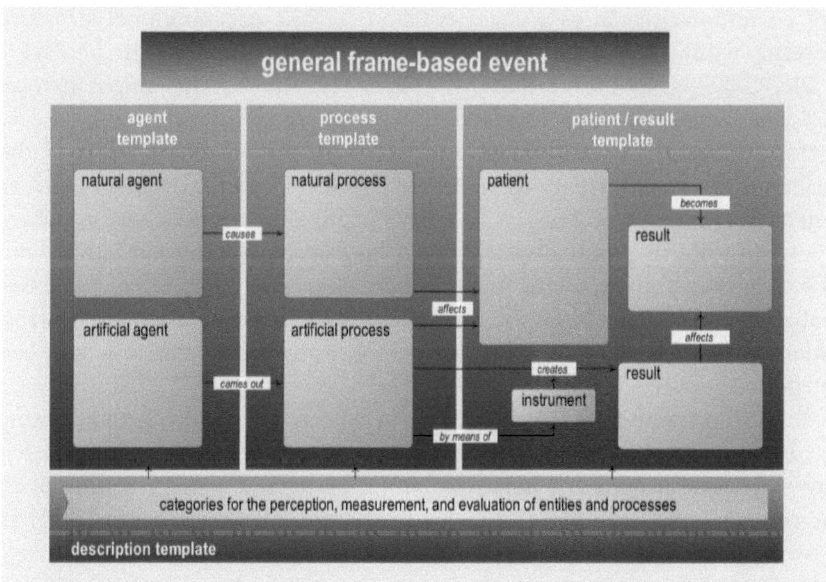

Figure 3.4. The General Frame-based Event developed byFaber & López Rodriguez (2012: 28)

L'Homme (2018) identifies two approaches to terminology, i.e. knowledge-driven and lexicon-driven. In the first, knowledge is the point of departure in analyses of the lexicon. Linguistic resources are compiled in term banks, thesauri, terminological knowledge bases, or domain ontologies. Such resources do not provide, however, information about the behaviour of terms, collocations, or the ways they are used. Data provided include definitions, synonyms, or some forms of relationships. Moreover, the majority of terms are nouns with few verbs and adjectives. On the other hand, the second perspective, the lexicon-based approach, starts with the lexicon, its manifestations in texts as well as properties in order to connect it with knowledge. Meanings of lexical units are connected with background knowledge which is 'built on previous experience, on beliefs, or on social conventions (2018: 6)'. Semantic frames constitute the structure of the background knowledge. They shape the situation; these in turn produce participants, tools, and other elements.

Specialised knowledge is regarded as a sequence of EVENTS and STATES, because every subject field is not static, but a dynamic process (Faber Benítez et al., 2005). The process is organised in the following way: an AGENT begins the process which influences a PATIENT and brings RESULTS in the end. It can be summarised in as a chain reaction, a basic organisational structure of terms within a domain which reflects their interrelationships: AGENT -> PROCESS -> PATIENT/RESULT. Moreover, some terms might involve peripheral categories, like INSTRUMENTS, which include concepts used to perform measurements, conduct analyses, and provide descriptions of the processes. One can distinguish NATURAL AGENTS and HUMAN agents, as well as NATURAL and ARTIFICIAL PROCESSES. In scientific writing, there is a trend towards nominalisation as a means of maintaining objectivity and to 'express description, connections, relationships and attributes of processes (Faber Benítez et al., 2005: 7)'. However, they necessitate the use of verbs, usually non-specialised, in order to demonstrate the interactions between categories.

To sum up, frame-based terminology is an approach that allows demonstrating the dynamic character of specialised domains. It does not show only terms, but also their relationships and hierarchy, and it provides a broader picture of all the processes that take place in each subject field. Moreover, corpus analyses allow for the production of a configuration of concepts in specialised knowledge fields in a valid way. The theory also proves that terminology is not only limited to nominal phrases, but also includes other parts of speech which illustrate the relationships between concepts and categories.

3.5. The connection between the interdisciplinarity of science and the project-specific terminology

Knowledge has been dynamically changing its character since 1945, which reflects its increasing complexity (Thompson Klein, 2004). Conceptualisation and perception of knowledge have evolved from a linear structure into a dynamic system. Moreover, the traditional division in disciplines is still in use, but it has been becoming more and more obsolete. As a result, new multi- or interdisciplinary, hybrid fields, even prima facie unrelated have emerged. Moreover, existing domains have been dividing into subdomains as a result of growing specialisation (Górnicz, 2019). These new domains have filled in the gaps that were created by the traditional division into disciplines. The emergence of such fragmentary and hybrid domains has led to the creation of intra-project terminology, used by individual research teams.

Interdisciplinarity in science is manifested in various ways. Subject fields become fragmentary, intertwine and create hybrids. Moreover, the complexity of research necessitates collaboration between specialists from different fields in international teams (Thompson Klein, 2004 2, Van Riper III, Powell, Machis, Van Wagtendonk, Van Riper, Von Ruschkowski, Schwarzbach & Galipeau, 2012: 216; Pelikan & Roelcke, 2015: 62). Interdisciplinary studies require combined efforts to deal with and solve too complex or interdependent problems for single-domain professionals (Polter & Rafols, 2009: 720; Thompson Klein, 2004: 2; Van Riper III et al., 2012; Pelikan & Roelcke, 2015). As a result, a new approach to problems has been developed that is based on the interaction between disciplines, especially in the domains with the majority of technological developments. Multidisciplinary teams are formed 'to solve problems whose solutions are beyond the scope of a single field or research practice' by using integrated scientific information (Polter & Rafols, 2009: 720; Van Riper III et al., 2012: 216). In addition, interdisciplinarity also pertains to languages. Nowadays, there is a need to link scientific with colloquial languages, i.e. scientists need to take unofficial languages and discourses of different groups of interest into account (Thompson Klein, 2004 7).

There are contradictory views concerning the status of interdisciplinarity, multidisciplinarity and transdisciplinarity. On the one hand, the closer related the disciplines are, the lower they score on interdsciplinarity, and consequently, the more remote they are, the higher the interdisciplinarity is (Polter & Rafols, 2009: 727). Thus, the MTCS domains are closely related, and therefore the disciplines are allegedly of little interdisciplinarity. However, scientific work or projects involve the efforts of international teams and the employment of multiple fields (typical for interdisciplinary studies), not only two (as in the multidisciplinary studies), and as such can be treated as interdisciplinary (Van Riper III et al., 2012: 217).

The MTCS domains have an interdisciplinary character as they are interdependent and also employ other disciplines. Microelectronics develops hardware for which computer science produces software, and telecommunication uses both hardware and software to develop communication solutions. Moreover, many applications are created to work in other fields, like medicine, energy production, banking, sports, etc., which proves Thomson Klein's (2004) claim that 'social, technical, and economic developments (…) interact with elements of value and culture in aging, energy, health care, and nutrition (Thomson Klein, 2004: 4)'. As a result, research teams consist of specialists of various disciplines and their choice depends on one's expertise (which was discussed in Chapter 1). Moreover, the multidisciplinary approach to problems leads to knowledge integration, and thus facilitates progress (Polter & Rafols, 2009: 722).

Conducting research and solving complex problems in collaboration among teams from various educational backgrounds leads to heterogeneity of terminology (Pelikan & Roelcke, 2015). Unlike corporations and business environments, in academic circles there is no drive to 'implement terminology specific to one research project', but there is a need for a common language. As a result, individual participants develop their own specialised idiolects, and may use idiosyncratically different terms for the same concepts, which might lead to miscommunication (Grucza, 2010: 43; Pelikan & Roelcke, 2015). However, in order to facilitate the success of the whole project, effective inner communication is indispensable (Pelikan & Roelcke, 2015). For this reason, project-specific terminology is developed automatically, but it is rarely written down and standardised. Idiosyncratic uses and idiolects overlap and a new project-specific variety of the specialised language is created. Moreover, idiosyncrasies and idiolects which reflect an individual researcher's conceptualisation of reality, lead to discrepancies between the definition of the term and its use.

Project-specific terminology, especially in highly innovative disciplines, is developed and used for a number of reasons. Working on novel solutions brings new concepts into existence which are not found elsewhere, and therefore require a name (Pelikan & Roelcke, 2015). The second reason is the language economy, i.e. reducing the linguistic effort in order to gain the maximum result. Moreover, sharing common project-specific terminology contributes to 'strengthening the team spirit', and facilitates collaboration among team members (Pelikan & Roelcke, 2015: 71). Researchers and engineers specialising in the MTCS domains work on state-of-the-art devices and technologies and "produce" new concepts that require new names.

Interdisciplinarity in the MTCS domains is manifested twofold: by developed research results or solutions and by interdisciplinary terminology. There are strict connections between hardware, software and communication devices. The equipment has to be designed, built and programmed to be compatible with other elements. Moreover, the development of new technologies involves applying phenomena described by other subject fields, such as, chemistry, physics, mathematics, geography, or mechanics with practical applications in medicine, sports, banking, mechanics, etc. This transdisciplinary character of the MTCS domains is reflected in the terminology, as key terms extracted via Sketch Engine show that a part of the MTCS terminology is borrowed from other disciplines.

Summing up, globalisation and dynamic scientific developments have led to a marked increase in collaboration on the international level. Communication problems, caused by different cultural, educational and linguistic environments, may affect the success of research. Therefore, scientists intuitively develop project-specific terminology to facilitate effective communication.

3.6. Migration of terminology as a manifestation of interdisciplinarity

Technological advances are followed by rapid development of scientific vocabulary. Moreover, globalisation exerts pressure on the creation of technical and scientific texts. One cannot speak of static, precise, neutral, and conventionalised scientific writing anymore, because it has to meet the demands of swift changes (Ijinska & Smirnova, 2014). As a result, modern science produces multifunctional and hybrid texts reflecting the intersection of cultures and conventions. Moreover, there is a tendency to use strongly context-dependent terms and across domains in such texts. It is referred to as migration of terminology, or transfer as a result of transferminologisation (Dury, 2005: Górnicz, 2019).

Nowadays, scientific domains are characterised by fuzzy boundaries 'which allow terms and concepts to be mobile and travel across various domains', which proves that 'inter-domain lexical and conceptual sharing exists (Dury, 2005: 37)'. Transfer of knowledge on the global scale has facilitated the exchange of interlingual, and inter-domain terminology. However, the terminological journey across specialised domains might bring about certain linguistic aftermaths. New concepts and names for them might appear, and coexist as synonyms for a given period of time, but later one alternative might change its meaning or disappear

(Dury, 2005). On the other hand, terms might be borrowed to different subject fields and be modified, be transferred with a metaphorical extension, with specialisation of meaning, or adapted without a change in the name (Dury, 2005; Górnicz, 2019). Finally, a concept might expand so that it had to be divided into subconcepts, such as *parasitism* in ecology which has been known since the ancient times (Dury, 2005). This term has also been borrowed by the MTCS domains, but as an adjective and applied to inanimate electronic objects. Its primary meaning of living at the expense of the other living organism[7] has been transferred to electronic devices to describe negative effects in a transistor or in a coil. Therefore, in electronics one speaks of *parasitic capacitance*, *inductance*, or *effects* which affect the performance of electronic devices negatively. As a result, technolectal metaphors are created (Górnicz, 2019).

In conclusion, terminological migration is one of the manifestations of the young discipline's interdisciplinary character. Terms in new domains might remain their original meaning, or acquire a new one. This phenomenon reflects changes in the creation of specialised texts, i.e. they have become multifunctional and hybrid. It also pertains to new scientific domains, like the analysed MTCS subject fields which also might be called hybrids, due to their interdisciplinary character with terminology borrowed from other, more traditional domains.

3.7. Multimodality in research papers

The need to convey messages precisely and explain novel ideas necessitates the use of intersemiotic communicative means in scientific writing. The more practical or experimental the domain is, the higher the level of multimodality and text hybridity. On the other hand, there is a need to facilitate the reader's understanding of the text, especially when the content contains various aspects of different sources (Bazerman, 1988 in Alvermann & Wilson, 2011).

Message construction depends on the complementarity of linguistic, visual, sonic and kinaesthetic resources, not only on the language (Lemke, 1998). Written messages contain linguistic and visual-graphological-typographical elements. Moreover, scientific texts are largely dependent on the visual content, since such a combination of verbal and graphical messages allows to 'multiply the meanings (Lemke, 1998)'. Visuals also depict abstract truth, because abstract modality is characteristic for scientific writing (van Leeuwen, 2005: 168). The combination of the verbal-typological aspects and visual-topological

7 https://www.ldoceonline.com/dictionary/parasitic, 2019.10.07.

components creates semiotic hybrids (Lemke, 1998). Thus, scientists juggle and connect verbal discursive elements with visual representations along with symbols and formulae, creating multimodal genres. As a result, complementary information in scientific writing is provided in the form of 'mathematical expressions, quantitative graphs, information tables, abstract diagrams, maps, drawings, photographs (Lemke, 1998)'.

In scientific texts, multimodal means have their own advantages, and convey specific meaning (Gibson, 1979; van Leeuwen, 2005 in Alvermann & Wilson, 2011; Lemke, 1998). Human comprehension of multimodal communication is driven by functional principles (Lemke, 1998). Meaning is a combination of linguistic typological principles and visual topological modalities via hybrid resources. Thus, understanding of the text requires the reconstruction of the writer's intended meaning in order to create or readers' own meanings, based on what they read and their own knowledge. As a result, the readers create a conceptual blend, re-conceptualise a given reality into a new meaning, and expand their knowledge (Fauconnier & Turner, 2003: 57–58). The process also takes place across languages, as scientists and engineers working in international teams structure their knowledge and experience individually on the basis of the language they speak – their own construal of the world, and finally re-conceptualise the 'old' and 'new' knowledge across languages (Langacker, 1987: 487–488; Lewandowska-Tomaszczyk, 2010: 106). Thus, visual representations of concepts are more thought-provoking and stimulating for readers' imagination to 'foster, monitor, regulate and maintain comprehension' than mere columns of texts (Dole, Duffy, Roehler & Pearson, 1991: 242 in Alvermann & Wilson, 2011: 120). For this reason, the authors decide to move away from the 'verbocentrism' and integrate two modes to convey meaning to make the decoding of the scientific texts more effective. However, the verbal content still remains the dominating one, but the comprehensive approach to the modes applied leads to the enrichment and complexity of readers' conceptualisation. Moreover, the use of multimodal communicative means affects the congruency of the decoded message.

Translation of one sign system into another is a comeback to the linguistic sources, and to the de Sausserian idea of the arbitrariness of the sign and its relationships with the signified and the signifier (Saussure, 1959: 67–68). The use of other communicative means also derives from the language economy. Therefore, scientists decide to decode information in a condensed way in a system of signs and symbols that are universally agreed upon, such as chemical compounds, mathematical algorithms, or physical formulae.

All in all, scientific writing makes an extensive use of multimodal communication. Written texts contain visual elements which complement the verbal content. Moreover, multimodality is manifested by various visual representations, like graphs, diagrams, graphics, photographs or even equations, but also by the use of symbols, all of which complement the verbal content and contribute to meaning-making.

3.8. Manifestations of scientific terminology

Research articles belong to highly specialised texts and, they are dense with technical terminology. Terms, being the biggest carriers of the information load, are the most distinctive feature of specialised texts that facilitate transfer of knowledge (Sager et al., 1980: 230; Zauberga, 2005: 107, in Mohammadi, 2013: 3; Gajda, 1990: 41). Technical revolutions and the expansion of knowledge have brought about the proliferation of terminology (estimated 90 % of new words are names for technical concepts) in order to describe concepts that have been developed in the process (Gajda, 1990: 39, 42).

There is no agreement, however, concerning the amount of specialised vocabulary in specialised texts. Terms account for the half of the total vocabulary of most linguistic communities in possession of modern technical knowledge' and are estimated to make from 5 % to 30 % of scientific texts. (Montgomery, 2000: 189). For example, Newmark (2004) states that 'terms usually consist of not more than 5 % of the text's vocabulary (2004: 12)'. On the other hand, Arsentyeva (2003) finds that 'terms constitute 20–30 % of the whole vocabulary of such texts (…) (Arsentyeva, 2003: 170–171 in Źrałka, 2007: 76)'. Moreover, scientific texts contain about 60–70 % of neutral words and 10 % of common literary vocabulary. Since terms are a distinguishing feature of specialised texts, therefore there is a need for studying them.

In terminology, there are two contradictory forces that are in a state of an instable balance (Gajda, 1990: 39). One brings chaos, but facilitates cognition and linguistic expression of new knowledge. The other force brings order, but it limits and corrects the area of the activity. However, total normalisation of terminology is not possible as there are subsequent or coexisting terms with a varied level of consistency. Moreover, the tendency to strict specialisation leads to the creation of domain-specific terms that might be understood only by insiders and totally incomprehensible for non-experts and professionals from other disciplines (Sager et al., 1980). The process of terminologisation includes transfers of meaning, derivation, new coinages or borrowings until standardisation. Moreover, terms may take the form of one-word units, multi-word units, abbreviations, acronyms in their strive for transparency, consistency, and precision.

Specialised vocabulary in science is discipline-dependent and has a different characteristic but it is not possible to distinguish general scientific and general technological vocabulary, since some lexemes are frequently used in various disciplines (Kozłowska, 2007; Sager et al., 1980: 237). In hard and technical sciences, which the MTCS domains fall into, concepts and terms are unequivocal, precise and clearly defined, and therefore easier to translate (Kozłowska, 2007: 125–126). Moreover, technical terms are a part of a finite system of terminological layers (Gajda, 1990: 42–43; Kozłowska, 2007: 126).

Terms in the MTCS domains can be considered interdisciplinary, 'which is proved by earlier studies. Hoffmann (1973 in Sager et al., 1980: 237) and Buchholz (1978) and Alekseev (1973 in Sager et al., 1980: 237) conducted research into various subject fields. Corpus analyses revealed the six most frequent words in each subject field, i.e. *current, temperature, voltage, cathode, energy, electrons*. The study reveals that in electronics a half of most frequent words were subject-specific, the other half, i.e. *temperature, energy, electrons*, also appear in Hoffman's physics list. Thus, microelectronics, one of the analysed subject-fields of the monograph, a part of electronics, shares some concepts and phenomena with other subject fields.

All in all, terms constitute the most salient feature of specialised texts, and scientific articles in particular. Terminology can take various forms, creating hybrids, and behave differently, which will be discussed in the following sections of this chapter.

3.8.1. Neologisms

The domains of new technologies are 'the creation of our epoch', and as a result deal with state-of-the-art solutions (Lavrova, 2013: 23). The innovative disciplines of new technologies are characterised by 'new discoveries, new science, new technologies' and produce a technological revolution. The language reflects their novel character: the need to name new concepts, i.e. objects, services, processes or phenomena in the world of technology (Sager et al., 1980: 280). Therefore, scientific language in these subject fields contains neologisms, i.e. non-literary, 'newly coined lexical units or existing lexical units that acquire a new sense' that act as a mirror of changes in the society or 'a lexical unit perceived as recent by language users (Newmark, 1988: 140; Rey, 1995: 64)'. Moreover, in hard and experimental sciences as well as medicine, there is an observable trend for the dominant position of English and the influence of English terminology over other languages (Linder & De Sterck, 2016).

Rey (1995) defines a neologism as 'a simple (morpheme-word) or a complex form (noun or verb phrase) (...) accepted by usage' which 'conform to grammatical rules (1995: 68)'. The author (1995) divides neologisms into formal, semantic and pragmatic. The first group entails the 'application of grammatical rules to the morpheme store of the language' as well as 'the integration or syllabification of the letters constituting abbreviations (Rey, 1995: 68)'. The latter appear frequently both alone and in noun phrases, especially in English, out of precision and language economy.

The second type is the semantic neology which, according to Rey (1995) 'is found in all neologisms without exception' and can be total, partial or very weak (1995: 70). This characteristics can be observed in borrowings – total novelties in the language system, in neologisms created by 'affixation, composition, agglutination into complex words or syntagmatic formations into word groups', which are partial novelties, and very weak in abbreviations and acronyms because their meanings is reduced to their original forms, but the shortening modifies the connotations (Rey, 1995: 70). Finally, pragmatic neology is related to communication, and it is basically the migration of lexemes among subsystems in which they are considered neologisms. This feature does not pertain to terminology, but terms cannot be analysed without their communicative aspects and term migration among specialised languages and to and fro the general variety is a well-known fact. Therefore, this feature should also include terminology. The three aspects decide on the novelty of the neologism.

Górnicz (2019) concentrates on terminological neologisms and defines them as potential lexical units, not used before, which are the result of combining units without a meaning, e.g. new sequences of speech sounds, or units that carry a meaning, i.e. morphemes or words. The most characteristic for specialised languages are multiword terms which appear rarely in the general language. Terms with a low information load form another category of terminological neologisms. Moreover, neosemantisms are created via metaphorical extensions of general language lexemes, but the changes in meaning can be summarised in the following way:

1. no change
2. narrowing of meaning (specialisation)
3. extension of meaning
   a) new meaning is closely related with the existing one (*adoption*)
   b) new meaning is hardly related with the existing one (*expansion*)
   c) metaphorical extension (…)
   d) metonymical extension (…)
4. extension by elision (Górnicz, 2019: 58–59).

There are a few classifications of neologisms, depending on the author and the language variety. Newmark (1988) identifies twelve types of neologisms:

A. Existing lexical items with new senses:
   1. old words with new senses which rarely appear in technological contexts because they rarely denote objects or processes,
   2. existing collocations with new senses that constitute 'normal descriptive terms which suddenly become technical terms' whose meaning sometimes becomes more general or figurative (Newmark, 1988: 142).

B. New forms:
   3. new coinages which are extremely rare unless they are brand names,
   4. words derived from Greek or Latin that become international and are used mainly in scientific and technological texts,
   5. abbreviations which, according to Newmark (1988), 'have always been a common type of pseudo-neologism (1988: 145)',
   6. collocations are frequent in scientific texts, especially in social sciences and information technology,
   7. eponyms, words created from a proper name, have been gaining in popularity,
   8. phrasal words which are a typically English phenomenon,
   9. newly transferred words remain their foreign origin and are not context-dependent, but do not refer to technology, and appear mainly in minority languages,
   10. acronyms i.e. lexemes, which 'designate products, appliances and processes', constituting of letters joined up and used in science internationally (Newmark, 1988: 148),
   11. pseudo neologisms which are defined as generic words that substitute specific words which rarely appear in academic texts since precision is of overriding importance,
   12. internationalisms which are limited by Newmark (1988) only to acronyms.

This detailed classification is only partially applicable to academic texts, which is pointed out by Newmark (1988), because the typology covers neologisms in the general language. Moreover, some categories, like internationalisms, are limited only to acronyms, but in fact this category should also cover lexemes of Greek and Latin origin, not to mention Anglicisms.

Sager et al., (1980), on the other hand, propose 5 sources of new specialised vocabulary in English (1980: 281):

(a) the neologism contains the elements of existing English and anglicised Greek or Latin elements,

(b) the lexeme comprises the Latin or Greek stem in its original form or modified,
(c) a blend of compressed existing terms, without losing the existence and meaning of its elements,
(d) eponyms use the names of people involved in the designation of the term, but do not provide its description nor relations with other terms,
(e) letters used individually or as compounds,
(f) totally new coinages 'which are not inspired in some way or other by an existing word, sound or image', are rather rare.

The classification of neologisms in specialised languages above proves that specialised vocabulary has a universal character with the tendency to the 'internationalisation of the language of science (Iljinska & Smirnova, 2010: 317–318)'. Neologisms except for the new coinages can be also treated as internationalisms which can be divided into the following groups:

1. lexical units of Greco-Latin origin;
2. words derived using Latin and Greek elements;
3. eponyms;
4. abbreviations (2010: 318).

The question remains: how long and far can these categories and examples be treated as new? Some of these are well-established lexemes, widely recognised by specialists, the others, like *microphone* have migrated to the general language, and they are a part of the popular general lexicon. Moreover, some terms, are created according to the rules above, but were coined in the past. For example, the terms *impedance,* a pseudo synonym of *resistance*, familiar to experts, but not popular to the general public, was created in 1886 by Oliver Heaviside from the Latin stem with a Latin/French suffix *–ance*[8].

Lukszyn and Zmarzer (2001) present a similar typology of new linguistic units within a terminological system, but they identify 4 categories with further subcategories (2001: 77–78):

1. neosemantisms
   (a) transterminologisation – term migration with its literal meaning, which is a result of interdisciplinarity, because some terms create one unity
   (b) terminologisation – migration of general language lexemes with a new figurative meaning,

8 https://www.etymonline.com/word/impedance, 27.08.2019

2. neologisms
   (a) units built entirely on the basis of the native language
   (b) units built on the basis of the native language with international terminological elements
   (c) units built on the basis of foreign terminological elements
3. borrowings
4. internationalisms.

Lukszyn & Zmarzer (2001), however, do not illustrate their classification of neologisms with examples, which makes their typology difficult to comprehend.

On the other hand, there are critical voices concerning the introduction of new lexicon, including terms, into scientific writing (Parysek, 2017). The abundance of new concepts and their proliferation lead to unnecessary disturbances in scientific communication. The introduction of many new terms is pointless, and it only brings about conceptual and terminological inflation. Parysek (2017) is an advocate of the traditional approach to terminology and to the scientific language, which, however, might have progress-inhibiting effects in science in the long run. The author's (2017) call to apply the principle of 'Ockham's razor' is, on the one hand, justified, since some scientists unnecessarily use too complex language in their articles, but, on the other, might lead to oversimplification of science (Parysek, 2017; Davis, 1998).

To sum up, the language of engineering, which the MTCS domains fall into, has been neglected in the literature on the subject of neologism. Therefore, the existing typologies either pertain to the general language or specialised language but analysed generally. Moreover, examples presented by the authors have lost their novel character, and have become an integral part of the specialised lexicon, or even migrated to the general language.

3.8.2. Borrowings

Borrowings from all contact languages, both direct and indirect, are the second source of language enrichment, beside neologisms, and have a long-lived tradition (Sager et al., 1980; Dunaj & Mycawka, 2017; Górnicz, 2019). They are words acquired from other languages, and are introduced mainly by bilinguals (Górnicz, 2019). New lexemes are introduced to the recipient language via code-switching and code-mixing. It is the effect of economic, cultural and linguistic contacts with other countries and intereferences (Bloomfield, 1933; Grónicz, 2019).

There are a few types of borrowings, depending on their lifespan in recipient languages as well as their character. On-the-spot borrowings are ephemeral phenomena, the effect of the temporary use of a donor language word by a bilingual, and it is treated as the first phase in the process of borrowing lexicon. Intimate or core borrowings supersede the native equivalent and become a part of lexicon (Bloomfield, 1933; Myers-Scotton, 1998 in Górnicz, 2019). Cultural borrowings allow for naming concepts unfamiliar in a given culture. Moreover, the most often borrowed lexemes are nouns which account for 70–75 %, followed by verbs – 18–23 %, adjectives 3–4 % and ending with adverbs and prepositions which make about 1 % of all borrowings (Górnicz, 2019).

Among borrowings, one can also distinguish semantic borrowings, semantic calques, syntactic-semantic calques, semicalques, syntactic calques, morphological borrowings of the word-formative model, pragmatic borrowings and formal borrowings (phonetic and orthographic) (Witalisz, 2016: 21–25 in Dunaj & Mycawka, 2017: 68–69; Górnicz, 2019). In order to determine whether a borrowing is justified, a set of criteria of assessment of linguistic forms has been developed: criteria of language sufficiency, economy, functionality, generality, cultural authority and aesthetics, with the first three being necessary (Dunaj & Mycawka, 2017: 69; Górnicz, 2019).

Terms are also subject to borrowing due to the development of the subject field and the emergence of the concept in the donor language that needs a designation in the recipient language to fill in the terminological gap (Górnicz, 2019). Yet, clarity of borrowings in specialised contexts might be questioned, especially in the case of monolinguals, but it is the definition that allows for the appropriate usage of the term. Borrowed terms might pertain to only one specialised subject field, called endoderivatives, and therefore they are not metaphorical. On the other hand, exoderivative terms are built from at least one element used in the general language. Moreover, borrowed terms are usually shorter, more economical and packed with meaning than native equivalents, which might not be morphologically possible in the recipient language. The use of internationalisms facilitates specialised communication on the international level. Surprisingly, a number of native terms are in fact borrowings, but created from native morphemes. Some terms might take the form of loan translations, and Górnicz (2019) differentiates loan renditions and loan creations. The first might be considered native terms with a borrowed concept, and the latter borrow the concept, but take a different form in the recipient language. Moreover, the phenomenon of borrowings creates internationalisms, to such an extent that practically every term may become international.

Sager et al. (1980) point out that the main sources of new vocabulary in English are predominantly loan translations from Latin and Greek. Moreover, specialised texts in English contain borrowings from other languages. In the fields of electrical engineering, there is a great number of borrowings from French. It, however, depends on a register, because as Górnicz points out (2019), in IT there is a diglossia, i.e. in informal IT nerd texts, the majority of borrowings are of Roman origin, whereas texts written in higher registers are dominated by English calques. Borrowings from German and other languages denote 'concrete objects, apparatus, and processes rather than concepts (Sager et al., 1980: 287)'. Anglicisation is the process of adaptation of spelling or pronunciation to the English rules and it is more often found in technology than in science.

In conclusion, borrowings constitute a quick form of language enrichment due to economic or cultural contacts. Terminology is also susceptible to taking designations from other languages for unfamiliar concepts, which leads to internationalisation. In scientific writing, most terms are of foreign origin, which facilitates international communication. However, there are doubts whether all borrowings are justified and indispensable, because the extensive use of this method might lead to the impoverishment of the recipient language.

3.8.3. Compression

Compression is nowadays a frequent phenomenon in technical, medical and scientific domains and is extensively used in computer science (Pop & Sim, 2009). Technological and scientific developments have brought about the creation of complex concepts and terms and abbreviation allows to 'denote terms and concepts as clearly as possible', which minimise the time needed to provide information, but short forms might be polysemous, ambiguous and familiar only to a narrow circle of experts in a given field (Pop & Sim, 2009; Mattiello, 2012; Sitkowski, 2008: 26).

In scientific texts, there are two quasi conflicting tendencies in terms of lexis. The trend is noticeable in the division of abbreviations into clear and unclear provided by Górnicz (1997: 27 in Sitkowski, 2008: 26). On the one hand, complex noun phrases are created, and the need to convey the possibly densest information load in limited space, on the other (Mattiello, 2012: 149). The compression process is performed by the 'abbreviation of existing words and expressions, by the omission of elements in compounds, by the creation letter symbols, by the combination of letters and numbers into short designations and by pictograms (Sager, et al., 1980: 277)'. Therefore, the use of abbreviations: initialisms, acronyms, clippings, and blends in research papers derives from the need to present information in a compressed form due to word limits and limited space imposed by publishers (Mattiello, 2012: 149). Even though these phenomena appear frequently in scientific writing out of economy, convenience and avoiding repetition, generative grammarians considered them to be 'oddities' 'of minor importance' (Pop & Sim, 2009: 557; Mattiello, 2012: 153). In terms of spelling, they behave unpredictably, irregularly, inconsistently and are formed irrespectively of rules (Mattiello, 2012: 153–154). Yet, initialisms and non-elliptic acronyms are considered prototypes, e.g. *IEEE* (*Institute of Electrical and Electronics Engineers*), an abbreviated eponym pronounced */I triple E/* which is an example of an alphabetism in which not all source words are graphically represented in the output.

In terms of their lifecycle, there are two types of abbreviations: temporary and permanent, i.e. they are either situationally, textually, or are subject-conditioned as well as those which replace the whole multi-word units in all instances (Sager et al., 1980: 277). Moreover, they are more frequent in writing than in speech, and may be restricted to a limited circle of specialists in a narrow subject field under time and space pressure (Sager et al., 1980; Mattiello, 2012: 150). However, some abbreviated forms might be ambiguous, stand for more than one term and need to be explained. Alphabetisms are divided into intitalisms, pronounced letter by letter, and acronyms, created from initial letters and are pronounced like normal words, e.g. MOSFET (Sager et al., 1980: 277–278; Pop & Sim, 2009: 557).

The problem with acronyms lies in their highly polysemous and homonymous nature. More than one meaning might be assigned to one set of letters and they are strongly context-dependent (Pop & Sim, 2009: 558). The acronym may have a meaning of its own because they are 'coined on the basis of an already existing word associations and information (Pop & Sim, 2009: 558)'. Moreover, some are not intuitive to decode, their meaning 'cannot be deduced from its base form but has to be learned', which might be challenging to less experienced readers, which contradicts the principles of logic and conciseness of terms (Sitkowski, 2008: 27).

Abbreviations share a set of characteristics, contradictory at times. One of the features is a degree of polarisation with regard to their expansion. On the one hand, they are familiar to a narrow inner circle of users, but, on the other, acronyms become known worldwide, and thus are treated as internationalisms (Sager et al., 1980: 277–278; Mattiello, 2012: 150). Moreover, acronyms also tend to acquire special meanings, not synonymous to their original full forms, and may undergo some stylistic changes (Mattiello, 2012: 150). Clippings, most prototypically formed by back-clipping, are originally characteristic for the colloquial language, but recently they have also been used in professional circles.

Blends, on the other hand, are a 'combination of compounding and compression' and can be analysed both as neologisms and abbreviations (Sager et al, 1980: 282)'. The most prototypical pattern in forming is by taking the first part of the first source element and the ending of the second. Their formation is limited to the most prototypical ones, blends 'are less regular than rules forming compounds (Mattiello, 2012: 153–154)'. Many abbreviations are a 'borderline case between acronyms and blends (Mattiello, 2012: 156)'.

Abbreviations serve three basic functions, i.e. lexical, naming, and as a reference at three levels: textual, social and pragmatic. At the textual level, abbreviations serve predominantly the naming function, which allows for labeling scientific and technological research, experiments and new discoveries with simple names easy to remember (Mattiello, 2012: 157). The second function is language economy. The choice of lexical items in the scientific texts is governed by the Principle of Least Effort, i.e. to convey the maximum content in a straightforward manner with the minimal amount of words (Zipf, 1949). Moreover, abbreviating affects text cohesion via anaphoric and cataphoric references (Mattiello, 2012: 160). In the first 'the full form is introduced first, and the shortened form is used afterwards to allude back to it', whereas in the latter the full form follows the abbreviation in the text (Mattiello, 2012: 160–161).

Summing up, abbreviation is a convenient way of conveying information in a compact way, especially in English which exhibits a tendency to compression. Abbreviations used by experts, such as scientists, facilitate professional closeness and 'cohesiveness among insiders', and might be 'obscure to non-experts (Mattiello, 2012: 159–160)'. The meaning of abbreviated forms, however, might be ambiguous and polysemous, and as such familiar only to a narrow circle of professionals. Moreover, in order to facilitate proper understanding of the text, the authors decide to use anaphoric reference along with the compressed term in their research papers.

3.9. Phraseology in scientific texts

Verbal communication is performed in units or chunks rather than in single words. Frequently used expressions facilitate its efficiency due to the functions they serve. Each discourse, form of communication or register develops its own characteristic phrases, scientific communication included. Therefore, there is a need to study phraseological units in scientific writing since they contribute to the development of meaning and the transfer of knowledge worldwide.

Phraseology can be loosely defined as 'the study of the structure, meaning, and use of word combinations (Cowie, 1994: 3168 in Granger & Paquot, 2008: 27)'.

It encompasses lexical units which are referred to as 'multi-word expressions, statistical phrases, chains, formulaic sequences, multi-word units, grouping, combinations of recurring words, lexical package, n-grams', or 'conventional expressions, lexicalized formulaic structures, prefabricated blocks, multi vocabulary lexical units, phrases, set phrases, etc. (Silva & Orenha-Ottaiano & Babini, 2017: 347)'. Generally speaking, phraseology in use encompasses different types of word units, like collocations, i.e. words that are used together, expressions, e.g. proverbs, etc., tendencies of use, such as passive voice, negative clauses, plural forms, or complementation patterns, like verbal and nominal regency (Hunston, 2010 in Silva et al., 2017).

In specialised languages, these entail not only terms, fixed expressions, but also word combinations, etc. usually used together in a language in order to verbalise specific senses which may undergo changes depending on the contextual needs, and idiolectal uses (Postolea, 2014; Müldner-Nieckowski, 2016; Podlecki, 2017). They are irregular, and do not have a systematic structure, as long as they meet the criterion of a multiword unit appearing with a high frequency, and they must be semantically specialised to be considered phraseological units (Müldner-Nieckowski, 2016; Silva et al., 2017).

Gledhill (2000) develops a hierarchy of systems of organisation in correlation with the levels of organisation, which is depicted in Figure 3.5. below. Specific expressions, e.g. lexical phrases to conventional sentence stems, possess distinct pragmatic and discoursal effects and occupy the highest position in the sophistication, and organisation hierarchy. The middle position is reserved for fixed expressions, like phrases and idioms. Collocations hold the lowest position, because they are only textually recurrent expressions.

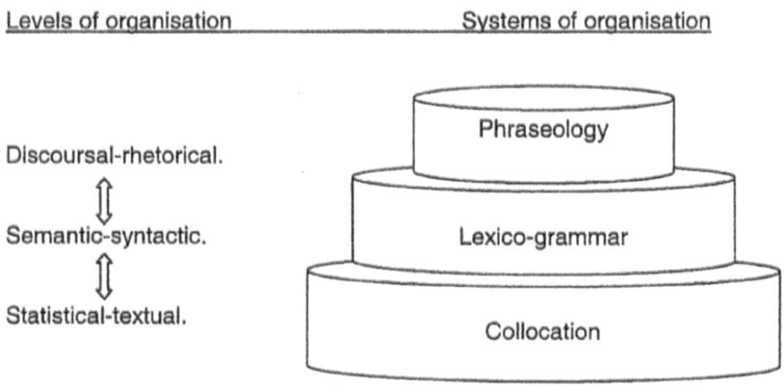

Figure 3.5. Gledhill's (2000) correlation between levels of organisation and systems of organisation (2000: 203)

Phraseology is a relatively new and complex field in which one can distinguish two approaches the traditional & corpus-driven, also called distributional or frequency-based (Granger & Paquot, 2008). The latter allows for identifying co-occurrences, such as 'frames, collocational frameworks, colligations and largely compositional recurrent phrases', and has moved the boundaries of phraseology towards free word combinations (Granger & Paquot, 2008: 29). The n-gram and co-occurrence analyses allow for putting forward a new typology based on the extraction procedure, which is depicted in Figure 3.6. below:

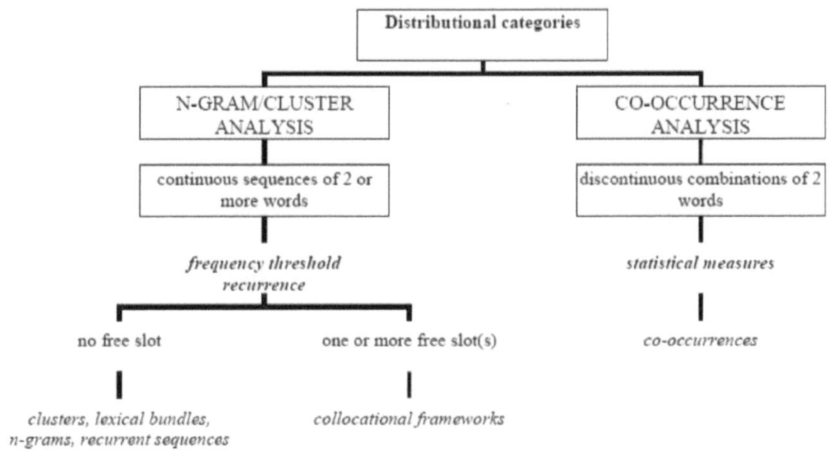

Figure 3.6. Distributional categories developed by Granger & Paquot (2008: 38)

N-gram extraction allows for the analysis of recurrent word sequences, regardless of their status, idiomacity or purposes (Granger & Paquot, 2008). On the other hand, co-occurrence analysis reveals the most frequent word combinations, which have been revealed via dedicated software, like Sketch Engine (the tool used in the analyses in this monograph).

In terms of morphology, phraseological units are word combinations comprised of at least two orthographic words (Granger & Paquot, 2008; Müldner-Nieckowski, 2016). Yet, some word combinations pose problems to this requirement. In English, compounds blur the borderline between phraseology and morphology due to their inconsistent spelling rules, i.e. being separate words, one word, or a hyphenated form. As a result, the traditional approach rejects them, and the corpus-driven analyses allow open compounds, some hyphenated in writing, and exclude the solid ones. Other problematic word categories include complex prepositions, adverbs and conjunctions, i.e. grammatical collocations, i.e. 'grammatical words collocating with lexical words' which play an important role in the scientific language, and yet are difficult to determine (Granger & Paquot, 2008; Gledhill, 2000: 12; Müldner-Nieckowski, 2016).

The borderlines between phraseology and syntax are also fuzzy (Granger & Paquot, 2008). The most debatable are less idiomatic expressions and collocations, in particular. Moreover, compound and syntactic phrases form other blurred areas. In this case, the important issue is to determine the variation level of syntactic changes that the phrases can undergo. Of the two approaches, the traditional one is stricter in terms of attitude towards distinguishing criteria whereas the distribution view is more concentrated on the lexico-grammatical patterns (Granger & Paquot, 2008; Gledhill, 2000).

Finally, phraseology is also connected with the discourse, and the two approaches concentrate on different aspects (Granger & Paquot, 2008). The traditional approach distinguishes formulae, i.e. expressions that reflect the interactive character of discourse, such as greetings, enquiries, or invitations, and the pragmatic functions of the formulaic expressions. The corpus-driven view shifts from pragmatic aspects to rhetorics and stylistics, and acknowledge multiword units that structure texts and perform major discoursal functions, such as hedging, organising, or referencing lexical bundles (Granger & Paquot, 2008; Biber, 2006). They are in the form of verbal or clausal units of speech, nominal and prepositional phrases (Granger & Paquot, 2008). They are also considered register markers, i.e. 'the preferred ways of saying things (Granger & Paquot, 2008: 34; Gledhill, 2000)'.

As mentioned above, there are different types of phraseological units, from very restricted and metaphorical in meaning to free word combinations normally used together, labelled 'lexical phrases, formulas, routines, fixed expressions and prefabricated patterns (Postolea, 2014; Müldner-Nieckowski, 2016; Biber, 2006: 133)'. Biber (2006) conducts thorough corpus studies of multiword units, and refers to them as lexical bundles. These are 'the most frequent recurring sequences of words' which are non-idiomatic and not complete in terms of grammatical structures, but salient (Biber, 2006: 133–134). They function as units in discourse, and are specific to different university registers. There are three main functions of lexical bundles, i.e.

1) stance expressions give information about the attitudes and degree of certainty:
   (a) epistemic bundles inform about certainty or its absence,
   (b) attitudinal or modality bundles provide speakers' attitudes, i.e. desires, obligation/directive, intention/prediction, or ability,

2) discourse organizers are a reflection of relationships between prior and forthcoming discourse elements
   (a) topic introduction/focus bundles signal the introduction of a topic
   (b) topic elaboration/clarification bundles provide additional information
   (c) identification/focus bundles emphasise the most important elements
3) referential expressions are a direct reference to physical or non-physical entities as well as other parts of the text:
   (a) imprecision bundles
   (b) bundles specifying attributes which specify procedures, quantities or descriptions of reality
   c) time/place/text-deixis bundles (Biber, 2006;).

The majority of these types of lexical bundles are found in scientific writing, unlike fixed metaphorical phrases, i.e. idioms. They constitute the most salient words for every section of the research paper (Gledhill, 2000).

In academic texts, phraseological units are key in the scientific expert-to-expert communication (Silva et al., 2017). In fact, phraseology plays 'an important role in the textual development of meaning' because the structure of scientific knowledge is related with the 'preferred ways of saying things (Gledhill, 2000: 206)'. Moreover, it significantly affects the rhetorical construction of the text. On the other hand, scientific articles are given more authenticity, which helps fulfilling target audience's expectations by using 'common vocabulary, terminological vocabulary and typical structures of academic-scientific communication' for both native and non-native speakers (Silva et al., 2017: 346; Chen & Baker, 2010).

In conclusion, phraseological units embrace a wide range of multiword units of a varied level of fixedness. Their usefulness and significance in specialised texts, and in scientific writing in particular, cannot be ignored. Lexical bundles facilitate communication in scientific writing for both native and non-native speakers, because communication in chunks is more effective than creating word combinations anew. Moreover, corpus analyses have revealed unknown facts about the language, which might affect the education process of potential members of academic circles, or non-native speakers.

3.9.1. Collocations in scientific writing

Academia, as a discourse community, are characterised by their specific language, which is manifested by the existence of collocations, since their members communicate via patterns, and not individual words (Gledhill, 2000;

Williams, 2002 in Peacock, 2012: 30). As a result, collocations, being members of a bigger group – phraseological units, are important linguistic means indispensable in knowledge transfer, which can be successfully achieved by using correct combinations of typical grammatical and lexical patterns (González & Verdaguer, 2016).

Collocations are responsible for the development of meaning in scientific writing (Gledhill, 2000; Peacock, 2012: 32). In addition, word combinations are not used accidentally, but contribute to lexical cohesion and allow to express one's messages in an economical way. They also facilitate the efforts of decoding the message by readers, which brings us back to the Principle of Least Effort (Zipf, 1949). Moreover, Peacock's study (2012) reveals that high-frequency noun collocations form domain-specific standard terminology, and they are indicators of different topics, research methods or discussion content. Therefore, it proves the need to study collocations in each discipline, like economics or IT, in isolation, and not to conduct one general study of all academic texts from all disciplines.

A collocation is comprised of 'words which tend to co-occur in recurrent, recognisable expressions', whose patterns are seen as 'fundamental units in the stylistic description of texts (Gledhill, 2000: 201; Menon & Mukundan, 2012)'. In German lexicology, it is defined as 'typical, usual, conventional and recurrent combination of lexemes (Gruntar Jermol, 2007: 137)'. It stays in relation to 'a range of commonly recognised multi-word phrases in language, including catchphrases, clichés, fixed expressions, formulae, free and bound collocations idioms, lexical phrases, turn-of-phrases, and so on (Gledhill, 2000: 7)'. On the other hand, in more recent studies, collocations are classified differently and are referred to as prefabricated language, phraseological units, lexical phrases, co-selection of words, conventionalised forms, ready-made utterances, naturally co-occurring strings of words, formulaic sentences, chunks or word partnerships (Menon & Mukundan, 2012; Peacock, 2012).

The borderline between a multiword term and a collocation is fuzzy or blurred. Gruntar Jermol (2007) points out the difficulty in determining the difference between the collocation and a multiword term which is particularly important for the specialised lexicology. In fact, 'high-frequency collocations of common nouns are part of favoured terminology by which disciplines can be differentiated (Groom, 2005 in Peacock, 2012: 42–43)'. However, it is not an easy task to draw a clear borderline between a multiword term, and a nominal collocation based on the definition (Gruntar Jermol, 2007). Nominal collocations become multiword terms when they meet a set of criteria, i.e. they express a well-defined reality, belong to a domain-specific conceptual system, and they are separated by their conceptual autonomy. However, there are problems with domain-specific collocations in certain areas, e.g. there is a lack of consistency in legal dictionaries, because they contain both terms and collocations which occupy too much space (Gruntar Jermol, 2007). Another problem relates to the place where collocations are listed, whether at the basis or collocates's entry.

Knowledge of collocations is also indispensable for a proficient command of language (Gledhill, 2000; Menon & Mukundan, 2012). Scientific texts are written both by native and non-native speakers (Peacock, 2012; Makowska, 2018). For example, in the MTCS domains, the number of non-native writers reaches the level of about 50 %. For them, learning and using collocations properly might pose a challenge (Peacock, 2012; Menon & Mukundan, 2012). Misuses might stem from the differences across languages, or the lack of awareness of the genre conventions. As a result, both native speakers and non-native scientists, creating scientific texts, are prone to the improper use of words in wrong contexts or to a narrow range of collocations. Nevertheless, their writing is later subject to language analyses and works as a language model for linguistic analyses.

All things considered, collocations are economical and domain-specific means of specialised communication. Yet, the borderline between a collocation and a multiword term is fuzzy since the most frequent nominal collocates prove to be parts of complex terms specific for domain-specific terminology. On the other hand, their knowledge is crucial both for experts, especially foreigners, as well as for translators.

3.9.2. Multiword terms

One of the manifestations of the need to compress information in scientific writing is the creation of multi-word terms, or compound terms. The other reason is the precision of expression as complex phrases allow for the exact denotation of particular, subordinate concepts in which every element gives an additional distinctive feature (Mazurkiewicz-Sułkowska, 2014: 29–30). Single-word terms denote predominantly superordinate general technical concepts (Mazurkiewicz-Sułkowska, 2014: 29–30). On the other hand, Sager et al. (1980) state that a syntagmatic unit combined of at least two elements has an independent meaning from its components that become parts of the whole terminological system (1980: 265–266), and unlike Mazurkiewicz-Sułkowska (2014), who describes explicitly the subordinate-superordinate single-word and multi-word term relationships, for Sager et al. (1980), a compound is an independent term entity with its distinct meaning of a broad concept. The authors (1980) contrast it with a phrase which is narrower, but constitutes the source of the compound term.

Compounds evolve 'from regularly occurring collocations and convert phrases into fully lexicalised or terminological units' with their meaning independent from their constituents (Sager et al.,1980: 265–266). This definition contrasted with that of a multi-word expression (MWE) is convergent in terms of meaning as MWEs are idiomatic and compositional, but it narrows compounds into terms (Sager et al.,1980; Hüning & Schlücke, 2015). Both phenomena stem from similar sources: chunks, collocations, extended lexical units, fixed expressions, lexical or lexicalised phrases, multi-word units, phraseological units, etc. However, multi-word terms are ingrained in the experts' minds in the same way as MWEs are 'stored in the Mental Lexicon of native speakers (Hüning & Schlücke, 2015: 450)'. All in all, both MWEs and multi-word terms form single lexical units with a distinct meaning which are syntactically fixed to some degree. For this reason, multi-word terms can treated as a MWEs, but are limited to specialised languages.

Multi-word terms have varied constituents. Among compound terms one can distinguish noun compounds, compound adjectives, compound verbs, compounds with particles, and multiple compounds in English (Sager et al., 1980). The first category of compound terms, noun compounds are formed by adding nouns, proper nouns or adjectives to the main, or a nuclear noun (Sager et al., 1980: 267–268). Complex terms created by adding eponyms appear quite frequently in scientific writing, e.g. *discreet Fourier transform*.

Terminological sets or categories are created by adding various determinants which assign the compound term to a given sub-category, i.e. provide a criterion for the subdivision (Sager et al., 1980). A constant nucleus placed in English at the end of the phrase 'indicates the category to which the concept belongs (Sager et al., 1980: 268)'. There are three main types of compound terms:

2. those which designate objects (substances, materials, products, apparatus)
3. those which designate properties (…)
4. those which designate processes and operations (Sager et al., 1980: 268).

In terms of the first type, compounds denoting objects, one can distinguish 9 subcategories, depending on the nucleus-determinant relationship:

(a) the comparison of the nucleus with another object,
(b) the specification of the material or substance used to make the nucleus,
(c) 'the inherent property of the new concept (Sager et al., 1980: 270)'
(d) the regular use of the nucleus,
(e) the product normally associated with the nucleus,
(f) the nucleus as the instrument used to operate on the determinant,

(g) the specification of the 'mode of operation of the nucleus (Sager et al., 1980: 270)';
(h) the determinant constitutes a whole whereas the nucleus might form a part,
(i) the identity of the nucleus is asserted by the determinant.

Sager et al. (1980) also identify relationships indicating place, time, properties or other relationships which are consistent with the patterns used in the general language, e.g. terms containing properties or disposition are created by adding a determinant which specifies the property of the term, such as a 'method apparatus and unit of measurement (1980: 271)'. Complex terms formed by the addition of the adjectival determinant are not considered compounds in morphological-syntactic terms, but terminologically speaking, they are full-fledged terms, e.g. *operating frequency*. Compound terms designating processes are formed from 'deverbal nouns and converted verbs (Sager et al., 1980: 271)'.

Sager et al. (1980) also classify terms in English formed by adding particles as compounds. These include terms written separately, together and with a hyphen.

Compounds may consist of more than two elements, with the predominant majority of 3- and 4-element phrases (36 and 40 % respectively according to Herzborg, 1971 in Sager et al., 1980: 272). However, long terms are usually mentioned in full in the attachments, or at the beginning of the text, and then shortened in the body of texts with the use of the anaphoric or cataphoric reference in order to avoid ambiguity (Mattiello, 2012: 160; Sager et al. 1980).

Apart from the above mentioned types of compounds, there are compound adjectives, but these rarely occur in the MTCS domains. One of the rare examples is *FInFET-based circuit*, formed by combining an abbreviation acting as a noun with a past participle, which is consistent with Sager et al.'s (1980) study. Howerver, long phrases are characteristic for the MTCS domains.

Compound verbs constitute the last category which are a typically English phenomenon. The predominant majority of verbs are of Latin origin. However, there are examples of one of the groups identified by Sager et al. (1980), i.e. compounds with particles. The nouns deriving from them appear among the keyword terms,

All things considered, complex phrases are used for two reasons: out of economical reasons and to avoid ambiguity and facilitate precision. Therefore, scientists in the MTCS domains make an extensive use of this language phenomenon, building either complex phrases or using compounds. The MTCS study confirms previous findings in this field.

3.10. Concluding remarks to Chapter 3

Chapter 3 is devoted to various aspects of scientific terminology and phraseology. Terminology, omnipresent in scientific articles, is the most salient feature of specialised texts, and acts as a reflection of each subject field. The traditional approach to terminology assumes the stability of term's meaning, its assignment to a given subject field, as well as clarity and precision, but it is a utopian vision, because it is not possible to record all changes in terminology the moment they occur. As a result, on the one hand, there are traditional, well-established standardised terms, and a constant influx of new terminology which reflects the innovations, on the other. The two conflicting tendencies in terminology descriptions: standardisation and metaphorisation constantly collide and coexist. Therefore, the safest attitude to modern terminology is to adopt a dual approach: take standardisation for granted and acknowledge typical linguistic phenomena in changing circumstances in terminology. Modern scientific disciplines have also a dual character: the disciplines are becoming narrower and more detailed, but at the same time draw concept from other subject fields and become interdisciplinary. In addition, multimodality is growing in importance. All these factors lead to terminological hybridity.

Finally, terms might not only be singleword units. In order to ensure precision, professionals build complex terminological phrases. However, it is difficult to differentiate between complex terms and collocations because the latter are often are constituents of the most salient domain-specific terms. Moreover, effective communication necessitates the use of specific lexical phrases that serve other important textual functions. Frequent word partnerships act as cohesion markers which facilitate the readers' encoding process.

Chapter 4 Corpora in analyses of scientific writing

The current chapter is devoted to the role of corpora in the studies of scientific texts. Corpora are bodies of naturally occurring texts which are subject of linguistic analyses (Bowker & Pearson, 2002). They reflect genuine communication between people. These large collections of authentic texts are in an electronic form which are gathered on the basis of definite, explicit criteria. Corpus analyses of the specialised language allow for the empirical studies of the language and verification of new meanings of words in professional contexts, like science, that are used instead of making hypothetical assumptions.

In addition, special purpose or specialised corpora focus on particular aspects of languages and their uses, in particular they allow for scrutinising terminology, phraseology, grammatical and rhetorical structures of particular text types. Yet, their compilation might pose a challenge for a number of reasons. Texts which are to be used in a corpus need to fulfil a set of criteria to ensure the representativeness of the corpus. One cannot escape the constraints at this point of research and should approach the corpus method with awareness of its limitations in order to ensure objectivity of the studies. Retrieved data might lead to interesting observations and conclusions on the condition that research questions and hypotheses are raised appropriately.

This chapter also presents ontologies as one of the methods of using corpus data which allow for structuring knowledge. They are particularly useful in terminological studies where full understanding of the domain depends on understanding the relationships between concepts and terms in authentic contexts.

Finally, corpus analyses also permit studying and determining recurrent features of the scientific language. Various aspects of the language of science have been analysed, starting from terminology, phraseology, discursive and rhetorical features ending with syntactic structures across domains in order to determine domain-specific nuances of the scientific language.

4.1. Corpora in analyses of specialised languages

Even though scientific and technical language should be objective, neutral, standardised and schematic in terms of text construction, there are context-dependent and domain-specific variations (Carrió Pastor, 2009). Its analysis should be carried out on authentic data which provide 'information about the most frequent language structures and rhetoric strategies (Carrió Pastor, 2009: 223–224)'. Generic conventions limit, however, linguistic resources and discoursal functional values.

Nowadays, corpora are treated as indispensable tools in linguistic studies which enable one to retrieve linguistic data from large bodies of authentic texts (López Mateo & Olmo Cazevieille, 2015). Among various types of corpora, the most useful in analyses of specialised languages, and terminology in particular, are specialised corpora (Waliński, 2005; Goźdź-Roszkowski & Witczak-Plisiecka, 2005; López Mateo & Olmo Cazevieille, 2015; Makowska, 2016). Similar texts are collected according to a set of predetermined criteria (Bowker & Pearson, 2002; Maia, 2003; Waliński, 2005; Johansson, 2007). They have to serve the same communicative purpose; need to be created at approximately the same time, share the same topic, functionality, style or a subject field. In order to obtain reliable results, input data must be as homogeneous as possible.

Corpora are more effective and extensive than other linguistic resources (Bowker & Pearson, 2002). Firstly, they provide fast access to research data, and research can be conducted in a very short time. Moreover, authentic research material provides information objectively and consistently about the authentic usage as well as meaningful linguistic patterns which are available. The body of texts is created by multiple authors, which prevents from linguistic idiosyncrasies. In specialised languages, corpora studies allow for analysing behaviour of lexemes and terms in authentic contexts. The borderline between the two is fuzzy, i.e. due to the de-terminologisation, i.e. the migration of terms into the general language, as well as the reverse trend, i.e. acquiring a specialised meaning by general language lexicon (Maia, 2003; Bowker & Pearson, 2002). Corpus analyses also enable observing patterns which otherwise would escape unnoticed (Johansson, 2007). Furthermore, corpora provide information about domain-specific collocations and other phraseological units typical for a given subject field. Finally, corpora help study and determine stylistic and grammatical features of specialised writing which are relevant to a given subject field.

In conclusion, scientific and technical language is prone to variations which can be analysed via corpus analyses. Corpora reveal interesting facts about different linguistic aspects of scientific writing. However, texts collections must not be accidental, but need to meet specific criteria in order to facilitate objectivity of the analysis and reliable results.

4.2. Building specialised corpora for terminological and phraseological analyses

Special purpose corpora constitute an indispensable tool in linguistic analyses of specialised varieties of language (Maia, 2003; Waliński, 2005). The term *corpus* seemed to cause confusion because the definition that a corpus was a collection of texts in an electronic form, meeting specific criteria to represent a language was deemed unsatisfactory (Pearson, 1998). Moreover, there is also a dilemma concerning other corpus terminology, i.e. whether a smaller, dedicated corpus should be called a subcorpus. Sinclair (1991 in Pearson, 1998) suggests that the term implies the corpus is a smaller version of a bigger one, and he puts forward the term *component* which illustrates the selection of a particular part of language and its homogeneity.

Specialised corpora are much smaller in size and concentrate on the language of specialised communication (Pearson, 1998). They are designed for a specific purpose, and therefore allow for analyses of unusual features of such communication which otherwise might be considered lexical deviations. They are restricted in terms of 'genre, author, period, or other criteria (...)' to serve their purposes (1998: 48). A set of pre-established criteria are necessary in order to design a representative corpus (Pearson, 1998; Bowker & Pearson, 2002; Maia, 2003; Waliński, 2005; López Mateo & Olmo Cazevieille, 2015). The criteria are divided into external and internal (Sinclair, 1991 in Pearson, 1998; Hundston, 2008). The first 'include genre, mode, origin and aims of the texts (Pearson, 1998: 52)'. Different types of publications, like newspapers or research articles in non-fiction, comprise genre category. The mode category determines whether the texts are written or spoken, but they must be in an electronic form, which nowadays has been taken for granted (Sinclair, 1991; Pearson, 1998; Bowker & Pearson, 2002; Hajnicz, 2011; Karpiński, 2017). Maia (2003) even specifies the necessity to obtain the right format of the content. Moreover, the criterion informs who has produced the text and other details concerning the people involved, like their age, education, etc. (Pearson, 1998). The aims include information about the target audience, their relationships with the authors and the purpose of the text, e.g. research articles provide information. Internal criteria include the topic which is a controversial issue, since it can be understood as the main theme of the text or the classification of the text (Pearson, 1998; Hundston, 2008). Moreover, text candidates must exhibit a certain level of similarity in terms of their structure and performed functions (Maia, 2003). Their identification should be performed by the examination of the lexical structure, and keywords of the text (Pearson, 1998). The choice of criteria depends on type of research that is going to be conducted (Hundston, 2008).

The compilation stage seems to be a straightforward task at face value, but in practice it appears to be much complex (Hundston, 2008). Hundston (2008) limits the criteria to three main ones that a corpus has to meet, i.e. size, representativeness, and balance. The first category, size, is the most controversial. On the one hand, it is said that the larger the corpus, the more representative it is, but on the other, smaller corpora allow for observing clearly how frequent words behave, which might be lost among countless instances. Moreover, both big and small corpora provide unique information which neither of them would give individually (Granath, 2007). Big corpora help identify meaningful structures, whereas small-size corpora concentrate on specific features which are characteristic for a given category of text. Moreover, large corpora are helpful in phraseological analyses and macro-patterning, but smaller ones focus on variation with the use of grammatical categories (Hundston, 2008). The constraints limiting size include software limitations, copyright and ethical issues as well as the availability of texts. Furthermore, the advent of the Internet has reshaped compilation of corpora due to easy access to its endless resources at an instant. The second criterion, representativeness, is the 'relationship between the corpus and the body of language is being used to represent (Hundston, 2008: 160)'. As a result, a corpus is a part, characteristic for a larger corpus. Special purpose corpora are controversial in terms of the comparison with the general ones. They are aimed at representing a specialised variety of a language, not the language as a whole, and they include a variety of the domain-specific texts which are allowed by the resources. The amount of texts in a given domain in a corpus reflects the importance of the domain in the society to which the corpus pertains. Moreover, in the case of problems with representativeness one should be aware of them and make all possible efforts in given circumstances, but 'be transparent about how the corpus has been designed and what is in it (Hundston, 2008: 162)'. The third criterion is the balance, i.e. 'the internal composition of the corpus (2008: 163)'. Yet, the imbalance in size can be overcome by frequency normalisation and it is not of overriding importance if the hypotheses made are modified accordingly. Yet, the corpus has to be 'large enough to make comparisons feasible (Hundston, 2008: 164)'.

Moreover, other professional corpus compilers list more detailed criteria concerning special purpose corpora at the compilation stage. There must be a balance among samples, i.e. there must be a comparable quantity of texts meeting the predefined criteria, which might be a challenging task in specialised languages due to the shortage of suitable texts (Maia, 2003; Waliński, 2005). The problem of size of the corpus seems to be a paradox, and seems to raise a degree of controversy, because 'small corpora tend only to be representative for certain high frequency linguistic features (Sinclair, 1991; McEnery & Wilson, 1996: 78; Maia, 2003; Hajnicz, 2011; Bowker & Pearson, 2002; Hundston, 2008). In the case of special purpose corpora it is believed that smaller size results from the problem of availability and copyright, but there might be problems with their representativeness, because a corpus must be a sample of a bigger population (McEnery & Wilson, 1996; Pearson, 1998; Bowker & Pearson, 2002; Biber, 2012). Gajek (2006) specifies the size of small corpora to be between 50,000 and 200,000 words, which is also subject to discrepancies due to different definitions of a word. Small corpora might face problems with representativeness, but they expand knowledge about the researched language sample, specific for a certain time, place or the speakers' social situation. Moreover, they must meet the expert-to-expert communication requirement, which means that the target audience should also possess a sufficient level of expertise, and be either fellow researchers, develop an interest in the topic, be trained professionals, or trainees (Pearson, 1998; Bowker & Pearson, 2002; Biber, 2012; López Mateo & Olmo Cazevieille, 2015). Moreover, the topic of the texts should be focused on a given subject field depending on the needs (Pearson, 1998; Waliński, 2005). Moreover, the corpus should also take the time of their inception into account. The texts which are to be included in the corpus should be created at a similar time in order to avoid discrepancies in the development of the subject field (Sinclair, 1991; Bowker & Pearson, 2002; Waliński, 2005). The choice of publications should possibly be limited to one genre so that it contains one type and style. Stylistic features of texts, as well as their intended function, or outcome ought to be homogeneous, and be used in an academic or educational setting (Pearson, 1998; Maia, 2003). Furthermore, Sinclair and Pearson (1998) advise to include whole texts from a variety of sources, e.g. in the case of a corpus made of research papers, entire documents need to be selected, in order to obtain a comprehensive view on the language. The texts have to be normalised and published in the written form, because they are easier to obtain and to ensure a satisfactory level of reliability of the material (Sinclair, 1991; Pearson, 1998; Bowker & Pearson, 2002; Karpiński, 2017). Moreover, selected texts must be written by a variety of acknowledged authors to be qualified to discuss specialised topics and to avoid idiosyncrasies. These texts ought to be rich in typical terminology to enable terminological studies (Pearson, 1998; Maia, 2003; Karpiński, 2017). The medium of publication should also be unanimous in order to maintain a high level of comparability (Waliński, 2005). However, in the case of multilingual comparable corpora text structures are neither identical nor even similar, but it is assumed that texts contain comparable domain-specific vocabulary and phraseology.

The criterion related to corpus usability in linguistic studies is representativeness which differentiates it from a free collection of texts (Pęzik, 2013; Biber, 2012). Therefore, a corpus must meet qualitative and quantitative criteria. These concern the representative number of various text types, their production level and readers' reception as well as the variety of linguistic distributions in a language. Yet, the appropriate level of variety of functional texts and specialised genres in reference corpora is difficult to attain (Pęzik, 2013). Therefore, the creation of smaller specialised corpora, concentrating on specific typology, genres, functionality or topicality, is fully justified. For example, home-grown corpora, created for the purpose of a single analysis, have both advantages and disadvantages. On the one hand, they provide interesting data leading to interesting research conclusions, but on the other, they are susceptible to disturbances of balance and representativeness.

However, the size of the corpus is not the key criterion and is subject to considerable dispute (Pęzik, 2013; Biber, 2012). Maia (2003) proposes the creation of small specialised corpora, strictly dedicated to a given specialised field. Such specialisation allows for answering more specific research questions as well as analyses of discourse, pragmatic, sociolinguistic aspects, or genres as well as the extraction of domain-specific terminology, retrieval of information and knowledge engineering (Maia, 2003; Hundston, 2008). The size of the special purpose corpus should be adjusted to the needs of research (Bowker &Pearson, 2002). Moreover, domain-specific comparable corpora, such as containing technical or scientific texts, are in demand due to their abundance of lexical and terminological units. Moreover, comparable corpora seem to answer 'perceived needs for texts as examples of 'natural' original text in the source language culture (Maia, 2003: 28)'. There are different writing conventions of scientific texts across cultures, which is reflected in the texts (Maia, 2003; Makowska, 2018).

Karpiński (2017) provides three parameters affecting the accuracy of the compiled corpus, i.e. quality and authenticity, documentation of data and the limited size. These three parameters are a summary of the discussion above, and have to be taken into account in order to compile a representative corpus. The amount of available research material makes the researcher modify their research methods (Hebal-Jezierska, 2013). There might be problem with the availability of specialised texts in a given domain, especially in minority languages, like Portuguese or Polish (Maia, 2003; Waliński, 2005; Carrió Pastor, 2009). Moreover, one can neither put too much trust into the corpus and its available tools nor choose the inappropriate material (Hebal-Jezierska, 2013). Another problem lies in the difficulty in obtaining the satisfactory amount, or a complete lack of appropriate texts needed to conduct research, or their heterogeneous character. In the case of specialised corpora, the size might be considered a hindrance, which excludes more advanced statistical analyses, or meaning partition of lexemes. In addition, comparable corpora are not ideal tools for cross-linguistic contrastive analyses, because there is no guarantee of text comparability across languages. As a result, they do not guarantee correspondences of lexical items or structures and they might be overlooked. Another problem might lie in annotation. Tagger's annotation errors must be predicted by the researcher, e.g. homonymous or syncretic forms. Moreover, search criteria need to be verified in terms of capital/small letters, orthographic variants or forms.

In conclusion, comparable corpora are particularly useful for studying specific aspects, like terminology or phraseology, in specialised languages. However, the creation and compilation of such corpora is limited by a set of constraints which text candidates need to meet. Moreover, apart from advantages of corpus analyses, there are numerous limitations, of which a corpus compiler has to be aware of in order to ensure the objectivity of their studies.

4.3. Terminological and phraseological data retrieval and analysis

Once a corpus is compiled, one can proceed to conducting studies on various aspects of a language in order to verify their research hypotheses (Lewandowska-Tomaszczyk, 2005). The analyses are performed on authentic linguistic structures and units in their natural contexts. There are two types of corpus analyses: corpus-driven which are the result of the scrutiny of corpus data and corpus-based, i.e. based on corpus data (Lewandowska-Tomaszczyk, 2005; Hebal-Jezierska, 2013). On the whole, corpus analyses allow for observing phenomena which might escape unnoticed otherwise, but they are not free from limitations.

Corpus analyses are divided into two categories – quantitative and qualitative studies. As mentioned above, they are not an easy task (McEnery & Wilson, 1996). The first deal with classifying features of the language which are found in the data on the basis of a particular scheme, and 'construct more complex statistical models in an attempt to explain what is observed (McEnery & Wilson, 1996: 76)'. Moreover, they allow for selecting the most important units and making comparisons between corpora. On the other hand, quantitative analyses are intertwined with the qualitative scrutiny. They also provide a wide perspective on the analysed data in terms of the typical behaviour, or accidental occurrences of analysed phenomena. Qualitative analysis is also responsible for detailed descriptions and drawing distinctions of the data. Yet, the conclusions drawn are limited to the analysed population, but are less likely to be expanded to bigger populations. On the other hand, they provide richer results and they are more precise than quantitative ones. However, the latter are of greater statistical reliability and allow for the higher level of generalisation of results.

Extracted lexemes or terminology can be researched in various ways (Lewandowska-Tomaszczyk, 2005). One of possible methods of corpora application in linguistics is analysing word combinations, starting from free combinations, through partly fixed, collocations up to idioms. Corpus analyses allow for confirming certain hypotheses concerning semantic phenomena at the lexical or sentence level, such as polysemy or synonymy. Meaning has, according to Lewandowska-Tomaszczyk (2005), a dispersed or distributional and not local character, which results in its encapsulation in bigger lexical groups. It is the situational context, or the context of use that provides information about a partial overlap of meaning or its exclusion. Corpus analyses are also useful in analysing synonymy, because a complete sameness of meaning is extremely rare, and polysemy especially in the case of antonymous polysemy. Moreover, corpora allow for studying the behaviour of defective lexemes which show inflectional irregularities or disturbances.

As mentioned in the previous chapter, word combinations might have a more fixed or a looser character. In the latter, the substitutability depends on the context (Lewandowska-Tomaszczyk, 2005). The frequency of various word partnerships as well as of word categories is different for different text types. Differences in the distribution of different parts of speech depend on the differences between languages. For example, English is an analytical language with a number of function words, like auxiliary verbs, prepositions or articles. The structural differences across languages also affect the frequency and structure of word partnerships. Collocations are formed from various parts of speech, such as verbs and nouns or adjectives and nouns, or even take the form of a full phrase. Apart from word combinations, corpora allow for analysing lexical bundles. They have irregular structures, but they are strictly connected with specific text types and discourses and perform specific functions (Biber, 2006). On the whole, the biggest advantage of corpus studies is the naturalness of the language. In other words, these are the specific linguistic choices in a given context made by native speakers in terms of morphology, syntax and meaning.

Corpora in the analysis of specialised languages concentrate on the scrutiny of the domain-specific terminology (Goźdź Roszkowski & Witczak-Plisiecka, 2005). The first stage is to identify potential terms. Frequency lists provide a proper overview about the overall topic of the texts in corpora. Moreover, concordance lists based on the most frequent vocabulary help identify the most often appearing collocates that accompany lexemes. In order to facilitate time efficiency of the study, two- or three-word frequency lists should be generated. Keyword analysis is one of the most effective methods of identifying domain-specific vocabulary. It also reveals characteristic, yet the most atypical vocabulary in comparison with the reference corpus.

Differentiating between a word and a term might be subject to considerable debate. As a result, corpus study should be supplemented with consultations with a subject-field expert. Since the results of analyses of various specialised domains can be used by specialised translators, it is important to determine which combinations a lexeme forms.

Pearson (1998) concentrates on terminology extraction from three corpora of different sizes (from 4.7 mln to 230,000 words) which are aimed at different target audiences, and discusses different approaches to it. The first method entails a manual analysis of composition of terms in a corpus before the study of frequency and collocational patterns was carried out. The justification for such an approach is that single-unit terms can be identified on the basis of frequency, and multiword terms are recognised by their collocates. The rationale behind the frequency approach lies in the fact that terms appear frequently in specialised texts.

Pearson (1998) believes that every domain has its own terminological profile which might differ from others. Since her study involved extraction of terms from three different corpora, the initial analysis entailed manually producing a potential term profile specific for each domain. A set of keywords was selected, and co-occurring lexemes were categorised as potential terms. These patterns were used as input data for the pattern matching program. The words and phrases which were extracted were term candidates of up to four components. The sequences of parts of speech included nominal and adjectival phrases with a determiner. It acts as a generic reference to the term, which is one of the tenets of the traditional approach to terminology. The distinction between a generic concept and the individual object is reflected in the ISO standard. However, Pearson (1998) prefers to distinguish between a generic and individual concept, latter of which would be given a name rather than acquire a status of a term. Moreover, in her corpora there are two types of terms, i.e. flagged and unflagged. The first might be preceded by any of the determiners, except for the indefinite article in order to provide specific reference, whereas the latter come after the indefinite or zero article, which indicates the generic reference. Pearson (1998) also provides linguistic signals in the text which indicate potential terms. such as *e.g. i.e. called, denotes, the term*.

Doing corpus research, one should be aware of its limitations when interpreting the results (Grabowski & Piotrowski, 2013). Firstly, conclusions should be drawn considering the differences across corpora. Raw frequency data might be misleading, and for this reason normalisation of search results is strongly advised to ensure balanced results. However, averaged or normalised data must also be verified due to huge discrepancies of corpus sizes. Moreover, the researcher needs to be aware that certain types of texts contain a specific frequency and ratio of parts of speech, e.g. technical or scientific texts. Data analyses can be enriched via text annotation which provides additional information concerning the details of the text (McEnery & Wilson, 1996; Grabowski & Piotrowski, 2013). However, the process is not free from mistakes, e.g. the tagger might not annotate the token properly, which might lead to the distortion of research results (Hebal-Jezierska, 2013; Grabowski & Piotrowski, 2013). Therefore, Sinclair (1991) advises the use of raw data, because the analysed lexeme might be mistakenly annotated. Although this process is automatic (manual annotation of a great number of texts is a time-consuming task), the analyst must be prepared to verify data and take possible mistakes into account during the interpretation of results. Therefore, researcher's intuition is of overriding importance, because at times corpus data need to be taken with a pinch of salt.

Even though specialised corpora attempt at describing the language used by a certain group of people, such as scientists, they pose a number of challenges to be faced with (Hebal-Jezierska, 2013). A small size corpus prevents from conducting more advanced statistical analyses and the partition of meaning of lexemes due to a lack of sufficient research material. Therefore, the subject of research should be chosen carefully in order to obtain necessary data, e.g. specialised vocabulary. Moreover, there is a danger of putting too much trust in corpora and their capabilities as well as available tools. Queries should contain information which allows for the optimal search of research material. Moreover, it might be difficult to automatically identify semantic equivalents in two texts loosely structurally correlated. At the sentence level, such texts are not structurally similar because they were created independently.

In conclusion, corpus analyses can reveal interesting facts about the specialised language of various nature, starting from lexical aspects, through syntactic up to discursive, or pragmatic. Yet, one should be aware of the limitations of statistical analyses, and take them into account in their research in order to ensure the objectivity of the study. Otherwise, the endeavours might be considered inconclusive.

4.4. Corpus linguistics in defining characteristic features of the scientific language

Scientific language is considered to be the most complex due to the high level of abstraction, high information load, high density of domain-specific terminology, and the expert audience. Therefore, it is dense in subject-field terminology, contains domain-specific word combinations, syntactic structures, discursive and pragmatic features, etc. Corpus linguistics enables extracting interesting facts about the language from authentic texts, giving an overview of the behaviour of vocabulary, most salient linguistic structures, and other features etc. in contexts, not in isolation in order to explain the ways knowledge is created and transferred via language (Hyland, 2015).

Corpora have revolutionised methods of studying the language of science, and changed the perspectives on the ways scientists communicate (Hyland, 2015). Corpus analyses allow for the empirical verification of hypotheses made on scientific writing, and act as a counterbalance to impressionistic, or observation methods of language studies which bring partial or prescriptive results. Statistical methods enable to compare all the communicative means across disciplines and genres in order to explain how scientists communicate knowledge to different audiences. Corpora have also proved that scientific texts, prima facie impartial, are in fact persuasive.

The most salient feature of the scientific language is terminology which can be studied extensively via corpora (Pearson, 1998). Their advantage lies in the fact that they allow for extracting terms from authentic texts and their natural contexts. Corpus analyses permit the observation of the behaviour of terms and drawing conclusions on the contextual examples. Each domain has its own term formation patterns which might contain even four or more elements. In scientific texts, terminology tends to form complex units preceded by a determiner. Moreover, there are unflagged terms which are used with an indefinite article or without any, and have a generic reference. In English, term patterns are identified by a set of linguistic signals, such as *called, known as, e.g. the term.*

As mentioned above, definitions are indispensable elements in scientific writing due to the function of scientific texts (Pearson, 1998). Corpus studies also allow for the identification of indicators of textual definitions. They are indispensable elements of the scientific language, and involve:

1. class words or generic terms, like *process*, *method*, *function*, or *property* preceded by the definite or indefinite articles;

2. two classes of connecting verbs and phrases, such as *comprise, consist, define, denote, describe* or *designate* for the first class, and the second consisting of *be, mean, consist of, know as, be used to* of which *be* gives intensional information, *consist* – extensional information, *known as* is used to indicate synonyms, *be used to* implies purpose or function, and these verbs may appear both in the active and the passive form;
3. phrases appearing before the definition that specify the subject field, or restrict the use of the term to the text, e.g. *for our purposes, here, as used here*;
4. focusing adverbs, i.e. *generally, usually, commonly*, which are used either 'to render a statement generally applicable or to restrict the scope of the reference (Pearson, 1998: 142)';
5. introduction of the distinguishing characteristic by the use of a preposition, relative pronoun or a past participle.

Definitions might also be signalled by complex sentential patterns. They are divided into two sentences in order to ensure better understanding. Pearson's (1998) corpora studies reveal typical patterns in scientific texts involving the introductory phrase *This is a/called/known as* which denote *processes, methods* or *products*. Semi formal definitions are indicated by the following verb phrases: *contain, have, be used to/for, include, involve, be characterised by, be described as, produce* or *provide*. Naturally, formal definitions are also revealed in scientific texts via corpus analyses.

In discourse studies, the way meaning is distributed over the whole text is of major concern (Biber et al., 2006). The overall meaning of the text is not limited only to individual sentences; it is the grammatical structures that play an active role in the meaning creation at the discursive layer (Biber et al., 2006; Lewandowska-Tomaszczyk, 2005). The choice of linguistic means depends on the communicative purpose of the text (Biber et al., 2006). Corpus analyses are very useful in determining which syntactic structures are characteristin for the scientific language, and are preferred in the IMRAD sections of the research paper in terms of the verb tense and voice. Their study into 19 research papers in medical research, published in 1985, reveals that present tense is mainly used in the discussion section and to a lesser extent in the introduction, which is depicted in Table 4.1. below.

Table 4.1. Biber et al.'s (2006) results of selected linguistic features in the IMRAD sections of research articles in medicine. The mean scores per 1,000 words in 19 research papers (2006: 124)

Linguistic feature				**RA Section**
	Introduction	**Methods**	**Results**	**Discussion**
Present tense	47.9	21.1	35.9	60.6
Past tense	20.7	48.5	40.3	13.0
Agentless passives	18.4	39.9	16.9	16.3

It indicates that the authors make reference to the present state of knowledge and the implications of conducted research. The section *methods* contains mainly verbs in the past form, which gives details of the conducted studies and procedures used, as well as the passive voice to remain impersonal and ensure objectivity.

Corpus study also allows for determining the most frequent academic word lists in academic texts as one of the features of the scientific language (Coxhead, 2012). Academic vocabulary, but not terminology, is not the most salient and central to the topics, yet it has to be acquired in order to understand scientific writing. Nevertheless, it poses a challenge especially for non-native speakers wishing to publish in English. Therefore, Coxhead (2012) compiled a corpus of various academic texts in English balanced in terms of the variety of authors and text length and identified 570 word families most frequent in scientific texts to serve as a basis for textbooks of Academic English. The study contributes to the support of the common-core hypothesis, which assumes the existence of 'a common core vocabulary across a range of academic texts and disciplines (Flowerdew, 2015: 101)'.

Biber, Conrad & Reppen (2006) point out that most of the linguistic research ignores quantitative methods of describing discourse characteristic features – the similarities and differences between texts and registers. Moreover, COTS corpus tools are not suitable for conducting research aiming at determining discourse features, but there are other computer programs to be used instead. Their study of scientific writing shows that 'noun phrases are the major grammatical device to refer to people, objects, or other entities in texts (2006: 108)'. However, there are major differences across registers in the way the referring expressions are used. Biber et al.'s (2006) study reveals that academic texts possess the lowest number of referring expressions in comparison with other researched registers. 65 % of these expressions provide new information in academic texts. Moreover, exophoric reference is absent in written registers with the exception of the author's self mention. The vast majority of anaphoric references in writing are comprised of full nouns, unlike in the spoken registers. The distance between the co-referential expressions is bigger in written texts than in spoken registers, because the receivers have no time limits in decoding the texts.

Corpora also facilitate studying pragmatic parameters of the scientific language which are used in order for the research papers to serve their communicative purpose, or function (Pérez-Llantada Aurìa, 2003). Such texts are created for expert audiences who 'share some common conceptual knowledge' with the authors (2003: 24). It was believed that technical texts should be written in the CBS style, i.e. provide clarity, brevity and sincerity and organised in the problem-solution pattern. However, Pérez-Llantada Aurìa's (2003) corpus study into technical research papers reveals that writers provide the readers with useful pragmatic hints to guide them through the text, and convince them about the validity of their hypotheses and research, i.e. objectivity and reliability of their observations or presented facts. In terms of politeness, scientists are rather categorical in terms of future of their research. Moreover, the authors make specific textual references regarding other researchers, and the need for interdisciplinary research. However, by using hedges and taxonomic statements they accept the limitations and show respect for the role of the scientific community in the society.

In addition, corpus studies are helpful in determining how scientists organise their writing in terms of rhetorical devices ensuring cohesion and expressing assessment in scientific texts (Argamon, Chase & Dodick, 2005). There are differences across disciplines in terms of the language style which stem from the different nature of scientific disciplines. For example, research papers in experimental disciplines, like the analysed MTCS subject fields, reflect their character based on the '"predict and test" methodology', i.e. scientists verify their predictions and hypotheses experimentally (2005: 158).

Moreover, experimental sciences are focused on spatiotemporal relationship by providing details of their projects and research results. Scientists in these subject fields make predictive comments, because they rely on predictive consistency, and they are open for discussions. In terms of modality, scientific writing in empirical domains is based on the assessment of facts based on evidence, because research manipulates the outcomes. The features of scientific texts in experimental science stem from the focus of these fields on 'repeatable series of controlled experiments' which lead to formulating general laws or truths (Argamon et al., 2005: 157)

It is widely believed that language is objective and impersonal in scientific writing (Hyland, 1995). Yet, scientists express their attitudes towards the messages they convey in their texts, e.g. interpretations, distance, evaluation, or vagueness, etc. Hedges perform three functions in scientific writing:

1. allow for expressing uncertainty about facts with caution and precision
2. enable scientists to protect themselves against losing their reputation from making categorical statements
3. help to develop relationships between writers and readers.

Corpus studies reveal that scientific language is extensively hedged with modal verbs and other forms:

1. lexical verbs, such as *indicate, suggest, appear, propose* which account for almost 56 % of instances
2. modal adjectives, like *likely, possible, most,* or *consistent with*
3. downtowners, e.g. *quite, almost, usually* lowering the verb force and distancing from the statement
4. epistemic modal verbs, accounting for over 76 % of the total number, such as *would, may, could*
5. modal nouns, like *possibility, assumption, estimate, tendency* are of lesser significance.

Corpus analysis also allows for the determining the distribution of hedges across the sections of the research paper. Hyland (1995) conducted the analysis of hedging devices in 26 research papers in molecular biology. The type of the hedging device depends on the rhetorical function of each section of the scientific article. The whole study proves that scientific language is more hedged than other language varieties.

As mentioned above, scientific writing is supposed to inform objectively about research results, and persuade the target audience about its relevance and novelty (Dontcheva-Navrátilová, 2013). The author's presence in scientific texts has been subject to debate, but the authorial voice is present in academic writing as 'the autobiographical self, the discoursal self and the authorial self' to serve one of two functions, i.e. to express stance and to engage the readers (Dontcheva-Navrátilová, 2013: 10). The author may play five roles in the text, i.e. be a representative, a discourse-organiser, recounter of the research process, opinion-holder and originator. Dontcheva-Navrátilová (2013) compiled comparative corpora of research articles written by native speakers and non-native speakers of English with major differences in design, i.e. there is a considerable difference in size, type of authorship and number of research articles in each corpus. Her study into the language of humanities shows that both native speakers and non-native speakers of English use personal pronouns in scientific articles. The most common are plural inclusive pronouns *we, us, our* in comparison with the singular exclusive *I, me, my*. The pronoun *we* refers either to the authors, or includes the audience to trigger interaction. Moreover, there is a difference in frequency of pronoun occurrence in articles written by native English speakers and Czech researchers. It stems from different writing styles, i.e. Saxonic and Teutonic (Galtung, 1981; Duszak, 1998). Czech scientists create scientific texts in the Teutonic style, where the author is not visible and the interaction with the reader is not assumed (Dontcheva-Navrátilová, 2013). On the other hand, articles written in the Saxonic style guide the readers through the line of research and the authors are open to discussions (Galtung, 1981; Duszak, 1998).

However, phraseology is the feature of the scientific language most extensively researched via corpus methods (Flowerdew, 2015). Corpus studies of lexical items are much easier than of grammatical structures. Corpora allow for delimiting the most frequently co-occurring lexemes, because people communicate in chunks, not in individual words. In addition, the core of scientific language consists of word combinations, because meaning is constructed, and decoded more easily when it comes in a bundle (Peacock, 2012). Peacock's (2012) analysis of 320 research articles in 8 domains shows sharp differences in the way words are combined across disciplines. As a result, scientific language has domain-specific varieties which should be analysed individually.

Moreover, Batista da Silva et al.'s (2017) study into academic texts from 8 domains reveals 100 most relevant phraseological units which are depicted in Figure 8.4. in Chapter 8. There is no division into categories, only a comparison of the results with other corpora, i.e. BNC, FLOB-J, BAWE-B and BAWE-C, which are consistent in the range of 31–46 % with specialised corpora, but there are significant differences when the results were compared with BNC. These phraseological units are called functional because they perform specific pragmatic functions in the scientific communication which are, however, not specified in the analysis.

Phraseological units, referred to by Biber (2006) as lexical bundles are considered important in the university language. They function as a bridge between structural units in academic writing. As mentioned above, Biber (2006) provides a whole classification with functions they serve (which was discussed in the previous chapter of the monograph), which is missing in Batista da Silva et al.'s (2017) analysis.

Moreover, collocations are also domain-specific, because they 'express differing terminology, different topics, different research methods, and differing content of discussions (Peacock, 2012: 42)'. Therefore, they constitute an important part of the scientific language, because it is difficult to differentiate a collocation from the most salient terminology, typical for a given subject field. Familiarity with high-frequency collocations has implications especially for non-native scientists, because they facilitate understanding of scientific writing.

All things considered, corpora have changed the linguists' perspectives on the scientific language, because they have enabled conducting empirical studies on authentic texts. Various aspects of the language of science have been scrutinised which reveal sharp differences in the language across domains. As a result, corpora have become a basic tool for academic textbook writers and scientific translators.

4.5. Building ontologies from terms extracted from a corpus

Ontologies have a long lived-tradition, and their roots in philosophy in the Aristotelian times (Gliński, 2005; Grzelak, 2013). They are a result of the need to create an autonomic system of classification and categorisation of concepts in order to produce a highly formalised, generally accepted model of specialised knowledge for natural language processing (Gliński, 2005; Grzelak, 2013; Bajerowska, 2017). In specialised communication, ontologies describe domain-specific fragments or conceptualisations of reality necessary for creating and processing knowledge (Gliński, 2005; Grzelak, 2013; Bajerowska, 2017). Keyword terminology generated from a corpus and concordances provide unique data concerning terms, their contextual meanings and relationships with other terms.

In order to achieve clarity of the message, two factors are of particular interest, i.e. categorisation and hierarchisation. The conceptual model has been acquired during the process of education, and Gliński (2005) compares these processes to the meaning triangle developed by Ogden & Richards (1923), which reflects the stages of assigning symbols to objects possessing specific features. Language is the tool in the subjectivisation of knowledge, i.e. assigning names to concepts and objects (Grucza, 2017).

However, Roche (2015) creates a double semtiotic triangle (depicted in Figure 4.3. below) reflecting the dual dimension of terminology: linguistic and conceptual, because 'conceptualization can be *uttered* in natural language, but it is *expressed* in formal language (2015: 132)'. Moreover, there is a discrepancy between the conceptual system retrieved from texts and the conceptual network defined by experts in a formal language. The double semiotic triangle developed by Roche (2015) aims at explaining the relations between notions: some belong to the conceptual dimension, i.e. ontology, and others belong to the linguistic dimension: LSP, which is shown in Figure 4.1. below. A concept can exist without a term, but not vice versa. In the ideal system, there is a one-to-one correspondence, but in natural languages terms can have a polysemic character, which is taken into account in Roche's model (2015).

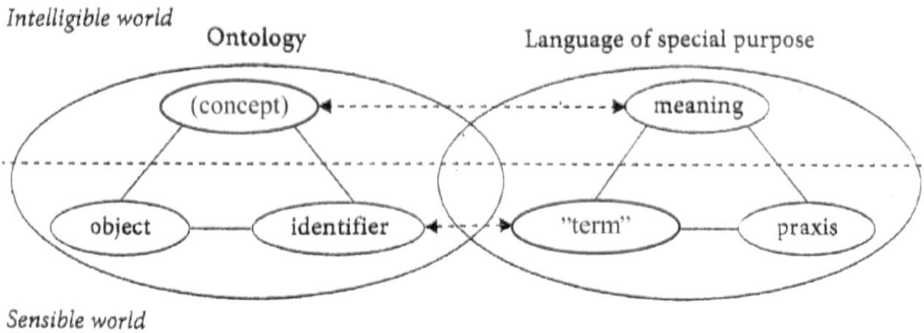

Figure 4.1. Roche's (2015) double semiotic triangle (2015: 132)

An ontology is seen as a formal, evident specification of a shared conceptualisation in order to ensure knowledge intelligible, and processable for communicating parties (Gruber, 1993 in Grzelak, 2013; Roche, 2015). It is a collection of informal rules which limit fragments of depicted reality aimed at reaching a consensus in understanding of knowledge accepted by knowledge users (Gliński, 2005; Bajerowska, 2017). This fragment of reality might be understood as specialised knowledge which at the individual level can be compared to specialised idioknowledge, and the collective level to specialists' polyknowledge (Grucza, 2017 B; Bajerowska, 2017). On the other hand, Roche (2015) identifies singular knowledge and knowledge of plurality of things. The first pertains to an individual object and its properties, whereas the latter refers to concepts which 'structure and organise the objects that inhabit the reality (2015: 138)'. Thus, concepts are helpful in organising reality because they group objects which share some characteristics. Moreover, they structure themselves into systems via arranging their properties in hierarchical relations. An ontology is a formal description of concepts in a given subject field gathered in a collection of classes along with their slot roles properties which depict the reality of a given community of practice, such as scientists and engineers (Gliński, 2005; Roche, 2015). It should also define its structure and its collection of lexicon (Bajerowska,

2017). Concept is seen as primary in ontologies and necessitates an ontological definition. (Roche, 2015).

Texts are seen as representatives of specialised knowledge, and the basis of quality assessment of specialised knowledge (Bajerowska, 2017). These texts constitute a base for the digital form of ontologies. In turn, ontologies are digital realisations of categorisations which reflect relations between terms in specialised texts, such as research articles. Specialised corpora, consisting of specialised texts, allow for term extraction which will helps create conceptual ontologies (Maia, 2003). Yet, bigger corpora are necessary for that purpose, otherwise data is too sparse (Li, Chubak, Lakshmanan & Pottinger, 2012). Moreover, there are othe problems, like extraction of only single-word terms or short phrases instead of complex terms.

Ontologies are created for a number of reasons (Gliński, 2005). The first reason is knowledge sharing, between both people and machines. Ontologies are knowledge bases, a part of language engineering, because they are conceptual maps showing how concepts are structured and related to each other (Toledo-Alvaro, Guzmán-Arenas & Martínez-Luna, 2012). Other main reasons entail multiple retrieval of knowledge in a given subject field or analyses of domain-specific knowledge (Gliński, 2005).

Creation of ontologies is more art than engineering, but their overall goal is knowledge sharing on a regular basis (Gliński, 2005; Grzelak, 2013). There are five rules in ontology assessment (Gliński, 2005; Grzelak, 2013): clarity, coherence, extendability, minimal encoding bias, and minimal ontological commitment. The process of ontology creation involves several stages (Grzelak, 2013), i.e. defining the classes, arranging the classes into hierarchical structures, defining class features and describing acceptable collections of values and providing values for each feature in appropriate class occurrences. The type of ontology and its range depend on its purpose.

There three approaches in ontology creation: the bottom-up, the top-down and a mixed method (Gliński, 2005; Grzelak, 2013). The bottom-up approach starts with concepts of higher granularity, whereas the starting point in the top-down method is definitions for more general concepts. In the third approach, the most obvious concepts are defined first, and then they are expanded. The first step is to define classes, and then their features should be provided. After that terms are added on the basis of their features: internal and external features, features of their parts, relations with other objects, and inherited features. Finally, class attributes are defined and class representations are chosen. However, every step in ontology creation should be supervised by an expert, or consulted with a dictionary (Toledo-Alvaro et al., 2012).

Roche (2015) identifies two types of ontologies, i.e. based on the traditional concept system, and defined by the frame language. Moreover, in the era of interdisciplinarity of science there grows a need to include and harmonise ontologies which reflect the interdisciplinary character of modern scientific disciplines. However, the goal of providing coherent, shareable and compatible model of knowledge cannot always be attained, because there will always be some degree of confusion (Roche, 2015).

On the other hand, Temmerman (2000) proposes a dual approach to ontologies. The author (2000) identifies three types of units:

> 'units of understanding which can be objectively perceived (…), units of understanding which are conceived in the mind (…) and units of understanding which in a first place acre conceived in the mind but which materialise and develop further thanks to experience (2000: 118)'.

The first type of units can be defined according to the tenets of the traditional approach to terminology because they are 'based on logical or ontological classification (2000: 119)'. The definition of these units can be based on a superordinate term with a set of characteristics. The remaining two types require other methods of description due to the interdisciplinary nature of science. The latter exhibit a prototype structure, i.e. family resemblance, fuzziness, etc., and as such can be described prototypically as part of frames or ICMs. The traditional definition based on the superordinate term would be too vague or too general to distinguish them from other units. Moreover, even clear-cut concepts may evolve in time and show a prototypical structure. As a result, Temmerman (2000) proposes a template helpful in describing units of understanding which template allows for describing repeating elements in entities, activities or collective categories which are 'understood within a frame or an ICM (Temmerman, 2000)'. The multidimensional nature of categories should be reflected in alternative perspectives which acknowledge cognitive forces in specialised languages and knowledge building, like metaphorisation or metonymy.

To sum up, ontologies allow for arranging concepts and terms into a systematic classification. It can be used by various groups of interests as well as machines. However, not all concepts can be organised into ontologies because of their prototypical and unstable nature. Moreover, ontologies are not perfect tools, and might lead to some confusion. Yet, keyword terminology generated by a corpus provides invaluable data for ontology creation from authentic sources, which might lead to a modification of reference materials, such as dictionaries or glossaries.

4.6. Concluding remarks to Chapter 4

The current chapter discusses various aspects concerning the analysis of scientific texts using corpus methodologies, starting from the corpora compilation, via potential difficulties up to data retrieval and possible types of analyses to be performed. Corpora are constrained by a set of requirements at the creation stage, but show facts about the language which could otherwise not be observed, because they contain authentic texts and reflect the way people communicate.

Terminology extracted from specialised corpora might be subject to a wide array of linguistic analyses in order to determine features of a given specialised language, or to be used for creating ontologies, i.e. formal conceptualisations, knowledge bases ordering concepts in specialised domains which ensure full understanding of the domain. However, like every tool, corpora are not free from limitations which need to be considered while conducting studies based on corpus data.

Chapter 5 The MTCS corpus, its design, tools and methodology

The current chapter discusses the phase of gathering research material that in order to conduct analyses of the scientific language in the domains of new technologies. Moreover, it also presents the details of the MTCS corpus design, based on the criteria available in the literature on the subject. It also includes the challenges and obstacles that had to be faced and overcome at the initial stage of research.

The chapter also deals with tools which were used to perform analyses, i.e. dedicated program and reference corpora that served as a comparison for the collected texts. The author explains her motivation for choosing Sketch Engine as the tool for extraction of domain-specific terminology. After that, there are details concerning the upload and compilation of collected research material into the MTCS corpus. They are followed by the methodology used to determine characteristic features of terminology, phraseology and other linguistic means used in the analysed research papers as well as the aims of the conducted study. The MTCS corpus design and methodology applied have been based on the theoretical assumptions discussed in the preceding chapters.

5.1. Research material: the MTCS corpus of research articles

The research idea stems from the author's practice as a translator and a proof-reader, and as a result she managed to collect material for the analysis which was later uploaded and compiled in the MTCS corpus. The analysis concentrates on the features of the language of new technologies: Microelectronics, Telecommunication and Computer Science (MTCS), relatively young, technical and empirical domains, embracing the elements of science and technology, and characterised by the dynamic development. As they belong to scientific subject fields, research requires conducting tests and experiments communicating it to the scientific community, and thus validating the results of performed analyses. As these domains have a practical and empirical character, scientists and engineers use specific means of communication in research articles, the basic genre for reporting research results.

In order to conduct the study of the scientific language, at the design stage, the corpus of research papers in English consisted of 219 scientific articles which were gathered from 3 sources and contained about 960,000 words before uploading and compilation. The publication time embraced the years 2007–2014 in order to reflect relatively recent changes in the scientific language in these domains. The articles pertain to the scientific disciplines, i.e. microelectronics, telecommunication and computer studies, which are interconnected and interdependent. However, two research papers had to be excluded from the body of texts since they did not fully meet the predetermined criteria.

At that point, the dominant position of English was clearly noticeable, because it was relatively easy to collect the required number of specialised texts to create a representative specialised corpus. The final composition of MTCS texts in the corpus is presented in Table 5.1. below.

Table 5.1. Composition of the MTCS corpus

English corpus		
Source	**No of articles**	**Number of words**
Mixdes 2013	105	336,525
Mixdes 2014	112	298,406
Total English	**217**	**634,931**

Table 5.1. above shows how the MTCS corspus is composed. The research papers, which are to be subject to analysis, are contained in two files, representing two sources in order to ensure both representativeness and homogeneity of research material.

In order to maintain homogeneity of data, and balanced distribution of results, the corpus contains research articles written by a sufficient number of authors representing different (often international) scientific institutions (working in international research groups). A wide range of authors of different nationalities (using international English) was also considered during the compilation in order to avoid idiosyncracies, which might affect the representativeness of the corpus. The year of publication is limited to the span of 2 years, namely 2013–2014, in order to include relatively recent changes in the dynamic language of new technologies.

5.2. The MTCS corpus design

MTCS corpus design is based on the criteria developed by Atkins, Clear & Ostler (1992) which provides a comprehensive set of criteria which helps determine the main aspects of the MTCS corpus, because the texts have to meet specific requirements to serve their purpose, i.e. internal (linguistic) and external (non-linguistic) criteria. The characteristics of the collection of MTCS research papers are presented in Table 5.2. below.

Table 5.2. Text attributes of research articles in the MTCS domains (Atkins, et al., 1992)

Text attributes of the MTCS corpus
Mode: written
Participation: 1-person, 2-person, 3-person, multi-person up to 39 authors
Preparedness: prepared (written, never spoken)
Medium: text
Style: prose
Genre: article
Constitution: composite
Factuality: fact
Setting: educational
Function: informative
Topic: telecommunication, computer science, microelectronics
Technicality: technical (specialist author – specialist target)
Date: date of publication from 2007 to 2014
Text status: original
Language: English
Language status: source language
Methodology approved: standardised or officially approved (research article)
Authorship: single, double, multiple
Sex of authors: male, female, mixed-sex groups
Nationality of authors: multiple
Authors' mother tongue: multiple
Authority of authors: research groups
Topic: telecommunication, microelectronics, computer science
Control parameters for written texts: external – research article, IMRAD format
Intended readership: 5 unrestricted heterogeneous
Education: 3–5 from BA – MA students to university doctoral level, post-doctoral level
Unknown: 3 group defined by lifestyle, profession, interests, etc.
Age: adults
Authorship: single and multiple
Format: length by word count
Explicit structure: 5 highly structured (IMRAD research papers)

The MTCS corpus contains samples of the language of new technologies. It consists of 217 research articles published in conference proceedings in English. The materials were obtained directly from conference organisers to enable the analyses of the scientific language in the domains of new technologies. The majority of texts come from two volumes of conference proceedings. The language of publication is English due to the fact that the majority of scientists decide to publish in English-speaking journals because of wider audiences and higher probability of citability. Moreover, the majority of researchers are not native speakers of English; therefore, they use the international variety of English.

Mode: written to be read

The mode of the MTCS corpus is written. Research papers are created to be read by professional target readers, such as other scientists and anyone interested so that they could reflect on research and provide feedback. Publication of research results is one of the stages of conducted studies, without which it is considered incomplete or invalid.

Participation: 1-person, 2-person, multi-person

Research in these engineering fields is conducted both individually and in research groups which consist of at least 2 participants up to even 40. There is a tendency to work in groups of 2 to 4 participants (46, 42 and 52 research papers respectively), and not individually, which is reflected in the authorship of the articles. Moreover, international and inter-institutional collaboration is also visible in the authorship, because 50 research papers are co-written by authors from various research institutions and countries. Of these, 26 are the result of international cooperation and 24 research papers present research conducted by inter-institutional research groups.

Preparedness: prepared (written)

Research papers are prepared (written) texts to be published in a journal or proceedings, but first they are spoken. The first draft is prepared and presented orally with visuals at a conference or workshop, and then the written version is elaborated to be published in a journal. The manuscripts are subject to peer revision, which results in the reediting of the draft before the research paper is published in a journal, monograph or proceedings.

Medium: text

As mentioned above, research articles are published manuscripts which were initially presented at conferences. Publications are an indispensable stage of conducting research, because they act as a report of conducted studies, communicate research results to the public, and validate the results worldwide, which allows for receiving feedback, and contribute to the success of the research group and the prestige of the research institution.

Style: prose

Research articles constitute a basic genre of scientific writing that communicate science worldwide. They are indispensable elements of conducting research, as they allow for publishing obtained results to the target audience.

Genre: article

The texts selected for the corpus are research articles in the engineering and applicative domains of new technologies which belong to hard sciences. The MTCS research papers generally follow the IMRAD format, i.e. Introduction-Methods-Results-Discussion and the authors are acquainted with the writing conventions of research papers in English. The compliance of the texts with the conventionalised pattern in such subject fields is higher than in humanities or social sciences. In contrast to the whole texts, not all abstracts and introductions are written according to the Swales' (1991) CARS Model (Create a Research Space of Research Introductions). Instead, they are summaries of conducted research. On the other hand, the abstracts that are compliant contain three elements (moves), i.e.

- establishing the territory
- establishing a niche
- occupying a niche.

Approximately, the word count for the texts reaches about 2900 words. The MTCS domains are based on 'experimental proof', which entails performing tests and experiments in order to empirically verify constructed hypotheses (Hyland, 2009). Therefore, the authors make frequent use of graphs, schemas, pictures, drawings, formulae or algorithms, which and might explain the low word-count. The complementary intersemiotic content makes the text multimodal and hybrydised.

Constitution: single composite

Research papers used in the MTCS corpus are integral and complete (Atkins et al., 1992). Moreover, they are created by multiple authors, but they are stylistically homogeneous due to the fact that they are written according to the MTCS pattern. They are organised into collections or composites, i.e. post-conference publications, monographs, proceedings or journals. Yet, every article constitutes a distinct text.

Format: length by word count

The 217 MTCS texts, selected according to a set of predetermined criteria, contain 634 931 words compiled in the MTCS corpus. A research paper contains on average 2900 words.

Explicit structure: 5 highly structured (IMRAD research papers)

The MTCS research papers are highly structured (5). The predominant majority of texts are written according to the IMRAD format, which constitutes a reflection of stages in conducted research. As a result, international authors are acquainted with the Saxonic writing convention. Moreover, articles's basic function is a report informing the audience about research results, The abstracts are written either as summaries or in accordance with Swales' (1990) CARS model. The analysis of the elements of abstracts and the macrostructure of the research article are presented in Chapter 6.

Factuality: fact

Research papers constitute a comprehensive report informing about conducted research and its results. Scientific writing is supposed to be factual, objective, precise and impersonal. However, the authors use personal pronouns to mark their presence as well as persuasion techniques to convince the audience about the presented facts and the validity of their research.

Setting: educational

Research papers also function as a form of reference books, because apart from conducting research, scientists' academic duties involve training other professionals. As tradition has it, knowledge is passed from experts to novices. Moreover, nowadays easy access to scientific texts due to online publications facilitates knowledge expansion among the people, both experts and novices interested in a particular subject, which contributes to higher readership.

Function: informative

Research papers are primarily created to inform the public about research results, therefore they function as reports of conducted studies. Publication of results is one of the stages of performing systematic scientific investigations in order to validate their results, incite discussion and gather feedback.

Topic: telecommunication, computer science, microelectronics

The articles pertain to three young, dynamically developing and closely intertwined disciplines of science and engineering, i.e. Microelectronic, Telecommunication and Computer Science. Microelectronics provides hardware, computer science creates software for hardware to function and operate, and telecommunication uses ready-made products of both domains to design communication solutions.

Technicality: technical (specialist author – specialist target)

MTCS articles are highly technical. They are written by experts and are targeted at experts (vertical communication). The writers are either scientists, engineers, professionals or final year university students who want to pursue a scientific career. The target audience includes other scientists, engineers, professionals from the industry, or anyone interested in the topic, since easy access to scientific texts has diversified the range of addressees, so that the group of addressees has become more heterogeneous (Pearson, 1998).

Date: date of publication from 2013 to 2014

Gathered texts were published between 2013 and 2014, so cover the span of 2 years.

Text status: original

MTCS research papers are originals, they were originally written in International English since the authors are of heterogeneous nationalities, often collaborating in international research groups and developing solutions for international research centres or companies.

Language: English

The language of the written publications which are subject to analysis is International English. The authors' nationality is heterogeneous, and therefore the texts are written in the international variety of the language. Only 4 texts were written by native speakers of English, either British or American.

Language links: stand-alone

The MTCS research articles are single, stand-alone texts. They are collected in journals, monographs or proceedings. As mentioned above, they were originally written and published in the International variety of English.

Language status: source language

Since the articles are published originals, then English constitutes the source language. As mentioned above, the nationalities of authors are diverse, which affects the language of publication. In this case, it is the international variety of English.

Methodology approved: standardised or officially approved (research article)

Research article is a conventionalised genre of scientific writing. Although there are no strict rules concerning the ways of writing scientific texts, the texts need to live up to the audience's expectations, because poorly written, unintelligible texts are not accepted for publication. For this reason, the scientists and engineers conform to the rules of the IMRAD-format, and prepare their texts accordingly. There might be slight domain-specific deviations from the standard, but the layout is easily noticeable.

Authorship: single, double, multiple

Research in the MTCS domains is mainly conducted in research groups, which is reflected in the authorship of the research articles. The majority of texts are written by 2- to 5-person research groups, which is reflected in the authorship of the analysed texts. The details of the authorship of articles are shown in Table 5.3. and Figure 5.3. below.

Table 5.3. Authorship of research papers in the MTCS corpus

No of authors	**English MTCS corpus**		
	Mixdes 2013	**Mixdes 2014**	**Total**
1	12	14	**26**
2	25	21	**46**
3	22	20	**42**
4	28	24	**52**
5	10	16	**26**
6	10	8	**18**
7	3	1	**4**
11	1		**1**
12		1	**1**
40	1		**1**
Total	**112**	**105**	**217**

The majority of texts were written by groups of 2–5 participants and only 26 texts were created by single authors, which is shown in Figure 5.1. below. In addition, 103 articles have at least four authors, the remaining 88 articles were written by 2 or 3 authors. The maximum number of authors is 40. Multiple authorship in this case reflects the international character of research, because 50 research papers were written by research groups which consisted of participants from other academic institutions at the national level, or from other countries, i.e. 24 research papers were written by researchers from various research centres within a country, and 26 texts are the result of international collaboration.

Figure 5.1. A pie chart representing the ratio of the number articles written by single, double and multiple authors in the MTCS corpus

Sex of authors: male, female, mixed

The analysis of the MTCS corpus of 217 articles shows that these highly technical, engineering subject fields are definitely dominated by men. Namely, 176 articles were written by male authors, only 2 texts were created by single female authors and 39 articles by mixed-gender research groups. One article is written by two female and one male co-authors.

Age of authors: adult

As mentioned above, scientific writing is an instance of vertical expert-to-expert communication. The texts in question are written by adult trained professionals and they are for adults: the professional audience.

Region of authors: standard

The authors use the international variety of English, because they are written and used mainly by proficient non-native speakers, which is consistent with the specificity of the disciplines, i.e. scientists work in international teams on international projects for international scientific institutions. The so-called standard has some deviations stemming from language interferences.

Nationality of authors: multiple

The origins of authors of the analyses research papers are diverse, they come from various countries, which is summarised in the Table 5.4. below. As indicated in literature on the subject, scientists strive to publish in English in order to ensure a higher Impact Factor, wider audience for their research. As a result, their scientific institutions gain prestige and they – a higher recognition.

Table 5.4. Nationality of authors in the MTCS corpus

Nationality	**MTCS corpus**		
	2013	**2014**	**Total**
Polish	199	170	**369**
Italian	7	19	**26**
Swiss	27	21	**48**
Iranian	18	34	**52**
Spanish	24	1	**25**
British	1		**1**
Estonian	11	6	**17**
Romanian	4		**4**
Ukrainian	3	10	**13**
Swedish	3	6	**6**
Japanese	4		**4**
Indian	8		**8**
German	36	17	**53**
Chinese		5	**5**
American	5		**5**
French	11	18	**29**
Bulgarian	2		**2**
Portuguese	21	16	**16**
Belgian	8	4	**12**
Czech	7		**7**
Egyptian		6	**6**
Greek		2	**2**
Montenegrin		1	**1**
Armenian		1	**1**
Austrian		9	**9**
Singaporean	6		**6**
Irish	1		**1**

As Table 5.4. above and Figure 5.2. below show, the authors' nationalities are heterogeneous, i.e. the authors represent 27 countries. Apart from Polish, the most frequent nationalities are: German (53), Swiss (48), Iranian (52), Spanish (25) and French (29), which is depicted in Figure 5.2. below. The predominant majority of Poles might stem from the fact that the proceedings followed up a conference held by the Polish organiser. In addition, high frequency of German, Swiss, Spanish and French scientists might reflect the core-periphery direction of knowledge transfer.

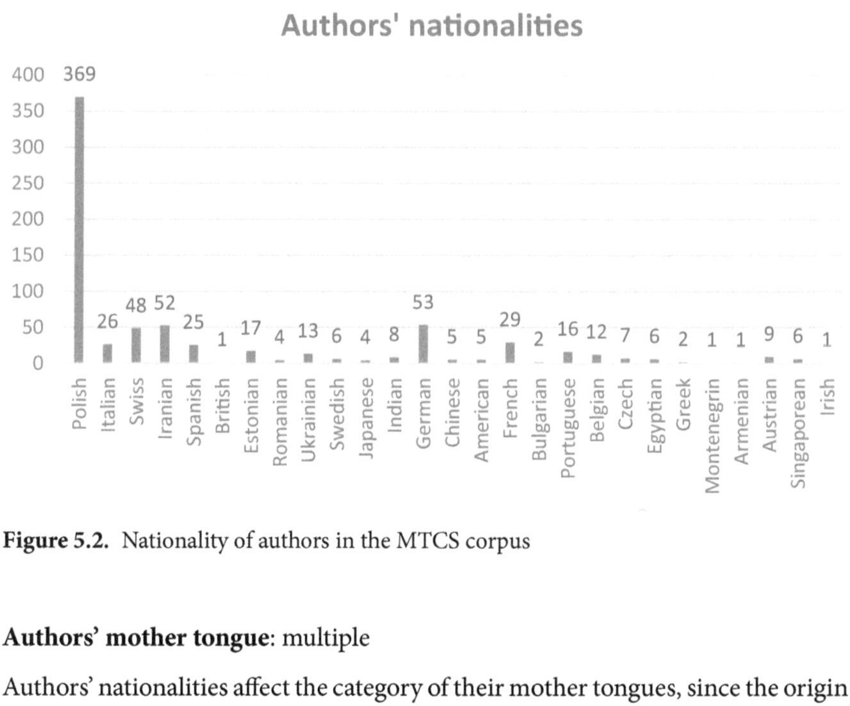

Figure 5.2. Nationality of authors in the MTCS corpus

Authors' mother tongue: multiple

Authors' nationalities affect the category of their mother tongues, since the origin decides about the authors' native language, which is summarised in Table 5.5. below. The authors in the MTCS corpus speak 21 different mother tongues. Apart from authors of the Polish origin, the papers were written by 110 authors who speak German as their mother tongue. There are also 52 speakers of Persian, 37 of Portuguese, 31 of French or 25 of Spanish. The other mother tongues, like English, are not that frequent, though.

Table 5.5. Authors' mother tongues in the MTCS corpus

Mother tongue	**MTCS corpus**		
	2013	**2014**	**total**
Polish	199	170	**369**
Italian	7	19	**26**
Portuguese	21	16	**37**
Persian	18	34	**52**
Spanish	24	1	**25**
English	7		**7**
Estonian	11	6	**17**
Romanian	4		**4**
Ukrainian	3	10	**13**
Arabic		6	**6**
Swedish	3	6	**9**
Japanese	4		**4**
Hindu	8		**8**
German	63	47	**110**
Chinese	6		**6**
Czech	7		**7**
French	19	22	**31**
Bulgarian	2		**2**
Montenegrin		1	**1**
Greek		2	**2**
Armenian		1	**1**

Authority of authors: research groups

Among the authors of the MTCS research papers one can distinguish scientists, engineers, professionals or university students forming research groups and working together on projects. The collaborative character of these domains is reflected in the authorship of the analysed texts. They are mainly written by groups of authors, individual authorship is rare among the MTCS texts.

Topic: microelectronics, telecommunication, computer science

The articles pertain to three disciplines: telecommunication, microelectronics, computer science. They have an interdisciplinary character, and they are closely related and interwoven so that it is difficult to draw a clear borderline between them.

Control parameters for written texts: external

The analysed research articles are mostly compliant with the IMRAD (Introduction-Methods-Results-and-Discussion) standard, either implicitly or more explicitly. The sections of the format reflect stages of conducted research, because research papers constitute reports from conducted research. However, there are domain-specific deviations from the widely-accepted, which better picture the specificity of scientists' work. In addition, there are a number of papers which are more narrative tackle legal issues or other phenomena not directly linked to stages in research.

Intended readership: 5 unrestricted heterogeneous

The texts are targeted at adult expert audience, but easy access allows practically anyone interested to become acquainted with the content as online publications have changed the character of the audience. Anyone expressing an interest in the topic can access it, and therefore intended readership has become heterogeneous.

Education: 3–5 from BA – MA students to university doctoral level

The target audience is expected to possess education at the university level, i.e. from BA or MA students to university (post-) doctoral level due to the highest level of complexity of the texts. The texts belong to the vertical expert-to-expert communication, and in the case of BA/MA students or readers reading the texts as a hobby – horizontal, since the addressees possess a comparable level of education.

Unknown: 3 group defined by lifestyle, profession, interests, etc.

The target audience the MTCS research papers are aimed at can be characterised by the profession and interests. The texts are predominantly written for experts: scientists, engineers or professionals working in the industry, for scientific institutions or research centres. Other groups of readers include people interested in technological novelties. The most essential prerequisite involves the level of education due to the level of complexity of the analysed texts.

Age: adults

Since the writers and readers' education is expected to reach the academic level, the MTCS texts are written by adult authors and aimed at adults due to the high level of complexity of discussed problems.

Text taxonomy:

The MTCS research papers can be classified as follows: they are written texts, published in journals. The texts present scientific facts and serve informational and educational purposes. The summary of the taxonomy is presented in Table 5.6. below:

Table 5.6. Taxonomy of the MTCS research papers (Atkins, et al., 1992)

Text taxonomy:
Written:
published:
journals
Non-fiction:
reference (discursive)
educational textbooks

In conclusion, the presented corpus design provides characteristics of the collection of scientific texts, gathered according to a set of criteria, as well as the authors and the target audience. It shows that the designed corpus contains homogeneous research papers since they were published in proceedings accompanying a conference on the subject. Moreover, it also reveals the diverse character of the authors and readers.

5.3. The tools used for the scrutiny

The tool chosen for the MTCS corpus management and statistical text analyses is Sketch Engine[9]. This computational program is designed for linguistists, translators or terminologists to conduct studies on large bodies of authentic texts on the individual word- or prase-level as well as the text. It allows for processing extensive data to determine the characteristic features of a language or its atypical use. The program generates frequency lists for morphological analyses and word concordances from the uploaded texts to verify the use of the lexeme in authentic contexts. Apart from typical features expected from such a tool, it possesses the unique function of terminology extraction which does not require further manual post-processing. This function was the determining factor in the decision-making process concerning the choice of a tool because the

9 https://www.sketchengine.eu/#blue, 05.05.2023

scrutiny concentrates on terminology and phraseology in the scientific language. Moreover, Sketch Engine allows for uploading PDF files without the need to convert them into TXT files, which was another reason for selecting this tool. Moreover, WordSketches provide lists of word combinations, i.e. collocations, which are idiomatically correct, which is of paramount importance in specialised communication. Finally, N-grams provide exhaustive data on word clusters or lexical bundles which are characteristic for the research articles which have been subject to analysis. Sketch Engine has beed constantly developing, and its latest versions are much more user-friendly than its previous versions. The intuitive Sketch Engine dashboard with its tools is presented in Figure 5.3. below.

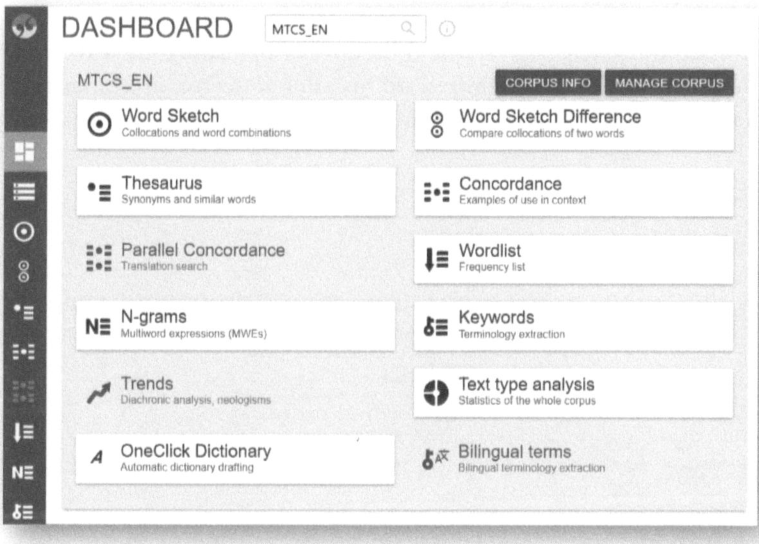

Figure 5.3. The screenshot of the Sketch Engine dashboard with its tools

The default reference corpus used by the Sketch Engine is English Web 2013 (enTenTen13) which contains 19,685,733,337 words. In terms of terminology Sketch Engine creators selected English Web 2013 sample with 204,976,089 words for English.

Moreover, the study required the comparison of the extracted terminology and phraseology with the general language. For this reason, the national corpus, BNC for English was used for the verification of the usage of the extracted terminology and phraseology. Additionally, Sketch Engine allows for conducting analyses on other uploaded and compiled corpora. Therefore, the results were also verified with Cambridge Academic English, a corpus of a written and spoken British academic language of 3,163,648 words. In the following sections, the details of the upload of research material and methodology will be provided in greater detail.

5.4. Text upload and MTCS corpus compilation

The current study is based on the analysis of English terminology and phraseology used in research papers presenting research results in practical and applicative MTCS disciplines. For this reason, a collection of homogeneous texts was gathered to constitute data for linguistic analyses which were uploaded and compiled in Sketch Engine. The procedure of uploading the texts into the program seemed to be a straightforward task due to its intuitive management bookmark presented in Figure 5.4. below, but the reality proved to be otherwise.

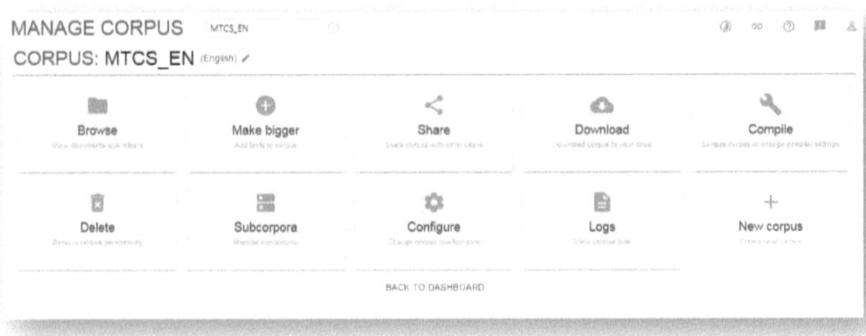

Figure 5.4. The screenshot of the Sketch Engine management bookmark with its tools

The corpus of 634 931 words was successfully uploaded and compiled, but two research papers had to be excluded since they were written by authors of Polish origin only. As a result, the English subcorpus contains 217 research papers and 627,000 words, stemming from two sources. Moreover, it a discrepancy between the word count calculated by Acrobat Reader and by Sketch Engine after the compilation of the corpus is noticeable.

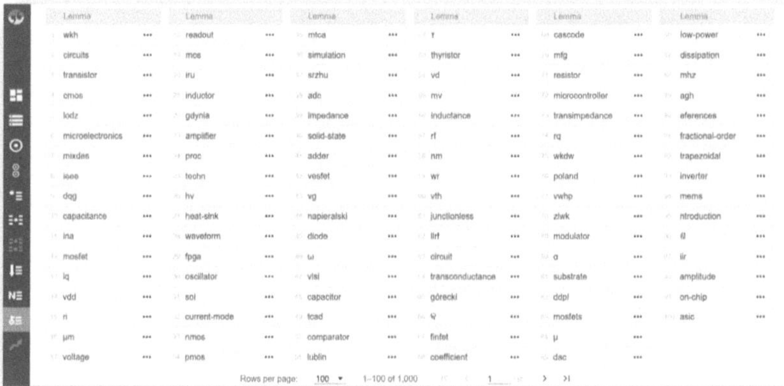

Figure 5.5. The list of 100 English singleword key terminology candidates extracted by Sketch Engine term extractor from the MTCS corpus

Even though the program creators promise trouble-free extraction of terminology and no need of its post-editing, key terms had to be revised and verified by the subject field expert. As shown in the screenshot of the Term Extractor results in Figure 5.5. above, decipheration of MTCS terminology proved to be a challenging task due to numerous multimodal elements and ancillary communicative means. It turned out to be a laborious and time-consuming task. In contrast, multiword terms were extracted practically without any problems, and Sketch Engine proves to be a reliable tool for terminology extraction of complex terms as shown in the Figure 5.6. below. The results of the process were reliable and needed very little post-editing but still required a subject-field expert's verification to determine whether a given candidate should be accounted for as a domain-specific term or should be treated as a collocation.

Figure 5.6. The list of 100 English multiword key terminology candidates extracted by Sketch Engine term extractor from the MTCS corpus

To sum up, according to the Sketch Engine technical specification, text uploading and corpus compilation should not pose any challenges and obstacles. The upload of the English research papers and the compilation process were trouble-free, but the list of keyword terminology had to be submitted for a subject-field expert's verification to perform analyses.

5.5. The aim of studies of the language of new technologies

Rapid advances in science and globalisation have resulted in the emergence of new empirical disciplines dealing with developing technologies and their practical applications as well as changes in the way languages are analysed. Modern computer methods allow for processing large bodies of authentic texts to draw conclusions how the language is really used.

The current study based on corpus analysis of research articles in the domains of new technologies is focused on terminology and phraseology used in the scientific language. It is based on the assumption that hybridity of these young and dynamic disciplines is manifested at various levels. In addition, all the analysed elements of the research paper contribute to communicating an unequivocal message to convince the reader about research results.

One of the main aims of the study is to delimit the characteristic features of the language of new technologies. The current study concentrates on various aspects of the domain-specific terminology problems of granularity of concepts, word combinations, borrowings, abbreviations, hybrids and neologisms created by international scientific communities. The current study also deals with polysemy and synonymy in terminology, rejected as unwanted by the advocates of the traditional approach to terminology, but considered desired in specialised communication by cognitivists (Temmerman, 2000).

This analysis is to determine the terminological status of the most frequent collocations appearing in the MTCS research papers and show how scientists maintain precision and clarity of expression via using multi-word combinations (including complex terms) in reporting results of their research to the public.

The analysis is also aimed at determining how the interdisciplinary and hybrid character of the MTCS disciplines is reflected in the subject-field terminology used in the analysed research papers. As the analysed texts were written by authors often belonging to international multidisciplinary research teams, who employ various disciplines in order to produce solutions to identified problems or gaps in knowledge, there is a need to investigate how it affects the terminology and phraseology (Van Riper III et al., 2012: 217). It can be analysed on a number of levels: as a combination of polilects within the domains, i.e. a logical sum of a collection of MTCS idiolects or borrowing terminology from traditional scientific domains, i.e. as a logical cross-section of other technolects and MTCS idiolects as well as the general language (Grucza, 2013).

Moreover, it aims at verifying whether the structure of the research article affects communication of results and which linguistic and multimodal elements the authors use to convey the cohesive and intended message to convince the target readers about research results. Finally, it investigates how the presence of authors in these highly technical and empirical domains, which belong to hard sciences, influences the objectivity of scientific texts in comparison to the results of a similar study into scientific texts dealing with soft sciences.

The results of the analysis are supposed to determine communicative means and characteristic features of terminology and phraseology in the language of new technologies. The outcomes of study are to be used by specialised translators dealing with scientific and technical texts (Byrne, 2012; Olohan, 2016).

5.6. Methodology

The rationale for the analysis of the language of new technologies has emerged from the gap in linguistic research on the subject. English studies embrace a wide array of languages specific to scientific disciplines ranging from strict humanities to hard sciences, but miss applicative domains being a hybrid of technical and academic disciplines. Therefore, the monograph attempts at delimiting characteristic features of terminology and phraseology of the language of new technologies. The author uses a a corpus-driven and a corpus-based approach and combined or hybrid methods, i.e. automated tools and manual analysis to determine how scientists and engineers communicate research results in English in the empirical and domains of Microelectronics, Telecommunication and Computer Science (MTCS), standing at the borderline of science and technology. The extracted data allowed for conducting both quantitative and qualitative analyses on the collected authentic texts, which aimed at answering research questions and verifying hypotheses about terminology and phraseology in the language of science and technology.

The study is based on keyword terminology extracted from the MTCS subcorpus via Sketch Engine's Term Extractor (Keywords), which is shown in Figure 5.7. below. The program allows for extracting single- and multiword term candidates.

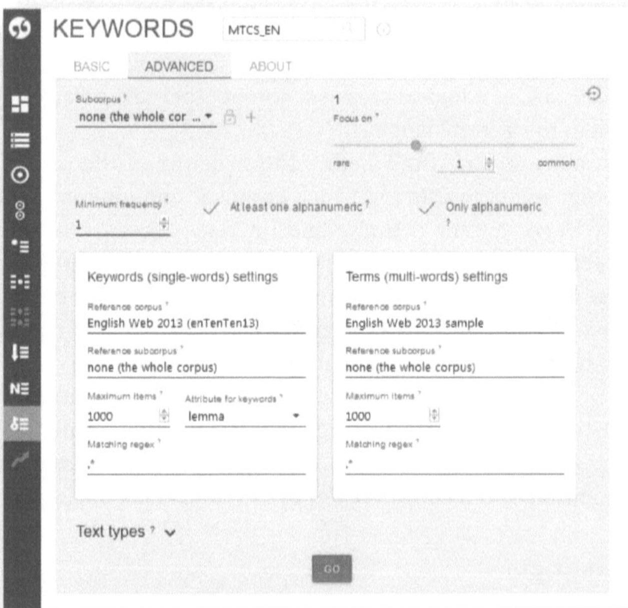

Figure 5.7. The screenshot of the settings of Sketch Engine's Term Extractor for keyword/term candidates

The operation was performed on the collection of the MTCS research papers to gather research data. As can be seen in the Figure 5.7. above, Sketch Engine uses a different reference corpus for extraction of single- and multi-word term candidates. Currently, the number of lemmas to be obtained can be determined, but the old version extracted 100 term candidates in each category. Lists of 100 keyword/term candidates generated by Sketch Engine are presented in Figures 5.5. and 5.6. in section 5.4. of the current chapter.

The obtained lists of keyword terminology generated by the Term Extractor contain terms which are more frequent and statistically important in the MTCS corpus than in reference corpora used by Sketch Engine. The program uses English Web 2013 (enTenTen13) for singleword terms and English Web 2013 sample for multiword terms. Sketch Engine allows for choosing other reference corpora, whose range has been expanded over time. Yet, the choice of other reference corpora, which was performed for further verification of results, did not affect the obtained keyword lists.

Keywords provide an insight into the topics as well as characteristic features of a given specialised language variety, speech community or a text type. Moreover, frequency lists are organised according to the diminishing frequency in the analysed texts, which relates them to the corpus-based approach. The analysis of research articles creates a perfect opportunity to draw comparisons between frequency lists extracted from the MTCS corpus and other corpora, like BNC or Cambridge Academic English to find similarities and differences in the distribution of terminology used in the analysed research papers in comparison with other texts.

On the other hand, concordances were used for the qualitative analyses, since they are an invaluable source of the use of terminology in its natural contexts. This way, the differences between the standardised dictionary definition and the experts' conceptualisation of the term could be detected. Concordance lines for and exemplary term *signal*, which shows how the term is used in the MTCS contexts, generated by Sketch Engine is presented in Figure 5.8. below.

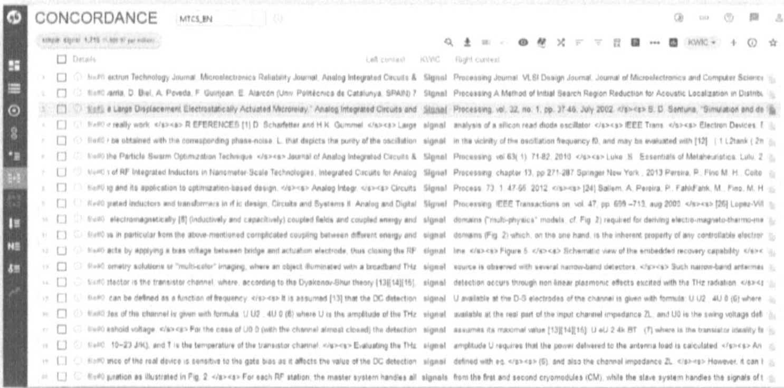

Figure 5.8. The screenshot of concordance lines for the term *signal* generated by Sketch Engine

The current analysis also entails collocations which are generated from the term's concordance, because correct combinations of typical grammatical and lexical patterns facilitate effective domain-specific communication (González & Verdaguer, 2016; Peacock, 2012). The scrutiny of collocation candidates is to verify what kind of word combinations terms form in the MTCS domains, and what their terminological status might be, whether it is a case of a collocation or a complex term, as indicated in the literature on the subject (Groom, 2005 in Peacock, 2012: 42–43; Gruntar Jermol, 2007). The collocations (KWIC) were extracted for the range -2/+2, because the majority of complex terms consist of 2–5 elements even though German language researchers limit their number to 2, but German has a unique feature to create complex nouns consisting of multiple elements, which is represented by complex multiword phrases in other languages, like English or Polish (Gruntar Jermol, 2007). The settings for the Sketch Engine's collocate extractor are presented in the screenshot below (Figure 5.9.).

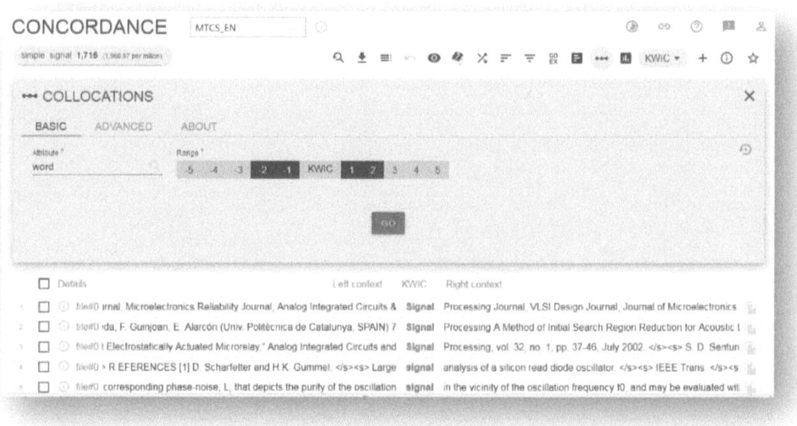

Figure 5.9. The screenshot of settings for Sketch Engine's Collocations

In addition, concordance lists allow for the extraction of word forms along with their frequencies, which enable to conduct quantitative analyses of a term's distribution in the corpus, in order to extract information about parts of speech terms acquire as well as types of word combinations terms form. In addition, concordance lines provide the insights of how the term is used in the analysed contexts, and allow for making comparisons with other copora to spot any deviations of use or domain-specific modifications of meaning. The screenshot for the frequency for the term *signal* is provided in Figure 5.10. below.

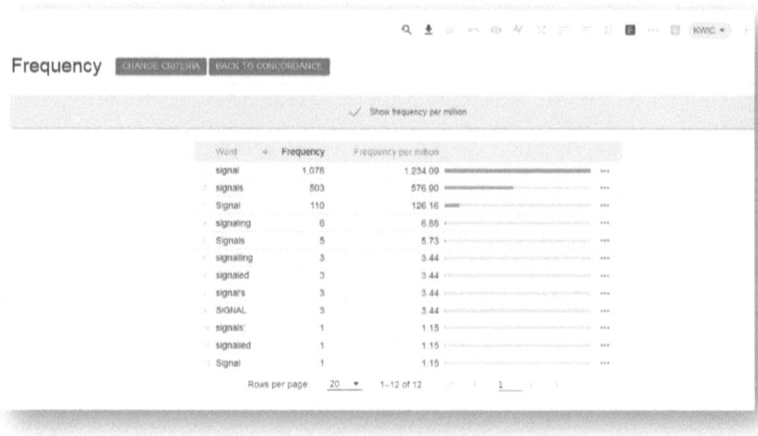

Figure 5.10. The screenshot of the frequency of word forms for the term *signal* generated by Sketch Engine

Finally, the scrutiny of the language of new technologies includes lexical bundles, which are called N-grams in the Sketch Engine. Their omnipresence and importance in various spheres of life, like business, science, etc. cannot be overlooked, since they perform specific communicative functions (Granger & Paquot, 2008; Biber, 2006). For this reason, the scrutiny of the language of new technologies also contains lexical bundles, or n-grams. Sketch Engine has a specific tool for generating the most recurring multiword expressions (NWEs) to perform further studies. The analyses of the scientific language conducted so far include non-idiomatic phrasemes consisting 4 elements, as the most frequently occurring, which are crucial in the creation of meaning above a word level in a given context and act as register markers (Gledhill, 2000; Lewandowska-Tomaszczyk, 2005; Granger & Paquot, 2008; Batista da Silva et al., 2017). Therefore, the author conducted a comparative analysis of 4-element bundles with other studies in English. The screenshot of the N-grams Extractor with the settings for the MTCS study is shown in Figure 5.11. below.

Figure 5.11. The screenshot of the Sketch Engine's N-gram Extractor with settings for the MTCS study

As a result, about 200 most common phrases selected in each language, for which Biber's (2006) criteria for communicative functions were applied for the analysis. The comparison of phraseological units in the MTCS domains with other scientific texts was conducted on the basis of Batista da Silva et al.'s (2017) study into academic texts.

Additionally, the author decided to perform supplementary analyses since they affect the obtained results. The study begins with a scrutiny of the structure of a research article in English, since the format determines the content and the way information is presented. Moreover, on the basis of the keywords, the author decided to include the analysis of multimodal elements because the analysed MTCS domains are fairly empirical and practical and rely heavily on numerical data. As a result, the authors include information in various graphical and numerical representations, creating hybrid texts. The results were compared with an analogous but less detailed scrutiny performed by Lemke (1998). In addition, the monograph contains a scrutiny of interdisciplinarity, due to the interdepent character and a short-lived tradition of the MTCS domains in the world of science. Finally, the study also includes the analysis of the presence of the author in research articles. On the one hand, the tests should be impersonal and objective, therefore deprived of the human factor. On the other, the authors mark their presence with the use of personal pronouns to perform specific pragmatic functions or to emphasise certain aspects. For thise reason, the author performed a study into the use of personal pronouns and compared the obtained results with Dontcheva- Navrátilová's (2013) analysis into the language of soft sciences.

5.7. Concluding remarks to Chapter 5

Research material posed a number of challenges that hindered the research process from its inception. As indicated in the literature, there were problems during the upload and corpus compilation stage. Even though Sketch Engine creators assure trouble-free automatic compilation without additional post-editing touches, the extracted single- and multiword term candidates required consultations with a subject-field expert, because the lists contained either inconclusive singleword term candidates or multiword units of the uncertain terminological status.

The procedures adopted to conduct analyses include quantitative and qualitative methods based on corpus data and were adopted from the leading specialists on the subject of corpus analysis and academic language. They were applied to perform a comprehensive study into the language of new technologies in the domains that create a hybrid between hard sciences and applicative, technical disciplines. The following chapters present the conducted analyses and the interpretation of the obtained results.

Chapter 6 Macrostructure and multimodality of the MTCS research articles

This chapter presents supplementary analyses of the scientific articles which are constituents of the created MTCS corpus, and yet constitute a valuable contribution to the communicated message. The investigations begin with the analysis of the structure of research articles in the domains of new technologies, whether they comply with the conventionalised IMRAD format in terms of the way information is presented to the target audience based on Branson (2004) and Hyland's (2009) criteria. The study also includes the scrutiny of the abstracts to verify whether they are written according to Swales' (1990) CARS model.

Moreover, the motivation for analysing multimodal elements in the MTCS research papers has arisen from the keyword results. An exceptionally high frequency of terms indicating the use of graphical representations in the MTCS texts led the author of the monograph to conducting study of all multimodal elements, like graphs, diagrams, schematic drawings, formulae, algorithms or tables as well as the comparison with another study of scientific texts performed earlier by a specialist in the field.

6.1. The macrostructure of the MTCS research papers

Technological revolution and globalisation have brought about an exponential increase in conducted scientific research. Its results require communication to the target audience worldwide. As a consequence, research papers have become the main genre of scientific writing, and constitute a written report communicating progress in research, a formal requirement to be fulfilled in scientific work. They are created according to a set of conventions, which might be peculiar to a given culture, or a writing style. Both the abstract, its indispensable forerunner, and the research paper, the main communicative vehicle, contain specific elements.

Abstracts were studied extensively by Swales (1990) who observed that abstracts are written according to a specific model which he calls Create a Research Space (CARS) Model of Research Introductions. There are three elements in the introductions of research papers which are called moves, i.e.

- establishing the territory – providing background information
- establishing a niche – finding a gap in research
- occupying a niche – filling the gap by conducting research.

However, Maferat & Mohammadzadeh's claim that (2013) not all abstracts are created according to the CARS model, which was the motivation for conducting study into abstracts of the MTCS research papers. The study entailed the identification of 5 categories, i.e. all CARS moves, only the 1st and 2nd moves, 2nd and 3rd moves, 1st and 3rd moves and a summary. All 217 abstracts were subject to analysis which is presented below. Table 6.1. presents the consistency of the MTCS abstracts with the Swales's CARS model.

Table 6.1. The consistency of the MTCS abstracts with the CARS model

CARS moves	**MTCS Research Articles**		
	Mixdes Proceedings 2013	**Mixdes Proceedings 2014**	**Total**
All moves	20	15	**35**
1&2 moves	0	0	0
2&3 moves	3	6	9
1&3 moves	5	3	8
Summary	84	81	**165**
TOTAL:	**112**	**105**	**217**

As can be seen in Table 6.1. above, the MTCS abstracts are mainly summaries which are focused on the description of state-of-the-art hardware or software with some references to the content of the article. Moreover, 35 research papers contain all elements of the CARS model and 17 contain only two moves. In addition, summaries amount to 76 %, which might reflect the authors' high level of awareness of the writing rules of research papers, which in turn might contribute to the high level of readership and citation of the paper.

As mentioned above, scientific writing is conventionalised in order to communicate research effectively to the public. Therefore, the MTCS corpus was analysed to check how consistent the texts with the format are. As a result, a set of 14 research article sections were identified, and the results of the analysis are presented in Table 6.2. below.

Table 6.2. The consistency of the MTCS research articles with the IMRAD pattern

No	Source of research papers	Introduction	Methods	Architecture/ Design	Prototypes/ Devices	Overview/ Structure	Parameters/ System	Models	Experiments/ Tests	Results	Application	Discussion	Conclusion	Acknowledgements	References
1	MIXDES 2013	112	13	22	31	48	30	38	50	56	15	13	103	47	112
2	MIXDES 2014	103	11	35	49	36	16	19	41	50	11	12	101	44	105
TOTAL		**215**	**24**	**57**	**80**	**84**	**46**	**57**	**91**	**106**	**26**	**25**	**204**	**91**	**217**

As Table 6.2. above shows MTCS research papers are consistent with the IMRAD pattern, but there are additional domain-specific sections, such as *prototype/device*, *model*, *architecture/design*. These elements emphasise the empirical character of the MTCS domains which rely heavily on the 'experimental proof (Hyland, 2009)'. On the other hand, they also confirm that the IMRAD format is treated as a convention and not as a standard. Moreover, they reflect the fact that scientists and engineers give details of the design stage of the production of new hardware or software solutions which are limited by a set of parameters as well as elaborate on new models, based on laws of physics and other phenomena. The frequency of occurrence of article sections and their titles shows that they are highly consistent with the format, which proves that the authors are acquainted with the Saxonic writing convention. It guides the readers through research details so that they are able to repeat the experiment or build the described prototype. Surprisingly, however, these domains score low on the *discussion* section which is specific for the Saxonic writing style. In this style, research papers are written to receive feedback from the target audience. It might stem from the fact that the analysed scientific articles are written by authors of heterogeneous origins (which was discussed in the chapter 5).

The structure of the MTCS research articles reflects the stages of conducting research, which is consistent with literature on the subject. However, the sections have been given alternative titles which illustrates how research is carried out from the inception, i.e. the design stage, simulations and tests, limited by a set of parameters up until the implementation phase when the developed either hardware or software starts operating. The papers contain the sections which are presented in Table 6.3. below:

Table 6.3. Identified sections of the MTCS research articles

Sections of the MTCS research articles
1. INTRODUCTION (background information)
2. DESIGN (equipment/program description, models, architecture)
3. PARAMETERS
4. SIMULATION/TESTS (experiments, tests, analyses)
5. RESULTS
6. IMPLEMENTATION (results of tests and the application of the study)
7. ACKNOWLEDGEMENTS
8. CONCLUSION
9. REFERENCES

The analysed articles have an explicit IMRAD structure which reflects stages in conducted research. The identified division into sections presented in Table 6.3. above also complies with Branson's study (2004) into research articles in which the author (2004) states that they act as a report of conducted research and are written according to the following order: IDEA – DESIGN STAGE – TESTS – RESULTS – APPLICATION (2004: 1222). However, the current study reveals that authors in the MTCS domains heavily support their results with previous findings, which is proved by high frequency of the section *references* in both languages. Moreover, 91 research papers contain the section *acknowledgements* which indicates that research was conducted collaboratively with other institutions, reflect collaborative international studies, or the study has been granted a subsidy. On the whole, the structure of the research paper emphasises the practical and empirical character of the MTCS domains which score high on the Hyland's criteria for the classification of the domains into hard and social sciences (2009: 9), which is summarised in Table 6.4. below:

Table 6.4. The evaluation of the MTCS domains according to Hyland's (2009) criteria

Empirical and objective +
Linear and cumulative growth of knowledge +
Experimental methods +
Quantitative methods +
More concentrated readership +
Highly structured genres +

The MTCS research articles present objective results of research based on empirical/experimental verification via quantitative methods. Research papers contain numerical data in the form of tables or graphs (which will be discussed in the next section of the chapter). Knowledge and boundaries are being expanded as the unknown areas are being diminished by empirical studies and practical applications of the developed solutions which fill up gaps in research. Moreover, it is expected from the audience to possess a sufficient level of expertise, but nowadays the range of target readers has become diversified due to easy Internet access to scientific writing (Pearson, 1998). Finally, scientific articles are highly structured, though at times implicit with respects to the IMRAD pattern (depending on the topic), in order to facilitate the decoding of the message by the target reader.

This study clearly indicates that the analysed research papers are written in the Saxonic style which is explicit and leads the reader through the text. In addition, the authors' nationality affects the structure of the text to a lesser extent. In the MTCS domains, the nationality of authors is diverse, yet they succumb to the Saxonic writing convention. As a result, the analysed papers are adjusted to the norms of the community of the addresses (Maferat & Mohammadzadeh, 2013).

To sum up, the study into abstracts and the structure of the research paper in the MTCS domains was conducted to indicate whether abstracts follow the CARS model and the body of the research paper is created according to the IMRAD format. The analysis has revealed that abstracts of the articles characterise developed solutions. In addition, the texts are more explicitly compliant with the pattern, which might stem from the fact that well-written scientific texts may ensure success after publishing.

6.2. Multimodality in the MTCS research papers

The MTCS domains have an empirical and practical character, because scientists and engineers develop practical solutions for identified problems and knowledge gaps. In order to prove that the solution is optimal, a set of tests and experiments are conducted before its final implementation. Therefore, the scientists and engineers rely heavily on numerical data and test results which prove the optimality of the proposed solution or a prototype. Moreover, the authors include schematic drawings and other multimodal information in their texts so that the reader could easily recreate the experiment using the set of given parameters. The supplementary intersemiotic means of communication lead to the creation of a hybrid text.

The analysed MTCS domains are one the one hand relatively young and interdisciplinary scientific disciplines, and strictly technical, practical engineering domains, based on experiments and belonging to hard sciences, on the other.

The use of intersemiotic means in the MTCS domains is manifested by a high frequency lexeme *figure* which appears 1236 times in the corpus, with the frequency 1,417.59 per million tokens, which indicates that arbitrary concepts and information are clarified with the use of visuals. Figure 6.1. below shows a word sketch for the analysed lexeme generated by Sketch Engine. The use of verbs with *figure* as an object, the use of the lexeme as a subject and the prepositional phrases prove that the authors illustrate their points with the visuals. Other grammatical structures give insights of the lexeme in question as part of the multiword term extracted as a keyword.

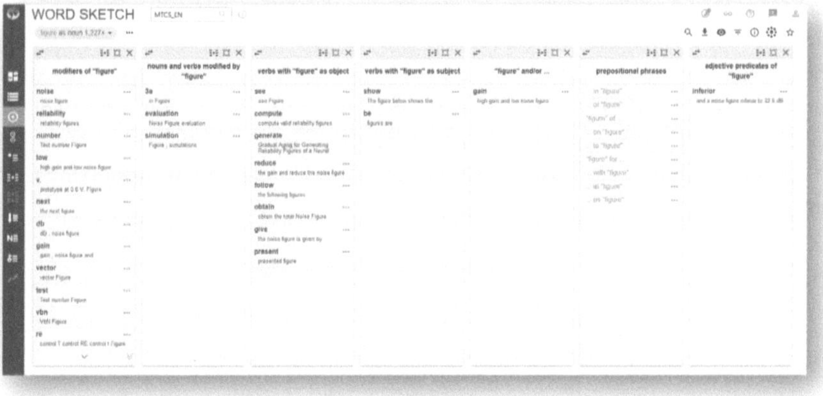

Figure 6.1. The Word Sketch for the lexeme *figure* generated by the Sketch Engine from the MTCS corpus

The use of the lexeme in the MTCS domains in the comparison to its general language corpus leads to the conclusion that these disciplines are based on experiments and technical data, the authors rely heavily on the visual content, and the frequency of the reference to the visual information exceeds significantly the general language. Moreover, collocation candidates, verbs used, also indicate that the authors direct the readers' attention to the visual content. The list of verbs that collocate with the above mentioned lexemes is provided in Table 6.5. below.

Table 6.5. The list of verbs co-occurring with the lexeme *figure* generated by the Sketch Engine from the MTCS corpus

Lexeme	***figure***				
verb	coocurrence count	candidate count	T-score	MI	logDice
shown	125	780	11.093	7.013	10.988
shows	64	358	7.944	7.171	10.361
presented	55	1,010	7.247	5.456	9.648
see	23	216	4.739	6.423	9.019
seen	17	154	4.076	6.475	8.646
presents	18	290	4.157	5.644	8.594
illustrated	11	78	3.287	6.828	8.099
represented	9	83	2.965	6.449	7.804
depicted	9	100	2.958	6.180	7.786
given	9	389	2.839	4.221	7.503
illustrates	6	30	2.434	7.332	7.278

The range of verbs collocating with the analysed lexemes is limited to 7 and provides details of how the authors refer to visual data. The statistical data measuring the strength of the collocation shows that the most frequent verbs form the strongest relationships with the analysed nouns. For example, the collocation list for the phrase *shown in figure* (Figure 6.2. below) reveals that the authors supplement verbal messages with the visual content supporting their points.

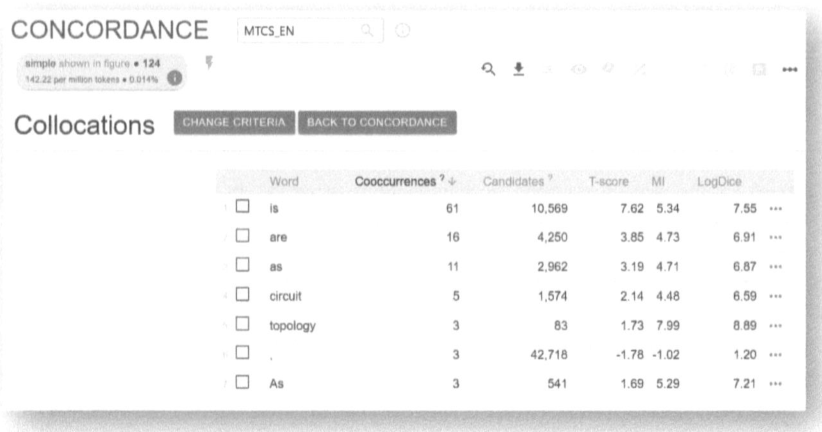

Figure 6.2. The list of collocates appearing in the position -1 with the lexeme *figure* Generated by the Sketch Engine from the MTCS corpus

The use of prepositions used with these lexemes also indicates that the authors make references to the visuals in the body of the text, by forming prepositional phrases listed in Table 6.6. below.

Table 6.6. The list of prepositions co-occurring with the lexeme *figure* generated by the Sketch Engine from the MTCS corpus

Lexeme	***figure***				
prep.	coocurrence count	candidate count	T-score	MI	logDice
In	286	10,996	16.104	4.390	9.581
In	24	1,913	4.414	3.338	7.964
Below	8	168	2.754	5.262	7.544
According	6	90	2.403	5.747	7.212
following	6	339	2.277	3.834	6.963

As shown above, the prepositions most often occurring with the analysed lexemes prove that the authors frequently use prepositional phrases, such as *in figure* or *the figure below* in which direct the reader's attention to the visual content. The summary of how the most frequent phrase *in figure* is used is summarised in Figure 6.3. below:

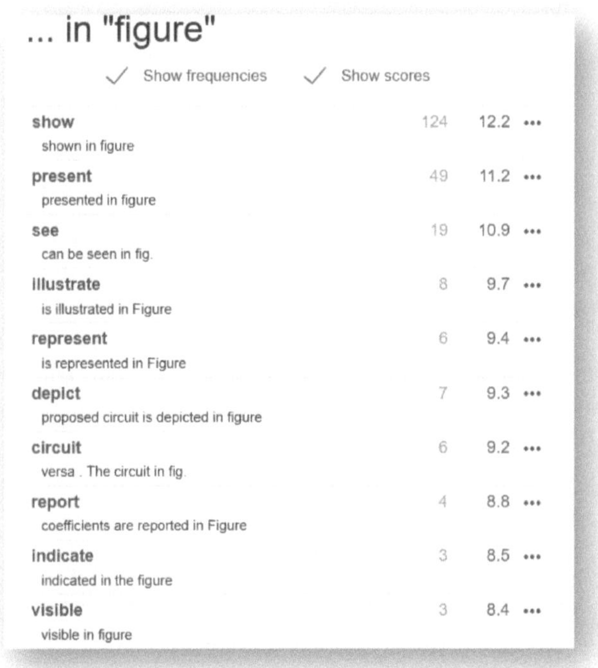

Figure 6.3. The summary of verbs co-occurring with the phrase *in figure* generated from the MTCS corpus by the Sketch Engine

The frequency list also reveals that the authors make verbal references to a given schemata or drawing, because the predominant majority of authors use the noun *figure* in Singular or as an abbreviation. Table 6.7. below shows the summary of how the noun in question is used.

Table 6.7. Frequency list for the lexeme *figure* generated by Sketch Engine from the MTCS corpus

Frequency list for the lexeme *figure*	
total frequency: 1,236	
Figure	840
figure	244
fig.	76
figures	60
Figures	11
FIGURE	2
FIG.	2
figured	1

Table 6.7. above illustrates that the analysed lexeme is mainly in the singular form. There are 1,164 Singular occurrences out of 1,236 in the full form. There are also abbreviated forms which appear 165 times. However, Sketch Engine treats the use of capital letters and abbreviated forms as separate forms. Therefore, the tabular summary contains 8 positions. Moreover, the lexeme appears in the past participle form, which suggests its use as a verb meaning *deciphered*, which is illustrated by Example (6.1.) below:

(6.1.) *Based on this figure, specifications for each sub-block of the NMS can be* ***figured out****.*

The list of multiword keyword candidates reveals that another way of presenting of information is conducted in graphs in the analysed research papers which supplement the verbal content. The term *block diagram* appears with the exceptionally high frequency of 122.72 per million tokens in comparison with the general language. A screenshot of a fragment of the concordance for this complex term is provided in the Figure 6.4. below.

Figure 6.4. The screenshot of the concordance for the term *block diagram* generated by Sketch Engine from the MTCS corpus

Again, it also suggests a frequent use of the visual representation of numerical data, which proves the empirical character of the MTCS domains. They are heavily dependent on 'experimental proof', and therefore contain results of experiments which confirm that the developed, tested and proposed solution is optimal (Hyland, 2009). The frequencies of the use of the lexeme *block diagram* in the MTCS domains and the general languages is shown in Table 6.8. below:

Table 6.8. The summary of the comparative general and specialised language corpus analysis of the lexeme *block diagram* generated by Sketch Engine and BNC

lexeme	***block diagram***	
corpus	MTCS EN	BNC
frequency	122.72	0.28

The range of verbs collocating with the noun phrase is limited, which stems from a rather low frequency of occurrence (Table 6.9. below). The verbs draw the reader's attention to the graphical content. Moreover, the verb *simplify* is used in the past participle form as an attributive informing that the graphics is a shortened or reduced version of the described phenomenon or problem.

Table 6.9. The list of verbs co-occurring with the lexeme *block diagram* generated by the Sketch Engine from the MTCS corpus

Lexeme	***block diagram***				
verb	coocurrence count	candidate count	T-score	MI	logDice
simplified	7	56	2.64	9.99	10.46
Simplified	4	21	2.00	10.60	10.00
shows	3	356	1.71	6.09	7.72

The range of prepositions is also limited to two. The prepositions place the details of the research results in the graphical representation and direct readers' attention to the visual content (Table 6.10. below).

Table 6.10. The list of prepositions collocating with the lexeme *block diagram* generated by the Sketch Engine from the MTCS corpus

Lexeme	***block diagram***				
prep.	coocurrence count	candidate count	T-score	MI	logDice
for	5	7,091	1.85	2.52	4.51
in	3	10,911	0.96	1.16	3.16

Frequency lists show that specific information is located in the specific graph, because the majority of occurrences of the phrase *block diagram* are in the Singular form. The details of the occurrences are presented in Table 6.11. below.

Table 6.11. Frequency list generated by Sketch Engine from the MTCS corpus for the lexeme *block diagram*

Frequency list	
block diagram **total frequency: 107**	
block diagram	71
Block diagram	34
block diagrams	1
Block Diagram	1

Word Sketch generated for the analysed phrase *block diagram* gives insights into how it is used by MTCS professionals (Figure 6.5. below).

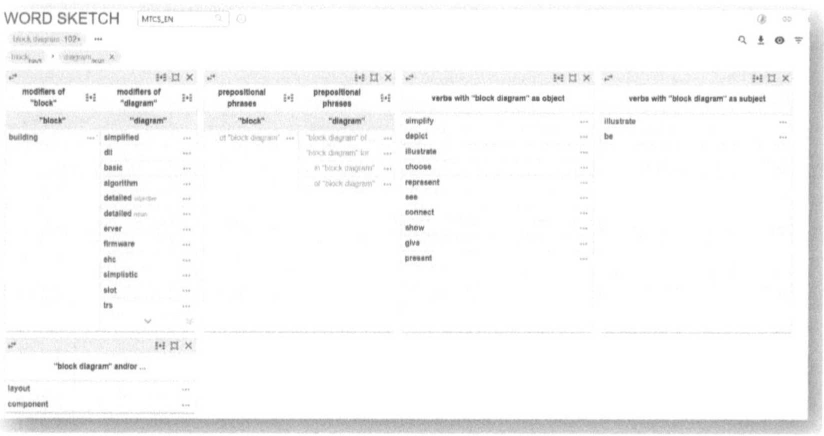

Figure 6.5. The Word Sketch for the phrase *block diagram* generated by the Sketch Engine from the MTCS corpus

The analysis of the Word Sketch reveals that the phrase is used to indicate graphical information that supplements the verbal content and acts as an argument for in the discussion about the proposed solution.

An analogous situation can be observed with the lexeme *table*. The authors of articles in the MTCS domains willingly present research results in the form of numerical data in tables, which is indicated by a high frequency of the lexeme (Table 6.12. below), but in these cases it does not appear as a keyword/term candidate.

Table 6.12. The summary of the comparative general and specialised language corpus analysis for the lexeme *table* generated by Sketch Engine and BNC

lexeme	***table***	
corpus	MTCS EN	BNC
frequency	661.39	198.70

Table 6.12. above demonstrates that the lexeme *table* in English is almost three times more frequent in the MTCS corpus than in the general language (BNC). The list of verb collocations direct reader's attention to the multimodal content supplementing the verbal message conveyed in the research paper.

Table 6.13. The list of verbs co-occurring with the lexeme *table* generated by Sketch Engine from the MTCS corpus

Lexeme	***Table***				
verb	coocurrence count	candidate count	T-score	MI	logDice
shown	36	780	5.914	6.124	9.679
presented	39	1,010	6.138	5.867	9.580
Listed	15	33	3.867	9.424	9.472
summarized	13	23	3.601	9.739	9.286
presents	18	290	4.197	6.552	9.279
summarizes	10	20	3.158	9.562	8.914
Given	13	389	3.534	5.659	8.667
shows	10	358	3.087	5.400	8.331
collected	7	63	2.630	7.392	8.311
see	8	216	2.777	5.807	8.226
gathered	5	17	2.231	8.796	7.921
seen	5	154	2.190	5.617	7.654
includes	4	99	1.967	5.932	7.433
compares	3	15	1.726	8.240	7.188

As indicated in Table 6.14. below, the list of prepositions is also limited and candidate lists contain only 2 potential collocates, namely *in* and *according.* Surprisingly, the preposition *to* which normally follows the lexeme *according* appears neither in the case of *table* nor *figure* in the MTCS corpus.

Table 6.14. The list of prepositions collocating with the lexeme *table* generated by Sketch Engine from the English MTCS corpus

Lexeme	***Table***				
Preposition	coocurrence count	candidate count	T-score	MI	logDice
In	186	19,996	13.104	4.676	9.030
According	4	148	1.951	5.252	7.343

The number of prepositions is very short-listed, which shows that the lexeme is less frequently used as *figure*, and as a result tabular information provided is less common among MTCS scientists than visuals, which is depicted in Table 6.15. below:

Table 6.15. Frequency list generated for the lexeme *table* by Sketch Engine from the MTCS corpus

Frequency list	
table **total frequency: 659**	
TABLE	298
Table	229
table	99
tables	32
TABLES	1

The results obtained from frequency lists also prove that the scientists specialising in the MTCS domains supplement verbal information with numerical data or summaries presented in the tabular form. The noun *table* is used 626 times out of the total 659 in the singular form in the MTCS research papers. The use of verbs and verb forms also indicates directing the readers' attention to the information summarised in tables.

As mentioned above, the MTCS domains are practical hard sciences, based on 'experimental proof (Hyland, 2009)'. For this reason, every study, aimed at producing practical solutions, is verified empirically in order to prove the solutions' efficiency. As a result, the authors describe stages of research step by step and include results of conducted experiments in the form of tables, graphs, photographs and other visual representations. The papers also contain equations, formulae, algorithms used to calculate the physical phenomena occurring during the experiments as well as electronic diagrams of developed hardware solutions. In order to perform the analysis of multimodal means used by scientists and engineers in the MTCS domains, Lemke's (1998) categories were used. Tables 6.16 and 6.17 below contain the results of the scrutiny. Table 6.16 below contains the results of each identified category broken down by the source of research papers. Authors of research papers in the MTCS domains frequently use intersemiotic means, which is proven by a high use of lexemes referring to visuals discussed above.

Table 6.16 Multimodal communicative means in the MTCS research papers (based on Lemke's (1998) cateogrisation)

category of visuals	**MTCS research papers**		
	Mixdes 2013	**Mixdes 2014**	**Total EN**
graphs	500	520	**1,020**
equations	658	457	**1,115**
diagrams	263	208	**471**
graphics	237	197	**434**
photographs	101	148	**249**
tables	165	124	**289**
other visuals	44	17	**61**

The use of multimodal communicative means is comparable between the analysed time span, with the majority of graphs and equations. Tables and photographs are less common, which is reflected in the lower frequency of the lexeme *table* (which is discussed above).

Table 6.17. Multimodal communicative means in the MTCS research papers in total and broken down by article (based on Lemke's (1998) categorisation)

category of visual representations	**total**	**total per article**
graphs	1,032	4.87
equations	1,115	5.26
diagrams	472	2.23
graphics	466	2.20
photographs	250	1.17
Tables	290	1.37
other visual representations	61	0.29
total visual representations	**3,686**	**15.19**

The authors in the MTCS domains rely most on graphs and equations as well as tables and graphics: schematic drawings, mind maps or more complex graphical representations. The structure of the visual content allows to draw the conclusion that numerical data and empirical verification of performed analyses play an important role in proving that the provided solution to a given problem is optimal.

A number of observations concerning the presentation of information is consistent with Lemke's study (1998). It also pertains to the layout of the research paper. The analysed articles are organised into double-column texts, which stems from the requirements of the publishing house. The exemplary layout research papers in these domains is presented in the Figure 6.6. below.

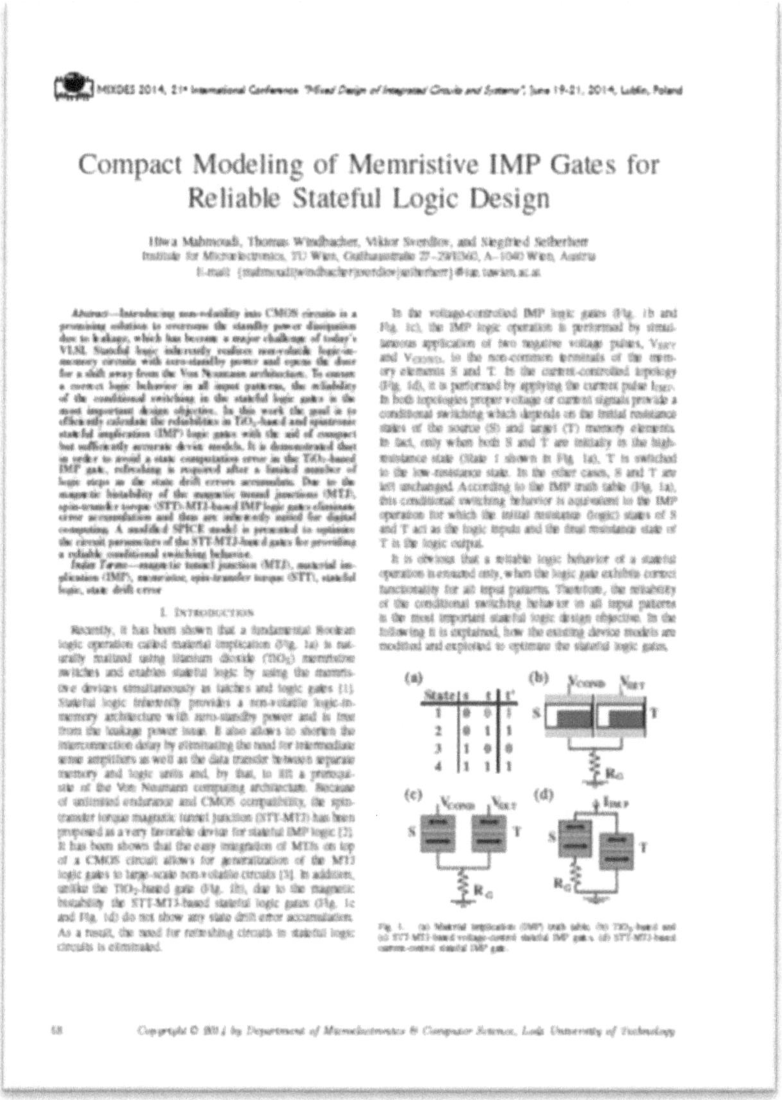
MIXDES 2014, 21st International Conference "Mixed Design of Integrated Circuits and Systems", June 19-21, 2014, Lublin, Poland

Compact Modeling of Memristive IMP Gates for Reliable Stateful Logic Design

Hiwa Mahmoudi, Thomas Windbacher, Viktor Sverdlov, and Siegfried Selberherr

Figure 6.6. Screenshot of the layout of an exemplary research paper from the MTCS corpus

Figure 6.6. above presents how the MTCS authors organise their texts. In the research papers under scrutiny, the font is rather small and a double-column structure of the text allows to fit in more text on a single page, which, however, requires more effort while reading, which is a manifestation of statistically longer texts (discussed in Chapter 5). Moreover, a high frequency of visual representations is also visible. Graphical information is integrated with the text and is not repeated in the verbal form, only referred to and commented upon. As a result, the multimodal content acts as a confirmation of what is being described. The use of equations is indispensable, otherwise the whole texts are deprived of the in-depth meaning (Lemke, 1998). Moreover, the current study was conducted with identical dilemmas as Lemke's (1998), i.e. how should equations be counted: line by line or following the numeration in the article, or whether integrated graphs should be counted as one or separately? Finally, the author of the monograph decided to comply with the numeration of equations and treat each graph separately. Another problematic area not mentioned by Lemke (1998) (due to the time span and technological advances) was the classification of screenshots: whether as photographs or as graphics. In the end, the author decided to categorise these visuals as graphics.

The current study of the visual content in the MTCS domains is parallel to Lemke's (1998) analysis, but is more exhaustive than the predecessor's. Lemke (1998) presents general data, not divided into categories and understands *graphics* as 'figures, charts, graphs. drawings, maps and specialized visual presentations'. The comparison between the analysis provided above and Lemke's study into 23 articles and chapters in the various domains (technical and natural sciences) shows that the number of the visual representations in the research papers almost equals the total amount of graphics used (16.2 per article in Lemke's study vs. 15.2 in the MTCS corpus). Moreover, the previous study shows that in the physical fields the number of the visuals reaches on average 3.8 and in technical reports 6.0 per article. In the MTCS domains the numbers of visuals exceed considerably in total the numbers provided in the preceding study. However, the number of equations is slightly lower, compared to 8.5 in Lemke's (1998) analysis of 20 articles in physics.

Multimodality in the MTCS domains is also manifested by the use of semiotic hybrid terms. One of the examples of such constituents appears in keyword term candidates, which is depicted in Table 6.18. below:

Table 6.18. A constituent of a semiotic hybrid term in the MTCS research papers appearing in the keywords extracted by the Sketch Engine

Semiotic hybrid term	meaning	MTCS Frequency	GL corpus frequency
ω	resistance, impedance	130.47	0.000

In the MTCS domains, the authors make use of Greek letter symbols, which are so frequent that they appear in the keyword candidates. However, these symbols cannot be ignored, because they are meaningful. Their meaning is, however, familiar only to specialists, since they are polysemous and their meaning might not be equivalent in all disciplines that they are used in. In the MTCS research papers they form constituents of complex terms, and as such create complex hybrid terms that ensure clarity and precision of expression.

In conclusion, the MTCS domains belong to empirical hard sciences as well as applicative technical disciplines in which research results are obtained through performing experiments in order to verify hypotheses. Consequently, scientists, preparing a written report from studies they conduct, rely heavily on intersemiotic communicative means to support the verbal content with visual means in order to persuade the target audience about the developed solutions. Thus, high frequency of visuals is reflected in key terminology extracted by Sketch Engine. The rationale for the use of multimodality is driven by the need to facilitate readers' comprehension of the text, and at the same time by the need to increase the credibility of the results. Moreover, multimodality is also manifested by the use of hybrid terms containing Greek letter symbols, which might pose a challenge to unexperienced readers, because their meanings is familiar to the inner circle of scientists and engineers working in these fields. As a result, the end product – research paper – is a hybrid at different levels: the structure of the text, the supplementation of information, or hybrid terminology.

6.3. Concluding remarks to Chapter 6

The rationale for conducting supplementary analyses has originated from various sources. The scrutiny of the research article structure is motivated by the need to verify how the scientists in the MTCS domain construct their message, which affects the language they use (Branson, 2004).

The remaining analyses in the chapter were the consequence of key terminology extraction via Sketch Engine. The use of multimodal information is reflected in the domain-specific terminology generated by Sketch Engine for the current study. It is the consequence of the fact that the MTCS domains are strictly empirical and rely on 'experimental proof', therefore contain information in graphical representation in various forms, i.e. graphs, tables, algorithms or even hybrid terminology, creating hybrid texts (Hyland, 2009; Lemke, 1998). The conducted study allows for drawing comparisons between the use of multimodal communicative means in the MTCS disciplines and the previous study. Both the structure and multimodality complement terminology and phraseology scientists use in the MTCS research articles in effective meaning-making, which will be discussed in the following chapters.

Chapter 7 The scrutiny of MTCS terminology

This chapter presents the analysis of the scientific terminology extracted from the MTCS corpus using Sketch Engine. The investigations begin with the overview of the obtained results and quantitative analysis of the forms the most salient terminology in the domains of new technologies take and the combinations it forms. Next, the chapter concentrates on different aspects of the MTCS terminology, such as neologisms, borrowings and compression, followed by the cognitive aspects, like metaphorisation, synonymy and polysemy. After that, the problems of standardisation of terminology are discussed due to the dynamic character of the MTCS domains. Moreover, the analysis also entails the verification of the extracted terms with the standard developed by the International Electrotechnical Commission (IEC) especially devoted to electronic and electrical terminology. The scrutiny also involves a comparison of definitions from the general language and specialised language dictionaries as well as the IEC standard. Finally, the ontology of the MTCS terminology are developed on the basis of the MTCS corpus data which are verified by dictionary definitions and a subject field expert. The analyses are conducted with a view to delimiting characteristic features of MTCS scientific terminology.

7.1. The MTCS terminology: an overview

The focus of the monograph is to delimit characteristic features of terminology in the MTCS domains. Sketch Engine has a unique tool, Term Extractor which allows for drawing out domain-specific key term candidates. The program extracted 100 singleword and 100 multiword key term candidates that were subject to expert evaluation. The screenshots of singleword keyword terminology is provided in Figures 5.5. on page 158, and multiword keywords are depicted in Figure 5.6. on page 159. For singleword terms, the cut-off frequency is 95.00 occurrences per million tokens. In the case of multiword term candidates the frequency is lower and amounts to 28.00 occurrences per million tokens. This method results in the extraction of 48 singleword terms and 72 multiword terms. The complete list of extracted MTCS terms is available in Appendix 1.

Overlaps of keyword terminology

The MTCS terminology overlaps within the two generated lists of terms, i.e. the same lexemes appear among key singleword terminology and as parts of complex terms. There are 9 singleword terms which are constituents of complex phrases either as a base or as a collocate. The list of simple terms contains nouns, abbreviations, and one symbol. The majority of complex terms are subordinate to the singleword units of specialised communication. The complete list of terminological overlaps is presented in Table 7.1. below.

Table 7.1. The list of terminological overlaps from keyword term candidates generated from MTCS corpus via Sketch Engine

Singleword terms	**Multiword terms**
circuit	readout circuit equivalent circuit integrated circuit circuit simulation
IC	integrated circuit
readout	readout circuit
RF (radio frequency)	sampling frequency operating frequency cut-off frequency clock frequency
voltage LV (low voltage)	threshold voltage supply voltage output voltage input voltage reference voltage control voltage low voltage voltage drop gate voltage voltage gain
ω (resistance, impedance)	thermal impedance transient thermal impedance input impedance thermal resistance
simulation	circuit simulation
pixel	pixel detector
doping	doping concentration

The overlaps suggest that the MTCS terminology has the tendency to form complex terminological phrases that are used to facilitate precision of expression, and legibility of the text. Moreover, multiword overlaps are subordinate terms which specify the type of the device or phenomenon.

Multiword terms are of finer granularity than singleword terminology. For example, the term *transient thermal impedance* contains two additional attributives *thermal* and *transient* which determine precisely the type of the phenomenon. In addition, terms also take the form of domain-specific abbreviations, like *RF* or *IC*, which is one of the manifestations of hybridity.

Syntactic characteristics

Syntactic characteristics of the MTCS terminology reflects earlier findings on the subject. Singleword terms consist of 22 nouns and 19 abbreviations as well as 4 units of measurement and 1 adjective.

Complex terms, extracted by Sketch Engine, are mainly noun+noun combinations (40), 23 adjective+noun phrases and 6 gerund+noun combinations.

In terms of number, 17 terms appear both in Singular and Plural but with the first form prevails. The list also contains 18 abbreviations in Singular and 6 abbreviations are both in Singular and Plural, because they denote devices. There are 5 Singular only terms including 1 countable noun used in singular the Singular form, but there are no Plural only terms. The list also contains one adjective.

The analysis of multiword MTCS terminology reveals that the Singular form prevails among the MTCS terminology. 51 terms appear both in Singular and Plural, but with the first form more frequent. 21 terms are Singular only, including 5 countable nouns.

In conclusion, this analysis is consistent with earlier findings that terms are mainly nouns in the Singular form. Moreover, terminological overlaps suggest the existence of a hierarchy of terms, which will be discussed in the following sections of the chapter.

7.2. The interdisciplinary character of the MTCS research papers

The MTCS domains are relatively young and dynamically changing, and these changes reflect the pace of developments in the globalised world. Moreover, they have a practical and applicative character, which entails creating solutions for implementation in various spheres of life. The developed devices or software have to meet specific criteria, be compliant with natural phenomena or operate under unfavourable conditions. For this reason, they are tested if the solution is optimal, and therefore physical and mathematical formulae are used. These developments are created for applications in various fields of life, like medicine, banking, sport, mechanics, or the industry.

The MTCS terminology is a blend of terms used in other fields of study, creating hybrid terminology. There are 29 multi-domain terms out of the list of single keyword terminology. The domains which are used entail engineering fields, but also science and social sicences. However, the most often appearing are terms from engineering and empirical domains, which emphasises the experiential character of the MTCS subject fields. Table 7.2. below presents the list of terms which are stem from and are used in other domains. They are multidisciplinary, which is characteristic for modern science.

Table 7.2. MTCS single word key terms extracted by the Sketch Engine from the MTCS corpus and classified according to their domains

MTCS term	**Origin**
CMOS	technology of production
microelectronics	subject field: electronics
transistor	electronics
IEEE	engineering, electronics, electricity
circuit	electricity, electronics, telecommunication
capacitance	physics
V_{DD}	physics
readout	researching method
MOSFET	electronics
Voltage	physics
amplifier	electronics
FPGA	electronics
oscillator	electricity
SOI	microelectronics
nMOS	electronics
pMOS	electronics
MTCA	microelectronics
simulation	CS, science, economics, technology
MOS	electronics
impedance	physics
ADC (converter)	electronics
VESFET	electronics
inductor	electronics, electricity
VLSI	electronics

Table 7.2. Continued

MTCS term	Origin
TCAD	electronics, computer studies
diode	electronics
capacitor	electricity, electronics
modeling	art, psychology, computer science, biology, engineering, mathematics, science,
optimization	aviation, chemistry, finance, economics, CS

Table 7.2. above shows that terminology in the MTCS domains is interdisciplinary, i.e. the disciplines under scrutiny borrow terms from other fields of study, but terms are rather restricted to hard sciences or social studies, but there is a considerable tendency to migrate within MTCS domains. It might prove the short-lived tradition of the analysed domains in the realm of knowledge.

In conclusion, interdisciplinarity of the MTCS domains stems from two sources. On the one hand, these subject fields are interdependent and share terminology, and draw from other, more traditional disciplines, due to a relatively short-lived tradition in the world of science on the other. However, the origins of terminology are limited to hard sciences up to social sciences.

7.3. Neologisms

The MTCS domains are relatively young scientific and technical disciplines which are developing dynamically. Therefore, new forms expression, new terms appear in the created texts, which emphasises the novel character of these domains. Moreover, new, state-of-the-art solutions require new names; the existing terms require modifications to adjust them to the changing reality.

The analysis of neologisms entails the typologies developed by Newmark (1988) and Sager et al. (1980). The following categories are present in the MTCS texts.

1. old words with new senses which are rare in technological contexts but they are present in the MTCS texts (Newmark, 1988: 141), which is presented in the table below:

Table 7.3. List of terms which contain existing lexemes with a new meaning generated from MTCS corpus via Sketch Engine

category of kewords	MTCS terms
Singleword	circuit doping
Multiword	power consumption current consumption current mirror noise figure thermal noise residual stress chip temperature

Table 7.3. above provides a list of terms which contain old words with a new meaning. These terms were created via metaphorical extenstions or polysemy (which will be discussed in the following sections of the chapter). For example, the term *noise* refers to disturbances or disruptions in the functioning of the device. The most ambiguous term, however, is *current consumption* which refers to the usage of the flowing current.

2. existing collocations with new senses constitute 'normal descriptive terms which suddenly become technical terms' whose meaning sometimes becomes more general or figurative (Newmark, 1988: 142).

There are two examples identified in the MTCS keyword terminology. The term mentioned above, *current consumption* which is basically the usage of the current, not the level of consumption at present whatsoever. Moreover, the term *low noise* denotes a low level of disruptions, and it is not connected with sounds.

3. new coinages which are extremely rare unless they are brand names. The current study proves that scientists avoid using brand names as terms, but they appear in texts to identify specific devices, which is illustrated in Example 7.1. below:

(7.1.) *The modules are connected to a main platform (Open Multimedia Application Platform -* ***OMAP*** *on* ***BeagleBoard*** *from* ***Texas Instruments****), which cooperates with the camera, a GSM module, SD card and Energy Harvesting Subsystem*

BeagleBoard is a type of a development platform whereas *OMAP* is an electronic circuit for programmers and electronics produced by an American company

Texas Instruments. These brands are used as alternatives for terms out of precision and economy.

4. international words derived from Greek or Latin and used mainly in scientific and technological texts, which appear frequently in the MTCS contexts, especially in the multiword combinations.

The keyword terminology includes 5 singleword terms of Greek origin and 12 taken from Latin. There are also combinations of Greek and Latin origin – 2 terms, and combinations of Greek and Latin with English – 3 terms. In terms of multiword combinations, the first element is mainly of Latin origin: 35 terms, followed by Greek – 8 terms and only one Latin-Greek combination. The second element is either Latin – 65 terms or Greek, only one term. As a result, Latin and Greek is present in the MTCS domains with the first being the most frequent donor language. It proves the traditional dominance of Latin and Greek in science.

5. abbreviations constitute 'a common type of pseudo-neologism (Newmark, 1988: 145)', are extensively used especially in the MTCS corpus (Table no 7.7. of abbreviated key terms in section *Compression* below). Abbreviations allow to compress the information, which is of overriding importance in scientific articles, in which every word counts in the drive to convey maximum content in the minimal amount of words.
6. collocations are frequently used in scientific texts, and they are domain specific. Like in other subject fields, the MTCS domains make frequent use of complex phrases to ensure precision of expression. However, it is difficult to determine where the boundary between a multiword term and a collocation lies (which will be discussed in the following chapter).
7. eponyms, or words created from a proper name, have also been found in the MTCS domains.

The list of keyword terminology contains two proper names, i.e. Fourier and Schottky. The term *Schottky diode* appears 48 times with the frequency 48.17 per million tokens. It is a diode that works under specific conditions due to its specific characteristics, and it is named after a physicist who made foundations for its creation. The term is often used with abbreviations, forming a multiword term, that determine the type of the device, such as in Example (7.2.) below:

(7.2.) *In this case, **the RF Schottky diode DM1** clips the output voltage at the level set by the Zener diode DM2, with the clipping amplitude defined by the modulation voltage.*

Moreover, *Fourier transform* is an algorithm and it was named after a French scientist who introduced it in studies of heat transfers. It appears in the MTCS research papers 27 times with the frequency 27.10 per million tokens.

8. phrasal words which are a typically English phenomenon occasionally appear in the MTCS corpus, e.g. the term *readout* whose frequency equals 290.94 per million is a noun created from a verb or an attributive being a part of a collocation *drop-out voltage*.
9. acronyms are also present in the MTCS disciplines, but their use is wider than categories identified by Newmark's (1988), i.e. products, appliances and processes, because they also denote institutions and technologies of production. The current analysis confirms previous studies in terms of their creation and use due to their international character. The MTCS acronyms are presented in Table 7.4. below.

Table 7.4. List of the MTCS acronyms extracted from keyword terminology and collocations generated from MTCS corpus by Sketch Engine.

Acronym	**Meaning**
ITER	International Thermonuclear Experimental Reactor is both a reactor and international research program created for finding a safe method of energy production from fusion, pronounced both */aɪtə/ or /ɪtə/*
CMOS	Complementary Metal-Oxide-Semiconductor is a technology of production of integrated circuits, pronounced as */cɪmɒs/*
MOSFET	Metal-Oxide Semiconductor Field-Effect Transistor is a technology of production of transistors, pronounced as /mɒsfət/
VeSFET	Vertical-Slit Field-Effect Transistor is a type of transistor, pronounced as */vesfət/*
HEMT	High-Electron-Mobility Transistor is a type of transistor, pronounced as */hemt/*
MESFET	Metal-Semiconductor-Field-Effect-Transistor is a type of transistor, pronounced as */mesfət/*

10. internationalisms which pertain to neologisms, include not only acronyms but also abbreviated terms and terms of Greek and Latin origin.

The MTCS corpus contains the predominant majority of internationally used terms. 17 singleword terms are of Greek and Latin origin, and there are 24 abbreviations, acronyms and symbols. Among multiword terms, there are 60 terms of Greek and Latin origin (either one or both elements), and 1 term is a symbol.

On the other hand, Sager et al.'s (1980) typology of neologisms in specialised contexts is divided into 5 categories, some of which overlap with Newmark's (1988), but better reflect some aspects of specialised vocabulary:

a) the neologisms that constitute a blend of Greek or Latin and English elements. Table 7.5. below presents the list of identified blended terms.

Table 7.5. The list of blends identified in MTCS keyword terminology generated from MTCS corpus via Sketch Engine

category of terms	term	languages involved	comments
singleword terms	voltage	Enlish+Latin	an English stem *Volt* derived from a name and ending with the Latin suffix *-age*
	microelectronics	Greek+Latin	a Greek prefix *micro-* with a modified Latin stem *electron* and ends with a Latin suffix *–ics* denoting a field of studies or sciences
	microcontroller	Greek+Latin	a Greek prefix *micro*-followed by a Latin stem *controller*

The analysis shows that terms are consistent with the previous study that terms were borrowed from traditional languages of science used in the past.

b) lexemes containing a Latin or Greek stem with modifications or maintaining its original form (which is depicted in Table 7.6. below). For example, a frequent in the MTCS corpus term *microphone* (appears 43 times with the frequency 43.16 .per million) contains a Latin stem *phon* with a prefix *micro-*, or *oscilloscope* (appears 43 times with the frequency 43.16 per million) which belongs to MTCS key terms. Table 7.6. below summarises terms of Greek and Latin origins which have undergone spelling modifications.

Table 7.6. The list of corresponding Greek or Latin terms with spelling modifications identified in MTCS keyword terminology extracted from the MTCS corpus via Sketch Engine

Category of terms	MTCS term
singleword	impedance
	simulation
	microelectronics
	optimization
	oscillator
	microcontroller
multiword	thermal
	control
	function
	detector

c) blends of compressed existing terms, maintaining their elements and meaning.

Among keyword terminology there are two examples. The term *pixel* is an abbreviation blend of English lexemes *picture* and *element* with a modification of spelling. The term was coined in the 1960s to denote small elements, dots, which a picture consists of. It appears in the MTCS corpus in single keyword terminology with the frequency 474.83 per million tokens, which suggests that these domains are inextricably connected with digital image processing. Moreover, the term *diode* which also appears in the MTCS research papers, is a blend of elements of Greek origin, i.e. of the prefix *de-*, meaning *two*, and the stem *odos*, meaning *the way*. It is an electronic device which allows current to flow one way and modifies it.

d) eponyms which were discussed above;
e) letters used individually or as compounds.

The domains of new technologies make an extensive use of numerical data due to their empirical nature. Therefore research papers contain units of measurement or symbols in the formulae which are also present in the keyword term candidate lists. There are 3 units of measurement, i.e. *GHz, Nm, dB* and a Greek letter ω which de notes resistance or impedance. Moreover, the MTCS domains make use of Greek alphabet letters as single terms or to form hybrid compounds, e.g. *neutron alpha particles*, *gamma radiation*, or *gamma function*.

f) totally new coinages 'which are not inspired in some way or other by an existing word, sound or image', are rather rare (Sager et al., 1980: 284).

The blend *RadMon* contains random elements of Latin origin and combined meaning of their sources which is a combination of *radiation* and *monitoring*, is a device that measures gamma radiation (Makowska, 2015). It can be classified both as a direct neologism and a blend.

In conclusion, dynamically developing domains of new technologies necessitate the use of novel means of communication which are abundant in the MTCS research papers. Practically every category of neologisms identified by language researchers is found in these texts, even though one of the typologies is created for the general language. Moreover, after the analysis, the direction of knowledge and language transfer is strongly visible, i.e. from traditional languages of science, i.e. Latin and Greek. It suggests that the disciplines are relatively young since they borrow terminology from other sources, creating hybrids manifested at morphological or lexical levels.

7.4. Borrowings

The international character of research in the MTCS domains can be manifested by a high frequency of borrowings in the created research papers. Borrowings, stemming from language contact, enrich the recipient language in communicative means which were missing (Sager et al., 1980; Dunaj & Mycawka, 2017; Górnicz, 2019). In specialised languages, borrowing terminology is the fastest method of expanding the terminological system (Lukszyn & Zmarzer, 2001). Thus, internationalisms are created. The directions of knowledge transfer in the MTCS domains are summarised in Figure 7.1. below.

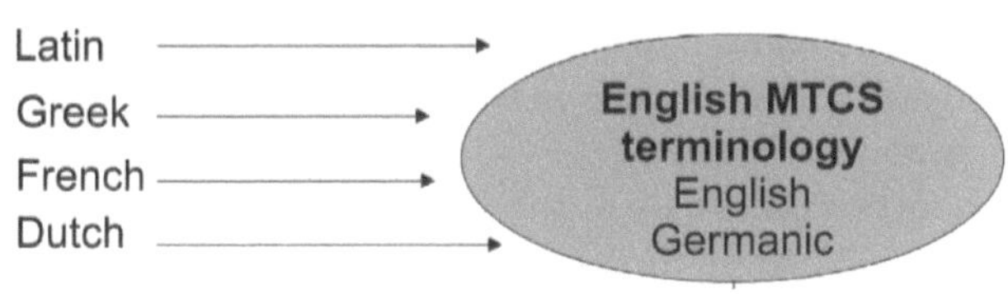

Figure 7.1. The direction of knowledge and terminology transfer in the MTCS domains developed on the basis of the analysis of the etymology of ectracted terminology

The MTCS domains contain terminology of foreign origin that in the predominant majority are of Latin origin. However, there are traces of other contact languages. There are 26 terms of English origin, including 16 English abbreviations. 22 terms were borrowed from other languages: 12 terms stem from Latin, 5 terms are of Greek origin, 2 terms are Latin and Greek combinations, and 3 terms are the result of mixing English with French or Latin. In terms of multiword English terms, 23 out of 72 contain an element of English origin. The fist elements are predominantly Latin – 34, followed by 13 English and 7 Greek terms, 5 terms of Germanic origin, then 4 French only, and another 4 together in a combination with English, and finally 2 Dutch. The second elements are mainly of Latin origin – 51 terms, 5 Germanic, 2 Greek and 2 French. 4 terms are English and French combinations as well as 1 English and Germanic combination. Finally, there are 2 terms of Dutch origin.

English exhibits a traditional tendency for a dominant language of science with respects to the sources of specialised vocabulary. There is a high frequency of terms of Latin and Greek origin, which indicates that these domains have been drawing on traditional sciences (Sager et al., 1980). The majority of terms are of Latin or Greek origin, which suggests that terms were borrowed from languages of science of the past, and along with the ratio of native and borrowed terms, it proves its majority status. The sentences might be filled to the brim with terms of Latin and Greek origin, as illustrated in Example (7.3.) below:

(7.3.) *The* ***photoelectric*** *effect dominates for low* ***energy radiation*** *and results in* ***absorption*** *of* ***photon*** *and* ***excitation*** *of* ***electron****. Excited* ***electron*** *takes all the* ***energy*** *of the* ***photon*** *and by* ***collision*** *with* ***semiconductor atoms*** *can generate more* ***electron****-hole pairs.* ***Detection*** *of the generated charge is practical only in the* ***depleted region*** *of backward* ***polarized diode*** *junction.*

Even though there are terms of Germanic origin, recent terminological inclusions from German have not been accounted for. For example, in other English texts on the subject, there commonly appears the German term *bremsstrahlung*, which verbatim in English means *'braking radiation'*, which however, does not appear in the MTCS keyword terminology.

The majority of borrowings are mainly loanwords adjusted to the orthographic rules the language. Moreover, there is a strong tendency to use internationalisms which are also created by blending. Blends, or hybrids, contain elements of various origins, such as Latin and Greek or German and French, e.g. the English term *microcontroller* contains a Greek prefix *micro-* followed by a stem of Latin origin *controller.* In addition, there are 3 singleword terms of combined origin, and 3 in the first element of multiword terminology and only 1 in the second.

To sum up, the MTCS domains heavily depend on borrowed vocabulary. Singleword terminology relies on native terms, which account for 48 % terms, which confirms the dominant position of English. Moreover, there is a trend to use internationalisms in science to ensure clarity and precision of expression.

7.5. Compression

Compression is a common strategy motivated by the need to squeeze the maximum capacity of information in scientific texts (Pop & Sim, 2009). On the one hand, they are clear for the inner circle of the speech community, but perplexing for the outsiders (Pop & Sim, 2009; Mattiello, 2012; Sitkowski, 2008). Yet, the MTCS domains make an extensive use of abbreviated forms that travel across languages, a typical phenomenon in specialised communication (Pop & Sim, 2009) which might reach a level of total incomprehension to non-experts (Example 7.4.).

(7.4.) *IDS-VGS characteristics of the FinFET-type JL MOSFET (channel length: nominal =3 m, actual =0.5 m); VDS=50mV.*

There are a few types of compressed forms in the MTCS domains, which is summarised in Table 7.7. below. The majority of abbreviated terms are compressed into acronyms, alphabetisms and other symbols.

Table 7.7. The list of abbreviated terms appearing in the MTCS corpus extracted via Sketch Engine

abbreviation	full name	Definition	frequency MTCS_EN	BNC Frequency
ACRONYMS				
CMOS	complementary metal–oxide–semiconductor	a technology of digital integrated circuit production	763.61	0.81
MOSFET	metal–oxide–semiconductor field-effect transistor	a type of transistor	263.95	0.24
VeSFET	Vertical-Slit Field-Effect Transistor	a type of transistor	103.37	0.000
HEMT	high-electron-mobility transistor	a type of transistor	16.06	0.000

(*Continued*)

Table 7.7. Continued

abbreviation	full name	Definition	frequency MTCS_EN	BNC Frequency
MESFET	metal–semiconductor field-effect transistor	a type of transistor	3.01	0.02
ALPHABETISMS				
IEEE	Institute of Electrical and Electronics Engineers	a non-profit institution established for setting standards in electrical engineering	991.58	0.466
FPGA	field-programmable gate array	a type of an integrated circuit	205.74	0.000
SOI	Silicon on Insulator	a technology in semiconductor production	198.72	0.041
pMOS	p-channel MOSFET	a subtype of transistor	119.43	0.02
nMOS	n-channel MOSFET	a subtype of transistor	119.43	0.01
MOS	Metal-Oxide Semiconductor	a type of transistor, a synonym for MOSFET	229.83	0.27
MTCA	MicroTCA	an open standard computing specification	111.4	0.000
ADC	analog to digital converter	a system that changes an analog signal to digital one	199.72	0.48
VLSI	very-large-scale integration	a process of combining millions of MOS transistors in the IC creation	107.39	0.031
TCAD	technology computer-aided design, technology CAD	a type of computer software for design purposes	96.35	0.000

Table 7.7. Continued

abbreviation	**full name**	**Definition**	**frequency MTCS_EN**	**BNC Frequency**
NLMS	normalised least mean squares filter	a variant of the LMS algorithm	26.09	0.01
DAC	digital to analog converter	a system that changes a digital signal to analog one	141.57	0.249
IVS	Intelligent Video Surveillance	image processing	0.000	0.041
PSAP	Presentation Service Access Point	an ID label used in open networks	0.000	0.031
RF	radio frequency	a physical quantity	351.27	0.478
LV	low voltage	a physical quantity	307.11	0.135
V_{DD}	Voltage Drain Drain	positive power-supply pin in field-effect transistors	203.7	0.02
PV	photovoltaic	an adjective referring to the solar energy	133.48	0.920
HV	high voltage	a physical quantity	195.71	0.041
IC	integrated circuit	a microchip used in electronics	261.95	0.633
CI	capacitance	a physical quantity	61.93	4.581
ABBREVIATIONS AND SYMBOLS				
GHz	Gigahertz	unit of measurement	183.66	0.093
AlGaN	aluminium gallium nitride	a chemical compound	21.08	0.000
nm	nanometre	a unit of measurement	458.77	1.984
dB	decibel	a unit of measurement	358.99	0.997
keV	kilo-electronvolt	a unit of measurement	5.02	2.16

The sections above show that abbreviations and acronyms are frequent in the MTCS corpus, and as a result 50 % of singleword terms are abbreviated. It might be linked to the fact that English is more prone to compression, because abbreviated forms are common even in the general language. On the other hand, MTCS domains are technical disciplines drawing on physical or chemical phenomena, which are quantities described in terms of units of measurement.

Abbreviations are more commonly used in the MTCS domains than in the general language, with w few exceptions. For this reason, it can be inferred that these abbreviations are domain-specific and familiar to the inner circle of scientists and engineers, e.g. *LV*, *IC* or *RF* which are unfamiliar to a non-expert reader. Example (7.5.) illustrates a pair of abbreviated terms referring to *high voltage* and *low voltage* electronic appliances.

(7.5.) ***HV** devices usually have some application drawbacks in comparison to their **LV** counterparts.*

The MTCS authors use polarising strategies with respect to abbreviations, i.e. either leave them compressed without further explanation or use the anaphoric reference strategy to ensure proper understanding of the text. It might stem from the fact that some terms might have been used earlier in the text, and as such familiar to the readers, while others have only been introduced and require proper clarification to be appropriately comprehended, which is shown in Example (7.6.) below:

(7.6.) *Among the several **analog/ RF receiver** components low noise **voltage controlled oscillators (VCO)** and highly selective bandpass filters are widely used.*

Alphabetisms are the most popular form of compression of complex terms, which is in alliance with Mattiello's (2012) findings that 'scientific contexts appear to favour the use of alphabetisms (2012: 159)'. In the MTCS domains, the names of some scientific organisations have been abbreviated and are pronounced like words, e.g. *CERN*, an abbreviation for the French name of the following scientific organisation: *Conseil Européen pour la Recherche Nucléaire. ITER* is another example of an acronym, but also an iconic alphabetism created from the initial letters of the full name in English of the international scientific research centre International Thermonuclear Experimental Reactor.

The abbreviations are of English origin and they have been borrowed directly into minority languages, like Italian, as it is indicated in Mattiello's (2012) analysis of the English and Italian scientific discourse which marks the direction of knowledge transfer from the majority language of science: English.

Moreover, abbreviations also pertain to physical quantities, units of measurement or chemical compounds that are more common in the general language. For instance, *nm, GHz* and *dB,* units of measurement present in the MTCS key terminology, appear relatively more frequently than others, like *keV*, due to their high usability in everyday life. On the other hand, there are alphabetisms, such as *IC* and *CI* which are polysemous, and ambiguous. They are present in the general language, but are used in different contexts with a different meaning. Such linguistic solutions allow for precision and economy of expression, and at the same time create hybrid subject-field terminology.

Apart from the compressed terms present in the keyword terminology, there are other interesting cases, such as blends. For example, the blend *MIXDES* stands for *Mixed Design of Integrated Circuits and Systems* and it is the name of the conference. It was created as a blend of and acronym *MIX* with an alphabetism *DES*. Moreover, the name of the research centre in Hamburg *DESY* is another blend created from an alphabetism and acronym from its extension in German *Deutsches Elektronen-Synchrotron*. The authors of the MTCS research papers assume that the readers are well acquainted with this research centre, and therefore they do not use the full name in texts, as shown in Example (7.7.) below:

(7.7.) *MTCA.4 Piezo Driver Another MTCA.4 RTM board is being developed at* ***DESY*** *for piezo control.*

A high frequency of abbreviated terms is dictated by the need to compress information due to limited publishing space. As a result, complex nominal hybrids with an abbreviation are created, i.e. *low level radio frequency (LLRF) control system -> LLRF control system*. They appear along with the anaphoric reference to facilitate decoding of the text by the target audience. Moreover, pleonastic nominal phrases, like *HEMT transistor* are a common phenomenon, because they specify the type of device or a process without using the extension, which might disturb the reading process and occupy too much space, as shown in Example (7.8.) below:

(7.8.) *Other effects, like series resistances, velocity saturation and channel length modulation –which are important when the* ***HEMT transistor*** *works at high voltage and high current– are also incorporated in the model.*

On the other hand, the authors decide to apply the anaphoric reference, which ensures proper reader's understanding of the text. The domains are highly technical and rely on the expected experimental results measured with mathematical precision. For this reason, the authors assume proper decoding of the text by applying this linguistic strategy. The anaphoric reference is shown in the example (7.9.) below:

(7.9.) *In the last few years, the* ***Tunnel-FET (T-FET)*** *is steadily gaining more attention as the possible successor of the standard* ***metal-oxide-semiconductor field-effect transistor (MOSFET)****.*

In the MTCS research papers, the most common type is the anaphoric reference, in which the abbreviation is provided in brackets, e.g. (Example 3.1. above) *metal-oxide-semiconductor field-effect transistor (MOSFET)*, to facilitate proper associations and avoid confusion, because abbreviations, and initialisms in particular, might be homonymous.

In conclusion, abbreviation allows for providing the maximum information load in limited space with maintaining a high level of precision. However, the majority of abbreviations are mainly used among the insiders, professionals, and are familiar to the MTCS community, therefore they are limited to the specialised language of new technologies. Moreover, English abbreviations migrate to minority languages, like Italian, and become internationalisms.

7.6. Metaphorisation of MTCS terminology

Metaphors as basic cognitive tools, allow for effective naming of new concepts or expressing ideas based on existing communicative means by juxtaposing two concepts, the existing one from the source domain with the new one in the target domain (Lakoff & Johnsen, 2003; Temmermann, 2000; Tabakowska, 2015; Siqueira et al., 2009). It is an efficient and clear method of expressing abstract ideas which are omnipresent in scientific texts (Temmermann, 2000; Pissolato, 2016 Pułaczewska, 2010; Ghajoyan, 2017). Also, terminology is created via metaphorical extensions on the basis of resemblance, connotation, allusions, or building new associations of already existing concepts (Iljinska & Smirnova, 2014; Pissolato, 2016).

In the MTCS research articles, metaphorical terms were identified from keyword terminology and collocations, which is presented in the Table 7.8. below. As can be seen from the table below, there are more metaphorical terms in multiword than in singleword terminology.

Table 7.8. Metaphorical terms in MTCS research papers extracted via Sketch Engine

category of terms	Terms
Singleword	circuit architecture
Multiword	behaviour/behavioural modeling delay line low noise clock frequency noise figure thermal noise residual stress parasitic capacitance particle swarm optimization current mirror (IC) ant colony optimization algorithm family logic/characteristics/member BSIM MOSFET family current starved inverter branch current method

The metaphorical mechanism which is the most widely used in the MTCS research papers is animation or personification. For example, electronic devices are assigned behaviour or features of living beings, i.e. a diode exhibits specific *behaviour* under specific circumstances (Example 7.10. below):

(7.10.) ***Diode behavior** becomes much more complex for MM (machine model) or CDM (charged device model)type discharges due to their oscillatory nature and high speed.*

(7.11.) *LLRF control system for XFEL accelerator is based on MicroTCA.4 (MTCA) **architecture** that is **flexible, reliable and manageable** solution derived from Advanced Telecommunication Computing **Architecture** (ATCA).*

In Example (7.11.) above, architecture is understood as a structure of something, and is personified by using the adjective *reliable*. Moreover, adjectives *flexible* and *manageable* give additional features, i.e. that the device is easy to operate, therefore is *flexible* (but not *elastic*). In addition, temperature may cause unwanted changes in the structure, called *stress*, which in the general language has a negative connotation, is it is illustrated by Example (7.12.) below.

(7.12.) *We analyze the bonding process performed in optimal* ***temperature*** *that* ***induces residual stress*** *as small as possible.*

Furthermore, electronic devices are animated, i.e. they behave like living organisms, since they may *absorb power*, which is shown in Example (7.13.).

(7.13.) *the inverter* ***absorbs power*** *when the output has a transition to a new logic state: if the transition is from 0 to 1, the output is loaded at the same voltage of the power supply bar, if the transition…*

The devices might also be affected by undesired phenomena, and *suffer* from delays caused by unwanted, *parasitic*, information, like wellbeing of living organisms is affected by parasites, which is exemplified in (7.14.) below:

(7.14.) *The NEMS start-up* ***suffers*** *a* ***latency*** *caused by the* ***parasitic information*** *carried by the capacitive feedthrough, which is considerably larger for square actuation.*

Also, different production methods and temperature conditions, or *variations*, are given the skill of influencing the test results, as shown in Example (7.15.). Similarly, the system of devices producing unavoidable, unwanted phenomena around the developed solution need to be kept under control, i.e. *simplified*, because the excess may affect its functioning (Example (7.16.) below).

(7.15.) ***Variations*** *within the* ***fabrication process*** *or* ***temperature variations*** *can* ***affect*** *the delay* ***values.***

(7.16.) *The* ***parasitic network*** *that* ***surrounds*** *the device is better to be kept as simple as possible because an increased complexity can* ***affect*** *the simulation* ***speed of a model.***

The second type of terminological metaphorisation in the MTCS research articles are metaphors based on symbolism. Terms draw on the general lexicon and metaphorical extensions in this case entail employing a familiar image, such as a feature, function, shape or type of movement, etc. to the target domain. The most common are similarities of function. The summary of terms is contained in Table 7.9. below.

Table 7.9. The characteristics of metaphorical terms based on different types of symbolism extracted by Sketch Engine from MTCS research papers

type of symbolism	term	explanation
function	current **mirror**	it is a circuit created to copy current to another device and ensures its stability. The idea of reflection of a *mirror*, i.e. its functions, is transferred to an electronic device
	output	The term concentrates on the idea of a product, like energy, power or information, of a device, but it also refers to a place, where something is released, which is indicated by attributives like *port* or *buffer*.
	filter	A *filter* or *filters* entail a group of devices in an electronic circuit that are responsible for blocking unwanted signals, just like a strainer which filters the desired contents from the unwanted.
	clock frequency	A computer's CPU is compared to a *clock* which repeats cycles in a given period of time, a second. Therefore, it works as a clock.
animal	particle **swarm** optimization	It is a method of calculating the best solution among possible solutions, called here particles which are countless like *bees* in a *swarm*, hence the animal metaphor.
	ant colony optimization algorithm	In computer science, it is a method of finding an optimal solution via graphical means from other options which are compared to the behaviour of *ants* looking for food. The successful ant finds the shortest way to its colony, which is later chosen by the rest of the ants.
	parasitic capacitance	It is an unavoidable and unwanted capacitance which is present in an electronic circuit and has to be considered or calculated when designing a given electronic device. For this reason, it is compared to a *parasite* feeding on a host or harming it.
shape	**branch** current method	It is the determination of the voltage between nodes. It is a comparison of current being divided into smaller parts, like a trunk of a tree with its branches.
	delay **line**	It is an electronic circuit that is designed to delay signals. The metaphor was coined on the shape symbolism, because it has an elongated shape.

(*Continued*)

Table 7.9. Continued

type of symbolism	term	explanation
	architecture	The idea of a design is extended to technical domains to denote 'the structure of a computer system and the way it works'[10], but is has been transferred to all electronic devices and parts not only a computer.
movement	circuit	The metaphorical extension is based on the type of movement, since the term refers to the circular movement of current in an electronic circuit.

Apart from different types of symbolisms, there are also metaphorical terms which are based on conceptual mappings, such as X is A FAMILY MEMBER, juxtaposing belonging to a group with having the same bloodlines. As the result, the term *family* appears with the frequency of 75.7 times per million tokens. Moreover, the term is used to denote a certain group of devices, characteristics and algorithms, such as a *families of microcontrollers* illustrated in Example (7.17.) below:

(7.17.) *Libraries for the most popular* ***families of microcontrollers*** *are available.*

It also exhibits the tendency to create eponyms with brand names, which is presented in the table 7.10. below.

Table 7.10. The comparison between the usage of the term *family* extracted by Sketch Engine from the MTCS corpus

type of attributives	extracted terms
devices	transistor logic family families of microcontrollers BSIM model family Analog Devices SHARC family processors newer Xilinx FPGA families
features	characteristics families
algorithms & formulae	ant colony algorithms family the Lanczos functions family

10 https://www.ldoceonline.com/dictionary/architecture, 17.05.2020.

However, the term is also used in its verbatim meaning, when the authors refer to a sample of people under scrutiny, as shown in Example (7.18.) below:

(7.18.) *Once they have been selected, a* ***family member****, a relative or a neighbour will* ***be contacted and offered to participate*** *in the study.*

The family might also be understood as patients' relatives when the developed solutions, like the *dispenser*, are to be implemented in the medical sector, or ease the effort necessary for patient care (Examples (7.19.) and (7.20.) below):

(7.19.) ***Family member*** *or doctor can be alarmed about the lack of patient reaction and local pharmacy can receive automatic order if the* ***dispenser*** *runs out of medicaments.*

(7.20.) *It may reduce the time devoted by* ***family*** *or hired supervisors to patient.*

The MTCS domains also make use of a CONTAINER metaphor. The term *data warehouse* appears with the frequency 3.01 times per million tokens and denotes a database that stores a lot of data from different sources. The metaphorical extension is based on the idea of a building used for storing goods. The term has only one collocation candidate due to its low frequency in the MTCS research papers. The characteristics of the term is presented in Table 7.11. below.

Table 7.11. The characteristics of the term *warehouse* extracted by Sketch Engine from the MTCS corpus

Lexeme		***warehouse***			
collocate	coocurrence count	candidate count	T-score	MI	logDice
Data	3	110	1.732	13.145	9.765

It is an example of a general term, identified by Byrne (2012), which might acquire special meanings in different contexts. The term is a metaphorical extension of a general lexeme *wholesaler* and is a CONTAINER metaphor describing a database that stores a lot of data from different sources. The idea metaphorically transferred is based on goods orderly disposed a building used for storing goods is used.

Metaphors are not only limited to nominal terms. The MTCS research articles contain also adjectives which have migrated from other domains into the language of new technologies to attribute nominal terms. Keyword terminology and collocation candidates contain three adjectives with metaphorical extensions of meaning, i.e. *parasitic* and *starved*.

The adjective *parasitic* appears in in the MTCS research papers with the frequency 149.1 per million, which is depicted in the concordance of the term in Figure 7.2. below.

Figure 7.2. The screenshot of the concordance for the adjective *parasitic* generated by Sketch Engine from the MTCS corpus

The frequency of the term occurrence in the analysed texts affects the number of collocation candidates and their distribution, which is presented in Table 7.12. below.

Table 7.12. Stems of the adjective *parasitic* generated by Sketch Engine from MTCS corpus

Stems of the adjective *parasitic*
parasitic effects
parasitic inductance
parasitic capacitance
parasitic elements
parasitic extraction
parasitic coupling
parasitic input

The negative meaning of the adjective *parasitic*, i.e. of a creature leaving at the expense of its host[11] is metaphorically transferred to the technical domains to denote unavoidable and unwanted phenomena which lower the efficiency of the electronic devices, and need to be taken into account during the design and test stage of research. Table 7.12. above shows that the adjective is used for attributing undesired elements, physical phenomena and processes.

11 https://www.ldoceonline.com/dictionary/parasitic, 19.05.2020.

Another example of an adjective which proves a relatively young age of the MTCS domains is *morphological* (Figure 7.3. below) which migrated from more traditional disciplines, like biology, geography or medicine. It acts as an attribute and forms complex terms, like *morphological operation* or *morphological opening and closing* which refer to digital data processing and denotes substantial changes in the image structure of form[12]. Therefore, the idea of structure is metaphorically transferred to technical domains from more physical objects, like organisms or geographical features.

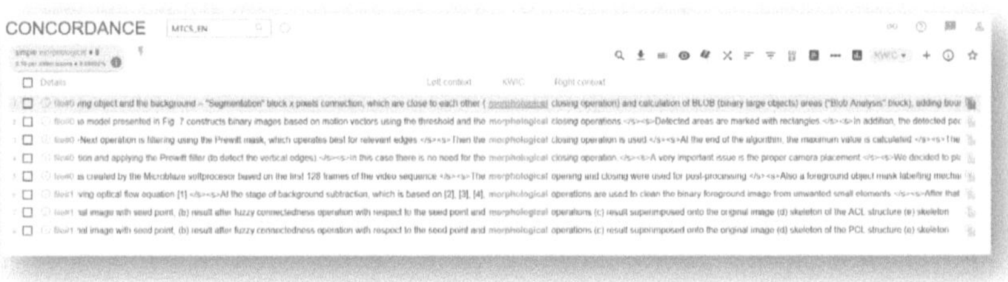

Figure 7.3. The screenshot of the concordance for the adjective *morphological* generated by Sketch Engine from the MTCS corpus

However, the most interesting is the adjective *starved* which is a constituent of a complex term *current starved inverter (CSI)*. It refers to a device which uses the barest minimum current to operate, analogous to living organisms that feed on the amount of food just enough to survive. It was coined to contrast with the term *current-limiting* which entails setting up the maximum limit of the supplied current. As shown in Figure 7.4. below, the adjective also forms other multiword combinations, like *linear current starved delay element* or *current starved cascaded inverters* which ensure precision of expression so necessary in research papers dealing with technical solutions that are to be implemented.

12 https://www.mathworks.com/help/images/morphological-dilation-and-erosion.html, 19.05.2020

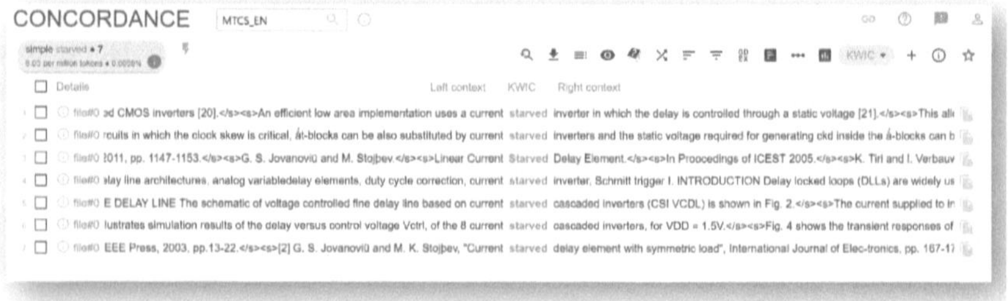

Figure 7.4. The screenshot of the concordance for the adjective *starved* generated by Sketch Engine from the MTCS corpus

All things considered, metaphors in specialised languages help conceptualise unfamiliar concepts since metaphorical terms juxtapose familiar concepts, e.g. from the general lexicon, with the new ones, which facilitates the effectiveness of communication. In the MTCS domains, source domains are taken either from the general lexicon or from subject fields with a long-lived tradition, such as geography, medicine or biology. Moreover, negative phenomena are expressed by negatively connotatively loaded lexemes.

7.7. Terminological synonymy

Synonymy in the traditional approach to terminology was considered undesired due to its allegedly negative impact on the efficiency of communication but this language phenomenon cannot be discarded from specialised communication (Lipka, 1992; Cruse, 2004: 156; Pearson, 1998: 169; Polackova, 2001: 174; *Čermák*, 2010 in Cocca, Kendzora, Řeřicha & Martínez, 2016: 22). However, proliferation of new concepts developed independently leads to the creation of lexical means that are close in meaning, but allow for expressing nuances in meaning (Cocca et al., 2016). Moreover, the existence of synonyms is a manifestation that a given subject field is still developing (Dury, 2005; Cocca et al., 2016).

The MTCS domains are technical and empirically verified engineering subject fields. Precision of expression is of overriding importance, enhanced by numerical data, graphs, algorithms or tables. Therefore, scientists and engineers working in these fields try to avoid ambiguous forms of expression and form unequivocal complex terms. However, the MTCS research articles contain a number of synonymous terms which are listed in Table 7.13. below.

Table 7.13. The list from keyword term candidates extracted from the MTCS research papers by Sketch Engine with possible synonyms

category of terms	**term**	**synonyms**
Singleword terms	inductor	coil
		reactor
		choke
	simulation	modeling
	impedance	resistance
		resistivity
	ADC	analog-to-digital converter (ADC)
		analog-to-digital converter (ADC)
Multiword terms	delay line	digital delay line
		delay filter
	fall **detector**	sensor
	clock signal	timepiece
		chronometre
	transfer function	system function
		network function
	supply/threshold/ input/output/low/ reference **voltage**	electric pressure
		electric tension
		electric potential difference
	gate oxide	gateway
		port
	voltage **drop**	fall
		decrease
		decline
	neural network	circuit of neurons
	wireless network	wi-fi

Table 7.13. above shows that the majority of terms selected from the MTCS terminology containing potential synonymous alternatives identified via standardised nomenclatures are surprisingly scarce among the multiword terms. Among MTCS terms, there are only 3 singleword terms with potential synonyms

and 9 complex terms with at least one synonymous alternative, of which 4 refer only to one element.

The range of potentially synonymous terms is limited in the MTCS domains, due to the fact that terminology was partially borrowed from more traditional disciplines. However, there are instances of synonymous terms which differ in terms of shades of meaning, distribution, and frequency of use.

The singleword term *inductor*, which denotes an electrical component, has three potential synonyms which are suggested by nomenclatures. However, their frequencies vary and corpus realisations present interesting results. Table 7.14 below constitutes the summary of the comparison between the keyword and its potential synonyms.

Table 7.14. The comparison between the keyword *inductor* and its potential synonyms extracted from the MTCS research papers by Sketch Engine

category	**inductor**	**coil**	**reactor**	**choke**
frequency per million tokens	232.82	32.11	2.29	1.15
collocation candidates -1 or +1	spiral, integrated, active, octagonal, square, passive, tapered	voltage, antenna	fusion, thermonuclear	N/A
function	main term	attributive	main term	main term
status	keyword	synonymous	non-synonymous	synonymous

The analysis of the term shows that it is the most frequently used by the MTCS authors in its primary meaning. Due to its high level of occurrence in the analysed texts, it has the longest list of collocation candidates (in the position -1 because it is used as a main term) which provide characteristics of the device. The remaining potential synonyms are either deprived of candidates in this category, they function as an attributive or have a completely different meaning. The term *coil* is used as an attributive, forming multiword terms, such as the one presented in Example (7.21.) below.

(7.21.) *The resonance circuit increases the amplitude of the weak input signal ui that is induced in the* ***tag coil antenna*** *by the continuous RF signal sent from the reader, before RF to DC conversion is achieved in the rectifier block*

Another potential candidate for a synonym appears only once in the whole corpus without any attributives, only with the definite article, which is illustrated in Example (7.22.) below.

(7.22.) *two low-impedance electrolytic capacitors have been chosen for the output and connected in parallel to decrease their equivalent series resistance; the* ***choke*** *has been wound with a wire cross-section greater than necessary.*

However, corpus realisations show that the term *reactor* is used by the MTCS writers to denote an apparatus enabling nuclear reactions, which is shown in Example (7.23.) below. Moreover, the lexemes co-occurring in its local context, i.e. *fusion* and *thermonuclear*, suggest its most iconic meaning that is used in nomenclatures.

(7.23.) *The diagnostic and control systems of large scale scientific experiments like particle accelerators, colliders or* ***fusion reactors*** *are in most cases complex distributed installations.*

As the literature on the subject suggests, synonymy can be graded, i.e. synonyms can be paired on the basis of a graded similarity or sameness of meaning. The MTCS research papers also contain quasi or pseudo synonyms whose equivalence of meaning is peripheral. One of the examples of pseudo synonyms are terms *simulation* and *modeling* which share a concept of reproducing, copying something, but their use is strictly conditioned. The first term is defined by LDCE as 'the activity of producing conditions which are similar to real ones, especially in order to test something, or the conditions that are produced'[13], whereas the latter is basically a computer representation or scientific description of a situation or event[14]. As a result, the term *simulation* focuses on copying specific conditions indispensable for performing experiments, and *modeling* deals with a digital mapping of a given situation.

The frequency of use determines the character of the MTCS domains. The scientists and engineers develop solutions to practical problems via performing tests and experiments in copied, simulated conditions. A part of their work is based on creating models or situations or events, which is depicted in Table 7.15 below.

13 https://www.ldoceonline.com/dictionary/simulation, 21.05.2020
14 https://www.ldoceonline.com/dictionary/model, 21.05.2020

Table 7.15. The comparison between the keyword *inductor* and its pseudo synonym extracted from the MTCS research papers by Sketch Engine

category	**simulation**	**modeling**
frequency per million tokens	1,580.46	379.63
collocation candidates -in position 1	numerical, TCAD, circuit, Sentaurus, device, computer, thermal, circuit-device, transient, aging	compact, behavioural, numerical, accurate analytical
function	main term	main term
status	keyword	pseudo synonym

Despite being pseudo synonyms, the terms share one collocation candidate, i.e. the adjective *numerical*, which also emphasises the empirical character of the MTCS disciplines as well as a strong dependence on *numerical* data. Other collocation candidates also underline that they are digital and modern. In addition, these terms cooccur with metaphorical collocates *aging* and *behavioural* which make them animated.

Concordance lines extracted from the MTCS research papers indicate that the authors use the analysed terms in their dictionary meaning, which is emphasised by the sentential context (Dash, 2008) as illustrated by Examples 7.24. and 7.25 below:

(7.24.) *A multi-physics model for the Colpitts oscillator circuit has been built in the developed* ***simulation*** *environment, and its self-excited resonance has been confirmed by the simulation.*

(7.25.) *A successful virtual design strategy requires* ***modeling*** *methodologies on different levels of abstraction and computational expense.*

In the MTCS tests, synonyms are also created via the use of anaphoric and cataphoric references, i.e. by using the full and abbreviated forms of terms. As a result, a set of real synonyms is created which are interchangeable in contexts within one domain provided that they refer to the same concept. For instance, the alphabetism *ADC* is used to denote two alternative full terms, i.e. *Analog-Digital Converter* and *Analog-Digital Controller* as absolute synonyms, with the first being more popular than the latter which is shown in Examples (7.26.) and (7.27.) below.

(7.26.) *Pipelined* ***analog-to-digital converter (ADC)*** *offers an attractive combination of speed (up to hundreds of Msamples/s) and resolution (up to 16-bit), which makes it widely used in nowadays applications.*

(7.27.) *The on-chip* ***Analog to Digital Controller (ADC)*** *has 10-bit resolution and is able to sample with rates up to 330 kHz.*

In addition, this abbreviation is also used as an attributive, also forming pleonastic multiword terminological combinations, such as the hybrid multiword cluster in Example (7.28.) below:

(7.28.) *The microcontroller is clocked at 16MHz and is running firmware written in C-language and compiled with* ***444 Controller*** *ADC Analog outputs Analog inputs.*

As mentioned above, research articles are carefully crafted texts with precisely used terminology. Therefore, the difference between near synonyms terms, sharing the concept of blocking something, the idea of resisting or becoming a barrier, *resistance, resistivity, impedance* will not be overlooked by the authors of the MTCS texts, because they are focused on different aspects. *Resistance* refers to the relationship between the voltage and the current, *resistivity* is a special type of resistance, a physical quantity that characterises the electrical resistivity of materials, whereas *impedance* is used when there is an opposition to a change in the current flow. As Table 7.16 below presents, the terms most often appearing are *resistance* and *impedance* which also share two collocation candidates. The authors, when using the term *resistivity*, refer to its level of performance.

Table 7.16. The comparison between the keyword *resistance* and its synonyms extracted from the MTCS research papers by Sketch Engine

category	**resistance**	**resistivity**	**impedance**
frequency per million tokens	497.76	28.67	302.79
collocation candidates -in position 1	<u>thermal</u>, feedback, series, electrical, <u>channel</u>,	high, low, average	<u>thermal</u>, input, load, optimum, <u>channel</u>, antenna
function	main term	main term	main term
status	keyword	synonymous	synonymous

The analysis of multiword terms also brings interesting results. The use of certain synonymous alternatives is strictly domain-specific and context-specific. The current study shows that some alternatives are used with varied frequencies and others are completely absent. For example, the term *clock signal* appears with the frequency 82.58 times per million tokens, but the synonymous alternatives for *clock* are not manifested in any way in the MTCS research papers. The absence of its synonyms might by explained by the fact that they belong to the general lexicon. Other terms also exhibit a similar tendency with its synonymous alternatives, such as the combination *transfer function*. The nomenclatures also suggest the following synonyms: *network function* and *system function*, but they are not used by the authors of the MTCS texts. In addition, the term *neural network*, a model of machine learning, has one potential synonymous alternative *circuit of networks* which, however, does not appear in the analysed texts.

Other terms and their synonyms are present in the analysed texts, such as the term *delay line* which is used to denote a specific element in a digital filter, and whose function is to delay a signal in order to synchronise the audio sound with visual elements. It can also be called *a digital delay line* or a *digital filter*. Yet, the authors of the MTCS texts opt for the first option, with the latter being marginally used.

Table 7.17. The comparison between the keyword *delay line* and its synonyms extracted from the MTCS research papers by Sketch Engine

Category	**delay line**	**digital delay line**	**digital filter**
frequency per million tokens	131.90	2.29	1.15
collocation candidates -in position 1	coarse, fine, tapped, external, variable, controlled	N/A	N/A
function	main term	main term	attributive
status	keyword	synonymous	synonymous

As Table 7.17 above shows, the MTCS authors use mainly the term which was extracted via Sketch Engine as keyword terminology. The other alternatives appear once or twice in the MTCS contexts. Even the list of potential collocates does not contain the adjective *digital*, but mainly refer to the type of tuning which this element is designed for. It can be polarising: *coarse* or *fine*, *controlled* or *tapped*, which is shown in Example (7.29.) below.

(7.29.) *Two phase detectors with two charge-pumps and low-pass filters generate two control voltages Vctrl_r and Vctrl_f to synchronize independently rising and falling edges as well in the* ***coarse*** *as in the* ***fine delay lines.***

In addition, as can be seen in Examples (7.30.) and (7.31.) below, the synonymous alternatives are used as a term and as an attributive.

(7.30.) *The accompanying datavalid signal is fed through edge detector and* ***digital delay line****, to compensate for the delay introduced by the pipeline ADC.*
(7.31.) *Splitting the unit delay - tools for fractional* ***delay filter design.***

The MTCS research papers are highly technical texts which require a high degree of expertise from the authors. For this reason, terminology which is used is the highest, professional and academic, level. Therefore, less professional terms will not appear in such texts, which is illustrated with the term *supply* ***voltage,*** with the emphasis on the second element in the combination, and its synonymous alternatives. Table 7.18 below shows the distribution of terms in the analysed corpus of academic texts.

Table 7.18. The comparison between the keyword *supply voltage* and its synonyms extracted from the MTCS research papers by Sketch Engine

category	**(supply) voltage**	**electric pressure**	**electric tension**	**potential difference**
frequency per million tokens	221.36	0.00	0.00	2.29
collocation candidates -in position 1	nominal, low, power, VDD, single, different	N/A	N/A	built-in, contact
function	main term	N/A	N/A	main term
status	keyword	N/A	N/A	synonym

As can be seen from Table 7.18 above, the most salient terminology in the MTCS domains also contains terminological alternatives which might not be readily evident to non-experts. In addition, the concordance lines imply some details which might suggest the use of the alternative as a synonym, which is illustrated by Example (7.32.) below:

(7.32.) *Simplification used in formula (8a) is well founded because gate doping is relatively high and the influence of the surface states charge is negligible in comparison with the* ***contact potential difference.***

Among MTCS multiword terminology, there is a term which is used both in the general language and in specialised varieties, namely the element *gate* in the multiword combination *gate oxide*. In addition, it contains two potentially synonymous alternatives, *gateway* and *port* which are also used in general and specialised languages. The three lexems, which potentially acquire the terminological status in the MTCS disciplines, are periferially connected with the idea of a connecting passage. In terms of the term *gate* it is 'the part of a fence or outside wall that you can open and close so that you can enter or leave a place'[15], whereas a *gateway* refers to the opening in a fence, wall etc that can be closed by a gate, or a 'way of connecting two computer networks'[16]. In contrast, the term *port* can be used in the language of new technologies to describe 'a part of a computer where you can connect another piece of equipment'[17]. The comparison between the lexemes is summarised in Table 7.19 below. The most frequently appearing are *gate* and *port*, and they also share collocation candidates that also allude to numerical data.

Table 7.19. The comparison between the keyword *gate* and its synonyms extracted from the MTCS research papers by Sketch Engine

category	**gate**	**gateway**	**port**
frequency per million tokens	760.41	9.18	92.90
collocation candidates -in position 1	transmission, logic, XOR, NOR, twin, NAND, double	TCP, mobile, translation	serial, debug, USB, output, two, input
function	main term	general lexicon lexeme	main term
status	keyword	pseudo synonym	pseudo synonym

As Table 7.15 above shows, the three lexemes are used differently by the MTCS authors. The keyword *gate* and its synonym *port* appear as terms in the analysed texts, whereas corpus realisations show that *gateway* is utilised in its general lexicon meaning, despite having a more technical one. As a result, all these analysed potential synonyms have their basic, general language meaning, metaphorically transferred in the first and third case into the MTCS domains, and they seem to act as pseudo synonyms. Their usage strictly depends on the conditions, which is indicated in literature on the subject. The differences are shown in Examples (7.33.-7.35.). The term *gate* appears to constitute the door preventing from or allowing passing it, *gateway* is simply the passage (in this

15 https://www.ldoceonline.com/dictionary/gate, 31.10.2019
16 https://www.ldoceonline.com/dictionary/gateway, 31.10.2019
17 https://www.ldoceonline.com/dictionary/port, 31.10.2019.

example, it is a smartphone that allows communication of symptoms), and finally, *port* is the place of connection which is also emphasised by collocation candidates, i.e. *USB, output* or *input.*

(7.33.) *The openings in LTO that enable the access to silicon source and drain pads were obtained with the same etching procedure as for the* ***gate opening*** *before gate stack fabrication but using a photosensitive resist mask patterned by standard 1 μm resolution photolithography.*
(7.34.) *All the symptoms processed from and to the immediate level will be distributed by a smartphone used* ***as a gateway.***
(7.35.) *The Bluetooth module is configured in bridge mode, so that it sends all the data received through the* ***serial port.***

MTCS terminology reveals that domain-specific terms form complex terms with general lexicon lexemes that have a number of synonyms, but none of them will acquire the terminological status. As a consequence, they are used as a word combination of a different category, which in this case is noun+verb co-occurrence. The term *voltage drop* refers to a decline in voltage in a circuit. Other potentially synonymous alternatives also share this idea, but the choice of words for a term cannot be accidental, which is shown in Table 7.20 below.

Table 7.20. The comparison between the keyword *voltage drop* and its synonyms extracted from the MTCS research papers by Sketch Engine

category	**voltage drop**	**voltage fall**	**voltage decrease**
frequency per million tokens	55.05	1.15	2.29
collocation candidates -in position 1	spiral, integrated, active, octagonal, square, passive, tapered	N/A	N/A
function	main term	N+V combination	N+V combination
status	keyword	synonymous	synonymous

The analysis shows that the scientists are fully aware of the context-dependent terminology, and use synonymous alternatives as different word categories in order to refer to a similar idea without resorting to the use of the term, which is illustrated by Examples (7.36.) and (7.37.) below.

(7.36.) *The circuit in Fig. 1 cannot operate at 0.6 V with high gain, due to the large* ***voltage drop*** *in the resistors.*

(7.37.) *Equation (1) clearly shows that the increase of the* ***gate voltage decreases*** *the threshold voltage (VTh), which can be used to improve the level of inversion under low voltage power supply conditions.*

This case raises the question whether the MTCS authors consciously avoid blending two terms, i.e. *gate voltage* and *voltage drop* and opt for a noun+verb combination, or the usage is dictated by the influence that *gate voltage* exerts on *threshold voltage*.

Finally, the tendency of English to compression and blending also results in the creation of synonyms. The term *wireless network* has an alternative blend *Wi Fi* or *wi-fi*, all of which is used interchangeably, and acts an example of a real synonym, but in this case, the term has also migrated to the general language (Cocca et al., 2016; Dury, 2005). In its full form, it is the most frequent in the MTCS research paper, but the compressed alternatives are also found.

In conclusion, synonymy in the MTCS research papers is rather limited, but synonyms exhibit all the aspects mentioned by the literature on the subject (Lipka, 1992; Pearson, 1998; Cocca et al., 2016). Terminology and its synonymous alternatives are carefully used, as scientists are expert users of the language of new technologies, and meticulously craft their scientific reports. The analysis also shows that not all the terminological options appear in the MTCS texts, despite being present in nomenclatures. Moreover, corpus realisations clearly indicate nuances of meaning of the vocabulary used, and in its local contexts in particular.

7.8. Polysemy

Polysemy, another undesired linguistic phenomenon in terminology description in the traditional approach, is the result of the evolution of meaning in time (Temmermann, 2000; Grinev-Griniewicz, 2016; Siqueira et al., 2009; Zolotukhin, 2016). It entails the extension of meaning to other concepts, but still maintaining a degree of relationship between them (Lipka, 1992; Pethő, 2001). Otherwise, it is the case of homonymy. However, in some cases it is difficult to make a clear distinction between these two notions (Lyons, 1968; Zolotukhin, 2016).

The MTCS research papers also contain inter-categorical polysemy of terminology, created via metaphorical extensions of meaning both from the general and specialised language as well as borrowing (Temmerman, 2000; Bursina, 2014 in Zolotukhin, 2016; Iljinska & Smirnova, 2014). In these domains, there are terms which migrate from other terminological systems and from the general language, due to the relatively young age of the MTCS domains as well as their interdisciplinary nature (Dury, 2005). The identified candidates for polysemous terms, extracted from keyword terminology generated by Sketch Engine from the MTCS research papers, are listed in the table 7.21. below.

Table 7.21. Polysemous terms identified from keyword MTCS terminology extracted via Sketch Engine

category	term
Singleword terms	**RF** (radio frequency, rheumatic fever, Russian Federation, etc.)
	ADC (a long list of terms and proper names)
	SoI (Silicone-on-Insulator), Statement of Intent, Severity of illness, Statistics of Income, sphere of influence, Segment Operating Income,
	IC (integrated circuit, infrastructure committee, etc.)
	HV (high voltage, high volume, home visit, half value, etc.)
	RI (resistor input, reference intake)
	MFG (manufacturing, mit freundlichen Grüßen, multi function generator)
	adder (circuit)
	circuit
	supply voltage
	current mirror
Multiword terms	thermal **noise**
	clock signal
	frame **grabber**
	image **acquisition**
	residual **stress**
	recording **channel**
	power **consumption**

There are three sources of potentially polysemous terms from the MTCS research articles. The first group consists of homonyms due to their multiple, but unrelated meanings (Lyons, 1968; Zolotukhin, 2016). Abbreviations and symbols have multiple meanings which are not connected and might create confusion, especially for novice readers. Two letter-aphabetisms, such as *RF*, *IC* or *HV* are used in various domains in English. The abbreviation *IC* stands for an *integrated circuit* in the electronic contexts, but there are other over 200 meanings in English. In addition, RF stands for *radio frequency* in the MTCS domains, and it is mainly used as an attributive of certain devices (Example (7.38.) below), but it is also used in business, chemistry, music, biology, politics, etc. and denotes various objects, substances or phenomena.

(7.38.) *The need for reducing the design time for* ***RF /analog circuits****, designers must adopt optimization based design methodologies.*

Similarly, the abbreviation *SoI* appearing in the MTCS research papers, meaning *Silicone-on-Insulator* (Example (7.39.) below), constitutes another instance of homonymy in specialised languages. As a result it is used in various domains and denotes different notions, ranging from business matters to medical applications.

(7.39.) *The application of* ***SoI processes*** *and current-mode processing for* ***HV IC*** *design has been shown as a choice widely increasing applicability of various ways of voltage and current signal amplification and processing in general.*

Compressed terms might also be used in different languages, such as the abbreviation *HV*. It is used to denote *high voltage* in both English, as indicated in Example (7.39.). above, but in German it refers to the *Hauptversammlung /Annual General Meeting/*. As a result, abbreviations can be considered the cases of homonymy, and not polysemy.

The second source of polysemous terms in the MTCS research papers is the general language. Lexemes from the general lexicon which are widely understood and used are borrowed into the MTCS language with an extension of meaning based on the resemblance of shape, function or manner of movement. They still maintain the main aspect of their sense, such as *mirror, channel, stress, grabber,* or *clock*.

The MTCS domains are relatively young, which results in borrowing terminology from other, more traditional disciplines. One of such examples is the term *circuit*, which belongs to the most salient terms in these disciplines, as it appears with the frequency of 2,776.69 times per million tokens. It is also used in the general language as well as other domains, like mathematics, biology, sports, law or even religious contexts, and shares the idea of a circle or a circular movement. It is metaphorically transferred to the device and refers to the movement of current within it, such as in Example (7.40.) describing *undesired current flows*:

(7.40.) *In such* ***circuits*** *the current-voltage conversion device is vulnerable to any* ***undesired current-flows****.*

As mentioned above, polysemous terms possess meaning which metaphorically transferred. Multiword terms contain general lexicon elements, mainly as the base, but also as collocates. The resemblance to familiar general language elements or phenomena allows for a better understanding of complex and abstract scientific concepts and technological details, such as in Example (7.41.) below:

(7.41.) *The clock tree circuits can add* ***jitter noise*** *and change the duty cycle of the* ***clock signal****.*

The terms *noise* and *clock* clearly communicate the message, i.e. *jitter noise* refers to disturbances in the electronic signal which can result in errors, whereas *clock signal* gives details of the type of signal appearing at regular intervals, like the clock.

Another example of a polysemous term, which is a hybrid of elements from the specialised and general lexicon is *frame grabber*. It refers to a type of device that allows for capturing picture frames from a camera. The idea of "grabbing" was metaphorically transferred from the informal register into the analogue-digital image processing. MTCS corpus realisations confirm the use of the analysed term in its definition meaning emphasised by the local context, such as in Example (7.42.) below:

(7.42.) *The library includes two separate sets of functions for* ***interaction*** *with camera and* ***frame grabber****.*

The meaning of lexemes from the general language might also be part of complex terms used in traditional disciplines, like physics, which are then borrowed by the MTCS disciplines. The term *residual stress* refers to a type of tension that is recorded after a material was subject to a force. The idea of a negative, unpleasant feeling is metaphorically transferred to denote an unwanted and unavoidable phenomenon occurring in specific conditions, which is illustrated in Example (7.43.) below:

(7.43.) *Concluding, the* ***residual stress*** *induced in bonding process significantly affects the membrane performance.*

On the other hand, the MTCS corpus contains terminology which is prima facie polysemous, but in fact it is the case of homonymy. A type of a circuit, an *adder circuit* is named after its primary function, i.e. performing calculations, and summing or adding, in particular. It has not connection with the general language meaning of the lexicon, a type of poisonous snake. Example (7.44.) below presenting a concordance line, shows that the term is used in its definition meaning, i.e. a device for calculations:

(7.44.) *Obtained results allow analyzing what structure of* ***full adder*** *should be used for* ***specific data summation.***

Polysemous terms also come from other specialised languages or the formal register, like *supply, acquisition*, or *consumption*. The term *acquisition* is used in business contexts, and to denote obtaining something in a formal register. The idea of obtaining of collecting is transferred with collocates specifying types of items that are gathered to be subjected to further processing, including *data* or *images*. Similarly, the term *supply voltage* uses the idea of 'an amount of something that is available to be used'[18], often appearing in the business language. In this case, it is *voltage* that exerts an influence on the performance of other elements, which is illustrated by Example (7.45.) below:

(7.45.) *The low* ***supply voltage limits*** *the biasing current and the load resistor values; both cannot be increased to have enough voltage head room or the MOSFET will enter the triode region.*

Finally, a formal language lexeme, *consumption*, becomes a part of the multiword keyword *power consumption* in the MTCS domains. The term denotes the usage of power by an appliance. The authors describe the combination of parameters for the proposed solutions which are personified and metaphorically consume supplies. The instance of personification is depicted in Example (7.46.) below:

(7.46.) *The proposed design* ***can operate*** *at higher frequencies and has* ***less power consumption***.

In conclusion, the existence of polysemy is a proof that meaning has been evolving in time. It also allows finding effective and familiar communicative means to name new objects or phenomena that are conceptually related to source domains. In the MTCS texts, there are two effective sources of polysemous terms, i.e. the general language (both the formal and informal registers) and specialised languages. Compressed terms, however, prove to be homonyms rather than instances of polysemy, which stays in alliance with literature on the subject. All in all, the cognitive aspects of MTCS terminology complement the process of its standardisation, which will be discussed in the following section.

---

18 https://www.ldoceonline.com/dictionary/supply, 20.04.2020.

7.9. Standardisation of MTCS terminology

The main aim of standardisation of terminology is to acknowledge a term and its meaning by a standardising body in order to unify concepts, their system and definitions to facilitate specialised communication (Pearson, 1998). Standardised terms are supposed to maintain its stable and monosemous character and eliminate homonymy, polysemy and synonymy. Moreover, in scientific and technical writing, standardised terminology is to reflect concepts precisely; it should also be neutral and context-free.

The majority of terminological systems is standardised with the ISO standard. However, the electrotechnical domains have developed their own standard for electric and electronic terminology. The International Electrotechnical Commission (IEC) has systematised and described electrotechnical terms, and compiled them into the International Electrotechnical Vocabulary (IEV) also published in the IEC 60050 series. As a result, their online glossary is available at http://www.electropedia.org/. As other nomenclatures, it contains 'historical' data, which are however, constantly updated. The screenshot of the Electropedia's browser is provided in Figure 7.5. below.

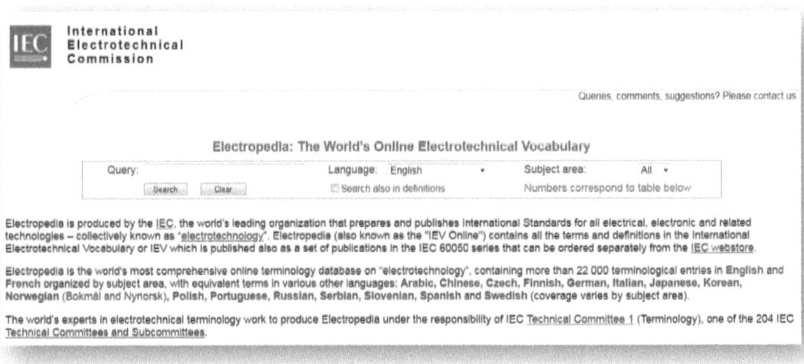

Figure 7.5. The screenshot of IEC's online technical dictionary available at http://www.electropedia.org/

The MTCS domains are relatively young, and therefore contain terminology from more traditional disciplines. They also belong to the electrotechnical disciplines, and as such they have an interdisciplinary nature. The practical and empirical aspects are depicted in the terminology used by the professionals. There are terms from hard sciences, like mathematics or physics, as well as mechanics, biology, medicine, or even banking due to the fact that the solutions are created for practical implementation and service. The list of disciplines involved in the MTCS subject fields which are a part of the electrotechnical disciplines recognised by IEC and categories of technical vocabulary and is shown in Figure 7.6. below.

102	Mathematics - General concepts and linear algebra
103	Mathematics - Functions
112	Quantities and units
113	Physics for electrotechnology
114	Electrochemistry
121	Electromagnetism
131	Circuit theory
141	Polyphase systems and circuits
151	Electrical and magnetic devices
161	Electromagnetic compatibility
171	Digital technology – Fundamental concepts
192	Dependabilty
195	Earthing and protection against electric shock
212	Electrical insulating solids, liquids and gases
221	Magnetic materials and components
311	Electrical and electronic measurements - General terms relating to measurements
312	Electrical and electronic measurements - General terms relating to electrical measurements
313	Electrical and electronic measurements - Types of electrical measuring instruments
314	Electrical and electronic measurements - Specific terms according to the type of instrument
321	Instrument transformers
351	Control technology
371	Telecontrol
395	Nuclear instrumentation: Physical phenomena, basic concepts, instruments, systems, equipment and detectors
411	Rotating machinery
415	Wind turbine generator systems
421	Power transformers and reactors
426	Equipment for explosive atmospheres
431	Transductors
436	Power capacitors
441	Switchgear, controlgear and fuses
442	Electrical accessories
444	Elementary relays
445	Time relays
447	Measuring relays
448	Power system protection
461	Electric cables
466	Overhead lines
471	Insulators
482	Primary and secondary cells and batteries
485	Fuel cell technologies
511	Nano-enabled electrotechnical products and systems
521	Semiconductor devices and integrated circuits
523	Micro-electromechanical systems (MEMS)
531	Electronic tubes
541	Printed circuits
551	Power electronics
561	Piezoelectric devices for frequency control and selection
581	Electromechanical components for electronic equipment
601	Generation, transmission and distribution of electricity - General
602	Generation, transmission and distribution of electricity - Generation
603	Generation, transmission and distribution of electricity - Power systems planning and management
605	Generation, transmission and distribution of electricity - Substations
614	Generation, transmission and distribution of electricity - Operation
617	Organization/Market of electricity
651	Live working
691	Tariffs for electricity
692	Generation, transmission and distribution of electrical energy – Dependability and quality of service of electric power systems
701	Telecommunications, channels and networks
702	Oscillations, signals and related devices
704	Transmission
705	Radio wave propagation
712	Antennas
713	Radiocommunications: transmitters, receivers, networks and operation
714	Switching and signalling in telecommunications
715	Telecommunication networks, teletraffic and operation
716	Integrated services digital network (ISDN) - Part 1 General aspects
721	Telegraphy, facsimile and data communication
722	Telephony
723	Broadcasting: Sound, television, data
725	Space radiocommunications
726	Transmission lines and waveguides
731	Optical fibre communication
732	Computer network technology
741	Internet of Things (IoT)
801	Acoustics and electroacoustics
802	Ultrasonics
806	Recording and reproduction of audio and video
807	Digital recording of audio and video signals
808	Video cameras for non-broadcasting
811	Electric traction
815	Superconductivity
821	Signalling and security apparatus for railways
826	Electrical installations
841	Industrial electroheat
845	Lighting
851	Electric welding
871	Active assisted living (AAL)
881	Radiology and radiological physics
891	Electrobiology
901	Standardization
902	Conformity assessment
903	Risk assessment
904	Environmental standardization for electrical and electronic products and systems

Figure 7.6. The screenshot of IEC's categories included in their online dictionary available at http://www.electropedia.org/

Terminology search in the glossary gives comprehensive results that include the keyword and the category or a discipline. Entries in the glossary are detailed and contain different sub-types of the term. For example, the term transistor has 18 hits in the IEC glossary, each of which has its unique reference number, which it is depicted in Figure 7.7. below. However, only one is the subordinate term *transistor* with the reference number *521-04-46* assigned to a category number *521 – Semiconductor devices and integrated circuits*. This classification does not reflect the conceptual structure of this terminological system, though.

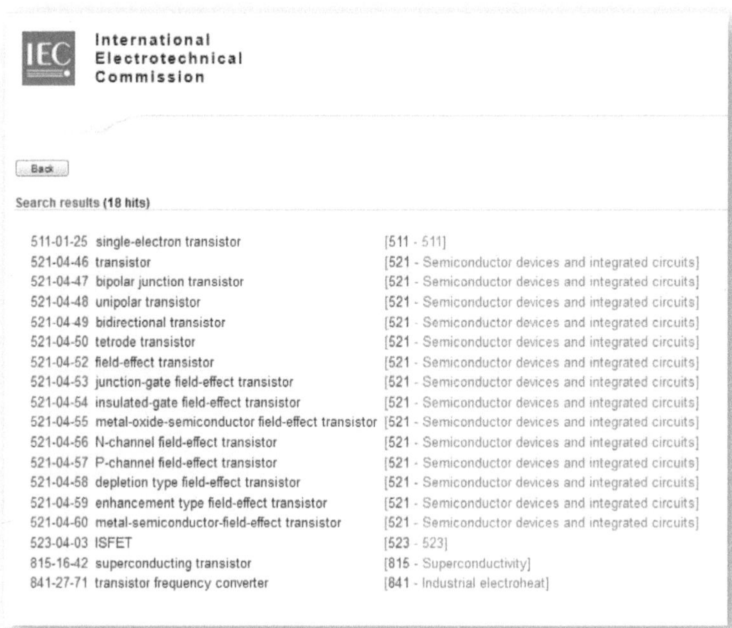
International
Electrotechnical
Commission

Back

Search results (18 hits)

511-01-25	single-electron transistor	[511 - 511]
521-04-46	transistor	[521 - Semiconductor devices and integrated circuits]
521-04-47	bipolar junction transistor	[521 - Semiconductor devices and integrated circuits]
521-04-48	unipolar transistor	[521 - Semiconductor devices and integrated circuits]
521-04-49	bidirectional transistor	[521 - Semiconductor devices and integrated circuits]
521-04-50	tetrode transistor	[521 - Semiconductor devices and integrated circuits]
521-04-52	field-effect transistor	[521 - Semiconductor devices and integrated circuits]
521-04-53	junction-gate field-effect transistor	[521 - Semiconductor devices and integrated circuits]
521-04-54	insulated-gate field-effect transistor	[521 - Semiconductor devices and integrated circuits]
521-04-55	metal-oxide-semiconductor field-effect transistor	[521 - Semiconductor devices and integrated circuits]
521-04-56	N-channel field-effect transistor	[521 - Semiconductor devices and integrated circuits]
521-04-57	P-channel field-effect transistor	[521 - Semiconductor devices and integrated circuits]
521-04-58	depletion type field-effect transistor	[521 - Semiconductor devices and integrated circuits]
521-04-59	enhancement type field-effect transistor	[521 - Semiconductor devices and integrated circuits]
521-04-60	metal-semiconductor-field-effect transistor	[521 - Semiconductor devices and integrated circuits]
523-04-03	ISFET	[523 - 523]
815-16-42	superconducting transistor	[815 - Superconductivity]
841-27-71	transistor frequency converter	[841 - Industrial electroheat]

Figure 7.7. The screenshot of the search results for the English term *transistor* generated from the IEC online glossary available at http://www.electropedia.org/

Terminology used in the MTCS disciplines exhibits a tendency towards unification and high level of precision, which is in alliance with Kozłowska's (2007) findings in terms the behaviour of terminology in hard sciences. On the other hand, cognitive methods of terminology creation cannot be ignored. The cognitive aspects are also present in the IEC glossary. There are instances of multiple entries for one term from the MTCS domains. The glossary contains 34 multiple entries. The multiword English term *cut-off frequency* is an example of the phenomenon. The glossary contains 8 hits with 7 entries for the very term, as it is presented in Figure 7.8. below. The detailed analysis of the phenomenon will be discussed in the next section of the chapter.

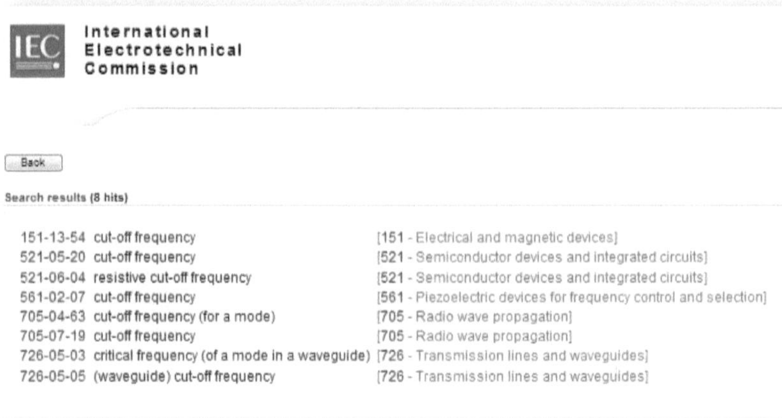

Figure 7.8. The screenshot of the search results for the English term *cut-off frequency* generated from the IEC online glossary available at http://www.electropedia.org/

Moreover, terminological synonymy is also reflected in the glossary. The entry contains a term with its synonymous alternative, and can be searched via each of them. The English MTCS multiword term *sampling frequency* is represented as *sampling rate* in the IEC glossary with the first term as an alternative. The screenshot of the IEC entry is shown in Figure 7.9. below.

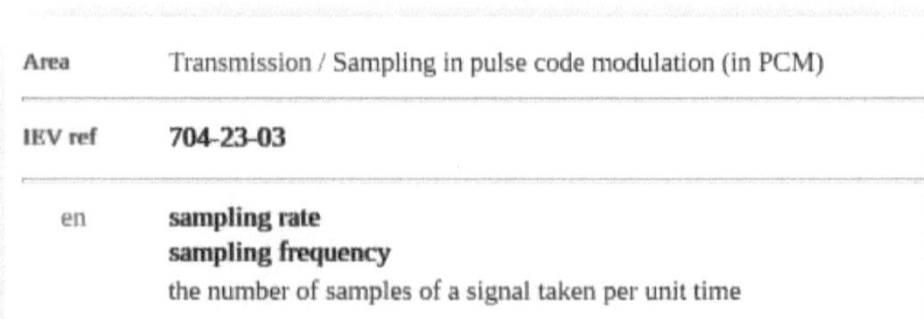

Figure 7.9. The screenshot of the search results for the English term *cut-off frequency* generated from the IEC online glossary available at http://www.electropedia.org/

The discrepancies between the IEC glossary and the MTCS research articles also concern extensions of abbreviations. In the analysed articles, the alphabetism *DAC* stands for the extension *Digital to Analog Converter*, whereas in the IEC glossary it refers to *derived air concentration*, as depicted in the Figure 7.10 below. Homonymy is a common phenomenon in compressed terminology, but it usually concerns terms in various disciplines. In this case, the compressed form has two different referents within a group of related subject fields.

Area	Nuclear instrumentation: Physical phenomena, basic concepts, instruments, systems, equipment and detectors / Radiation protection instrumentation and dosimetry
IEV ref	**395-05-28**
en	**derived air concentration** DAC air concentration of a single radionuclide, that if present for 40 hours per week over 50 weeks and inhaled at 0,020 $m^3 min^{-1}$ by reference man, will result in the uptake of one Annual Limit on Intake (ALI)

Figure 7.10. The screenshot of the entry of the English term *DAC* generated from the IEC online glossary available at http://www.electropedia.org/

Other differences between terminology in the MTCS texts and the IEC glossary pertain to different word combinations, which result in forming completely different terms. For example, one of the eponym MTCS corpus realisations *Schottky*, being an attributive of the term *Schottky diode* contains other eponym combinations in the IEC glossary, such as *Schottky barier* or *Schottky effect*. The multiword combination *common mode* is another interesting example. In the MTCS research papers there are combinations with *rejection*, *feedback*, *voltage*, *control* or *output*, but the IEC glossary contains 10 terminological combinations, which are presented in Figure 7.11 below, of which only two overlap: *rejection* and *voltage*.

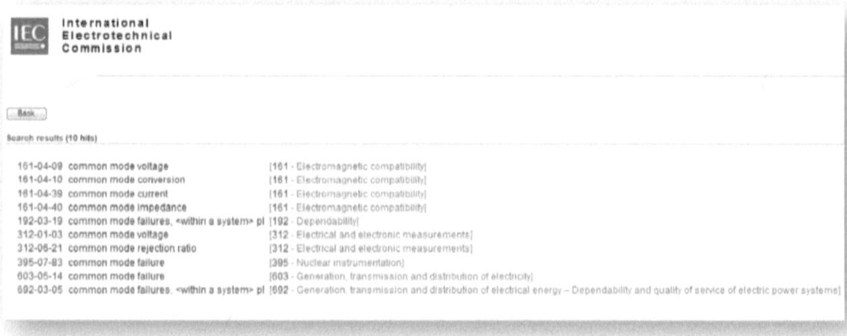

Figure 7.11. The screenshot of the search results for the English term *common mode* generated from the IEC online glossary available at http://www.electropedia.org/

However, there are also cases of a lack of the IEC entry for a term. It concerns mainly multiword MTCS terminology, adjectives, verbs as well as abbreviations and symbols. Among the terms extracted from the analysed research papers via Sketch Engine, there is a lack of 23 singleword and 40 multiword terms, which accounts for 48 % and 56 % respectively. The differences might have various reasons, but it is worth mentioning that the electrotechnical domains pertain to electronics and telecommunication, and do not cover computer science.

All things considered, the domains of new technologies are relatively new empirical and practical, thus borrowing terminology from other, more traditional subject fields. The fields are strictly connected and it is difficult to draw a definite borderline between disciplines. Terminology used in the MTCS research papers is interdisciplinary, which reflects such a character of these closely related subject fields and their practical character. Terminology in the fields of electrical engineering and electronics is standardised by the International Electrotechnical Commission (IEC), but the developed glossary does not fully reflect the domain-specific terminology extracted via Sketch Enging, which suggests the retrospective character of the standard.

7.10. Definitions

Definitions are a manifestation of terminological work and determine its quality (Suonuuti, 2001). For the purpose of the analysis, Lukszyn & Zmarzer's (2001) classification of definitions was taken into account as well as Löckinger et al. (2015), Suonuuti (2001), Lušicky & Wissik's (2015) understanding of the intensional definition. As a point of reference, a general language dictionary was included, i.e. Longman Dictionary of Contemporary English for the extracted MTCS terms. In addition, specialised language dictionaries were consulted to draw comparisons. The departure points were the definitions included in the IEC glossary, but they were compared with specialised dictionaries available online, such as TechTerms The Computer Dictionary and Wikipedia as a last resort. The definitions exhibit major differences depending on the dictionary and they are shown on the example of the term *diode* for each type of the dictionary in Figures 7.12, 7.13 and 7.14 below.

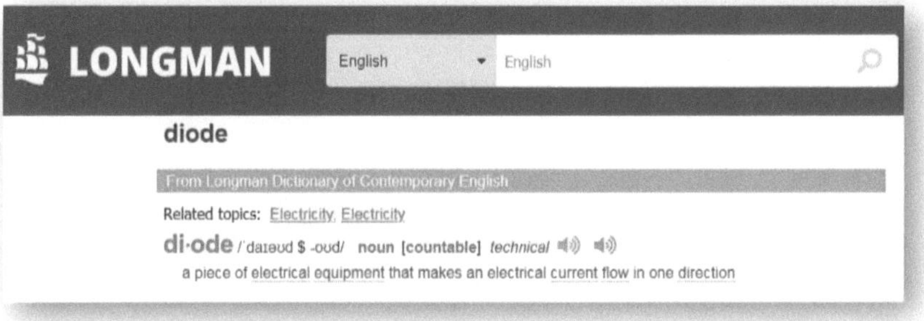

Figure 7.12. The screenshot of the entry of the English term *diode* generated from the LDCE online dictionary available at https://www.ldoceonline.com

The LDCE definition provides a general idea of the meaning of the term followed by the general language corpus examples which show how to use the word. General language dictionaries are created for non-experts who want to verify what a word means. On the other hand, more specialised dictionaries, like TechTerms or Wikipedia contain very detailed, descriptive, and informative definitions aimed at non-experts interested in the topic who wish to acquire specialised knowledge. They constitute an instance of vertical communication, because they are written in the general language and provide thorough explanation. The screenshot of an exemplary definition from TechTerms dictionary is provided in Figure 7.13 below.

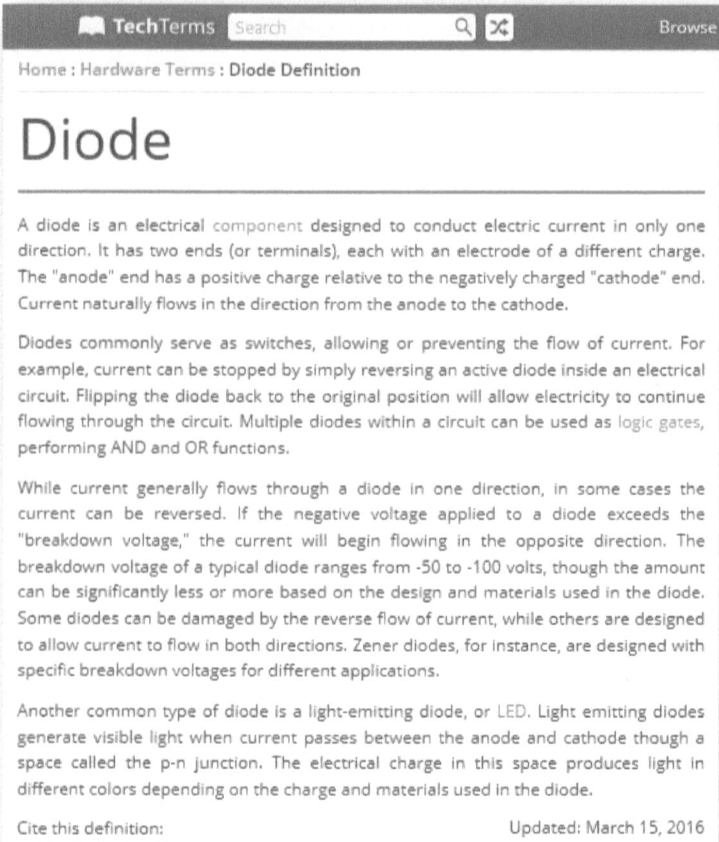

TechTerms Search Browse

Home : Hardware Terms : Diode Definition

Diode

A diode is an electrical component designed to conduct electric current in only one direction. It has two ends (or terminals), each with an electrode of a different charge. The "anode" end has a positive charge relative to the negatively charged "cathode" end. Current naturally flows in the direction from the anode to the cathode.

Diodes commonly serve as switches, allowing or preventing the flow of current. For example, current can be stopped by simply reversing an active diode inside an electrical circuit. Flipping the diode back to the original position will allow electricity to continue flowing through the circuit. Multiple diodes within a circuit can be used as logic gates, performing AND and OR functions.

While current generally flows through a diode in one direction, in some cases the current can be reversed. If the negative voltage applied to a diode exceeds the "breakdown voltage," the current will begin flowing in the opposite direction. The breakdown voltage of a typical diode ranges from -50 to -100 volts, though the amount can be significantly less or more based on the design and materials used in the diode. Some diodes can be damaged by the reverse flow of current, while others are designed to allow current to flow in both directions. Zener diodes, for instance, are designed with specific breakdown voltages for different applications.

Another common type of diode is a light-emitting diode, or LED. Light emitting diodes generate visible light when current passes between the anode and cathode though a space called the p-n junction. The electrical charge in this space produces light in different colors depending on the charge and materials used in the diode.

Cite this definition: Updated: March 15, 2016

Figure 7.13. The screenshot of the entry of the English term *diode* generated from the TechTerms online dictionary available at https://techterms.com/

Finally, the IEC definitions differ from the latter two in a number of respects. On the one hand they are brief and laconic, and provide the very core of the term. On the other, more complex terms are thoroughly defined and contain formulae and schematic drawings. Each term has its unique reference number, which is a key to access the definition. However, they are written in the specialised language, because they are created to facilitate horizontal expert-to-expert communication. The glossary creators assume a certain level of expertise among target users. In addition, the definitions are only in English and French, which is the reflection of Graddol's (2000) hierarchy of languages with English and French on top of the pyramid as big languages. The exemplary definition from the IEC glossary is provided in Figure 7.14 below.

Figure 7.14. The screenshot of the entry of the English term *diode* generated from the IEC online glossary available at http://www.electropedia.org/

However, the MTCS realisations indicate that the authors assume a sufficient level of expertise on diodes from readers and do not provide definitions in their texts. The only working definition which was provided pertains only to a specific type of diode along with its characteristics, as illustrated by Example (7.47.) below:

(7.47.) *As a consequence, there were produced the first (p-n)-(l-h) diodes [31,32,33] with reduced, by two orders of magnitude, the reverse currents and with linear in five decades characteristics of the logarithm forward current vs the voltage,* ***so-called logarithmic diodes.***

Instead, the scientists describe the details of performed experiments, and the procedures that diodes were subjected to, which is shown in Example (7.48.) below interpreting the visual content:

(7.48.) *Each time the DMOS turns off, the* ***diode*** *takes over (blue diamonds) and conducts the current flowing through the inductor (yellow triangles).*

On the other hand, the authors of MTCS texts include context definitions, like the one which is provided in Example (7.49.):

(7.49.) *The* ***CIC filters*** *are a class of finite impulse response (FIR) filters designated for multi-rate signal processing.*

The definition written by the scientists is focused on the type and the purpose of the filters, whereas the one developed in Wikipedia gives details of their structure and the way they operate, and therefore is only partially compatible, i.e. Example (7.50.):

(7.50.) *In digital signal processing, a* ***cascaded integrator–comb (CIC)*** *is an optimized class of finite impulse response (FIR) filter combined with an interpolator or decimator.*
A CIC filter consists of one or more integrator and comb filter pairs. In the case of a decimating CIC, the input signal is fed through one or more cascaded integrators, then a down-sampler, followed by one or more comb sections (equal in number to the number of integrators).

However, it needs to be pointed out that Wikipedia cannot be fully trusted as practically anyone can make their contributions, and it was created for non-experts, hence the lack of compatibility. Yet, the analysis of context definitions in the MTCS research papers is consistent with earlier corpus studies (Pearson, 1998).

The comparison between definitions from general and specialised dictionaries as well as a dedicated standardised glossary reveals considerable differences.

There are 18 general language definitions for singleword terms, 16 specialised language definitions and 25 included in the IEC glossary out of 48 identified terms. In addition, 4 terms are defined more than once in the IEC glossary, and one definition pertains to a different extension of the abbreviation *DAC*, which was discussed in the previous section and shown in Figure 7.10. In terms of the type of definitions, the majority of them are intensional (30) and 4 factual from all analysed dictionaries. The latter define extracted adjectives, since it is difficult to place them in the terminological system. Moreover, one of the terms in the IEC, *frequency* is defined by an antonym, as shown in Figure 7.15 below.

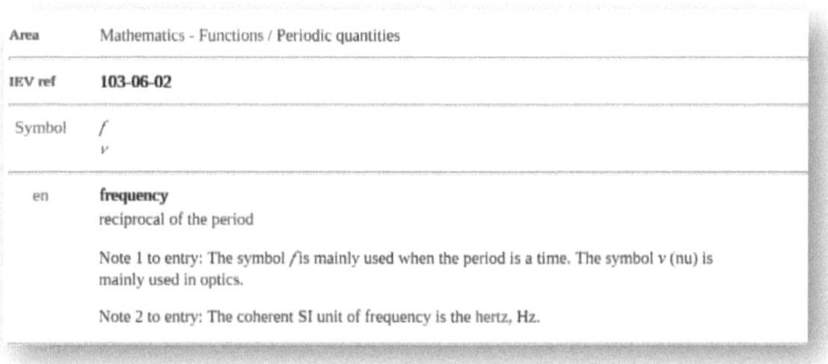

Area	Mathematics - Functions / Periodic quantities
IEV ref	**103-06-02**
Symbol	*f* *ν*
en	**frequency** reciprocal of the period Note 1 to entry: The symbol *f* is mainly used when the period is a time. The symbol ν (nu) is mainly used in optics. Note 2 to entry: The coherent SI unit of frequency is the hertz, Hz.

Figure 7.15. The screenshot of the definition for the term *frequency* generated from the IEC online glossary available at http://www.electropedia.org/

Abbreviations and symbols frequently occurring in the MTCS research articles are not included in any nomenclature. The probability of occurrence of definitions for multiword terms is even lower. There are only 3 general language definitions, 2 specialised language definitions and 32 IEC definitions, but interestingly 22 terms contain multiple definitions in the IEC glossary, ranging from 2 to even 10. Like in the case of singleword terms, there is a predominant majority of intensional definitions (33), followed by 4 factual definitions.

As mentioned above, the IEC glossary contains multiple definitions for terminology. They focus on different aspects of the term. The core or centre of the term remains stable, but there are peripheral aspects, like coefficients, components or specific applications. However, multiple definitions are not always compatible with the MTCS realisations. For example, the multiword term *common mode* generated via Sketch Engine from the English MTCS subcorpus forms complex terminological combinations with nouns *rejection*, *feedback*, *voltage*, and *control* to form the following terms:

common mode rejection,
common mode feedback,
common mode voltage,
common mode control.

However, only two of them are represented among the 10 definitions provided in the IEC glossary, which is depicted in Figure 7.16 below.

Figure 7.16. The screenshot of the definition for the English term *common mode* generated from the IEC online glossary available at http://www.electropedia.org/

Moreover, there are two definitions for *common mode voltage* and the term *common mode rejection* acts as an attributive for *ratio*. The differences might stem from the fact that the glossary contains historical data, whereas research papers describe prototype solutions, which is reflected in novel use of terminology.

The lack of terms might be motivated in a number of ways. MTCS research papers contain new terminology that is not yet included. Moreover, terms might reflect too low frequency of occurrence. Multiword terms might either be newly coined or be of an unsure status between a collocation and a term. On the other hand, they might constitute a subordinate term, of higher granularity in the system or a strictly domain-specific complex term.

In conclusion, the comparative analysis of definitions of MTCS terminology reflects the adjustments dictionary and glossary writers make to tailor the contents to the needs of the target users. General language and specialised language dictionaries created for non-experts are written in a plain language, whereas the IEC glossary is aimed at professionals, and therefore the language is highly specialised. On the other hand, the latter contains either very laconic, brief definitions or very explanatory with multimodal elements along with equivalents in 18 languages but the definitions are provided only in English and French. The majority of definitions, regardless of the type of the reference, are intensional, giving insights of term's characteristics and its place in the terminological system.

7.11. The ontology of MTCS terminology

Ontologies are an answer for the need for an independent system of classification and categorisation of the terminological system in order to facilitate processing of knowledge (Gliński, 205; Grzelak, 2013; Bajerowska; 2017). There are two factors necessary for the clarity of expression, i.e. categorisation and hierarchisation (Gliński, 2005). Moreover, there are differences between the conceptual network provided by experts and textual realisations that can be verified by an ontology (Roche, 2015).

Terminology in the MTCS domains can also be categorised and hierarchised into ontologies. The author decided to take a mixed approach to the process of creation: both top-down and bottom-up approaches, but the most obvious terms were classified first and then followed by the less evident (Gliński, 205; Grzelak, 2013). The ontologies were consulted with specialised dictionaries and verified by a subject-field expert as advised by the literature on the subject (Toledo-Alvaro et al., 2012).

MTCS terminology generated by Sketch Engine from the collection of scientific texts exhibits a considerable variety. At the first stage of developing an ontology, categories of terms were identified. MTCS terms can by classified into 9 categories, i.e. hardware, software, processes, physical quantities, units of measurement, image processing, standards, properties and technology of production, which is depicted in Figure 7.17 on page 234. Singleword terms constitute the level of superordinate terminology of lower granularity and multiword terms, of higher granularity, occupy the second and third level of subordinate terms.

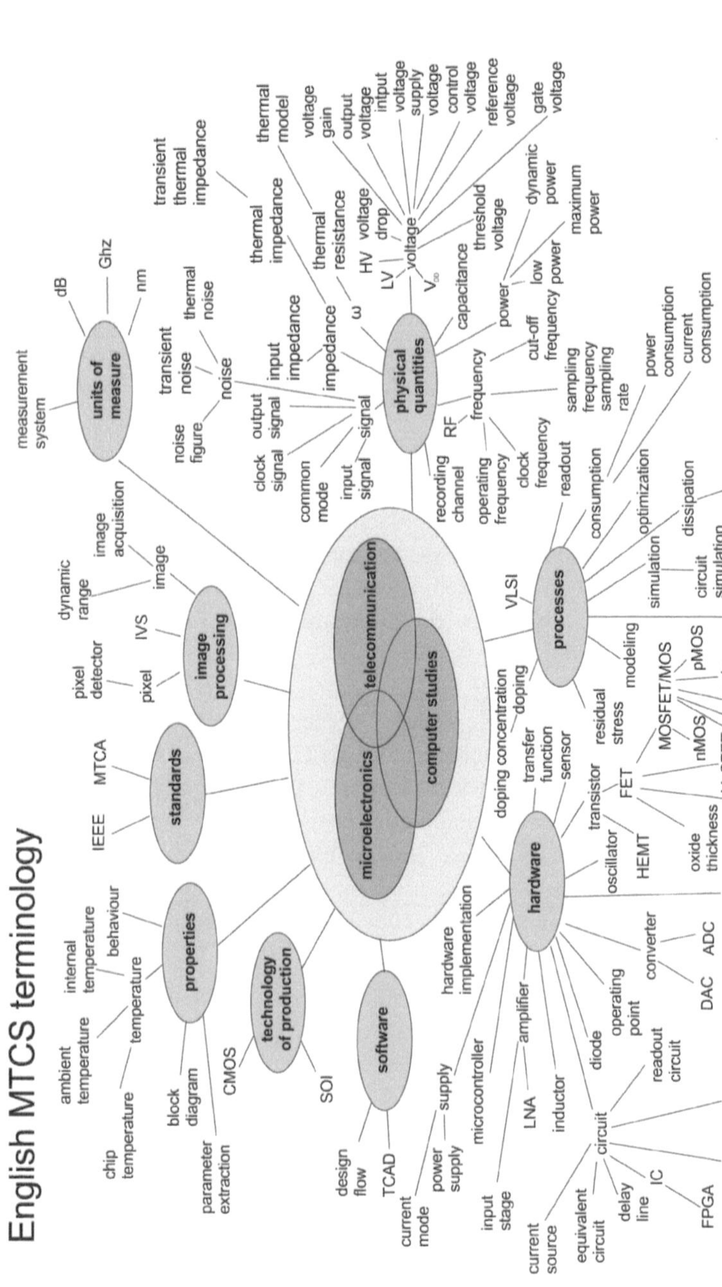

Figure 7.17. The ontology developed from keyword terminology generated by Sketch Engine from the MTCS corpus

Categories exhibit discrepancies in terms of the number of constituents. The MTCS domains make an exceptionally frequent use of terms referring to hardware, physical quantities, processes and properties which emphasise their practical and empirical nature. Moreover, terms denoting hardware contain strictly electronic devices. In terms of units of measurement, the category contains 3 items, which act as a confirmation of the existence of hybrid terms, and a higher reliance of scientists and engineers on results of measurements or finding optimal parameters to proposed solutions. Terminology concerned with physical quantities is focused on the aspects of the electric current, whereas the terminology categories referring to software and physical phenomena differ completely in the number of identified terms.

The biggest advantage of ontologies lies in the precise placement of ambiguous or vague terms in the correct place of the whole system. This is especially crucial for translators, purportedly non-experts in a given subject field, who want to render the source text into the target language. For example, the term *delay line* would suggest a dimension property, or a *filter order* might be understood as an arrangement of filters, whereas in fact the first is a kind of an electronic component that causes delays in the system and the latter refers to elements that cause delays in a circuit which can be calculated, and therefore predicted, as shown in the concordance lines below (Examples 7.51. and 7.52.).

(7.51.) *Output pulse of a basic topology generator based on the 2N2369 transistor using a discrete 10 pF capacitor instead of the* ***delay line****.*

(7.52.) *Calculation of FIR* ***filter order*** *requires solution of quadratic equation.*

Moreover, the term *channel region* might imply a reference to image processing, but in fact it is an element of a transistor, which is best illustrated by example (7.53.) from the concordance line below:

(7.53.) *In the TFET, this mechanism can be switched on and off abruptly by controlling the band bending* ***in the channel region*** *by means of the gate* ***bias****.*

Also, the term *bias* might imply an abstract notion, but in electronics it is a type of current that flows through transistors and other devices.

The most surprising are, however, the discrepancies in corpus realisations of abbreviations, i.e. CMOS, nMOS, pMOS or MOS/MOSFET. Definitions suggest that these are different types of technology, but in the MTCS corpus the first is directly referred to as *technology of production* (Example 7.54), whereas the latter are used to denote different types of transistors. For this reason, they were assigned to different categories (Example (7.55.) below).

(7.54.) *The rapid evolution of* ***CMOS technologies*** *has made the development of fully integrated circuits yield the implementation of telecommunications systems where fully integrated wireless receivers.*

(7.55.) *Also, it should be noted that the sizes of* ***NMOS and PMOS transistors*** *that are utilized in TGs are considered the same in this proposed design.*

In some of these cases, definitions do not reflect the contextual meaning and the place of terms in the whole terminological system, only concordance lines give clues about their relations with other terms and where they should be placed in the system.

In conclusion, ontologies, a method of knowledge into a systematic and autonomic representation, are based on contextual meaning and relationships between terms deriving from authentic texts which are verified with dictionary definitions and subject-field experts. The MTCS terminology organised into an ontology shows surprising relationships between terms, which is particularly useful for users who need to become fully acquainted with the terminological system, like for example translators.

7.12. Concluding remarks to Chapter 7

This chapter presents analyses of different aspects of technical terminology in the domains of new technologies. The behaviour of terminology in the MTCS domains reflects both approaches to terminology description. On the one hand there is a strong tendency to use standardised terms, but the cognitive mechanisms cannot be discarded since they are productive and effective in terminology creation. As a result, they allow for better cognition and understanding of novel aspects of research and proposed solutions.

In terms of their structure, terms mainly appear to be nominal and in the Singular form, which is consistent with earlier studies (Sager et al., 1980). The language of new technologies tends to form multiword terminological units (complex terms) which ensure precision of expression, which will be studied in the following chapter. In addition, the tendency to create hybrid terminology containing abbreviations and/or units of measurement also needs to be emphasised as a domain-specific feature of the MTCS terminology.

Moreover, the majority of terms are borrowed, forming internationalisms, and the source languages suggest the dominant position of English in science as terminology has its roots mainly in classical languages of science, such as Latin and Greek, and rather restricted to hard sciences. There is also a considerable number of neologisms, but there is an overall tendency to use internationalisms.

Both borrowings and neologisms suggest the young age and interdisciplinarity of the MTCS disciplines, as terms are borrowed from more traditional disciplines. Migration of terminology from one domain to another is a common phenomenon. As a result, terms expand their range of usage to new domains and become interdisciplinary. Terminological synonymy and polysemy are also present in the analysed texts, despite a strong tendency to standardisation. Nevertheless, there is as strong tendency to use well-established terminology due to the empirical nature of the MTCS domains.

Definitions found in the dedicated IEC nomenclature are adjusted to the needs of target users, but they constitute rather partial reflection of terminology, which suggests two reasons: rapid development of these disciplines and/or lack of engagement from the glossary creators. Dictionaries aimed at less professional target readership contain more thorough explanations, yet not all terms can be found there, either. Finally, MTCS terminology extracted by Sketch Engine and its corpus realisations have allowed for developing an ontology, which shows surprising relationships between terms. Singleword terms constitute superordinate categories whereas multiword terminology allows for a precise assignment of subordinate terms in the whole terminological system.

Yet, it is not terminology alone that accounts for meaning-making in the MTCS research papers. It is supplemented with other devices, like lexical bundles and persuasion techniques which allow for convincing the target readers about research results and proposed practical solutions to identified problems. Phraseological units and other linguistice vehicles are discussed in Chapters 8 and 9.

Chapter 8 Phraseology in the MTCS research articles

The current chapter is focused on complex phrases that facilitate communicating science to wide audiences in the MTCS domains. Communication in the scientific community is conducted via lexical units, patterns that are peculiar to a given subject field rather than individual words. Therefore, the analysis entails domain-specific collocations and other phraseological units in the quantitative and qualitative approach. The scrutiny of collocations also attempts at drawing a borderline between a collocation and a multiword term.

Moreover, the author also conducted the analysis of lexical bundles, or n-grams, scientists and engineers use to successfully convey their messages. The scrutiny is to determine the differences in the types and functions of lexical bundles which are found in the analysed research papers. In addition, the generated n-grams by Sketch Engine from the MTCS corpus are contrasted with a parallel study to find the most common forms of expression among scientists.

8.1. Collocations in the MTCS research papers

Scientists as a community develop specific forms of communication, and are more likely to communicate via specific linguistic patterns rather than single words. As a result, collocations hold responsibility for the creation of meaning (Gledhill, 2000; Peacock, 2012). In specialised communication, collocations form typical and recurrent word combinations, and therefore need to be studied within each domain because a number of collocations form domain-specific complex terms. As a result, the borderline between a collocation and a multiword term is fuzzy (Gruntar Jermol, 2007; Peacock, 2012). For this reason, the analysis of the most frequently appearing word combinations in the MTCS texts was conducted.

According to Gruntar Jermol (2007), the study of collocations should be limited to two-word combinations, i.e. a base and a collocate, the first context-free and the latter context-dependent, but complex terminology is often comprised of 3 or 4 elements (Sager et al. 1980). Therefore, due to the need to achieve a high level of precision in conveying the message, the authors of the MTCS research articles decide to form complex multiword phrases, not only restricted to two-word combinations. For this reason, the author decided to analyse collocations within the range of -2 to +2. The number of singleword terms was limited to about 40. The cut-off frequency was set at. 100.00 times per million tokens in.

As a result, 40 singleword terms were generated from the MTCS corpus. For each term, 4 collocation candidates were extracted from the list. The full list of collocation candidates in provided in Table 8.1. below.

Table 8.1. The list of keyword terminology with the most frequent collocation candidates generated from the corpus via Sketch Engine

No	English	Frequency	Collocation candidates
1	circuit	2438,82	integrated, proposed, readout, analog
2	voltage	2027,33	supply, threshold, low, gain
3	simulation	1384,00	results, TCAD, performed, numerical
4	transistor	1325,79	MOS, PMOS, NMOS, bipolar, situated, point-contact, field-effect
5	technology	1321,78	CMOS, SOI, nm, trends, process
6	sensor	837,03	wireless, temperature, Hall, smart, pressure
7	CMOS	763,61	technology/technologies, nm, process, SOI
8	amplifier	738,67	operational, AC, chopper, charge
9	capacitance	443,60	parasitic, equivalent, detector, feedback
10	pixel	415,50	detector/detectors, readout, active, hybrid
11	Nm	401,45	130/65/180/200, etc., CMOS, technology
12	capacitor	358,30	sampling, MIM, CDET, unit
13	RF (radi0o frequency)	351,27	backplane, receiver, signals, station
14	dB	343,24	NF, gain, temperature, below
15	modeling	341,23	compact, simulation, analytical, behavioural
16	diode	325,18	rectifier, MOS, silicon, MBR1045
17	LV (low voltage)	307,11	circuitry, devices, range, transistors
18	impedance	294,96	transient, thermal, input, matching
19	oscillator	264,96	ring, temperature-controlled/controlled, relaxation, quadrature
20	MOSFET	263,95	Models, transistor, integrated, operation
21	IC (integrated circuit)	261,95	mA, multichannel, readout, collector
22	readout	260,94	electronic, pixel, circuit, chip
22	MOS	229,83	transistor/transistors, resistances, diode
24	optimization	224,81	swarm, particle, ant, methodologies
25	inductor	203,74	tapered, spiral, integrated, square
26	VDD	203,70	supply, voltage, increases, μm
27	inverter	201,73	cascaded, starved, chain, mirror

Table 8.1. Continued

No	English	Frequency	Collocation candidates
28	ADC (converter)	199,72	pipelined, 10-/12-bit, channels, designed
29	SOI	198,72	FD, MOSFETs, technology, double, CMOS
30	HV (high voltage)	195,71	ICs, switches, current-module, space, buffers
31	ehaviour/ behaviour	193,70	conditional, switching, age-dependent, best, similar
32	GHz	183,66	2.4/1.3, frequency, band, bandwith
33	doping	171,62	concentration/concentrations, profie/profiles, density, ND, level
34	microcontroller	144,52	AVR/Octalynx/RISC/Atmel, families presented
35	DAC	141,51	6-/7-bit, primary, trim/trimming, steering
36	NMOS	119,43	transistors, THz, detectors, branches, mirror
37	pMOS	119,43	transistors, branches, mirror
38	MTCA	111,40	backplane, crate/crates, digitizer, fast, architecture
39	VLSI	107,39	fuzzy, systems, CMOS, circuits,
40	VESFET	103,37	JL/junctionless, transistor, FET, n-type

In the MTCS research papers, the most common lexemes collating with keyword terms are nouns, adjectives and verbs, but there are also other collocates, like abbreviations, symbols, or chemical formulae. Moreover, there are also proper nouns, because eponyms occur frequently in technical scientific disciplines. The full list divided into individual parts of speech is provided in Table 8.2. below.

Table 8.2. The list of collocates divided into parts of speech generated from the MTCS corpus via Sketch Engine

Parts of speech	Collocates
nouns	readout, supply, threshold, gain, results, point-contact, field-effect, trends, process, temperature, pressure, technology, chopper, charge, detector, feedback, hybrid, unit, backplane, receiver, signal, station, simulation, rectifier, silicon, circuitry, device, range, transistor, input, ring, quadrature, model, operation, multichannel, collector, electronics, pixel, chip, restistance, diode, swarm, ant, methodology, square, voltage, chain, mirror, channel, 12-bit, current-module, space, frequency, band, bandwith, concentration, profile, density, level, family, branches, backplane, crate, digitizer, architecture, system
proper nouns	Hall
adjectives	analog, low, numerical, bipolar, wireless, smart, operational, parasitic, equivalent, active, analytical, behavioural, transient, thermal, spiral, conditional, best, age-dependent, similar, primary, fuzzy, JL/junctionless, compact, double
verbs	presented, proposed, performed, situated, steering, settling, sampling, matching, controlled, tapered, increases, cascaded, starved, pipelined, switches, buffers, designed, trim
other	TCAD, MOS, PMOS, NMOS, SOI, CMOS, nm, AC, MIM, CDET, FD, MOSFET, ICs, mA, NF, ND, FET, below

As can be seen from Table 8.2. above, the predominant majority of collocates are nouns, followed by adjectives, which confirms the quantitative analysis of multiword terminology, which was described in Chapter 7. The extracted collocate candidates are comprised of 66 nouns and 24 adjectives. Verbs as are used as collocates in 17 cases, and other parts of speech account for 18. As a result, the total number of collocates generated from the MTCS research papers amounts to 125.

Of the whole list of collocates generated by Sketch Engine, the most frequent collocates can be identified which are nouns and verbs, which is shown in Table 8.3. below.

Table 8.3. The summary of most common collocates divided into parts of speech generated from the MTCS corpus via Sketch Engine

parts of speech	the most frequent collocates
nouns	gain, MOS, CMOS, SOI, process, temperature, technology, detector, readout, backplane, transistor, circuit, NMOS, PMOS, device, supply, mirror, branches
verbs	Integrated

The empirical and practical character of the analysed disciplines of new technologies is emphasised by the use of scalar and construction collocates. As a result, there are 18 scalar collocates and 16 construction collocates of MTCS terminology. The list of identified scalar and construction collocates is presented in Table 8.4. below.

Table 8.4. The summary of scalar and construction collocates generated from the MTCS corpus via Sketch Engine

type of collocates	collocates
scalar collocates	range, level, frequency, readout, temperature, controlled, unit, 130.180, etc. bipolar, threshold, density, numerical, results, trends, analytical, increases, feedback, thermal, detector,
construction collocates	performed, module, architecture, profile, technology, square, operation, model, ring, silicon, sampling, space, steering, quadrature, pipelined, tapered

In conclusion, the quantitative analysis of the generated collocates for singleword terms shows that the majority of collocates are nouns and adjectives, which is consistent with previous studies on the subject. Moreover, scalar and construction collocates emphasise the empirical and practical character of the MTCS disciplines.

8.2. Drawing a borderline between a collocation and a multiword term

MTCS research articles are written to communicate results of research verified empirically in a precise manner. For this reason, scientists use specific word combinations, ranging from free combinations, restricted collocations to multiword terms (Menon & Mukudan, 2012). Moreover, as literature suggests, collocations, being the most recurrent word combinations, are in fact domain-specific terminology (Gledhill, 2000; Peacock, 2012). However, it is difficult to determine the difference between a collocation and a multiword term, because complex noun phrases often constitute standard multiword terminology (Gruntar Jermol, 2007; Peacock, 2012). As a result, word combinations and terms in scientific texts consist of 3 or 4 elements, even hybrids with chemical formulae, symbols, units of measurement, etc. to ensure precision and clarity (Sager et al., 1980). For this reason, the author decided to determine which of the identified word combinations are collocations, complex terms, or perhaps a borderline case. The study entailed the consultation of corpus realisations with a specialised language dictionary and the dedicated IEC glossary. Moreover, the developed ontology, discussed in the previous chapter, acted as an additional reference. The results of the analysis are provided in Table 8.5. for the analysed terminology.

Table 8.5. English collocations, terms and borderline word combinations generated from the MTCS corpus via Sketch Engine

MTCS terms	complex terms	collocations	borderline
circuit	integrated circuit readout circuit analog circuit	proposed circuit	
voltage	supply voltage threshold voltage voltage gain		low voltage
simulation		simulation results TCAD simulation performed simulation numerical simulation	
transistor	MOS transistor pMOS transistor nMOS transistor bipolar transistor field-effect transistor point-contact transistor	transistor situated	
technology		number+nm technology technology trends technology process	CMOS technology – domain specific SOI technology

Table 8.5. Continued

MTCS terms	complex terms	collocations	borderline
sensor	wireless sensor (network) temperature sensor Hall sensor smart sensor pressure sensor		
CMOS		number+nm CMOS technology CMOS process CMOS SOI	CMOS technology
amplifier	AC amplifier chopper amplifier operational amplifier charge amplifier		
capacitance	parasitic capacitance equivalent capacitance feedback capacitance	detector capacitance	
pixel	pixel readout (chip) active pixel (sensor APS) hybrid pixel detector		
nm		65/130/180/200 nm CMOS technology	
capacitor	MIM capacitor	sampling capacitor capacitor CDET unit capacitor	
RF	RF backplane RF receiver RF station	RF signal	
dB		gain (dB) NF temperature 125^0 (dB) below ± 0.5 dB	
modeling	compact modeling analytical modeling behavioural modeling simulation modeling		
diode	rectifier diode MOS diode silicon diode	MBR1045 diode – model, brand	

(Continued)

Table 8.5. Continued

MTCS terms	complex terms	collocations	borderline
LV	LV transistor	LV circuitry LV devices LV range	
impedance	transient thermal impedance input impedance impedance matching		
oscillator	Ring oscillator (voltage) controlled oscillator (VCO) Temperature-controlled oscillator (TCO) Relaxation oscillator quadrature oscillator		
MOSFET	MOSFET model MOSFET transistor	integrated MOSFET MOSFET operation	
IC	readout IC collector current Ic	mA IC	multichannel IC
readout	readout chip (single) pixel readout circuit	electronic readout	
MOS	MOS transistor	MOS based resistance	MOS diode
optimization	Particle Swarm Optimization Ant Colony Optimization (ACO)		optimization methodology
inductor			integrated inductor tapered inductor spiral inductor square inductor
V_{DD}	Supply voltage V_{DD} V_{DD} voltage supply	µm V_{dd} Supply voltage V_{DD} inceases	
inverter	(current) starved inverter Cascaded inverter	Inverter chain	switched-current mirror inverter
ADC	Pipelined ADC* – pipeline ADC	10-/12-bit ADC (model) designed ADC	ADC channel
SOI	SOI technology *FD SOI MOSFETs*	*SOI CMOS* technology	double SOI wafer

Table 8.5. Continued

MTCS terms	**complex terms**	**collocations**	**borderline**
HV		HV ICs HV current module	HV switch HV buffer HV space
behaviour		similar behaviour the best behaviour	*age-dependent behaviour* conditional switching behaviour
GHz		2.4 GHz 2 GHz bandwidth 2.4 GHz band 3.5 GHz frequency	
doping	doping profile doping concentration (ND) doping density	doping level	
microcontroller		OctaLynx/ AVR Atmega/Atmel AVR microcontroller family presented microcontroller	
DAC	current-steering DAC	primary DAC 6-/7-bit trimming DAC (in-channel) trimming DAC	
NMOS	NMOS transistor	NMOS THz detector NMOS current mirror NMOS branch	
PMOS	PMOS transistor	PMOS current mirror PMOS branch	
MTCA		MTCA.4 crate fast MTCA MTCA.4 architecture MTCA backplane MTCA Fast Digitizer	
VLSI		VLSI fuzzy (processor architecture) VLSI circuits VLSI CMOS circuits	VLSI systems
VeSFET	Vertical-slit FET (VeSFET) Vertical-Slit Field-Effect Transistor (VeSFET)		junctionless VeSFET n-type junctionless VeSFET

The analysis shows that 28 word combinations out of 40 analysed singleword terms are in fact subject field terminology. 9 multiword terms are reflected in the multiword key terminology generated by Sketch Engine, i.e. *threshold voltage, supply voltage, voltage gain, thermal impedance, transient thermal impedance, readout circuit, integrated circuit, doping concentration,* and *pixel detector*. Of these 28 terms, 10 terms form adjective+noun combinations and 15 terms are abbreviation+noun terminological hybrids, which is not fully consistent with Peacock's (2012) findings. Moreover, the list contains one eponym, *Hall sensor*, named after an American physicist. There are 30 combinations which were evaluated as collocations and 14 borderline word combinations between a collocation and domain-specific term. In terms of the terminological deviations, one of the abbreviations, *IC,* has two unrelated extensions, i.e. either *integrated circuit* or *collector current,* but spelled *Ic*. The term *pipelined ADC* is spelled without the *–ed* suffix as *pipeline ADC* in reference materials.

Collocations are also formed from more general terms, like *technology, simulation*. Similarly to complex terms, there are either noun+noun combinations or adjective+noun combinations but there are also hybrid combinations with numbers (*6-/7-bit trimming DAC*), units of measurement (*3.5 GHz frequency, μm* V_{dd}), brand names (*OctaLynx/ AVR Atmega/Atmel AVR microcontroller, MTCA.4 architecture*), product reference number (*MBR1045 diode*) and other symbols (*temperature 125⁰ (dB), below ± 0.5 dB*). There are also combinations which are the result of anaphoric reference, such as *Vertical-Slit Field-Effect Transistor (VeSFET)*

However, the borderline word combinations are the most interesting cases. They are domain-specific, but it might be difficult to determine whether they fulfil Gruntar Jermol's (2007) three criteria, i.e. whether they express a well-defined reality, belong to a domain-specific conceptual system, and they are separated by their conceptual autonomy. There is a definite lack of definition in reference materials, but they meet at least two conditions. For example, the combination *low voltage* can be treated as a term, because scientists and engineers are implicitly acquainted with the range of voltage and the current frequency. As a result it meets the three criteria mentioned above. Moreover, an *ADC channel* describes a specific point in the *device*, and for professionals it is a term as well as *junctionless VeSFET*, a type of a transistor, in reference materials called *JL transistor*. However, there are borderline cases, like the *multichannel IC* – a type of an integrated circuit which also meets the requirements, but it is a proposed, novel solution, and therefore used idiosyncratically, i.e. (Example 8.1. below)

(8.1.) *The architecture of the proposed prototype of the* ***multichannel IC****, called Optical Radiation Readout Circuit (ORRC), is presented schematically in Fig. 1.*

But there are combinations, like *CMOS technology* or *SOI technology* in which the attributive cannot function on its own, but they are inseparable parts of partnerships, as in Example (8.2.) below:

(8.2.) *The rapid evolution of* ***CMOS technologies*** *has made the development of fully integrated circuits yield the implementation of telecommunications systems where fully integrated wireless receivers.*

These two partnerships meet two criteria, and are very frequent in the MTCS texts. However, another hybrid, *MOS diode*, has a more unsure status. On the one hand, there is no definition, but it constitutes a specific type of a diode. Finally, an adjective+noun combination *age-dependent behaviour* which is used not in medical contexts, but it refers to an integrated circuit, and as such it is more a collocation than a term, e.g. (Example 8.3. below)

(8.3.) *As a result the ADRSMBM of the VGA can switch from one AD-RSM to another to simulate the* ***age-dependent behavior****.*

In conclusion, collocations in the MTCS research articles play an important role in meaning-making. Frequently occurring word combinations allow for precise and efficient means of communication and provide evidence for the common-core hypothesis. On the other hand, a number of extracted collocates constitute domain-specific terminology, which is reflected in multiword terms generated by Sketch Engine. It amounts to 12.5 % of analysed multiword terminology, which is consistent with previous studies on the subject (Gledhill, 2000; Peacock, 2012). However, the types of word combinations are more diverse than only nominal phrases and include a frequent use of adjectival attributives. In addition, the authors build complex 3- or 4-word combinations as well as hybrids with numbers, units of measurement, chemical formulae, and other symbols to facilitate understanding and efficiency. The use of multiword phrases contradicts, however, earlier assumptions about the constitution of collocations (Gruntar-Jermol, 2007).

8.3. Multiword terms

Multiword terms are formed to convey the maximum information load in limited space in scientific writing. Additionally, complex terms facilitate precision of subordinate terms. It is due to the fact that multiword terms are of higher granularity, and concentrate on a given aspect of a superordinate term, whereas the latter denotes the general concept (Mazurkiewicz-Sułkowska, 2014). Moreover, complex terms can be divided into categories with regard to their constitution.

The MTCS terminological system, which was organised into ontologies from the keyword terminology generated by Sketch Engine, and presented in the previous chapter, contains superordinate and subordinate terms divided into a set of identified categories. Moreover, this hierarchy of terms is even expanded by collocates generated by Sketch Engine Collocate. The analysis of multi-word terms and collocations in the MTCS domains confirms Mazurkiewicz-Sułkowska's study (2014). For example, the single-word term *transistor* denotes a device which controls the flow of current or voltage, and acts as a superordinate term that encompasses various types of transistors which are used in the MTCS domains, as shown in Table 8.6. below.

Table 8.6. The comparison of compounds created from the term *transistor* generated by the Sketch Engine from the MTCS corpus

Multiword options for the term *transistor*	
determinant	**nucleus**
NMOS	transistor
field-effect	transistor (FET)
junctionless	transistors (JLT)
bipolar	transistors transistor
PMOS	transistors transistors
HV	transistors
LV	transistors transistor
cascade	transistor
input	transistor
feedback	transistor
nanowire	
point-contact (germanium)	
elementary	

Moreover, for the purpose of the analysis, the 9 subcategories identified on the basis of the nucleus-determinant relationship developed by Sager et al. (1980) were used. The list of categories and the results of the analyses are presented in Table 8.7. below.

Table 8.7. The division of multiword terms appearing in the MTCS research papers generated by the Sketch Engine from the MTCS corpus divided into Sager et al.'s (1980) categories

category	multiword term
the comparison of the nucleus with another object	clock frequency clock signal channel region current consumption frame grabber recording channel delay line current mirror common mode
the specification of the material or substance used to make the nucleus	oxide thickness doping concentration
the inseparable feature of the new concept	thermal noise (pulse analysis) thermal impedance transient thermal impedance low voltage low noise dynamic range
the regular use of the nucleus	integrated circuit analog circuit dynamic power power consumption digital circuit internal temperature low voltage low power maximum power supply voltage thermal time (constant) dynamic power
the product normally associated with the nucleus	measurement system block diagram power supply

(*Continued*)

Table 8.7. Continued

category	multiword term
the nucleus as the instrument used to operate on the determinant	chip temperature pixel detector design flow parameter extraction image acquisition hardware implementation image processing signal processing
the specification of the mode of operation of the nucleus	operating frequency operating point sampling rate sampling frequency circuit simulation
the nucleus might form a part whereas the determinant constitutes a whole	input voltage output voltage input charge input signal output signal noise figure voltage drop voltage gain cut-off frequency power dissipation gate oxide
the identity of the nucleus is asserted by the determinant	readout circuit thermal model reference voltage thermal resistance drain current ambient temperature transfer function equivalent circuit current source input impedance control voltage input stage current mode gate voltage channel length

Table 8.7. above presents the division of MTCS multiword terminology into categories identified by Sager et al. (1980). However, due to a high level of abstraction, some of these need to be treated metaphorically, such as *the nucleus as the instrument used to operate on the determinant*. Moreover, some terms might be assigned to more than one category, because they meet the criteria, such as *thermal resistance* in which the adjective *thermal* might act as a determiner of the nucleus as well as its feature. On the other end, there are a few trends noticeable in the analysed terms. The majority of terms belong either to the category of *the regular use of the nucleus* or *the identity of the nucleus is asserted by the determinant*, which suggests that the authors communicate in well-known and widely-used patterns as well as strive to ensure precision. This categorisation differs from the ontology presented in the previous chapter in terms of their main focus being placed on the nucleus-determinant relationships and not the term's position in the terminological system.

Sager et al.'s (1980) classification also includes relationships indicating place, time, properties or other relationships which are consistent with the patterns used in the general language, e.g. terms containing properties or disposition are created by adding a determinant which specifies the property of the term, such as a 'method apparatus and unit of measurement (1980: 271)'. Complex terms formed by the addition of an adjectival determinant are not considered compounds in morphological-syntactic terms, but they are full-fledged terms terminologically speaking, e.g. *operating frequency*. Such terms are quite frequent in the MTCS research articles, as it was indicated.

In MTCS domains, authors form compounds which consist of more than two elements, with the predominant majority of 3- and 4-element phrases (36 and 40 % respectively according to Herzog, 1971 in Sager et al., 1980: 272), such as *designed front-end readout electronics*. However, long terms are usually mentioned in full in the attachments or at the beginning of the text and then compressed in the body of texts with the use of the anaphoric or cataphoric reference in order to avoid ambiguity (Mattiello, 2012: 160; Sager et al. 1980).

Apart from the above mentioned types of compounds, there are compound adjectives, but these rarely occur in the MTCS domains. One of the rare examples is *FInFET-based circuit* formed by combining an abbreviation acting as a noun with a past participle, which is consistent with Sager et al.'s (1980) study.

Compound verbs, an English phenomenon, comprise the last category and appear rather seldom in the MTCS research papers. However, there are examples of one of the groups identified by Sager et al. (1980), i.e. compounds with particles. The nouns deriving from them appear among the keyword terms, i.e. *readout* (298.20 times per million tokens) and *cut-off* (111.25 times per million words), which derive from the tendency to nominalisation in the scientific writing. The verbs are used quite infrequently, i.e. the verb *to cut off* appears in the MTCS corpus 6 times (6.88 times per million tokens), 4 times in the present simple form and twice as a gerund. The details are provided in the screenshot of the concordance in Figure 8.1. below.

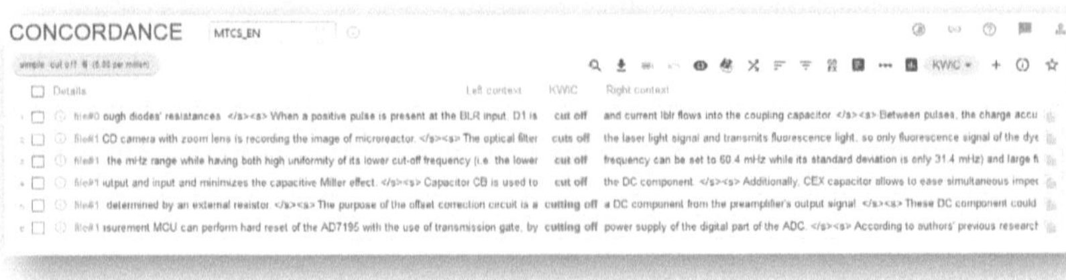

Figure 8.1. The screenshot of concordance lines for the verb *to cut off* generated from the MTCS corpus via Sketch Engine

The second verb *to read out* appears 11 times, 10 times in the present simple form and once as a gerund. The verb forms confirm the emphasis of the recentness of conducted research. The details are provided in the concordance list below (Figure 8.2.).

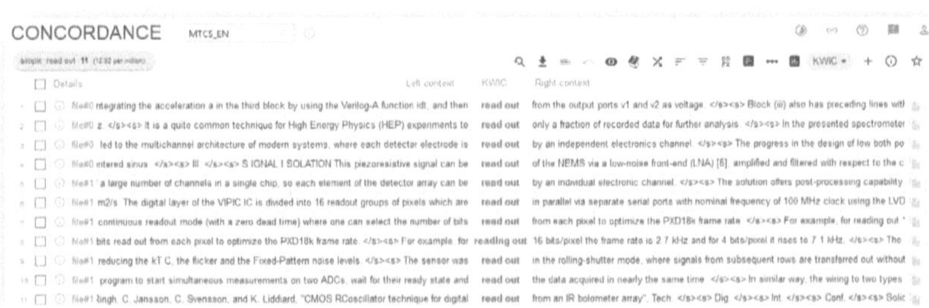

Figure 8.2. The screenshot of the concordance for the verb *to read out* generated from the MTCS subcorpus via Sketch Engine

However, the lexeme *outline* is a more interesting case, since it can be used both as a noun and as a verb. Out of 22 times in the MTCS corpus, there are 8 nouns, of which one is an attributive, and 14 verb forms: 9 in the Present Simple tense and 5 in the Passive Voice. It is an instance of the English free categorisation into parts of speech due to scarce suffixation. The details are provided in Figure 8.3. below.

Figure 8.3. The screenshot of concordance lines for the lexeme *outline* generated from the MTCS corpus via Sketch Engine

In conclusion, multiword terms in the MTCS domains fit within the identified categories of complex terms with respects to the nucleus-determinant relationships. However, the division should be treated more metaphorically due to the abstract nature of the MTCS terminology. Yet, terms alone will not allow efficient communication without the use of specific lexical bundles which perform specific functions.

8.4. Lexical bundles in the MTCS research articles

The corpus-driven approach to phraseological studies has changed the scope of interest towards free word combinations which appear frequently in authentic texts. Moreover, such non-idiomatic expressions are salient constituents of texts and perform important functions, i.e. allow for expressing authors' attitudes, act as cohesion markers, or help organise the text, and thus enhance readers' comprehension. These phraseological units are called differently, Sketch Engine uses the term *n-grams*, but in this monograph they will be referred to after Biber (2006) as *lexical bundles*.

The analysis of the MTCS research articles cannot miss the scrutiny of lexical bundles in order to provide a comprehensive view of the language of new technologies and means of communicating science to the general public. For this reason, Sketch Engine N-gram was used to generate 4-word sequences, as the most often studied (Biber, 2006; Batista da Silva et al., 2017). Moreover, the cut-off frequencies were set at the minimum frequency of 10 times per million tokens. The literature on the subject suggests the minimum frequency at the level of 40 times per million tokens, but it was set for bigger corpora (Biber, 2006). As a result, 203 most common non-idiomatic phrases were selected from the generated list of n-grams. The complete list of lexical bundles is available in Appendix 3. In addition, the list of lexical bundles was compared with Batista da Silva et al.'s (2017) list of 100 most common phraseological units in 8 scientific articles in different disciplines, like natural sciences, engineering, health sciences and agriculture. The comparison reveals that 41 phrases from that study are present on the list of MTCS lexical bundles. The results of the comparative study are presented in Figure 8.4. below. However, a few other units differ only with respects to an article or a preposition, such as *the form of a* in the previous study and the example from the MTCS list *the form of the* or *as a function of* in the first study and *a function of the* in the latter. The 59 % of non-convergent lexical bundles might stem from the fact that the earlier study was conducted on heterogeneous data, whereas English MTCS texts are exclusively engineering subject fields. Yet, 41 % of the phrases confirm that the language of science is to some extend universal, which proves earlier studies (Montgomery, 2000: 255; Gnutzmann & Rabe, 2014: 33; Seweryn, 2010; Gajda, 1990).

IN THE CASE OF; AS A RESULT OF; ~~AT THE END OF~~; THE END OF THE; AT THE SAME TIME; AS WELL AS THE; IN THE FORM OF; ON THE BASIS OF; CAN BE USED TO; ONE OF THE MOST; ~~IT IS IMPORTANT TO; IS ONE OF THE~~; IN TERMS OF THE; ~~A WIDE RANGE OF~~; IN THE PRESENCE OF; ~~THE NATURE OF THE~~; IT IS POSSIBLE TO; ~~IN ADDITION TO THE; IN THE ABSENCE OF~~; THE SIZE OF THE; ~~IN THE CONTEXT OF~~; A LARGE NUMBER OF; IS BASED ON THE; WITH RESPECT TO THE; ~~AS A FUNCTION OF~~; THE FACT THAT THE; ~~AT THE TIME OF~~; THE REST OF THE; THE USE OF THE; ~~THE BEGINNING OF THE; A WIDE VARIETY OF; AT THE BEGINNING OF; IN THE DEVELOPMENT OF~~; THE DEVELOPMENT OF THE; CAN BE FOUND IN; ~~TO BE ABLE TO~~; THE BASIS OF THE; ~~THE TOP OF THE~~; IN THIS CASE THE; THE USE OF A; AS PART OF THE; THE VALUE OF THE; ~~AN IMPORTANT ROLE IN; IN A VARIETY OF~~; THE CENTER OF THE; ~~THAT THERE IS A~~; A RESULT OF THE; ~~IN RELATION TO THE; IN A NUMBER OF; THE STRUCTURE OF THE~~; IN SUCH A WAY; ~~THE CASE OF THE; TO THE DEVELOPMENT OF; THE EXTENT TO WHICH; AS WELL AS IN~~; THE TOTAL NUMBER OF; ~~A GREAT DEAL OF; THE PRESENCE OF A; IT IS CLEAR THAT; AN EXAMPLE OF A; REFERRED TO AS THE; OF THE MOST IMPORTANT~~; TO THE FACT THAT; AN INCREASE IN THE; ~~IN THE SAME WAY~~; IT IS NECESSARY TO; ~~IN THE COURSE OF; THE ROLE OF THE; IT IS DIFFICULT TO; THE FORM OF A; AS WELL AS A; THE QUALITY OF THE; AND THE USE OF; THE SUM OF THE; IS REFERRED TO AS; OF A NUMBER OF; THE DIFFERENCE BETWEEN THE; THAT THERE IS NO; THE RELATIONSHIP BETWEEN THE; IS AN EXAMPLE OF~~; IS DETERMINED BY THE; ON THE OTHER HAND; ~~IN THE PROCESS OF~~; BE FOUND IN THE; ~~SUCH A WAY THAT; FOR THE PURPOSE OF; AS A RESULT THE; WITH THE EXCEPTION OF; THE BOTTOM OF THE; IN CONTRAST TO THE; ON THE ONE HAND; A MEMBER OF THE~~; IT SHOULD BE NOTED; CAN BE USED FOR; ~~IS LIKELY TO BE~~; AT THE LEVEL OF; ~~THE RESULTS OF THE~~; THE LENGTH OF THE; ~~THE WAY IN WHICH~~; IS RELATED TO THE

Figure 8.4. The results of the comparative study of most relevant lexical bundles with Silva et al.'s (2017) study and the MTCS corpus

The author also decided to develop the lists of the most recurrent lexical bundles in the MTCS domains, parallel to Batista da Silva et al.'s (2017), but the analysis is limited to 50 4-word combinations. Moreover, the list contains a high frequency of terms, which had to be manually removed in order to concentrate on only the phrases of interest. The results are provided in Table 8.8. below.

Table 8.8. The most recurring lexical bundles generated from the MTCS corpus via Sketch Engine N-gram

The most recurrent lexical bundles in MTCS research articles
is shown in Fig.
is presented in Fig.
as shown in Fig.
on the other hand
as a function of
in the case of
is based on the
with the use of
on the basis of
the value of the
the use of the
the case of the
as well as the
with respect to the
can be used to
as the same time
are shown in Fig.
the influence of the
it is necessary to
block diagram of the
presented in this paper
is organized as follows
is based on a
can be used for
the performance of the
in the form of
it can be seen
the basis of the
is one of the
can be seen in
can be used in
one of the most
the values of the
by means of the
the size of the
simulation results of the
is proportional to the
can be found in
block diagram of the

Table 8.8. Continued

The most recurrent lexical bundles in MTCS research articles
to the fact that
is the number of
in the range of
can be seen that
a function of the
the fact that the
should be noted that
results are presented in
is due to the

In addition, the MTCS domains have an empirical and practical character, which is also depicted in the phrases used. The authors make references to the details of solutions that they provide, such as dimensions, ingredient, structure, measurements, shape, function, or application. The list of lexical bundles referring to the proposed prototypes is provided in Table 8.9 below.

Table 8.9. The list of lexical bundles referring to the proposed prototypes extracted from the MTCS corpus via Sketch Engine N-gram

lexical bundle	the operation of the; the design of the; at the level of; at the end of; the total number of; the calculation of the; the length of the; the difference between the; the shape of the; the impact of the; an increase in the; is a function of; the structure of the; the properties of the; the parameters of the; the measurement of the; part of the system

With regard to the structural characteristics, MTCS lexical bundles are predominantly noun phrases with a few verb phrases in both languages. In the analysed MTCS research papers, they are comprised of either noun phrases with a postmodifier or prepositional phrases, which is in alliance with other studies, like Biber's (2006) study of academic registers or Granger & Paquot's study (2008). Moreover, research papers in English are written in the impersonal style achieved via the use of the Passive Voice, which is confirmed by the MTCS corpus realisation in Example (8.4.). Such a structure of forms confirms earlier studies, such as Biber (2006) or Granger & Paquot's (2008) on the subject.

(8.4.) *In addition,* ***it should be noted that*** *sudden cardiac arrest (for a patient treated in hospital) is still difficult to predict and to treat.*

Grammatically, the phrase *it should be noted that* in Example 8.6. above is in the Passive Voice, which creates the impersonal mood and makes the text more formal. Functionally, however, as an *epistemic impersonal stance bundle (discussed below),* draws the readers attention to an important condition, which needs to be taken into account during the study.

Moreover, MTCS lexical bundles can also be categorised with regard to the functions they perform. For this reason, Biber's (2006) classification of primary functions of lexical bundles was applied in the current analysis. The results of the division are provided in Table 8.10. below.

Table 8.10. The most recurring lexical bundles generated from the MTCS corpus via Sketch Engine N-gram

functions of lexical bundles		lexical bundles
epistemic stance bundles	impersonal bundles	it is possible to can be used to can be used for can be seen in can be used in can be found in to the fact that can be seen that It can be seen As it can be which can be used can be divided into would like to thank can be considered as As can be seen can be expressed as authors would like to due to the fact cannot be used can be described by can be approximated by can be achieved by
modality stance bundles	obligation /directive bundles	it is necessary to should be noted that it should be noted it is worth noting that be taken into account

Table 8.10. Continued

functions of lexical bundles		**lexical bundles**
	intention /prediction bundles	
	ability bundles	in order to obtain to be used in to take into account in order to minimize in order to provide in order to calculate
discourse organising bundles	topic introduction focus bundles	presented in this paper is organised as follows paper is organized as results are presented in This paper presents a In this paper we This paper is organized described in this paper of this paper is paper presents the design
	topic elaboration/ clarification bundles	on the other hand as well as the as a result in this case the is due to the in such a way as a result of
	identification/ focus bundles	is one of the one of the most of the most important is the most important The main advantage of is the same as is applied to the is related to the The architecture of the

(*Continued*)

Table 8.10. Continued

functions of lexical bundles		lexical bundles
referential bundles	bundles specifying attributes	as a function of is based on the on the basis of is based on a in the form of the basis of the by means of the with the use of the value of the the influence of the the size of the is proportional to the is the number of in the range of a wide range of in the value of a large number of in the field of the end of the the gain of the the center of the of the number of the operation of the the design of the at the level of at the end of the total number of the calculation of the the length of the the difference between the the shape of the the impact of the an increase in the is a function of the structure of the the properties of the the parameters of the the measurement of the

Table 8.10. Continued

functions of lexical bundles		lexical bundles
		part of the system in terms of the in relation to the as a way of as a part of based on the moduli the value of the the main goal of the performance of simulation results of the for different values
	time/place/text- deixis bundles	is shown in Fig. is presented in Fig. as shown in Fig. at the same time are shown in Fig. is depicted in Fig. block diagram of the are presented in Table is used in the circuit shown in Fig. As it was mentioned is illustrated in Fig. results are shown in is presented in the in the previous section

As can be seen in Table 8.10. above, the predominant majority of lexical bundles are referential bundles, and bundles specifying attributes in particular as well as deixis bundles. They provide details of the solutions the scientists and engineers develop, i.e. construction and functioning as well as help reader find interesting information by references to visuals and numerical data, which confirms the empirical nature of the MTCS domains. The second place with respects to the number of bundles occupy discourse organising bundles which guide the reader through the text via maintaining topic continuity, i.e. informing the reader about the structure of the article and keep the reader focused on the content, an suggest the authors' familiarity with the Saxonic writing convention (Duszak, 1998; Dontcheva- Navrátilová, 2012). Finally, there are attitudinal bundles which mark the authorial presence and their attitudes. These are particularly noticeable as the authors seem to make frequent use of mitigation strategies. According to Carrió Pastor (2009), hedging is more conventional in soft sciences, but authors in the MTCS research articles make surprisingly a frequent use of epistemic impersonal stance bundles as well as obligation bundles, which is shown in Table 8.10. above. One of the possible reasons of using them is drawing the readers' attention to specific details, as shown below in Examples (8.5.) & (8.6.) below:

(8.5.) *It* ***can be seen that*** *the circuit structure inadvertently becomes more complex.*

(8.6.) *A survey about integrated inductor state-of-the-art* ***can be found in*** *[8].*

To sum up, lexical bundles play an important role in meaning-making in the MTCS research articles. As indicated in the literature on the subject, there are three main functions of phraseological units, but there is a significant number of lexical bundles referring to the proposed solution, which emphasises the practical character of the MTCS domains. In general, there is a strong tendency to nominalisation and frequent references to multimodal contents. In addition, there is a high density of text cohesion markers and as well as hedges, which reflects the writing style of scientific texts in English – more dialogous Saxonic that guides the readers through the text and stages of research.

8.5. Concluding remarks to Chapter 8

This chapter is devoted to complex lexical units, from free lexical bundles to more and more restricted, like collocations and multiword terms. The current analysis confirms that scientists and engineers communicate in chunks or linguistic patterns in order to achieve a cohesive and coherent written report of conducted research which is communicated worldwide. The most recurrent word combinations often form domain-specific terminology, and the borderline between a collocation and a complex term can be fuzzy. For example, the phrase *low frequency* is a multidomain combination, but in the MTCS domains it has gained a status of a term due to a determined and clearly defined range of frequency to be considered low. In addition, multiword terms are also subject to classification, but due to a high level of abstraction of terminology, the applied categories need to be treated metaphorically.

In addition, lexical bundles are non-idiomatic phrases that perform important functions and contribute to meaning-making in the MTCS research articles. The extraordinary high frequency of referential bundles confirms the empirical and practical nature of the MTCS domains. A frequent use of epistemic stance bundles indicates that the authors present their attitudes towards the written content more openly, which will also be tackled in the following chapter. In addition, discourse organising bundles are extensively used in the MTCS texts, which shows that the authors guide the readers through the text and stages in research. The distribution of bundles suggests the acquaintance with and the adherence to the writing conventions in English, i.e. the Saxonic style. Subject-specific terminology together with n-grams used by the authors communicate the results of conducted research to the public, which constitutes an obligatory condition in scientific work. Finally, lexical bundles making frequent references to multimodal contents prove the multimodal, hybrid character of the MTCS research articles.

Chapter 9 Supplementary analysis of the MTCS research articles

This chapter presents a supplementary scrutiny of the authorial presence and references to the audience in the analysed MTCS scientific articles as a means of meaning-making and creating cohesion and coherence of the communicated message. The investigations begin with the quantitative analysis of personal pronouns and possessive adjectives used in the MTCS research papers. Their use in scientific texts indicates the presence of authors in purportedly objective and impersonal scientific texts that communicate research results that are verified empirically.

The quantitative analysis is followed by the comparison of the use of personal pronouns and possessive adjectives as well as the indication of their pragmatic functions in the texts (Hyland, 1995). Finally, the author compares the results with Dontcheva-Navrátilová's (2013) study into scientific articles written by native and non-native authors speakers of English.

9.1. Presence of the author in the MTCS scientific texts

Research papers are supposed to present facts, and therefore they should be written according to the scientific paradigm (Dontcheva-Navrátilová, 2013). As a result, they should be precise, objective and impersonal. Yet, linguistic studies have shown that authors of scientific texts use a number of devices which perform specific linguistic functions, such as persuasion in order to convince the audience about proposed solutions or to validate research results. The use of personal pronouns also performs a range of functions in scientific articles (Hyland, 1995).

The author of the monograph conducted a study into the use of personal pronouns in disciplines which belong to hard sciences, and compared the results with Dontcheva-Navrátilová's (2013) analysis of the use of personal pronouns in research articles in soft sciences in English written by native speakers of English and Czech authors, as well as with Hyland's (1995) study into 26 research papers. The current study also includes the pronoun *you* and possessive adjective *your* which were not included in the preceding analyses. The results of the study of personal pronouns and possessive adjectives in MTCS research articles are presented in Table 9.1. below:

Table 9.1. The results of the study of the use of personal pronouns and possessive adjectives in the MTCS domains conducted by the author of the monograph

pronouns /adjectives	**number of occurrences**	**rate per million tokens**
I	15	17.20
my	17	19.50
me	10	11.47
we	969	1,111.37
our	247	283.29
Us	88	100.93
you	26	29.82
your	6	6.88
Total	**1,378**	**1,580,45**

The study of the frequency of personal pronouns and possessive adjectives in the MTCS domains reveals that it is more common to make use of pronouns in plural forms are more common than singular, which is consistent with Dontcheva-Navrátilová's (2013) findings. The avoidance of the first person singular pronoun is supposed to prevent the scientist from taking the risk of the face-threatening strategy and potential subjectivity. Moreover, the first person singular pronoun *I* appears 15 times and there are 5 instances of the object pronoun and 19 examples of possessive adjective in the first person *my*. However, the most frequent is the first person plural pronoun *we* and the possessive adjective *our*. There are three explanations for the use of pronouns, i.e. the first lies in the multiple authorship of analysed materials, reflecting the cooperative character of research in these fields. The second lies in the writing convention concerning research papers, and the Saxonic writing style in English which is more dialogical and direct. The third one stems from the language system itself, as English belongs to North-Germanic languages and is an analytic language with scarce inflectional affixation. For this reason, pronouns function as subjects and objects and are indispensable for the grammatical correctness, according to the syntactic rules.

The pronoun *I* is used for three reasons in the MTCS domains:

1. to describe one's experience or education (9 times)
2. to talk about one's achievements (1 time)
3. to express gratitude (2 times)
4. to explain or justify the choice of procedures or line of research (3 times)

However, the first person personal pronoun is used in the biographical section to establish the author as a representative of the scientific community (point 1, 2 and 3 above) and to describe research (point 3 above), in which the author adopts a role of the recounter of the research process (Dontcheva-Navrátilová, 2013) which are illustrated by Examples (9.1.), (9.2.), (9.3.) and (9.4.) below:

(9.1.) *construction of this measuring equipment,* ***I*** *owe thanks to Mr. Leonard Pogorzałek, an*

(9.2.) *. II. INITIAL REASERCH During my B.Sc. studies,* ***I*** *had chosen for the specialisation technical*

(9.3.) *touching the germanium plate surface (b)* ***I*** *used for this purpose two measurement*

(9.4) ***I*** *succeeded by using an l-h junction [29,30] and developed its technology to a proper level.*

The findings are similar to previous studies which show that authorial presence is used as a persuasion technique. The pronoun *I* is more frequently used by native speakers due to the compliance with the Saxonic writing style which assumes dialogicity.

The first person possessive adjective *my* is more frequent as it it appears with the frequency 19.50 per million tokens. The list of collocates are shown in Table 9.2. below:

Table 9.2. The list of collocates co-ocurring the possessive adjective *my* extracted from the MTCS corpus by Sketch Engine

Keyword: *my*		
Collocate	**Frequency**	**Score**
	15	88,2
B.Sc.	2	11,9
colleague	2	11,7
work	3	11,1
semester	1	11
staff	1	11
thesis	1	11
opinion	1	10,9
degree	1	10,9
interest	1	10,9
team	1	10,8
knowledge	1	10,6

As presented in Table 9.2. above, possessive adjective *my* refers mainly to conducted research (*my work*), obtained degrees (*my diploma work, my master thesis*, etc.) or the research team (*my colleagues, my team, my limited laboratory staff*) who conduct studies. However, there are two instances, where the authors refer to their knowledge (*utilising my knowledge*) and express opinions, i.e. *in my opinion it seems*, but due to hedging expressed in the verb which follows the categorical statement of a stance is softened in order not to risk face-threatening (Hyland, 1995; Dontcheva-Navrátilová, 2013). The results of the query are presented in the screenshot of the concordance for the analysed possessive adjective in the Figure 9.1. below.

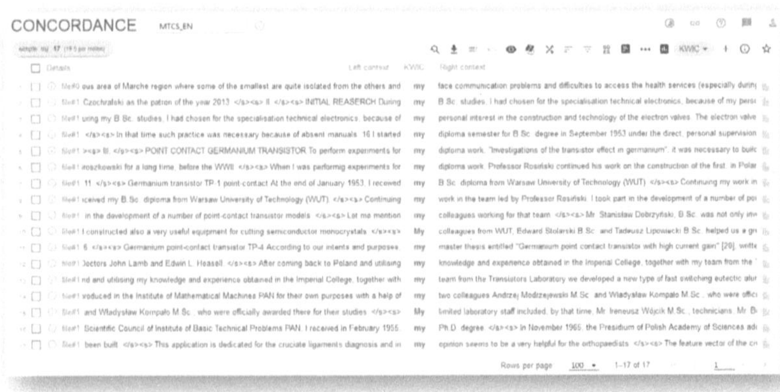

Figure 9.1. The screenshot of the concordance for the possessive adjective *my* generated by Sketch Engine from the MTCS corpus

Another pronoun, which is rather underrepresented in the MTCS domains, but more frequent than in the Czech studies, is the object pronoun *me*. In alliance with Dontcheva-Navrátilová's (2013) analysis, it appears rather rarely, with the frequency 11.47 per million tokens, but only a half of the examples provided are used as a pronoun, and therefore relevant for the study. The occurrences, which can be accounted for an object pronoun, explain mainly one's motivation for taking certain actions, as shown in the examples (9.5.)-(9.7.) below.

(9.5.) *In April 1958, thanks to the endeavours of Professor Groszkowski, the Polish Academy of Sciences (PAN)* ***delegated me*** *to Imperial College of Science and Technology in London for postgraduate studies. Later, in September*

1959, I protected with a black paint Reflecting further, I will return to the 1957 year, when Professor B.M. Wuł ***invited me*** *to visit the Physics Institute (FIAN) of Soviet Academy of Sciences (SAS) in Moscow.*

(9.6.) *It was also* ***an occasion for me*** *to me to visit the Physics Institute (FIAN) of Soviet Academy of Sciences (SAS) in Moscow. It was also* ***an occasion for me*** *to visit there the Radiotechnic Institute of SAS, where I met Dr N.A. Pienin, who introduced his new theory of the p-n*

(9.7.) *for an influence of the minority carrier recombination velocity at the base contact [28]. This theory* ***fascinated me*** *and I started to look for the way of making such contact, which would present a very low value of the surface*

However, the most frequent in the MTCS corpus is the personal pronoun *we*. In the MTCS research papers, it appears exceptionally frequently (1,111.37 per million tokens). An excerpt of concordance lines is presented in the Figure 9.2. below.

Figure 9.2. The screenshot of the concordance for the personal pronoun *we* generated by Sketch Engine from the MTCS subcorpus

As shown in Figure 9.2. above, the pronoun refers mainly to the research team, and emphasises the collaborative character of conducting research in the MTCS disciplines. The details of the potential authors' roles are provided in list of collocations. Sketch Engine Collocator provides extensive information about lexemes that are frequently appear with the pronoun *we*. The list of collocates is given in Figure 9.3. below.

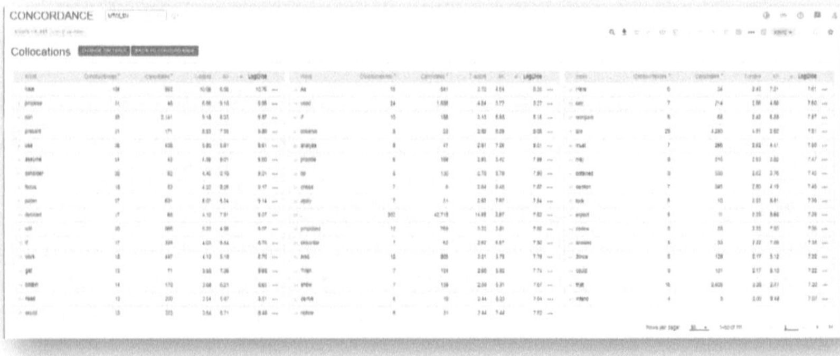

Figure 9.3. The screenshot of the collocates of the personal pronoun *we* generated by Sketch Engine from the MTCS corpus

The list of collocates allows for the determination of the authors' roles listed by Dontcheva-Navrátilová (2013), from the safest to the most face-threatening, which are provided in Table 9.3. below:

Table 9.3. The roles that the authors take in the English MTCS research papers with examples of verbs generated by Sketch Engine Word Sketch and KWIC

Authors' role	**Verbs which follow the pronoun *we***
representative	consider, know
discourse-organiser	describe, show, proceed, report demonstrate
recounter of the research process	focus, intend, decided, obtain, observe, analyse, provide, chose, apply, invstigate, performed, notice, compare, look
opinion-holder	conclude, assume
originator	propose, present, review, developed, designed

Table 9.3. above demonstrates that the authors of MTCS research papers take the whole range of roles, from the least to the most face-threatening. The most widely represented is the role of the recounter of the research process, which proves that a scientific article constitutes a report of the whole research process. Moreover, it also emphasises the empirical and practical character of the MTCS domains. Surprisingly, the MTCS authors also adopt the most risky role of an originator, which confirms the novel character of developed solutions. In addition, the authors are also familiar with the Saxonic writing convention

because they act as discourse organisers and guide the reader through the text. They also position themselves among representatives of the scientific community and express their opinions. The list of collocates of the pronoun *we* also contains auxiliary and modal verbs, such as *can, need, would, do, must* or may.

The phrase *we can* is fairly frequent in the MTCS scientific texts, as it appears 89 times with the frequency 102.08 times per million tokens. The pronoun *we* refers either to the research team when followed by verbs *to increase, to use*, or *to calculate,* and thus, the authors provide details of their research, i.e. the possibility to apply a method or use an apparatus with a view to obtaining results with the use of hedging. On the other hand, *we* is used as the inclusive pronoun which pertains to both the authors and the readers when followed by verbs *to observe, to see* or *to notice.* Finally, the writers provide details of the assumptions they made before or during conductin research by using verb *to assume* together with the phrase *we can*. Table 9.4. below provides details of collocation candidates of the analysed phrase.

Table 9.4. The list of collocates of the phrase *we can* generated by Sketch Engine Word Sketch and KWIC

Collocate of *we can*	Frequency	Coll. freq.	T-score	MI	logDice
observe	5	23	2,235	11,0564	10,5146
see	12	214	3,4578	9,10157	10,3418
notice	4	31	1,9984	10,3039	10,0931
assume	3	42	1,7296	9,45071	9,55154
calculate	4	100	1,9949	8,61421	9,43776
increase	3	281	1,7155	6,70861	8,05358
use	5	538	2,2115	6,50854	8,02961
not	3	1123	1,6659	4,70989	6,34179

Another modal verb which follows pronoun *we* is *to need* which imposes an obligation on readers and writers. The choice of verbs that follow the phrase indicates the need to apply certain procedures, perform certain activities, or to use specific devices in the research process. The list of concordances illustrating the use of the phrase in question is shown in Figure 9.4. below.

Figure 9.4. The screenshot of concordance lines of the phrase *we need* generated by Sketch Engine from the MTCS corpus

Another epistemic modal verb expressing expressing expectation in a combination with a personal pronoun is *would*. In the MTCS texts, it appears 13 times with the frequency of 14.91 times per million tokens, mainly in the verbal phrase *would like to*. Moreover, there are two instances of expectation, i.e. *we would use* and *we would define*, the other occurrences are a part of a verb pattern *would like to do something*, used when expressing polite wishes, which is shown in Figure 9.5. below.

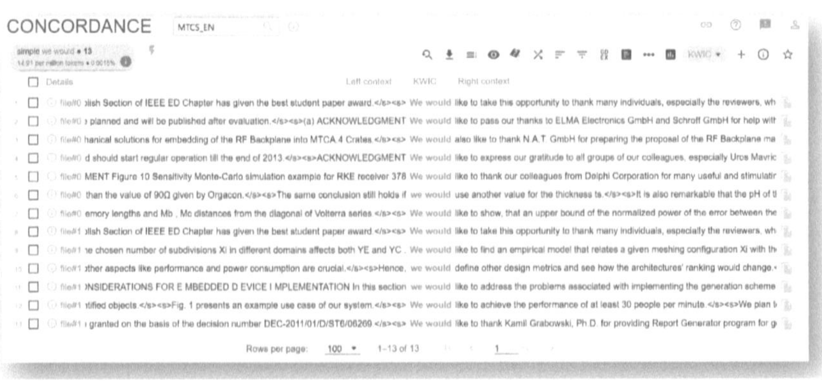

Figure 9.5. The screenshot of concordance lines of the phrase *we would* generated by Sketch Engine from the MTCS corpus

Moreover, the most salient modal verb used for hedging *may* appears with the pronoun *we* only 8 times in the MTCS texts. By using it, the scientists try to avoid their research paper from being rejected by reviewers, and finally by the target audience. The examples of hedging, presenting research results are presented in Figure 9.6. showing concordance lines for the phrse *we may* below.

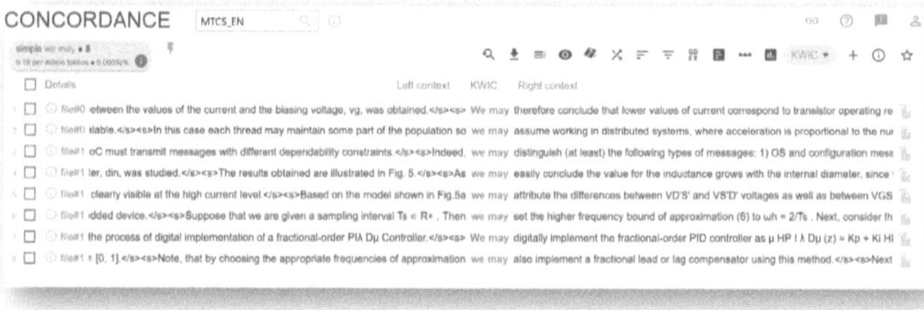

Figure 9.6. The screenshot of concordance lines of the phrase *we may* generated by Sketch Engine from the MTCS corpus

In addition, the MTCS commit themselves strongly to performing specific activities by using the combination of a pronoun *we* and the deontic modal verb *must*. The obligations include either tasks connected with research or the necessity to put special emphasis on a specific detail of research reported in the research paper. The details of the use of the analysed phrase is shown in Figure 9.7. below:

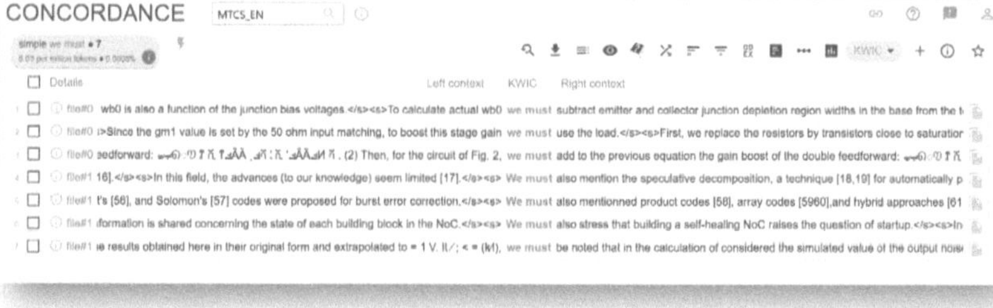

Figure 9.7. The screenshot of concordance lines of the phrase *we must* generated by Sketch Engine from the MTCS corpus

This leads to the investigation of the use of the object pronoun *us* in the MTCS corpus. It is the third most frequent pronoun which appears 103 times in the corpus with the frequency 118.13 times per million tokens. The most often coocurring lexemes include verbs *to let, to allow* and *to give* as well as a preposition *for*, which is shown in Table 9.5 below:

Table 9.5. The list of collocates of the pronoun *us* generated by Sketch Engine Word Sketch and KWIC

Collocates of the pronoun *us*	**Freq**	**Coll. freq.**	**T-score**	**MI**	**logDice**
Let	16	29	3,99914	12,1893	11,9556
let	14	17	3,74112	12,7672	11,9005
give	5	52	2,23332	9,66879	10,0458
allow	6	131	2,44317	8,59884	9,7146
allowed	3	37	1,72953	9,42281	9,45568
allows	6	284	2,43579	7,48252	8,98877
for	3	7091	1,24842	1,84049	3,77238

Collocation candidates generated by Sketch Engine indicate that the pronoun *us* is used to refer both to researchers as a group and the research process in terms of methods and equipment involved, obtained research results or assistance in the study (Examples (9.8.)-(9.10.) below).

(9.8.) *The balanced structure of the comparator allows* ***us*** *to use only one Schmitt trigger connected between both (inverting and noninvertig) inputs of the comparator.*

(9.9.) *The obtained results are very encouraging for further development and allow* ***us*** *to draw a number of conclusions in context of our system.*

(9.10.) *We are also happy to see the latest Ngspice supports dynamic loading functions [3] which are quite helpful for* ***us*** *to get the model authoring kit.*

In addition, the pronoun is also used as inclusive *us* to treat readers and researchers as one group, which involves the audience in the process of conducting research because it stimulates readers' imagination to recreate the situation, which is shown in Figure 9.8. below.

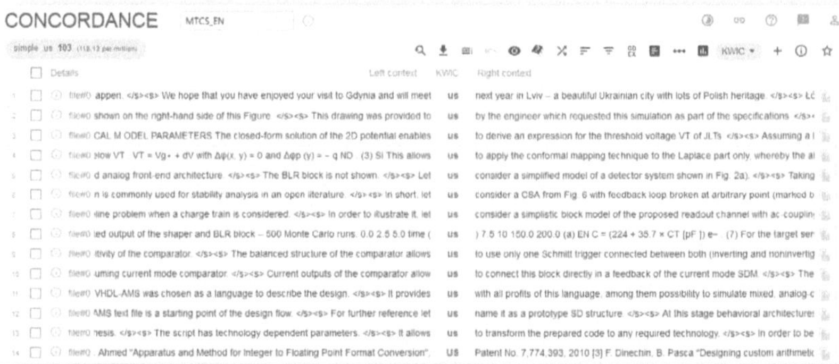

Figure 9.8. The screenshot of the concordance for the object pronoun *us* generated by Sketch Engine from the MTCS corpus

Figure 9.9. The screenshot of the concordance for the possessive adjective *our* generated by Sketch Engine from the MTCS corpus

In addition, possessive adjective *our* refers exclusively to the authors and to their expertise, research or developed solutions, as indicated in the collocation list presented in Figure 9.10. below. The use of modal verbs *can, would,* or *need* indicates softening the utterance by hedges and taking a low risk strategy (Dontcheva-Navrátilová, 2013; Hyland, 1995).

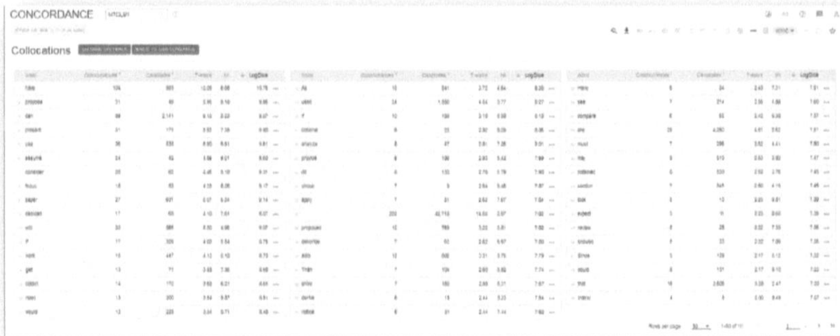

Figure 9.10. The screenshot of the collocates of the possessive adjective *our* generated by Sketch Engine from the MTCS corpus

Moreover, the authors make direct references to the audience in the MTCS research papers by using pronoun *you* and possessive adjective *your*. By doing so, they address the readers as professionals, engage them and start a dialogue with them, direct their attention to certain details of their studies or call for action, as in Examples (9.11). and (9.12.). The use of these pronouns stays in alliance with the Saxonic writing style which is dialogical, and texts guide readers through the contents.

(9.11.) *Now,* ***we get your attention to*** *the Min & Max circuit's simulation results.*
(9.12.) *If* ***you as model developers or users*** *have any requirements which are not included here, please do not hesitate to contact us.*

In addition, the pronoun and the adjective in question are used to talk impersonally in order to make generalisations, which is illustrated by Examples (9.13.)-(9.15.) below:

(9.13.) *The pheromone* ***helps you select*** *an edge.*
(9.14.) ***You could say*** *that ant algorithms are algorithms.*
(9.15.) *In each iteration, the quantity of ants* ***create your path****.*

However, according to the scientific paradigm, scientific texts should be written in such a way so as to maintain objectivity and to avoid the presence of the author (Dontcheva-Navrátilová, 2013). Therefore, the MTCS texts infringe the rule via the use of personal pronouns. Moreover, scientific writing should be deprived of complex figures of speech and rhetorical devices in order to communicate science precisely and impartially. However, scientists make use of rhetorical devices in a fairly technical text, such as a rhetorical question which remains unaswered (Example (9.16.) below):

(9.16.) *Although such a disagreement is not surprising, considering both models used differ in structure and complexity, it poses nevertheless an interesting question:* ***where does this difference come from?***

Another surprising aspect is the register. Scientific texts should be written in a formal language. Yet, the authors make frequent use of auxiliary verb *do* in the informal, contracted negative form, which appears 34 times in the corpus with the frequency 38.99 times per million tokens, as in Examples (9.17.) and (9.18.) below:

(9.17.) *This difference* ***doesn't*** *affect significantly the CSA performance, because nearly all of electron-hole pairs flows into the input stage of the frontend electronics.*

(9.18.) *The CIC filters are significantly smaller then FIR (Finite Impulse Response) or IIR (Infinite Impulse Response) filters because they* ***don't*** *use multiplier.*

In addition, the writers address the audience by using the phrase *the reader*, creating a distance between them in order to call for action, i.e. referring to the literature on the subject (Examples (9.19.) and (9.20.) below). This indirectness can be emphasised by the use of the passive voice which in fact functions as a call for action, as illustrated by Example (9.21.):

(9.19.) *For further information on AES,* ***the reader can see*** *the paper by J. Daemen and V. Rijmen.*

(9.20.) *Regarding the mathematical processing of the data in this way obtained,* ***the reader should refer to the work*** *of Kocher et al.*

(9.21.) *For the complete set of closed-form equations* ***the reader is asked*** *to refer to references.*

On the other hand, the noun *reader* constitutes one of the subject field terms, which is definitely more frequent than the lexeme from the general lexicon, but does not appear in the keyword terminology. Example (9.22.) shows one of such instances.

(9.22.) *During the charge-up phase* ***the reader*** *sends a continuous RF signal to generate the DC supply voltage in the rectifier block, while the rest of the functional blocks on the tag remain in stand by mode.*

On the whole, the frequency of occurrence of personal pronouns in the MTCS research articles is higher than in Dontcheva-Navrátilová's (2013) study. The pronouns considered by her irrelevant are more frequent in the MTCS corpus realisations. The MTCS authors, however, take more face-threatening functions, and their presence is to add the human factor in the description of performed experiments and tests, i.e. they act like pointers that show the way through the process, and as such contribute to meaning-making and the creation of a cohesive and coherent message which communicates research results.

To sum up, corpus analysis of the MTCS research papers has revealed that the author's presence is more visible in the MTCS scientific articles than in the parallel study. Moreover, the heterogeneous discourse community writing in these domains generally conforms to the Saxonic writing style and use all possible devices that help the readers decode the whole research process. In order to convince the audience about their research and obtained results, the scientists and engineers resort to various linguistic strategies, within and beyond the English writing convention, i.e. lexical bundles help shape the structure of the message, and the use of personal pronouns gives a research paper a more personal touch. Moreover, the writers smuggle in informal language structures in order to create a more dialogic style in scientific texts, technical and empirical in nature.

9.2. Concluding remarks to Chapter 9

This chapter is devoted to the authorial presence in the MTCS research papers. The presence of the author is a manifestation of domain-specific communication, which is not expected from scientific texts, and in strictly technical and empirical disciplines. Even though research articles should be written according to the scientific paradigm, i.e. they should be objective and impersonal, the authors mark their presence and express certain attitudes towards the presented content via hedging, which stays in the connection with phraseology discussed in the preceding chapter, and stance bundles in particular. In addition, the scientists draw the readers attention to particular details of research, or conduct a dialogue with readers to make them more involved in the article. As a result, the use of personal pronouns and possessive adjectives, along with other elements, like the macrostructure of the research paper, multimodal elements, domain-specific terminology, or lexical bundles, contributes to meaning-making and creating a cohesive, hybridised text which effectively communicates science.

Final remarks

Scientific writing in major disciplines has been extensively studied in English, but so far language researchers have devoted little attention to the language of new technologies. Moreover, the language of electronics, telecommunication and computer science (MTCS), disciplines undergoing dynamic changes, has not been addressed in the corpus-driven and corpus-assisted perspective yet. The analyses presented in the monograph are, to date, the first attempt to provide a comprehensive description of the characteristic features of terminology and phraseology in technical MTCS domains by applying a range of corpus linguistic methodologies with a set of terminological, phraseological and textual typologies. The study is based on a body of carefully selected authentic texts which constitute substantial and representative samples of quite recent scientific writing in English. The first four chapters of the monograph provide a theoretical framework and a review of literature on the subject in English, Polish and German. They are followed by Chapter Five which describes research material, applied research tools and methodologies. The following chapters (from Six to Nine) concentrate on various aspects of scientific terminology and phraseology in English, i.e. macrostructure, terminology, phraseology and pragmatic aspects in research articles. The study bridges the gap in literature on scientific writing, scientific language, terminology and phraseology in science, but it also points out current trends in science, scientific texts and scientific language. The practical part provides detailed characteristics of the terminology and phraseology taking into consideration macrostructural aspects and the influence of the standard writing conventions as well as the evolution of scientific disciplines, i.e. them becoming more detailed, interdisciplinary and hybridised.

Firstly, the study has shown that corpora compilation and upload is not always automatic trouble-free and not requiring any additional post-editing touches, as indicated by Sketch Engine technical support[19]. The computational program supports a range of formats and works with 85 languages, with all options available for English, as shown in Figure 1 below. In addition, until recently, the problem with the conversion of PDF files containing complex data has not been by Sketch Engine indicated.

19 https://www.sketchengine.eu/what-can-sketch-engine-do/, 18.06.2020

LANGUAGE	POS TAGGING	LEMMATIZATION	WORD SKETCHES	TERMS
English	✓	✓	full	✓

Figure 1. The screenshot from the Sketch Engine's webpage confirming all options available for English

The program is cut out for working with analytical languages, such as English, because the upload and compilation of the MTCS corpus was almost free from obstacles even though the PDF files contained multiple columns of texts, complex phrases or headings. In addition, lists of terminological candidates extracted by Sketch Engine required verification of the subject-field expert due to their diversity. Given the challenges and obstacles faced, the study should be considered a success.

The analyses revealed that at the macrostructural level English research papers conform to the publisher' requirements, but the titles of individual sections are domain-specific. The analysed research articles are rather homogeneous in terms of the way the authors structure their message, both the abstract and the contents of the research paper. The analysis has shown that both abstracts are predominantly summaries, but they also present an overview of the proposed solution. As a result, the dedicated Swales' (1990) CARS model is of limited application for the MTCS abstracts. In addition, scientific articles are consistent with the IMRAD pattern whose sections are overtly present in the texts.

The analysed scientific texts emphasise the practical and empirical nature of these domains because the texts reflect the stages of conducted research. However, there is an alternative division into sections to the IMRAD format which better mirrors the empirical and applicative nature of the analysed domains. Therefore, MTCS research articles act as reports of performed studies, or even as advertising spots persuading about the validity of the prototype or a proposed solution.

The investigation has also shown that the experimental verification of developed systems or methods in the MTCS research papers is validated via the use of multimodal communicative means, such as graphs, schematic drawings, graphics, algorithms or formulae, creating a hybrid text. In fact, the MTCS authors rely heavily on the intersemiotic elements which supplement the verbal content, and their use is indicated by keyword terminology. The conducted analysis was more detailed than the one published before and has shown that the use of multimodal elements is almost equally frequent as in the previous study. Yet, symbols, formulae, or units of measurement, etc. are crucial due to the creation of domain-specific hybrid terminology. As a result, the scientific articles become hybridised, which has been considered a trend in modern science.

The scrutiny of MTCS terminology has indicated that there are polarising trends in the creation and validation of terminology. On the one hand, cognitive mechanisms are clearly visible, but on the other there is a strong drive for maintaining a high level of precision via the use of stndardised terminology. As a result, there is a marked tendency towards standardisation, which is reflected in the creation of a dedicated and interdisciplinary IEC standard for electrotechnical domains. Yet, term coverage in the standard is far from being desired, especially in the case of multiword terms, which reflects its retrospective and historical character. Cognitive phenomena, like metaphorisation, polysemy, and synonymy are functional in the creation of MTCS terminology since they effectively 'translate' abstract concepts via extensions of familiar meaning to new concepts in the case of the first two as well as allow for expressing specific terminological nuances via the latter. Moreover, synonymy and polysemy are present but limited among MTCS terminology. The synonyms originate either from other domains or from the general language lexicon, whereas, polysemy is based on a metaphorical transfer from familiar general language concepts or intercategorial, as these disciplines draw on more traditional sources of vocabulary. On the other hand, terminological metaphors are rather common, and are based on familiar symbolisms, like animals, family, shape, movement, functions, or CONTAINER metaphors. The discussed cognitive aspects are reflected in the IEC standard, a distinct nomenclature for eletrotechnical disciplines, which is a proof that cognitive mechanisms in terminology creation cannot be ignored. In addition, the developed ontology for the analysed terminological system has revealed unexpected relationships between the terms, and prove the superordinate character of singleword terminology generated by Sketch Engine as well as the subordinate relation of multiword terms.

The general characteristic features of MTCS terminology is summarised in Table 1. below.

Table 1. The summary of characteristic features of MTCS terminology

Terminological aspect	Characteristics of MTCS terminology
syntactic characteristics	• nominal singleword terms • mainly noun phrases • high frequency of abbreviations • a tendency to use hybrid terms with units of measurement and symbols • the predominant majority of singular terms
neologisms	• creating neologisms by extension of meaning of GL lexemes • using old words in new meanings • using brand names as new coinages • Latin & Greek as sources of new specialised vocabulary • eponyms as neologisms • acronyms • internationalisms • Latin&Greek blends or modifications as neologisms • blends of existing terms • hybrid terms containing symbols, chemical formulae, units of measurement, etc.
borrowings	• higher reliance on native terminology in singleword terms • borrowing terminology from traditional languages of science as well as French and Dutch
metaphorisation	• metaphorisation of terminology more common among multiword terms • using metaphorical adjectives
synonymy	• more synonymous terms • synonyms created via anaphoric or cataphoric reference
polysemy	• homonymous abbreviations • intercategorial polysemy • borrowing terms from the general language
definitions	• high frequency of multiple definitions in the IEC standard • intracategorial homonymy • higher level of IEC definition coverage • mainly intensional definitions with a number of factual ones
ontologies	• 9 ontological categories with singleword terms as superordinate terms and multiword terms as subordinate ones

As can be inferred from Table 1 above MTCS terminology behaves in a consistent manner, which can also stem from the specificity of the language, and the fact that it enjoys its majority status. In terms of cognitive aspects, MTCS terminology is based on polarising mechanisms in terminology creation, as it relies both on standardisation and the sociocognitive vehicles. In addition, definitions are well-depicted in reference resources. However, in terms of origins, terms were borrowed from traditional languages of science, which again indicates the majority status of English (measured by the volume of publications in the MTCS domains).

The analysis has demonstrated that meaning in research articles in the MTCS domains is conveyed not only via terminology. Phraseological units are important participants in meaning-making due to their unique textual functions in these respects. The analysis of the most recurrent word combinations confirms a high frequency of nominal phrases among keyword terminology, followed by adjectival phrases as well as hybridised forms. On the other hand, there is a degree of overlap between generated collocations and multiword key terminology, which confirms previous studies on the subject, but their structure is more diverisifed. In addition, the predominant majority of scalar and construction collocates confirm the empirical and practical nature of the MTCS disciplines.

Research articles in these domains act as a spokesman that announces the success of the solution's implementation based on results of tests and experiments. A part of collocations forms domain-specific terminology with a number of complex keyword terms. Yet, the adopted categorisation needs to be treated metaphorically due to a high level of abstraction of MTCS terminology. Finally, lexical bundles present in the MTCS research articles predominantly concern the proposed solution, either hardware, software or developed methods, and contribute to the cohesion and coherence of the communicated message. Thus, the focus on the product confirms the claim that research is treated as a product for sale. Moreover, the authors guide the readers through the text via discourse organising bundles, which is consistent with the Saxonic writing convention. In addition, MTCS research articles also contain a high frequency of hedges, epistemic stance bundles, which indicates the author's reserved and cautious attitude towards the content in order to avoid face-threatening acts and prevent their studies from being rejected. The study of lexical bundles stays in the connection with the analysis of the authorial presence in the research article, a purportedly objective text, whose content is based on empirical verification. Yet, authors mark their presence with the use of personal pronouns and possessive adjectives. In addition, the authors use strategies to include the readers by referring to their experience or to call for feedback, or use specific linguistic means to distance themselves from the readers.

Returning to the hypothesis posed at the beginning of the study, it can be stated that scientific texts are cohesive and coherent, persuasive hybrid pieces of writing, in which hybridisation is manifested at various levels: the macrostructure of the text, terminology, the use of multimodal elements or even the presence of the author. Moreover, terminology is interdisciplinary, mainly borrowed from well-established disciplines, which confirms the disciplines' short-lived tradition as well as their dynamic development. Terms tend to form complex, multiword combinations, often hybridised (containing units of measurement, abbreviations or physical quantities) to ensure precision of expression and adhere to tight publisher's limits in the word count. Singleword terms in the analysed languages build word combinations which are domain-specific and they are not reflected in nomenclatures. In addition, they are used in either modified or completely new meanings which are not yet reflected in existing refence material. Moreover, singleword terms constitute superordinate terms in the MTCS terminological system, whereas multiword terms are subordinate, which was verified by the developed ontology.

The study also aimed at determining the degree of terminological standardisation. Surprisingly, the level of terminology description in the IEC glossary is low, which suggests dynamic changes in these disciplines as well as the retrospective and historical character of the nomenclature. On the end, cognitive mechanisms of terminology creation, like metaphorisation, synonymy and polysemy, are noticeable, and even reflected in the dedicated IEC standard. In addition, the analysis of aspects of technical terminology, like neologisms, borrowings, compression, or etymology of terms, indicates the English origin of terminology, which might suggest that it acts as a donor language in these disciplines. In addition, interdisciplinarity consitutes another feature of MTCS terminology, because the domains of new technologies draw on concepts from other, more traditional, disciplines. The feature also confirms the practical character of these subject fields, because they provide solutions that are implemented in various spheres of life. It is also manifested both through migration of terminology across domains and borrowings from traditional languages of science, all of which results in hybridity of the MTCS terminology. As it was discussed, terms in the analysed MTCS domains have a more complex syntactic structure than it is indicated in literature on the subject. A high frequency of abbreviated terms, combinations of terms with abbreviations, symbols, or units of measurement, etc. are also manifestations of hybridity in science.

The study also entailed the verification of phraseological units as participants in meaning-making. Non-idiomatic word combinations used in the MTCS research articles mainly refer to the proposed solutions, which puts emphasis on the products of research and proves the practical nature of the analysed domains, as they are supposed to convince the reader about the validity of the novel alternative. Lexical bundles play important textual roles in the analysed scientific articles, i.e. facilitate readers' comprehension of texts by ensuring text cohesion, and inform about the authors' attitudes towards the provided contents. The latter are connected with the authorial presence in the analysed texts which, prima facie, are intended to maintain objectivity. However, applied linguistic means perform persuasive functions, which confirms previous studies on the subject. Phraseological units together with the structure of the research paper contribute to the success of research, i.e. promoting the solutions as the most relevant alternative in the scientific arena.

Finally, domain-specific collocations comprise to a large extent complex terms with a different degree of formalisation, but their structure differs from the one described in literature on the subject. Collocations in the domains of new technologies consist of nominal or adjectival phrases as well as hybrids, and not only nouns phrases, as literature suggests. As a result, hybridity in the MTCS is manifested at different levels, which complies with earlier studies on technical and scientific communication.

Future directions would include the extension of the analysis of scientific texts and the inclusion of an additional subcorpus in another language. It would require a compilation of a subcorpus of research articles in German or other minority language. This would allow comparing trends in terminology creation the use of phraseology in three languages, two of which considered languages of science, which might prove to be helpful for scientific and technical translators. Such an extensive comparative study of technical terminology and phraseology in science would also contribute to a better understanding of contemporary scientific and technical communication, considered the most prestigious and at the same time demanding and complex in the translation process.

Bibliography

Adajian, T. (2005). On the Prototype Theory of Concepts and the Definition of Art. In *The Journal of Aesthetics and Art Criticism*. Vol. 63. No. 3. pp. 231–236.

Agrifoglio, R. (2015). Knowledge Preservation Through Community of Practice Theoretical Issues and Empirical Evidence. In: *SpringerBriefs in Information Systems*. Vol. XIV. No. 83. pp. 25–46.

Alekseev, P.M. (1973). Lexikalische und morphologische Statistik der Subsprache der Elektronik. pp. 157–169

Alvermann, D.E. & Wilson, A.A. (2011). *Comprehension* Strategy Instruction for Multimodal Texts in Science. In: *Theory Into Practice*. Vol. 50. Ohio: Routledge. pp. 116–124.

Ammon, U. 1998. *Ist Deutsch noch internationale Wissenschaftssprache? Englisch auch für die Lehre an den deutschsprachigen Hochschulen*. Berlin: de Gruyter.

Ammon, U., Dittmar, N. & Mattheier, K.J. (eds.). (1987). *Sociolinguistics. An International Handbook of the Science of Language and Society.* Berlin, New York: Walter de Gruyter.

Argamon, S., Chase, P. & Dodick, J. (2005). The Languages of Science: A Corpus-Based Study of Experimental and Historical Science Articles. In: *Proceedings of the Annual Meeting of the Cognitive Science Society*. Vol. 27. pp. 157–162.

Arsentyeva, Elena (2003). "Scientific and technical texts as an object of study and analysis." In: Kielar, B.Z. & Grucza,S. (eds) (2003). *Języki specjalistyczne 3. Lingwistyczna identyfikacja tekstów specjalistycznych.* Warszawa: Katedra Języków Specjalistycznych – Wydział Lingwistyki Stosowanej i Filologii Wschodniosłowiańskich UW. pp.169–176.

Atkins, S., Clear, J. & Ostler, N. (1992). Corpus Design Criteria. In: *Literary and Linguistic Computing*, Vol. 7. No. 1. pp. 1–31.

Bajerowska, A. (2017). Ontologie terminologiczne jako cyfrowe reprezentacje wiedzy. In: *Lingwistyka Stosowana / Applied Linguistics / Angewandte Linguistik*. Vol. 21. pp. 1–8.

Bakhtin, M. Discourse in the Novel. In The Dialogic Imagination: Four essays by M.M.Bakhtin. Holquist, M. (ed.). ([1935]1981). Emerson, C & Holquist, M. (trans.). Austin, TX: University of Texas Press.

Bartmiński, J. & Niebrzegowska-Bartmińska, S. (2009). *Tekstologia*. Warszawa: Wydawnictwo Naukowe PWN.

Batista da Silva, E., Ottaiano, A.O. & Babini, M. (2017). Identification of the most common phraseological units in the English language in academic texts: contributions coming from corpora. In: *Acta Scientiarium. Language and Culture*. Vol. 39. No. 4. pp. 345–353.

Baumann, K.D. (1997). Fachsprachliche Phänomene in den verschiedenen Sorten von populärwissenschaftlichen Vermittlungstexten. In: Hoffmann, Lothar et al.: *Fachsprachen. Handbücher zur Sprach- und Kommunikationswissenschaft 14*. Berlin: de Gruyter, pp. 728–735.

Baumann, K.D., Dörr, J.E. & Klammer, K. (2014). *Fachstile. Systematische Ortung einer interdisziplinären Kategorie*. Berlin: Frank & Timme Verlag für wissenschaftliche Literatur.

Bazerman, C. (1988). *Shaping written knowledge: The genre and activity of the experimental article in science*. Madison, WI: University of Wisconsin Press.

Belt, P., Mottonen, M. & Harkonen, J. (2011). Tips for Writing Scientific Journal Articles. In: *Industrial Engineering and Management Working Papers*, Vol. 5, Oulu: University of Oulu.

Biber, D. & Reppen, R. (2012). *Corpus Linguistics. Vol. IV. Methods and Applications*. London: SAGE Publications Ltd.

Biber, D. & Reppen, R. (2015). *The Cambridge Handbook of English Corpus Linguistics*. Cambridge: CUP.

Biber, D. (2006). *University Language. A Corpus-Based Study of Spoken and Written Register*. Amsterdam & Philadelphia: John Benjamins Publishing Company.

Biber, D. Representativeness in Corpus Design. In: Biber, D. & Reppen, R. (2012). *Corpus Linguistics. Vol. IV. Methods and Applications*. London: SAGE Publications Ltd. pp. 3–34.

Biber, D., Conrad, S. & Reppen, R. (2006). *Corpus Linguistics. Investigating Language Structure and Use.(Fifth printing)*. Cambridge: CUP.

Bilut-Homplewicz, Z. Czachura, W. & Smykała, M. (eds.). (2009). *Lingwistyka tekstu w Polsce i w Niemczech. Pojęcia, problemy, perspektywy*. Wrocław: Wrocławskie Wydawnictwo Oświatowe.

Bizzell, Patricia. *Academic Discourse and Critical Consciousness*. Pittsburgh: University of Pittsburgh Press, 1992.

Bloomfield, L. (1933) *Language*. London: George Allen & Unwin Ltd.

Borowiak, M. (2008). Przyszłość językowa Unii Europejskiej: mit wielojęzyczności czy dominacja języka angielskiego? In: *Investigationes Linguisticae*, Vol. XVI. pp. 1–15.

Bowker, L. & Pearson, J. (2002). *Working with Specialized Language. A practical guide to using corpora*. London & New York: Routledge.

Branson, R.D. (2004). Anatomy of a Research Paper. In: *Respiratory Care*. Vol. 49. No. 10, pp. 1222–1228.

Brutt-Griffler, J. (2006). Languages of Wider Communication. In: Brown, K. (ed.). *Encyclopaedia of Language and Linguistics*. Boston: Elsevier

Buchholz, E. (1978). Beispiele für bildliche Darstellung in englischen Fachtexten der Technik. In: *Berichte der Sektion Fremdsprachen*. Lepizig: Karl-Marx-Universität. pp. 111–127

Budinsky, K.G. (2001). *Engineer's Guide to Technical Writing*. Materials Park: ASM International.

Bursina, O.A. (2014). *Termiology of social work: structure, semantics, functioning [Terminogija social'noj roboty: struktura, semantika i funcionirovanie]*. Doctoral thesis. Saint-Petersburg: SPSU. (in Rus.).

Byrne, J. (2012). *Scientific and Technical Translation Explained. A Nut and Bolts Guide for Beginners*. London & New York: Routledge.

Cabré Castellví, M. T. (2003). Theories of Terminology. Their Description, Prescription and Explanation. In: *Terminology*. Vol. 9: 2. pp. 163–199.

Cabré, M. T. et al. (2006). 10 anys del Corpus de l'IULA. Barcelona: Institut Universitari de Lingüística Aplicada - Universitat Pompeu Fabra.

Cabré, T. & Sager, J.C. (ed.). (1998). *Terminology. Theory, Methods and Applications*. Amsterdam & Philadelphia: John Benjamins Publishing Company

Campos, A.A. & Tormer Castells, S. Adjectives and Collocations in Specialized Texts: Lexicographical Implications. In: Dykstra, A. & Schoonheim, T. (eds.). (2010). *Proceedings of the 14th Euralex International Congress*. Leeuwarden: Fryske Akademy. pp. 872–881.

Carrió Pastor, M.L. (2009). Contrasting Specific English Corpora: Language Variation. In: *International Journal of English Studies. Special Issue*. pp. 221–233.

Čermák, F. (2010) *Lexikon a semantika* [Lexicon and semantics]. Lidové noviny: Praha

Chen, Y.H. & Baker, P. (2010). Lexical Bundles in L1 and L2 Academic Writing. In: *Language Learning & Technology*.Vol. 14. No. 2. pp. 30–49.

Chitez, M., Doroholschi, C.I., Kruse, O., Salski, Ł. & Tucan, D. (eds.). (2018). *University Writing in Central and Eastern Europe: Tradition, Transition, and Innovation*. Cham: Springer.

Chlebda, W. (2013). *Na tropach korpusów. W poszukiwaniu optymalnych zbiorów tekstów*. Opole: Wydawnictwo Uniwersytetu Opolskiego.

Chromá, M. (2006). Synonymy and Polysemy in a Bilingual Law Dictionary. In: *Proceedings of Euralex 2006*. pp. 730–741.

Chromá, M. (2011). Synonymy and Polysemy in Legal Terminology and Their Applications to Bilingual and Bijural Translation. In: *Research in Language*, Vol. 9. No. 1. pp. 31–50.

Claessens, M. (2020). *ITER. The Giant Fusion Reactor. Bringing a Sun to Earth.* Cham: Springer.

Clancey, W.J. (2007). The knowledge level reinterpreted: Modelling socio-technical systems. *International Journal of Intelligent Systems.* Vol. 8(1). pp. 33–49.

Cocca, M, Kendzora, T.J., Řeřicha, V. & Martínez, E.A. (2016). Terminological synonyms in Czech and English sport terminologies. In: *Linguistica Pragensia.* Vol. 2. pp. 21–32.

Collier, J.H. & Toomey, D.M. (eds.). (1997). *Scientific and Technical Communication: Theory, Practice, and Policy.* Thousand Oaks: SAGE. Retrieved from: https://www.collier.sts.vt.edu/stc/index.htm

Collier, J.H. & Toomey, D.M.. Scientific and Technical Communication in Context. Retrieved from: http://www.faculty.english.vt.edu/Collier/stc/. Accessed 1 October, 2013

Copek, T., Barker, K., Delisle, S., Szpakowicz, S. & Delannoy, J.F. (1997). What Is Technical Text?. In: *Language Sciences*, Vol. 19. No. 4, pp. 391–423.

Cowie, A.P. (1994). Phraseology. In Asher, R.E. (ed.). *The Encyclopedia of Language and Linguistics.* pp. 3168–3171. Oxford: Oxford University Press.

Coxhead, A. A New Academic Word List. In: Biber, D. & Reppen, R. (2012). *Corpus Linguistics. Vol. IV. Methods and Applications.* London: SAGE Publications Ltd. pp. 249–274.

Cruse, A.D. (2004). *Meaning in Language. An Introduction to Semantics and Pragmatics.* Oxford: OUP.

Crystal, D. (1997). English as a Global Language. Cambridge: Cambridge University Press.

Crystal, D. (2003). *English as a Global Language. Second Edition.* Cambridge: CUP.

Dash, N.S. (2008). Context and Contextual Word Meaning. In: *SKASE Journal of Theoretical Linguistics.* Vol. 5. No. 2. pp. 21–31.

Davis, W.A. (1998). Implicature. In: *Routledge Encyclopedia of Philosophy.* London and New York: Routledge. pp. 89–93.

Day, R.A. How to Write a Scientific Paper. In: Scanlon, E., Hill, R. & Junker, K. (1999A). *Communicating Science: Professional Contexts.* London & New York: Routledge. pp. 89–100.

de Swaan, A. (2001). *Words of the World: The Global Language System.* Cambridge: Polity Press.

Dogan, M. (1996). The Hybridization of Social Science Knowledge. In: *Literary Trends.* Vol. 45. No. 2. pp. 296–314.

Dole, J. A., Duffy, G. G., Roehler, L. R., & Pearson, P. D. (1991). Moving from the old to new: Research on reading comprehension instruction. *Review of Educational Research, 61*, 239–264.

Dontcheva- Navrátilová, O. (2012). Lexical Bundles in Academic Texts by Non-Native Speakers. In: *Brno Studies in English*. Vol. 38. No. 2. pp. 37–58.

Dontcheva- Navrátilová, O. (2013). Authorial Presence in Academic Discourse: Functions of Autor-Reference Pronouns. In: *Linguistica Pragensia*. Vol. 1, pp. 9–30.

Dörr, J.E. Die Herausbildung von Fachdisziplinen. In: Baumann, K.D., Dörr, J.E. & Klammer, K. (eds.). (2014). *Fachstile, Systematische Ortung, einer interdisziplinären Kategorie*. Berlin: Frank & Timme Verlag für wissenschaftliche Literatur. pp. 11–26.

Drubin, D.G. & Kellogg, D.R. (2012). English as the Universal Language of Science: Opportunities and Challenges. In: *Molecular biology of the cell*. Vol. 23(8): 1399.

Dubuc, R. (1997) *Terminology: A Practical Approach*. Quebec: Linguatech Editeur Inc.

Dunaj, B. & Mycawka, M. (2017). O potrzebnych i niepotrzebnych zapożyczeniach z języka angielskiego. In: *Studia Linguistica XII. Annales Universitatis Paedagogicae Cracoviensis*. pp. 67–80.

Dury, P. (2005). Terminology and Specialized Translation: The Relevance of the Diachronic Approach. In: *LSP & Professional Communication*, Vol. 5. No. 1, pp. 31–41.

Duszak, A. (1998). *Tekst, dyskurs, komunikacja międzykulturowa*. Warszawa: Wydawnictwo Naukowe PWN.

Duszak, A., Gajek, E. & Okulska, U. (2006). *Korpusy w angielsko-polskim językoznawstwie kontrastywnym*. Kraków: Universitas.

Duszak, A., Jopek-Bosiacka, A. & Kowalski, G. (eds.). (2015). *Tekst naukowy i jego przekład*. Kraków: Universitas.

Eckert, T., Johann, A., Känzig, A., Küng, M., Müller, B., Schwald, C. & Walder, L. (2014). Is English a 'Killer Language'? The Globalisation of a Code. In: *eHistLing*. Vol. 1. pp. 106–118.

Ehlich, Konrad (2006), Mehrsprachigkeit in der Wissenschaftskommunikation – Illusion oder Notwendigkeit? (in:) K. Ehlich/ D. Heller (red.), Die Wissenschaften und ihre Sprachen. Bern, Peter Lang: s. 17–38.

European Commission. (2007). *Improving Knowledge Transfer Between Research Institutions and Industry Across Europe: Embracing Open Innovation. Implementing the Lisbon Agenda*. EUR 22836 EN, Office for Official Publications of the European Communities, Luxembourg.

Evans, V. & Green, M. (2006). *Cognitive Linguistics: an Introduction.* Edinburgh: Edinburgh University Press

Evans, V. (2007). *A Glossary of Cognitive Linguistics.* Salt Lake City: The University of

Faber Benítez, P., Márquez Linares, C. & Vega Expósito, M. (2005). Framing Terminology: A Process-Oriented Approach. In: *Meta: journal des traducteurs/ Meta: Translators' Journal.* Vol. 50. No. 4.

Faber, P. & López Rodriguez, C.I. Terminology and Specialized Language. In: Faber, P. (ed.). (2012). *A Cognitive Linguistics View of Terminology and Specialized Language.* Berlin: De Gruyter Mounton.

Faber, P. (2015). Frames as a framework for terminology. In: Kockaert, H.J. & Steurs, F. (eds.). (2015). *Handbook of Terminology. Volume I.* Amsterdam and Philadelphia: John Benjamins Publishing Company.

Faber, P. (ed.). (2012). *A Cognitive Linguistics View of Terminology and Specialized Language.* Berlin: De Gruyter Mounton.

Facchinetti, R. (ed.). (2007). *Corpus Linguistics 25 Years on.* Amsterdam: Rodopi B.V.

Falahati Qadimi Fumani, M. R. & Abdollahpour, S. (2017). Translation of Neologisms in Fishery-Engineering based on Kurki's (2012) Framework: A Strategy-Based Analysis. In: *International Journal of English Language & Translation Studies.* Vol. 5. No. 2. pp. 43–52.

Fathalla, M.F. (2004). *A Practical Guide for Health Researchers.* Cairo: World Health Organization Regional Office for the Eastern Mediterranean.

Fauconnier, G. & Turner, M. (2003). Conceptual Blending, Form and Meaning. In: *Recherches en Communication.* No. 19. pp. 57–86.

Felber, H. (1984). *Terminology Manual.* Paris: International Information Centre for Terminology (Infoterm) & UNESCO.

Felber, H. Basic Principles and Methods for the Preparation of Terminology Standards. In: Interrante, C.G. & Heymann, F.J. (eds.). (1983). *Standardization of Technical Terminology:Principles and Practices.* Toronto: ASTM STP 806. pp. 3–14.

Fillmore, C.J. & Atkins, B.T. (1992). Toward a Frame-based Lexicon: The Semantics of RISK and its Neighbors. In: Lehrer, A. & Feder Kittay, E. (eds.). *Frames, Fields and Contrasts.* New Jersey: Lawrence Erlbaum Assoc.

Fischer, G. (2000). Symmetry of Ignorance, Social Creativity, and Meta-design. In: *Knowledge-Based Systems.* Vol. 13. pp. 527–537.

Fischer, G. (2001A). *Communities of Interest: Learning Through the Interaction of Multiple Knowledge Systems.* In: 24th Annual Information Systems Research Seminar In Scandinavia (IRIS'24), pp. 1–14. Available at: http://www.cs.colorado.edu/~gerhard/papers/iris24.pdf

Fischer, G. (2001B). External and Sharable Artifacts as Sources for Social Creativity in Communities of Interest. In: Gero, J. S. & Maher, M. L. (eds.). *Computational and Cognitive Models of Creative Design V, Key Centre of Design Computing and Cognition* Sydney, Australia: University of Sydney, pp. 67–89. Available at: http://www.cs.colorado.edu/~gerhard/papers/ccmcd2001.pdf

Fischer, G. (2005). Social creativity: Making All Voices Heard. In: *Proceedings of the HCI International Conference (HCII)*. Retrieved from: https://pdfs.semanticscholar.org/d87e/2c3684da038afc99bb6d76a145292ddf8f95.pdf, 25.10.2018

Fischer, G. Learning, Social Creativity, and Cultures of Participation. In: Sannino, A. & Ellis, V. (eds.). (2014). *Learning and Collective Creativity. Activity-Theoretical and Sociocultural Studies*. New York: Routledge. pp. 198–215.

Fishman, J.A. Domains and the Relationship Between Micro- and Macrosociolinguistics. In: Gumperz, J. & Hymes, D. (eds.). (1972). *Directions in Sociolinguistics. The Ethnography of Speaking*. New York: Holt, Rinehart and Winston, pp. 407–434.

Flowerdew, L. (2015). Corpus-based Research and Pedagogy in EAP: From Lexis to Genre. In: *Language Teaching*. Vol. 48. No. 1. Cambridge: CUP. pp. 99–116.

Gafiyatova, E.V., Korovina, I.V., Solnyshkina, M.I. & Yarmakee, I.E. (2017). Deictic Elements as Means of Text Cohesion and Coherence in Academic Discourse. In: *Journal of Social Studies Education Research*. Vol. 8. No. 3. pp. 190–200

Gajda, S. (1982). *Podstawy badań stylistycznych nad językiem naukowym*. Warszawa/Wrocław: Państwowe Wydawnictwo Naukowe.

Gajda, S. (1990). *Współczesna polszczyzna naukowa. Język czy żargon?* Opole: Instytut Śląski w Opolu.

Gajda, S. (ed.). (1999). *Dyskurs naukowy – tradycja i zmiana*. Opole: Uniwersytet Opolski– Instytut Filologii Polskiej.

Gajda, S. Styl naukowy. In: Bartmiński, J. (ed.). (2001). *Współczesny język polski*. Lublin: Wydawnictwo Uniwersytetu Marii Skłodowskiej-Curie. pp. 183–199.

Gajda, S. Styl naukowy. In: Malinowska, E., Nocoń, J. & Żydek-Bednarczuk, U. (eds.). (2013). *Przewodnik po stylistyce polskiej. Style współczesnej polszczyzny*. Kraków: Universitas.

Gajek, E. Zasoby i narzędzia internetowe w językoznawstwie korpusowym. In: Duszak, A., Gajek, E. & Okulska, U. (2006). *Korpusy w angielsko-polskim językoznawstwie kontrastywnym*. Kraków: Universitas. pp. 311–327.

Gallego Hernández, D. (2015). The Use of Corpora as Translation Resources. A Study Based on a Survey of Spanish Professionals Translators.

In: *Perspectives: Studies in Translation Theory and Practice*. Vol. 23. No. 3. pp. 375–391.

Galster, C. Hybrid genres. In: *Routledge Encyclopedia of Narrative Theory*. Herman, D., Jahn, M. & Ryan, M.L.(eds). (2005). pp. 226–227. London: Routledge.

Galtung, J. (1981). Structure, Culture, and Intellectual Style: An Essay Comparing Saxonic, Teutonic, Gallic and Nipponic Approaches. In: *Social Science Information*. SAGE: London and Beverly Hills. Vol. 20, No. 6, pp. 817–856

Geeraerts, D. (1989). Prototype Theory. Prospects and Problems of Prototype Theory. In: *Linguistics*. Vol. 27. No. 4. pp. 587–612.

Ghajoyan, H. (2017). The Role of Metaphor in Technical Term-Formation. In: *Armenian Folia Anglistika*. Vol. 1. No. 15. Yerevan: YSU. pp. 27–38.

Gibson, J.J. (1979). *The Ecological Approach to Visual Perception*. Boston: Houghton Mifflin

Gledhill, C.J. (2000). *Collocations in Science Writing*. Tübingen: Gunter Narr Verlag.

Gliński, W. (2005). Ontologie-próba uporządkowania terminologicznego chaosu. In: *Od informacji naukowej do technologii społeczeństwa wiedzy. Nauka-Dydaktyka- Praktyka*. pp. 163–175.

Gnutzmann, C. & Rabe, F. (2014). „Das ist das Problem, das hinzukriegen, dass es so klingt, als hätt' es ein Native Speaker geschrieben". Wissenchafltiches Schreiben und Publizieren in der Fremdsprache Englisch. In: *Fachsprache*, Vol. 1–2/2014, pp. 31–52.

Godin, B. & Gingras, Y. (2000). What is Scientific and Technological Culture and How Is It Measured? A Multidimensional Model. In: *Public Understanding of Science*. Vol. 9. pp. 43–58.

Gonzalez, W.J. (ed.). (2005). *Science, Technology and Society: A Philosophical Perspective*. Bern: Netbiblio.

Göpferich, S. (2000). Analyzing LSP Text Types: From Descriptive to Prescriptive Text(-Type) Linguistics. In: Trosborg, A. (ed.). *Analysing Professional Genres*. Amsterdam: John Benjamins Publishing Company

Górnicz M. (1997) Sposoby i granice kompresji terminów (na podstawie terminologii medycznej– nazwy nowotworów. W: *Poradnik Językowy*. Nr 2 (541).

Górnicz, M. (2019). *Wewnątrzjęzykowe uwarunkowania zapożyczeń technolektalnych w języku polskim. Sudi@ Naukowe pod redakcją naukową Sambora Gruczy*. Warszawa: Instytut Komunikacji Specjalistycznej i Interkulturowej Uniwersytet Warszawski.

Goźdź-Roszkowski, S. & Witczak-Plisiecka, I. (2005). Korpusy a języki specjalistyczne. In: Lewandowska-Tomaszczyk, B. (ed.). *Podstawy językoznawstwa korpusowego*. Łódź: Wydawnictwo Uniwersytetu Łódzkiego. pp. 174–200.

Grabowski, Ł & Piotrowski, T. Interpretacja danych frekwencyjnych z korpusów językowych : opis pewnych problemów (na kilku przykładach z życia wziętych). In: Chlebda, W. (2013). *Na tropach korpusów. W poszukiwaniu optymalnych zbiorów tekstów*. Opole: Wydawnictwo Uniwersytetu Opolskiego. pp. 59–71.

Graddol, D. (2000). *The Future of English? A Guide to the Popularity of the English Language in the 21st Century*. London: The British Council, The English Company (UK), Ltd.

Granath, S. (2007). Size Matters – Or Thus Can Meaningful Structures Be Revealed in Large Corpora. In: Facchinetti, R. (ed.). *Corpus Linguistics 25 Years on*. Amsterdam: Rodopi B.V. pp. 169–184.

Granger, S. & Paquot, M. (2008). Disentangling the Phraseological Web. In: Granger, S. & Meunier, F. (eds.). *Phraseology: An Interdisciplinary Perspective*. Amsterdam & Philadelphia: John Benjamins Publishing Company. pp. 27–49.

Grinev-Griniewicz, S. (2016). Polysemy in Language and Thought. In: *CROSSROADS. A Journal of English Studies*. No. 12. pp. 19–30.

Groom, N. (2005). "Pattern and meaning across genres and disciplines: an exploratory study". *Journal of English for Academic Purposes* 4: 257–277.

Gross, A.G., Harmon, J.E. & Reidy, M.S. (2002). *Communicating Science. The Scientific Article from the 17th Century to the Present*. Oxford: OUP.

Gruber T.R.(1993). *Toward Principles for the Design of Ontologies Used for Knowledge Sharing*, Stanford Knowledge Systems Laboratory. http://tomgruber.org/writing/onto-design.pdf, [Accessed: 5.05.2013].

Grucza, F. & Wiśniewski, W. (eds.). (2005). *Teoria i praktyka upowszechniania nauki wczoraj i jutro*. Warszawa: Polska Akademia Nauk, Rada Upowszechniania Nauki przy Prezydium PAN

Grucza, F. (2017A). *Dzieła wybrane. Tom 8. Zagadnienia metalingwistyki. Lingwistyka – jej przedmiot, lingwistyka stosowana. Wydanie jubileuszowe z okazji 80. rocznicy urodzin*. Warszawa: Wydawnictwo Naukowe Instytutu Komunikacji Specjalistycznej i Interkulturowej.

Grucza, F. (2017B). *Dzieła zebrane. Tom 3. O języku, językach i lingwistyce. Wydanie jubileuszowe z okazji 80. rocznicy urodzin*. Warszawa: Wydawnictwo Naukowe Instytutu Komunikacji Specjalistycznej i Interkulturowej.

Grucza, S. (2009). O nieporozumieniach w sprawie siły lingwistyki. In: *Lingwistyka Stosowana / Applied Linguistics / Angewandte Linguistik*. No. 1, pp. 99–113

Grucza, S. (2010). Główne tezy antropocentrycznej teorii języków. In: *Lingwistyka Stosowana*. No. 2. pp. 41–68.

Grucza, S. (2013). *Lingwistyka języków specjalistycznych*. Warszawa: Wydawnictwo Naukowe Instytutu Kulturologii i Lingwistyki Antropocentrycznej Uniwersytet Warszawski.

Grucza, S. (2015). Języki jako instrumenty predykcji wiedzy przyszłości. In: Duszak, A. Jopek- Bosiacka, A. & Kowalski, G. (eds.). *Tekst naukowy i jego przekład*. Kraków: Universitas.

Gruntar Jermol, A. (2007). Fachsprachliche Kollokationen: Schwerpunkt Deutsch- Slowenisch. In: *Linguistica*, Vol. 47. No. 1. pp. 137–144.

Grzelak, W. (2013). Ontologia – próba usystematyzowania pojęć. In: *Informatyka ekonomiczna (Business Informatics)*, Vol. 4. No. 30. pp. 159–168.

Gumperz, J.J. (1968). The Speech Community. In: Duranti, A. (ed.). (2001). *Linguistic Anthropology. A Reader*. Oxford: Blackwell Publishing, pp. 43–52.

Hajnicz, E. (2011). *Najbardziej znane korpusy tekstów. Opracowanie przeglądowe. Nr 1021*. Warszawa: Wydawnictwo IPI PAN.

Halliday, M.A.K. (1973). *Explorations in the Functions of Language*. London: Edward Arnold.

Hamel, R.E. (2007). The Dominance of English in the International Scientific Periodical Literature and the Future of Language Use in Science. In: *AILA Review 20*. John Benjamins Publishing Company. pp. 53–71.

Hebal-Jezierska, M. (2013). Podstawowe zasady korzystania z korpusów przy badaniu języka. In: Chlebda, W. *Na tropach korpusów. W poszukiwaniu optymalnych zbiorów tekstów*. Opole: Wydawnictwo Uniwersytetu Opolskiego. pp. 17–30.

Hengl, T. & Gould, M. (2002). *Rules of thumb for writing research articles*. Retrieved from: https://www.researchgate.net/publication/228549945. 18.10.2016.

Henri, F. & Pudelko, B. (2003). Understanding and Analysing Activity and Learning in Virtual Communities. In: *Journal of Computer Assisted Learning*, Vol. 19. Wiley: Blackwell Publishing, pp. 474–487.

Herzberg, B. (1986). The politics of discourse communities. Paper presented at the CCC Convention, New Orleans, La, March 1986.

Herzog, R. (1971). Gegenwärtige Tendenzen in der terminologischen Wortbildung. In: *Mitteilungsblatt für Dolmetscher und Übersetzer*. Vol. 17. 9/10 pp. 3–6.

Hoffmann, L. (1985). Vom Fachwortschatz zum Fachtext. In: *WZ der PH Zwickau*. Vol. 1. pp. 117–121.

Hoffmann, L. (ed.). (1973). Fachwortschatz Chemie, Häufigkeitswörterbuch Russisch, Englisch, Französisch. Leipzig.

Hüning, M. & Schlücke, B. Multi-word Expressions. In: Müller, P.O., Ohnheiser, I., Olsen, S. & Rainer, F. (eds.). (2015). *Word Formation, An International Handbook of the Languages of Europe [HSK series]*. Berlin: De Gruyter. pp. 450–467.

Hunston, S. (2008). Collection Strategies and Design Decisions. In: Lüdeling, A. & Kytö, M. (eds.). *Corpus Linguistics. An International Handbook. Volume 1.* Berlin: De Gruyter Mouton. pp. 154–167.

Hunston, S. (2010). Corpora and language teaching: issues of language. In S. Hunston. *Corpora in applied linguistics* (p. 137–169). Cambridge, MA: Cambridge University Press.

Hyland, K. & Shaw, K. (eds.). (2016). *The Routledge Handbook of English for Academic Purposes.* London: Routledge

Hyland, K. (1995). The Author in the Text. Hedging Scientific Writing. In: *Hong Kong Papers in Linguistics and Language Teaching.* Vol. 18. pp. 33–42.

Hyland, K. (1998). Persuasion and Context: The Pragmatics of Academic Metadiscourse. In: *Journal of Pragmatics*, Vol. 30. pp. 437–455.

Hyland, K. (2009A). *Academic Discourse. English in a Global Context.* London: Continuum

Hyland, K. (2009B). Writing in the Disciplines: Research Evidence for Specificity. In: *Taiwan International ESP Journal*, Vol. 1. No. 1, pp. 5–22

Hyland, K. (2011). Disciplines and Discourses: Social Construction of Knowledge. In: Starke-Meyerring, D., Paré, A., Artemeva, N., Horne, M. & Yousoubova, L. (eds.). *Writing in the Knowledge Society.* West Lafayette: Parlor Press and The WAC Clearinghouse. pp. 193–214.

Hyland, K. Corpora and Written Academic English. In: Biber, D. & Reppen, R. (2015). *The Cambridge Handbook of English Corpus Linguistics.* Cambridge: CUP. pp. 292–308.

Hymes, D. (1972). Models of the Interaction of Language and Social Life. In: Gumperz, J.J. & Hymes, D. (eds.). (1972). *Directions in Sociolinguistics: The Ethnography of Communication*. New York: Holt, Rinehart & Winston. pp. 35–71. http://orfeo.tessitures.org/actes-de- langage/scene-langagiere/speech-community-hymes/ available 19.07.2018

Iljinska, L. & Smirnova, T. (2010). Pragmatic Aspects of Scientific Technical Text Analysis. In: Witczak-Plisiecka, I. (ed.). *Pragmatic Perspectives of Language and Linguistics* Vol. II: Pragmatics

Iljinska, L. & Smirnova, T. (2014). Conflicting Tendencies in the Development of Scientific and Technical Language Varieties: Metaphorization vs. Standardization. In: *Research in Language*. Vol. 12. No. 1, pp. 93–111.

Interrante, C.G. & Heymann, F.J. (eds.). (1983). *Standardization of Technical Terminology: Principles and Practices*. Toronto: ASTM STP 806.

Janda, L. A. 2000. Cognitive Linguistics. Paper presented at SLING2K Workshop (February 2000). Available at: http://www.seelrc.org/glossos/issues/8/janda.pdf.)

Jeż, M. Problemy współczesnej terminologii turystycznej w języku polskim i ukraińskim. In: Łukasik, M. & Mikołajewska, B. (eds.). (2014). *Studi@ Naukowe 17. Języki specjalistyczne wczoraj, dziś i jutro*. Warszawa: Wydawnictwo Naukowe Instytutu Kulturologii i Lingwistyki Antropocentrycznej, Uniwersytet Warszawski.

Jiao, X. & Wenjing, Z. (2013). English Dominance and Its Influence on International Communication. In: *Theory and Practice in Language Studies*. Vol. 3. No. 12. pp. 2262–2266.

Johansson, S. (2007). Seeing Through Multilingual Corpora. In: Facchinetti, R. (ed.). *Corpus Linguistics 25 Years on*. Amsterdam: Rodopi B.V. pp. 51–71.

Johnson, M. (1987). *The body in the mind: The bodily basis of meaning, imagination, and reason*. Chicago: University of Chicago Press.

Johnstone, B. & Marcellino, W. Dell Hymes and the Ethnography of Communication. In: Wodak, R., Johnstone, B. & Kerswill, P. (eds.). (2010). *The Sage Handbook of Sociolinguistics*. London: Sage Publishers.

Kamberelis, G. & Wehunt, M.D. (2012). Hybrid Discourse Practice and Science Learning. In: *Cultural Studies of Science Education*. Vol. 7, pp. 505–534.

Karpiński, Ł. (2017). *Systemy leksykalno-komunikacyjne*. Warszawa: Wydawnictwo Campidoglio.

Kerswill, P. (1994). *Dialects Converging: Rural Speech in Urban Norway*. Oxford: Oxford University Press.

Klégr, A. (2004). Intralingual and interligual synonymy. *An Online Journal of Modern Philology*. Retrieved from: http://philologica.net/studia/20

Klemensiewicz, Z. (1953). *O różnych odmianach współczesnej polszczyzny*. Warszawa: PIW.

Klemensiewicz, Z. (1956). Zagadnienia i założenia historii języka polskiego. In: *Pamiętnik Literacki: czasopismo kwartalne poświęcone historii i krytyce literatury polskiej*. Vol. 47. No. 3. pp. 86–137.

Klimova, B.F. (2013). Scientific Prose and Its Specifics. In: *Procedia – Science and Behavioral Sciences*, Vol. 83, pp. 52–55.

Kockaert, H.J. & Steurs, F. (eds.). (2015). *Handbook of Terminology. Volume I.* Amsterdam & Philadelphia: John Benjamins Publishing Company.

Kołupajło, K. Język naukowy jako autonimiczny przedmiot badań naukowych. In: Łukasik, M. & Mikołajewska, B. (eds.). (2014). *Studi@ Naukowe 17. Języki specjalistyczne wczoraj, dziś i jutro.* Warszawa: Wydawnictwo Naukowe Instytutu Kulturologii i Lingwistyki Antropocentrycznej Uniwersytet Warszawski.

Kontutytė, E. (2017). *Einführung in die Fachsprachenlinguistik.* Vilnus: Vilniaus universiteto leidykla.

Kosova, M.V. (2003). Russian linguitic terminology: semantic process [Russkaja lingvisticheskaja terminologija: semanticheskie processy]. Volgograd: VSU (in Rus.)

Kozłowska, Z. (2007). *O przekładzie tekstu naukowego (na materiale tekstów językoznawczych) Wydanie II.* Warszawa: Wydawnictwa Uniwersytetu Warszawskiego.

Krapivkina, O.A. (2015). Verbalization of the Writer in Academic Prose. In: *Journal of Siberian Federal University. Humanities and Social Science.* Vol. 8. pp. 1625–1634.

Kristeva, J. (1986). *The Kristeva reader* (Ed. T. Moi). Oxford: Blackwell.

Kruger, A., Wallmach, K. & Munday, J. (eds.). (2011). *Corpus-Based Translation Studies. Research and Applications.* London & New York: Continuum International Publishing Group.

Kublikowski, R. (2012). Definicja perswazyjna –niemanipulacyjna czy manipulacyjna. In: *Przegląd Filozoficzny – Nowa Seria.* No. 3. pp. 273–282.

Kuhi, D. (2017). Hybridity of Scientific Discourses: An Intertextual Perspective and Implications for ESP Pedagogy. In: *The Journal of Applied Linguistics and Applied Literature: Dynamics and Advances.* Vol. 5. No. 2, Summer and Autumn, pp. 61–80.

Kulikova, I.S. & Salmina, D.V. (2002). *Introduction into the metalinguistics: lexographical and communicative pragmatic system aspects. [Vvedenie v metalingvistiku; sistemnyj leksikograficheskij i kommunikativno-pragmaticheskij aspekty].* Moscow: Vertikal (in Rus.).

Kurkowska, H. & Skorupka, S. (2001). *Stylistyka polska. Zarys. Wydanie V uzupełnione.* Warszawa: Wydawnictwo Naukowe PWN.

L'Homme, M.C. (2018). Maintaining the Balance Between Knowledge and the Lexicon in Terminology: A Methodology Based on Frame Semantics. In: Lexicography. Vol. 4. pp. 3–21

Labocha, J. (2008). *Tekst, wypowiedź, dyskurs w procesie komunikacji językowej.* Kraków: Wydawnictwo Uniwersytetu Jagiellońskiego

Labov, W. (1982). Building on empirical foundations. In W. P. Lehmann and Y. Malkiel (eds.), *Perspectives on Historical Linguistics*. Amsterdam: Benjamins. 17–92.

Lakoff, G. & Johnsen, M. (2003). *Metaphors We Live By*. London: The University of Chicago Press.

Lakoff, G. (1987). *Women, Fire, and Dangerous Things: What Categories Reveal about the Mind*. Chicago & London: The Chicago University Press.

Landheer, R. (1989). L'importance des relations hyponymiques dans la description lexicographique. *Actes du XVIIIe Conres International de Linguistiquw et de Philologie Romanes. Université de Trèves. Tübingen*: Max Niemeyer Verlag. pp. 139–151.

Langacker R. (1987). *Foundations of Cognitive Grammar*. Vol. 1. Stanford University Press. International Publishing Group. pp. 13–32.

Laponce, Jean. (2003). Babel and the market: Geostrategy for minority languages. 58–63. 10.1017/CBO9780511613739.005.

Lavrova, A. IT Engineering Specialized Language Manifestations. In: Budin, G. & Lusicky, V. (eds.). (2013). *Languages in for Special Purposes in a Multilingual, Transcultural World. Proceedings of the 19th European Symposium on Languages for Special Purposes. LSP 2013, Vienna, Austria*. pp. 23–28.

Lehrer, A. (2010). Problems in the Translation of Creative Neologisms. In: Lewandowska- Tomaszczyk, B. & Thelen, M. (eds.). *Meaning in Translation*. Frankfurt am Mein: Peter Lang. pp. 293–303.

Lemke, J.L. (1990A). *Talking Science: Language, Learning and Values*. Westport: Ablex Publishing.

Lemke, J.L. (1990B). Technical Discourse and Technocratic Ideology. In: Halliday, M.A.K., Gibbons, J. & Nicholas, H. (eds.). *Learning, Keeping and Using Language: Selected papers from the Eighth World Congress of Applied Linguistics*, Sydney, 16–21 August 1987. Vol. 2. pp. 435–460.

Lemke, J.L. (1995). *Textual Politics: Discourse And Social Dynamics*. London: Taylor & Francis.

Lemke, J.L. Multiplying Meaning: Visual and Verbal Semiotics in Scientific Text. In: Martin, J.R. & Veel, R. (eds.). (1998). *Reading Science. Critical and Functional Perspectives on Discourses of Science*. London: Routledge.

León Araúz, P. & San Martín, M. (2011). Distinguishing Polysemy from Contextual Variation in Terminological Definitions. In: *Actas del X Congreso de la Asociación Europea de Lenguas para Fines Específicos: La investigación y la enseñanza aplicadas a las lenguas de especialidad y a la tecnología*. pp. 173–186.

Lesser, E.L. & Storck, J. (2001). Communities of Practice and Organizational Performance. In: *IBM Systems Journal*. Vol. 40. No. 4. pp. 831–841.

Levická, J. (2009). Terminology Variation: On the Concept of Synonymy in the Light of an Interlingual Analysis of a Terminology Field. Retrieved from: https://www.semanticscholar.org/paper/Terminology-Variation%3A-On-the-Concept- of-Synonymy-a-Levick%C3%A1/c6d2d4f505e553e30390a9e8bb6ce5d8b54764a2, 21.12.2019.

Lewandowska-Tomaszczyk, B. & Thelen, M. (eds.). (2010). *Meaning in Translation*. Frankfurt am Mein: Peter Lang

Lewandowska-Tomaszczyk, B. (ed.). (2005). *Podstawy językoznawstwa korpusowego*. Łódź: Wydawnictwo Uniwersytetu Łódzkiego.

Lewandowska-Tomaszczyk, B. Re-conceptualization and the emergence of discourse meaning as a theory of translation. In: Lewandowska-Tomaszczyk, B. & Thelen, M. (eds.). (2010). *Meaning in Translation*. Frankfurt am Mein: Peter Lang.

Li, T. Chubak, P., Lakshmanan, L.V.S. & Pottinger, R. (2012). Efficient Extraction of Ontologies from Domain Specific Text Corpora. In: *Natural Language Processing and Chinese Computing*. In: *CIKM '12: Proceedings of the 21st ACM international conference on Information and knowledge management*. pp. 1537–1541.

Linder, D. & De Sterck, G. (2016). Non-native scientists, research dissemination and English neologisms: What happens in the early stages of reception and re-production?. Iberica. 2016. pp. 25–58.

Lindsay, D. (1995). *Dobre rady dla piszących teksty naukowe*. (K. Pesz Trans.) Wrocław: Oficyna Wydawnicza Politechniki Wrocławskiej.

Lipka, L. (1992). *An Outline of English Lexicology. Lexical Structure, Word Semantics and Word-Formation*. Tübingen: Max Niemeyer Verlag.

Livnat, Z. (2012). *Dialogue, Science and Academic Writing*. Amsterdam & Philadelphia: John Benjamins Publishing Company.

Löckinger, G., Kockaert, H.J. & Budin, G. Intensional Definitions. In: Kockaert, H.J. & Steurs, F. (eds.). (2015). *Handbook of Terminology. Volume I*. Amsterdam/Philadelphia: John Benjamins Publishing Company. pp. 60–81.

López Mateo. C. & Olmo Cazevieille, F. (2015). Compiling Texts for a Specialized Corpus in the Biochemistry Domain: Theoretical and Methodological Aspects. In: *Procedia – Social and Behavioural Sciences*. Vol. 198. pp. 300–308.

Losee, R.M. (1999). Communication Defined as Complementary Informative Processes. In: *Journal of Information, Communication and Library Science*. Vol. 5, pp. 1–15.

Lüdeling, A. & Kytö, M. (eds.). (2008). *Corpus Linguistics. An International Handbook. Volume 1*. Berlin: De Gruyter Mouton. pp. 154–167.

Lukszyn, J. & Zmarzer, W. (2001). *Teoretyczne podstawy terminologii.* Warszawa: Wydział Lingwistyki Stosowanej i Filologii Wschodniosłowiańskich.

Lušicky, V. & Wissik, T. (2015). *Procedural Manual on Terminology. Translation-Oriented Terminology Work.* Skopje: Secretariat for European Affairs & Deutsche Gesellschaft für Internationale Zusammenarbeit.

Lyons, J. (1968). *Wstęp do językoznawstwa (Introduction to Theoretical Linguistics).* Warszawa: PWN

Lyons, J. (1977). *Semantics Volume 2.* Cambridge: CUP.

Lyons, J. (1995). *Linguistic Semantics: An Introduction.* Cambridge: CUP

Łukasik, M. & Mikołajewska, B. (eds.). (2014). *Studi@ Naukowe 17. Języki specjalistyczne wczoraj, dziś i jutro.* Warszawa: Wydawnictwo Naukowe Instytutu Kulturologii i Lingwistyki Antropocentrycznej Uniwersytet Warszawski.

Łukasik, M. & Zych, M. (2014). Detailed Terminographic Analysis of „Glossary of Terminology Used in the Standardization of Geographical Names". In: *Activities relating to the Working Group of Toponymic Terminology.* New York: 28th Session of United Nations Group of Geographical Experts.

Łukasik, M. (ed.).(2008). *Debiuty Naukowe II. Terminologia – Translatoryka – Terminografia.* Warszawa: Katedra Języków Specjalistycznych, Wydział Lingwistyki Stosowanej i Filologii Wschodniosłowiańskich UW.

Maćkiewicz, J. (1996). *Jak pisać teksty naukowe.* Gdańsk: Wydawnictwo Uniwersytetu Gdańskiego.

Maferat, H. & Mohammadzadeh, S. (2013). Genre analysis of literature research article abstracts: A cross-linguistic, cross-cultural study. In: *Applied Research on English Language.* Vol. 2, pp. 37–49.

Maia, B. (2003A). What are Comparable Corpora? In: *Proceeding of the Corpus Linguistics Workshop on Multilingual Corpora: Linguistic Requirements and Technical Perspectives.* pp. 27–34.

Maia, B. (2003B). *Using Corpora for Terminology Extraction. Pedagogical and computational approaches.* Retrieved from: http://repositorio- aberto.up.pt/bitstream/10216/14010/2/usingcorpora000072829.pdf, 10.05.2015.

Makowska, A.B. (2015). Hybrid, Borrowing, or Code-Switching? The Analysis of Selected Terminology of State-of-the-art Technologies in Polish. In: Kwiatkowska, A. & Stanecka, A. (eds.). *Hybrids and Hybridity.* Piotrków Trybunalski: Naukowe Wydawnictwo Piotrkowskie przy Filii Uniwersytetu Jana Kochanowskiego. pp. 191–207.

Makowska, A.B. (2016). Conceptual Discrepancies of Polish-English Terminology. Designing a Corpus of Microelectronics, Telecommunication and Computer

Science for Scientific Translation. In: Bogucki, Ł, Lewandowska-Tomaszczyk, B. & Thelen, M. (eds.). *Translation and Meaning. New Series*. Vol. 2 Part 2. Frankfurt am Mein: Peter Lang GmbH. pp. 263–284.

Makowska, A.B. (2016). Creating Multilingual Corpora to Teach Scientific Translation. In: Gallego- Hernández, D. (ed.). *New Insights into Corpora and Translation*. Newcastle upon Tyne: Cambridge Scholars Publishing. pp. 57–78.

Makowska. A.B. (2018). Research Articles as a Means of Communicating Science: Polish and Global Conventions. In: Chitez, M., Doroholschi, C.I., Kruse, O., Salski, Ł. & Tucan, D. (eds.). *University Writing in Central and Eastern Europe: Tradition, Transition, and Innovation*. Cham: Springer.

Malinowska, E., Nocoń, J. & Żydek-Bednarczuk, U. (eds.). (2013). *Przewodnik po stylistyce polskiej. Style współczesnej polszczyzny*. Kraków: Universitas

Martín-Martín, P. (2003). Genre and Discourse Community. In: *ES Revista de filología inglesa*. No. 25. pp. 153–166.

Mattiello, E. (2012). Abbreviations in English and Italian Scientific Discourse. In: *ESP Across Cultures*. Vol. 9. pp. 149–168.

Mazurkiewicz-Sułkowska, J. (2014). *Słowiańska terminologia techniczna na materiale polskim, rosyjskim i bułgarskim*. Łódź: Wydawnictwo Uniwersytetu Łódzkiego.

McEnery, T. & Wilson, A. (1996). *Corpus Linguistics. An Introduction. Second Edition*. Edinburgh: Edinburgh University Press.

Meadows, A.J. (1998). *Communicating research*. San Diego: Academic Press.

Medawar, P. (1999). Is the Scientific Paper a Fraud? In: Scanlon, E., Hill, R. & Junker, K. *Communicating Science: Professional Contexts*. London & New York: Routledge. pp. 27–31.

Menon, S. & Mukundan, J. (2012). Collocations of High Frequency Noun Keywords in Prescried Science Textbooks. In: *International Education Studies*. Vol. 5. No. 6. pp. 149–160.

Mentrup, W. (1976). Gemeinsprache und Fachsprachen. Überlegungen zur Methodik ihrer lexikographischen Erfassung. In: *Wirkendes Wort*. Vol. 26. No. 6 pp. 431–443.

Mikołajczak, S. (1990). *Składnia tekstów naukowych. Dyscypliny humanistyczne*. Poznań: Wydawnictwo Naukowe Uniwersytetu im. Adama Mickiewicza.

Miller, C.R. & Fahnestock, J. (2013). Genres in Scientific and Technical Rhetoric. In: *Poroi. The Interdisciplinary Journal of Rhetorical Analysis and Invention*. Vol. 9. No. 1. pp. 1–4.

Mohammadi, M. (2013). Meeting Translator's Terminological Needs. In: *Proceedings of the 4th Ottawa Student Colloquium on Terminology, Lexicology and Technologies*.

Möhn, D. & Pelka, R. (2007). *Fachsprachen. Eine Einführung*. Tübingen: Max Niemeyer Verlag.

Moles, A. (1962). La cite scientifique en 1972. In: Bulletin Societe d'Etudes et Documentation Economiques et Sociales. Paris

Montero-Martínez, S. & Faber Benítez, P. (2009). Terminological Competence in Translation. In: *Terminology*. Vol. 15. No. 1. pp 88–104.

Montgomery, S.L. (2000). *Science in Translation. Movements of Knowledge through Cultures and Time*. London: The University of Chicago Press

Morgan, M. (2004). Speech Community. In: Duranti (ed.). *A Companion to Linguistic Anthropology*. Oxford: Blackwell Publishing. pp. 3–22.

Müldner-Nieckowski, P. (2016). Schemat procedury definiowania znaczeń związku frazeologicznego. In: Dziamska-Lenart, G. & Liberek, J. (eds.). *Perspektywy współczesnej frazeologii polskiej. Geneza dawnych i nowych frazeologizmów polskich*. pp. 209–227.

Myers-Scotton C. Code switching. In: Coulmas, F. (red.). (1998). *The Handbook of Sociolinguistics*. Hoboken: Blackwell Publishing.

Nair, P.K.R. & Nair V.D. (2014). Organization of a Research Paper: The IMRAD Format. In: *Scientific Writing and Communication in Agriculture and Natural Resource*. Switzerland: Springer International Publishing, pp. 13–25.

Nakos, D. (1983). Is Standardization Always Necessary? In: Interrante, C.G. & Heymann, F.J. (eds.). *Standardization of Technical Terminology: Principles and Practices*. Toronto: ASTM STP 806. pp. 40–45.

Newmark, P. (1988). *A Textbook of Translation*. Hempstead: Prentice Hall

Newmark, P. (2004). Non-literary in the Light of Literary Translation. In: *Journal of Specialised Translation*. No. 1, pp. 8–13.

Nilsson, H. (2015). Enumerations Count. Extensional and Partitive Definitions. In: Kockaert, H.J. & Steurs, F. (eds.). *Handbook of Terminology. Volume I*. Amsterdam & Philadelphia: John Benjamins Publishing Company. pp. 82–100

Ning, Z. (2008). A Genre-based Analysis of English Research Article Abstracts and the Linguistic Feature of Personal Pronouns for Financial Economics. In: *US-China Education Review*, Vol. 5. No. 7, pp. 62—65

O'Conner, M. and Woodford, F.P. (1976). *Writing scientific papers in English*. Amsterdam: Elsevier

Ogden, C.K. & Richards, I.A. (1923). *The Meaning of Meaning. A Study of the Influence of Language upon Thought and of the Science of Symbolism*. New York: Harcourt, Brace &World, Inc.

Okoń, W. (ed.). (1979). *Teoria i praktyka upowszechniania wiedzy*. Warszawa: Wiedza Powszechna.

Olohan, M. (2016). *Scientific and Technical Translation*. Oxon & New York: Routledge.

Olohan, M. Scientific and Technical Translation. In: Baker, M. & Saldanha, G. (eds.). (2011). *Routlegde Encyclopaedia of Translation Studies Second Edition*. London & New York: Routledge Taylor & Francis Group. pp. 246–249.

Olszewska, D. (2009). Teksty naukowe jako przedmiot badań tekstologicznych. In: Bilut- Homplewicz, Z. Czachura, W. & Smykała, M. (eds.). *Lingwistyka tekstu w Polsce i w Niemczech. Pojęcia, problemy, perspektywy*. Wrocław: Wrocławskie Wydawnictwo Oświatowe. pp. 163–175.

Olszewska, D. (2010). Czy język naukowy jest wyłącznie językiem "ratio"? In: Łopuszańska, G. & Wilma, D. (eds.). *Studia Germanica Gedanensia*. Vol. 22. pp. 169–175.

Owen, S. (2014). Teacher professional learning communities: Going beyond contrived collegiality toward challenging debate and collegial learning and professional growth. In: *Australian Journal of Adult Learning*. Vol. 54. No. 2. pp. 54–77.

Parysek, J.J. (2017). Metafory i neologizmy współczesnego języka nauk społecznych i ekonomicznych. In: *Ruch Ekonomiczny i Socjologiczny*. Vol. 79. No. 3. pp. 175–192.

Patrick, L.P. The Speech Community. In: J. K. Chambers, J.K., Trudgill, P. & Schilling, N. (eds.). (2004). *The Handbook of Language Variation and Change*. Hoboken: Wiley- Blackwell.

Peacock, M. (2012). High-frequency Collocations of Nouns in Research Articles across Eight Disciplines. In: *Ibérica*. Vol. 23. pp. 29–46.

Pearson, J. (1998). *Terms in Context*. Amsterdam: John Benjamins Publishing Co. Press.

Pelikan, K. & Roelcke, T. (2015). Is There a Project-specific Terminology? Considerations Focusing a Public Health Project. In: *Fachsprache*, Vol. 1–2. pp. 62–82.

Pérez- Llantada Aurìa, C. (2001) Designing New Genre Identities in Scientific and Technical Discourse: Cognitive, Social and Pedagogical Implications. In: *Journal of English Studies*. Vol. 3. pp. 251–263.

Pérez- Llantada Aurìa, C. (2003). Social Pragmatics in Technical Writing: A Corpus-based Analysis of Thematic Articles. In: *Ibérica*. Vol. 5. pp. 19–34.

Pethő, G. (2001). What is Polysemy? – A Survey of Current Research Results. In: Németh, E.T. & Bibok, K. *Pragmatics and the Flexibility of Word Meaning*. Amsterdam & New York: Elsevier Science. pp. 175–224.

Pęzik, P. (2013). Wybrane aspekty reprezentatywności małych i średnich korpusów. In: Chlebda, W. *Na tropach korpusów. W poszukiwaniu optymalnych zbiorów tekstów*. Opole: Wydawnictwo Uniwersytetu Opolskiego. pp. 17–30.

Picht, H. & Schmitz, K.D. (Hrsg.). (2001). *Terminologie und Wissensordnung. Ausgewählte Schriften aus dem Gesamtwerk von Eugen Wüster*. Wien: TermNet Publisher.

Pieterse, J.N. (1994). Globalization as Hybridization. In: *International Sociology*. Vol. 9. No. 2. pp. 161–184.

Piotrowski, T. & Grabowski, Ł. (2013). Interpretacja danych frekwencyjnych z korpusów językowych: opis pewnych problemów (na kilku przykładach z życia wziętych). In: Chlebda, W. (ed.). *Na tropach korpusów. W poszukiwaniu optymalnych zbiorów tekstów*. Opole: Wydawnictwo Uniwersytetu Opolskiego. pp. 58–71.

Pissolato, L. (2016). Communicative Perspective of Terminological Metaphors. In: *Nueva Revista del Pacifico*. No. 64. pp. 150–167.

Podlecki, M. (2017). Frazeologia jako tworzywo komunikacji między sportowcami. In: *Zeszyty Naukowe Uczelnianej Rady Doktorantów UKW*. Vol. 4.

Polackova, G. (2001). Synonymy of Medical Terminology from the Point of View of Comparative Linguistics. In: *Bratisl Lek Listy*. Vol. 102. No. 3. pp. 174–177.

Pop, A.M. & Sim, M.A. (2009). The Use of Acronyms and Initialisms in Business English. In: *Annals of Faculty of Economics*, University of Oradea, Faculty of Economics. Vol. 1. No. 1. pp. 557–562.

Postolea, S. (2014). The Phraseology of General Use ICT Texts and its Translation from English into Romanian – A Corpus-based Analysis. In: *Studii de ştiinţă şi cultură*. Vol. X. No. 2. pp. 231–242.

Pułaczewska, H. (2010). Metaphors, Particles, Terminology: from Objectivist to Cognitivist Approach in Physics and Linguistics. In: Witczak-Plisiecka, I. (ed.). *Pragmatic Perspectives on Language and Linguistics. Vol. II: Pragmatics of Semantically-Restricted Domains*. Newcastle upon Tyne: Cambridge Scholars Publishing.

Reinbothe, R. Geschichte des Deutschen als Wissenschaftssprache im 20. Jahrhundert. In: Eins, W., Glück, H., & Pretscher, S. (eds.). (2011). *Wissen schaffen – Wissen kommunizieren. Wissenschaftssprachen in Geschichte und Gegenwart*. Wiesbaden: Harrassowitz Verlag. pp. 49–66.

Rey, A. (1995). *Essays on Terminology*. Amsterdam & Philadephia: John Benjamins Publishing Company

Richter, B. (1995). The Role of Science in our Society. In: *Physics Today*. Vol. 48. No. 9.

Rincke, K. (2010). Alltagssprache, Fachsprache und ihre besonderen Bedeutungen für das Lernen (Everyday and special language and their role in science education). In: *Zeitschrift für Didaktik der Naturwissenschaften*. JG 16. pp. 235–260.

Roberts, S.M. & Pruitt, E.Z. (2003). *Schools as Professional Learning Communities. Collaborative Activities and Strategies for Professional Development*. Thousand Oaks: Corwin Press, Inc. A Sage Publications Company.

Roche, C. (2015). Ontological Definition. In: Kockaert, H.J. & Steurs, F. (eds.). *Handbook of Terminology. Volume I*. Amsterdam & Philadelphia: John Benjamins Publishing Company. pp. 128–152.

Rosch, E. (1978). Principles of categorization. In E. Rosch and B. B. Lloyd (eds.), *Cognition and Categorization*. Hillsdale, NJ: Erlbaum, 27–48.

Rowe, W. & Schelling, V. (1991). *Memory and Modernity: Popular Culture in Latin America*. London: Verso.

Rowland, F. (1999A). Scientists in Communication. In: Scanlon, E., Hill, R. & Junker, K. *Communicating Science: Professional Contexts*. London & New York: Routledge. pp. 55–60.

Rowland, F. (1999B). Methods and Motives for Publishing Original Work in Science. In: Scanlon, E., Hill, R. & Junker, K. *Communicating Science: Professional Contexts*. London & New York: Routledge. pp. 61–71.

Rus, D. (2014). Technical Communication as Strategic Communication. Characteristics of the English Technical Discourse. In: *Procedia Technology*. Vol. 12. pp. 654–658.

Sager, J. (1983). Terminology and the Technical Dictionary. In: *1st EURALEX International Congress Proceedings*, pp. 315–326.

Sager, J.C. (1990). *A Practical Course in Terminology Processing*. Amsterdam & Philadelphia: John Benjamins Publishing Company.

Sager, J.C., Dungworth, D. & McDonald, P.F. (1980). *English Special Languages, Principles and Practices in Science and Technology*. Amsterdam & Philadephia: John Benjamins Publishing Company.

Sanchez-Stockhammer, C. (2012). Hybridization in Language. In: Stockhammer, P.W. (ed.). *Conceptualizing Cultural Hybridization. A Transdisciplinary Approach*. Heidelberg: Springer.

Santos, C. & Costa, R. (2015). Domain Specificity. Semasiological and Onomasiological Knowledge Representation. In: Kockaert, H.J. & Steurs, F. (eds.). *Handbook of Terminology. Volume I*. Amsterdam & Philadelphia: John Benjamins Publishing Company.

Saussure, F. D. (1959). *Course in General Linguistics*. New York: Philosophical Library.

Schiffrin, D., Tannen, D. & Hamilton, H.E. (eds.). (2001). *The Handbook of Discourse Analysis*. Malden & Oxford: Blackwell Publishers, Inc.

Schmidt-Rohr, G. (1933). *Mutter Sprache – Vom Amt der Sprache bei der Volkwerdung*. Jena: Eugen Diedrichs Verlag

Selinker, L. (1972). *Interlanguage*. In: *IRAL; International Review of Applied Linguistics in Language Teaching*. Vol. 10: 3. pp. 209–231.

Servage, L. (2009). Who is the „Professional" in a Professional Learning Community? An Exploration of Teacher Professionalism in Collaborative Professional Development Settings. In: *Canadian Journal of Education*. Vol. 32. No. 1. pp. 149–171.

Seweryn, A. (2010). Dominacja języka angielskiego we współczesnej komunikacji naukowej – bariera czy usprawnienie cyrkulacji naukowej. In: Pietruch-Reizes, D., Babik, W. & Frączek, R. (eds.). *Zarządzanie informacją w nauce*. Katowice: Wydawnictwo Uniwersytetu Śląskiego. pp. 75–93.

Silva, E., Orenha-Ottaiano, A. & Babini, M. (2017). Identification of the most common phraseological units in the English language in academic texts: Contributions coming from corpora. *Acta Scientiarum. Language and Culture*. 39. 345. 10.4025/actascilangcult.v39i4.31811.

Simavi, S., Tangri, K., & Grigorov, M. (eds.). (2013). *Art of Knowledge Exchange. A Primer for Government Officials and Development Practitioners*. Washington, DC: The World Bank Institute. Available at: https://openknowledge.worldbank.org/handle/10986/16506 License: CC BY- NC-ND 3.0 IGO.

Sinclair, J. (1991). *Corpus, Concordance, Collocation*.Oxford: OUP.

Sinclair, J. (2004). *Trust the Text. Language, Corpus and Discourse*. London & New York: Routledge.

Siqueira, M., Flávia Souto de Oliveira, A., Dienstbach Hubert, D., Faé de Almeida, G. & Moreira Brangel, L. (2009). Metaphor Identification in a Terminological Dictionary. In: Ibérica. Vol. 17. pp. 157–174.

Sitkowski, K. (2008). Kompresja w tekstach specjalistycznych. In: Łukasik, M. (ed.). *Debiuty Naukowe II. Terminologia – Translatoryka – Terminografia*. Warszawa: Katedra Języków Specjalistycznych, Wydział Lingwistyki Stosowanej i Filologii Wschodniosłowiańskich UW. pp. 26–30.

Snyder, W.M., Wenger, E. & McDermott, R. (2014). *Seven Principles for Cultivating Communities of Practice*. Retrieved from: https://www.researchgate.net/publication/265678077_Seven_Principles_for_Cul tivating_Communities_of_Practice, 10.02.2018

Steiner, G. (1975). *After Babel: Aspects of Language and Translation*. Oxford: OUP

Stevens, J.P. (1992). *Applied Multivariate Statistics for the Social Sciences* (2nd edition). Hillsdale, NJ: Erlbaum.

Stockhammer, P.W. (ed.). (2012). *Conceptualizing Cultural Hybridization. A Transdisciplinary Approach*. Heidelberg: Springer.

Strehlow, R.A. (1983). Terminology and the Well-Formed Definition. In: Interrante, C.G. & Heymann, F.J. (eds.). *Standardization of Technical Terminology: Principles and Practices*. Toronto: ASTM STP 806. pp. 15–25.

Suchodolski, B. (1979). Perspektywy popularyzacji nauki. In: Okoń, W. (ed.). *Teoria i praktyka upowszechniania wiedzy*. Warszawa: Wiedza Powszechna.

Suonuuti, H. (2001). *Nordterm 8. Guide to Terminology*. Helsinki: Tekniikan Sanastokeskus.

Swales, J. (1988). Discourse Communities, Genres and English as an International Language. In: *World Englishes*. Vol. 7. No. 2 pp. 211–220

Swales, J.M. (1990). *Genre Analysis. English in academic and research settings*. Cambridge: CUP

Swales, J.M. (1997). English as *Tyrannosaurus Rex*. In: *World Englishes*. Vol. 16. No. 3. pp. 373–382.

Tabakowska, E. (2015). Status metafory w języku naukowym. Oryginał i przekład. In: Duszak, A. Jopek-Bosiacka, A. & Kowalski, G. (eds.). *Tekst naukowy i jego przekład*. Kraków: Universitas. pp. 37–51.

Taylor J. R. (1995). *Linguistic Categorization: Prototypes in Linguistic Theory*. Oxford: Oxford University Press.

Tehan, T.M. (2009). *SIL Electronic Book Reviews 2009-007. Communicating science: The scientific article from the 17th century to the present by Alan G. Gross, Joseph E. Harmon, and Michael Reidy*. pp. 1–4.

Temmerman, R. (1997). Questioning the Univocity Ideal. The Difference Between the Socio- cognitive Terminology and traditional Terminology. In: In: *Hermes, Journal of Linguistics*. Vol. 18. pp. 51–90.

Temmerman, R. (2000). *Towards New Ways of Terminology Description. The Sociocognitive Approach*. Amsterdam & Philadelphia: John Benjamins Publishing Company.

ten Hacken, P. (2008). Prototypes and Discreteness in Terminology. In: *Proceedings of EURALEX 2008*. pp. 979–987.

Thelen, M. (2015). The Interaction between Terminology and Translation. Or Where Terminology and Translation Meet. *trans-kom*. Vol. 8. pp. 347–381.

Thompson Klein, J. (2004). Interdisciplinarity and Complexity: An Evolving Relationship. In: *E:CO Special Double Issue*. Vol. 6. Nos. 1–2, pp. 2–10.

Tincheva, N. (2017). Prototypes in Text-Types: Political Discourse. In *International Journal of Language and Linguistics*. Vol. 4. No. 1. pp. 23–29.

Todorović, L. (2003). Original (scientific) Paper – The IMRAD Layout. In: *Archive of Oncology*, Vol. 11. No. 3, pp. 203–5.

Toledo-Alvaro, J.I., Guzmán-Arenas, A. & Martínez-Luna, G.L. (2012). Automatic Building of an Ontology from a Corpus of Text Documents Using Data Mining Tools. In: *Journal of Applied Research and Technology*. pp. 398–404.

Trimble. L. (1985). *English for Science and Technology: A Discourse Approach*. Cambridge: Cambridge University Press.

Trosborg, A. (ed.). (1997). *Text Typology and Translation*. Amsterdam: John Benjamins Publishing Company.

Trosborg, A. (ed.). (2000). *Analysing Professional Genres*. Amsterdam: John Benjamins Publishing Company.

Trosborg, A. Text Typology: Register, Genre and Text Type. In: Trosborg, A. (ed.). (1997). *Text Typology and Translation*. Amsterdam: John Benjamins Publishing Company Utah Press.

Van Leeuwen, T. (2005). *Introducing Social Semiotics*. London: Routledge.

Van Riper III, C., Powell, R.B., Machlis, G., Van Wagtendonk, J.W., Van Riper, C.J., Von Ruschkowski, E., Schwarzbach, S.E. & Galipeau, R.E. (2012). Using Integrated Research and Interdisciplinary Science: Potential Benefits and Challenges to Managers of Parks and Protected Areas. In: *The George Wright Forum*. Vol. 29. No. 2. pp. 216–226.

Varantola, K. (1987). Popularization Strategies and Text Functional Shifts in Scientific/Technical Writing. In: *Unesco Alsed-LSP Newsletter*. Vol. 10. No. 2 (25). pp. 33–52.

Verdaguer, I. & González, E. (2016). A lexical database of collocations in scientific English: preliminary considerations. In: *Euralex 2004 Proceedings*. pp. 929–934

Vincente, A. & Falkum, I.L. (2017). Polysemy. In: *Oxford Research Encyclopedia of Linguistics*. Retrieved from: http://linguistics.oxfordre.com/, 20.01.2020.

Waliński, J. (2005). Korpusy wielojęzyczne – równoległe i porównywalne. In: Lewandowska- Tomaszczyk, B. (ed.). *Podstawy językoznawstwa korpusowego*. Łódź: Wydawnictwo Uniwersytetu Łódzkiego. pp. 42–60.

Wardhaugh, R. (2006). *An Introduction to Sociolinguistics. Fifth Edition*. Oxford: Blackwell Publishing

Wenger, E. (1998). *Communities of Practice Learning, Meaning and Identity*. New York: CUP.

Wenger, E., McDermott, R. & Snyder, W. (2002). *Cultivating communities of practice: a guide to managing knowledge.Boston, MA*, Harvard Business School Press.

Wenger-Trayner, E. & Wenger-Trayner, B. (2015). *Communities of practice. A brief introduction*. Retrieved from: http://wenger-trayner.com/wp- content/uploads/2015/04/07-Brief-introduction-to-communities-of-practice.pdf, 02.02.2018

Whorf, B.L. (1939). The Relation of Habitual Thought and Behaviour to Language. In: Carroll, J.B. (ed.). (1956). *Language, Thought, and Reality*. Cambridge, MA: MIT Press, pp. 134–159.

Wilkoń, A. (2000). *Typologia odmian językowych współczesnej polszczyzny*. Katowice: Wydawnictwo Uniwersytetu Śląskiego.

Williams, G. (2002). "In search of representativity in specialised corpora: categorisation through collocation". *International Journal of Corpus Linguistics* 7: 43–64.

Witalisz A. (2016) *Przewodnik po anglicyzmach w języku polskim*. Kraków.

Witczak-Plisiecka, I. (ed.). (2010). *Pragmatic Perspectives on Language and Linguistics. Vol. II: Pragmatics of Semantically-Restricted Domains*. Newcastle upon Tyne: Cambridge Scholars Publishing.

Wu, J. (2011). The Writing of Research Papers: IMRAD and Beyond. In: *Landscape Ecology*, Vol. 26. No. 10, pp. 1345–1349

Wüster, E. (1953). Die terminologische Sprachbehandlung. In: Picht, H. & Schmitz, K.D. (Hrsg.). (2001). *Terminologie und Wissensordnung. Ausgewählte Schriften aus dem Gesamtwerk von Eugen Wüster.*Wien: TermNet Publisher. pp. 11–20.

Wüster, E. (1955). Standardization of Technical Terms – Problems and Progress. In: *Sprachforum*. Vol. 1. No. 1.

Wyroba, E. Tajniki sukcesu w upowszechnianiu wiedzy. In: Grucza, F. & Wiśniewski, W. (eds.). (2005). *Teoria i praktyka upowszechniania nauki wczoraj i jutro*. Warszawa: Polska Akademia Nauk, RadaUpowszechniania Nauki przy Prezydium PAN, pp. 211–216.

Wytrębowicz, J. (2009). O poprawności językowej publikacji naukowo-technicznych. In: *Zagadnienia Naukoznawstwa*. Vol. 1. No. 179.

Zauberga, I. (2005). Handling terminology in translation. In K. Károly, & Á. Fóris (Eds.). *New trends in translation studies: in honour of Kinga Klaudy*. pp. 107–116. Budapest: Akadémiai Kiadó.

Zdunkiewicz-Jedynak, D. (2008). *Wykłady ze stylistyki*. Warszawa: Wydawnictwo Naukowe PWN.

Zipf, G.K. (1949). *Human Behavior and the Principle of Least Effort. An Introduction to Human Ecology*. Cambridge, MA: Addison-Wesley Press, Inc.

Zolotukhin, D. (2016). Polysemy in Linguistic Terminological Systems Based on the Analysis of French Linguistic Terms. In: *Journal of Language and Education*. Vol. 2. No. 2. pp. 68–74

Źrałka, E. (2007). Teaching Specialised Translation Through Official Documents. In: *The Journal of Specialised Translation*. Vol. 7. pp. 74–91.

Internet resources:

http://www.electropedia.org/

http://www.nkjp.uni.lodz.pl

https://auth.sketchengine.eu

https://old.sketchengine.co.uk

https://sj.umg.edu.pl/

https://www.desy.de/

https://www.dmcs.pl/

https://www.english-corpora.org/bnc/

https://www.iter.org/

https://www.mixdes.org/

Appendix 1

Keyword term candidates extracted by Sketch Engine Term Extractor

No	English Singleword Terms		Score	frequency	F	RefF
1	IEEE	W	704.24	991.58	988	46
2	CMOS	W	444.37	763.61	761	25,088
3	analog	W	377.71	440.59	439	19
4	modeling	W	314.26	341.23	340	10
5	transistors	W	304.37	1325.79	730	28,720
6	LV (low voltage)	W	273.97	307.11	306	14
7	circuit	W	207.69	2438.82	1,348	114,698
8	LNA	W	206.59	281.00	236	1,815
9	readout	W	205.30	260.94	260	10,934
10	voltage	W	204.20	2027.33	1,865	243,088
11	FPGA	W	201.73	205.74	200	13,322
12	VDD	W	201.16	203.70	203	2
13	impedance	W	199.93	294.96	250	31,803
14	simulation	W	197.20	1384.00	1,021	192,929
15	sensor	W	194.99	837.03	553	208
16	SOI	W	192.85	198.72	198	15,293
17	RF (radio frequency)	W	192.73	351.27	350	93
18	HV (high voltage)	W	188.33	195.71	195	11,418
19	microelectronics	W	175.11	409.48	408	5,342
20	MOS	W	173.64	229.83	229	26,044
21	MOSFET	W	169.94	263.95	203	4,832
22	GHz	W	169.94	183.66	183	10
23	inductor	W	160.14	203.74	193	8,831
24	optimization	W	154.96	224.81	218	47
25	amplifier	W	152.07	738.67	601	71,457
26	IC (integrated circuit)	W	150.05	261.95	243	71
27	capacitances	W	147.92	443.60	112	518
28	nm	W	147.11	401.45	400	195
29	dB	W	139.44	343.24	342	165
30	technology	W	134.48	1321.78	133	512
31	oscillator	W	134.24	264.96	228	20,181

No	English Singleword Terms		Score	frequency	F	RefF
32	ADC (converter)	W	133.28	199.72	185	17,604
33	inverter	W	124.41	201.73	134	10
34	CI (capacitance)	W	123.18	61.93	621	61,405
35	ω (resistance. impedance)	W	122.44	130.47	121	7,354
36	nMOS	W	119.37	119.43	119	426
37	diode	W	119.29	325.18	230	32,726
38	pMOS	W	118.33	119.43	119	909
39	VESFET	W	117.96	103.37	100	4
40	microcontroller	W	117.76	144.52	132	19,631
41	pixel	W	117.06	415.50	343	219
42	doping	W	114.52	171.62	171	57
43	MTCA	W	112.40	111.40	111	207
44	behavior	W	111.95	193.70	188	78
45	VLSI	W	111.33	107.39	106	2,368
46	DAC	W	110.80	141.51	132	23
47	capacitor	W	110.11	358.30	227	36,267
48	TCAD	W	105.60	96.35	96	204

No	English Multiword Terms		Score	Frequency	F	RefF
1	power consumption	W	266.15	356.29	335	30
2	threshold voltage	W	153.55	176.64	152	0
3	supply voltage	W	116.75	193.70	165	48
4	block diagram	W	84.79	109.40	103	26
5	thermal resistance	W	84.63	92.33	84	1
6	delay line	W	80.62	115.42	95	22
7	power dissipation	W	79.91	92.33	85	9
8	low power	W	78.35	160.58	109	46
9	current mirror	W	77.28	112.41	76	0
10	cut-off frequency	W	68.47	76.28	69	3
11	current source	W	68.47	84.30	69	3
12	voltage gain	W	65.20	72.24	68	7
13	output signal	W	60.47	86.31	71	22
14	output voltage	W	60.27	89.32	82	43
15	power supply	W	59.27	176.64	150	175
16	input signal	W	58.54	106.40	76	36
17	thermal impedance	W	53.19	60.22	52	0

No	English Multiword Terms		Score	Frequency	F	RefF
18	transient thermal impedance	W	52.19	59.21	51	0
19	readout circuit	W	51.18	60.22	50	0
20	input voltage	W	50.68	64.23	54	10
21	signal processing	W	49.27	137.50	59	25
22	low noise	W	46.94	70.25	52	15
23	clock frequency	W	46.43	58.21	51	14
24	integrated circuit	W	45.43	174.63	64	49
25	clock signal	W	44.98	72.26	47	8
26	circuit simulation	W	43.15	63.23	42	0
27	input impedance	W	41.58	59.21	57	45
28	reference voltage	W	41.44	44.46	41	2
29	noise figure	W	41.15	58.21	40	0
30	gate oxide	W	41.15	47.17	40	0
31	thermal time (constant)	W	41.15	41.15	40	0
32	operating frequency	W	39.03	51.19	41	9
33	design flow	W	38.83	48.17	38	1
34	dynamic power	W	38.70	55.20	41	10
35	channel region	W	38.13	37.13	37	0
36	control voltage	W	38.12	61.22	39	6
37	equivalent circuit	W	37.20	51.19	40	12
38	internal temperature	W	36.84	39.14	37	4
39	low voltage	W	36.70	61.22	45	29
40	input stage	W	36.19	40.15	36	3
41	thermal model	W	36.13	58.21	35	0
42	current consumption	W	35.90	44.16	44	29
43	voltage drop	W	34.34	48.17	39	19
44	thermal noise	W	33.85	34.12	33	1
45	mesurement system	W	33.73	63.23	35	8
46	current mode	W	33.64	44.16	34	5
47	doping concentration	W	33.12	48.17	32	0
48	image processing	W	33.07	65.24	51	65
49	transfer function	W	32.85	51.19	46	49
50	hardware implementation	W	32.56	41.15	32	2
51	oxide thickness	W	32.11	37.13	31	0
52	frame grabber	W	31.58	39.14	31	2
53	v supply	W	31.58	32.12	31	2
54	gate voltage	W	31.33	44.16	33	10

No	English Multiword Terms		Score	Frequency	F	RefF
55	operating point	W	31.18	44.16	32	7
56	channel length	W	31.11	37.13	30	0
57	transient noise (pulse analysis)	W	31.11	30.11	30	0
58	sampling frequency	W	31.03	33.12	31	4
59	recording channel	W	30.86	52.19	30	1
60	image aquisition	W	30.76	41.15	31	5
61	ambient temperature	W	30.46	38.14	35	21
62	residual stress	W	30.11	31.11	29	0
63	chip temperature	W	30.11	31.11	29	0
64	sampling rate	W	29.80	41.14	30	5
65	maximum power	W	29.19	40.15	33	19
66	input charge	W	29.10	37.13	28	0
67	dynamic range	W	28.52	45.16	36	34
68	common mode	W	28.35	36.13	29	7
69	drain current	W	28.10	104.38	27	0
70	pixel detector	W	28.10	54.20	27	0
71	parameter extraction	W	28.10	34.12	27	0
72	filter order	W	28.10	28.10	27	0

Appendix 2

The list of lexical bundles generated by the Sketch Engine

No	lexical bundle	frequency
1	is shown in Fig.	116
2	is presented in Fig.	83
3	it is possible to	81
4	as shown in Fig.	72
5	On the other hand	70
6	as a function of	66
7	in the case of	64
8	is based on the	60
9	with the use of	59
10	on the basis of	53
11	the value of the	47
12	the use of the	47
13	the case of the	46
14	as well as the	45
15	with respect to the	42
16	In the case of	41
17	can be used to	40
18	at the same time	39
19	are shown in Fig.	33
20	the influence of the	32
21	it is necessary to	32
22	block diagram of the	32
23	presented in this paper	31
24	is organized as follows	31
25	is based on a	31
26	can be used for	31
27	the performance of the	30
28	paper is organized as	30
29	in the form of	30
30	it can be seen	29
31	work was supported by	28
32	the basis of the	27

No	lexical bundle	frequency
33	of the collector current	27
34	can be used in	27
35	can be seen in	27
36	This work was supported	27
37	one of the most	26
38	is depicted in Fig.	26
39	the values of the	25
40	by means of the	25
41	the size of the	24
42	simulation results of the	24
43	is proportional to the	24
44	can be found in	24
45	Block diagram of the	24
46	was supported by the	23
47	to the fact that	23
48	is the number of	23
49	in the range of	23
50	can be seen that	23
51	a function of the	23
52	One of the most	23
53	the fact that the	22
54	should be noted that	22
55	results are presented in	22
56	it was decided to	22
57	is shown in figure	22
58	is due to the	22
59	be taken into account	22
60	a wide range of	22
61	is shown in Figure	21
62	in the value of	21
63	It can be seen	21
64	As it can be	21
65	the rest of the	20
66	the accuracy of the	20
67	in order to obtain	20
68	be used in the	20
69	are presented in Table	20

No	lexical bundle	frequency
70	This paper presents a	20
71	In this paper we	20
72	the gain of the	19
73	a large number of	19
74	As a result of	19
75	the end of the	18
76	on the other hand	18
77	in the field of	18
78	It is based on	18
79	to take into account	17
80	to be used in	17
81	the results of the	17
82	the center of the	17
83	of the number of	17
84	of the most important	17
85	is given by the	17
86	is equal to the	17
87	It should be noted	17
88	which can be used	16
89	the operation of the	16
90	the design of the	16
91	is used in the	16
92	is shown in fig.	16
93	is controlled by the	16
94	circuit shown in Fig.	16
95	can be divided into	16
96	are presented in Fig.	16
97	It is possible to	16
98	As it was mentioned	16
99	would like to thank	15
100	the calculation of the	15
101	taking into account the	15
102	is illustrated in Fig.	15
103	is connected to the	15
104	in this paper is	15
105	in the order of	15
106	in such a way	15

No	lexical bundle	frequency
107	for different values of	15
108	can be considered as	15
109	at the level of	15
110	at the end of	15
111	as a result of	15
112	The paper is organized	15
113	As shown in Fig.	15
114	As can be seen	15
115	the total number of	14
116	described in this paper	14
117	can be expressed as	14
118	and the number of	14
119	In this case the	14
120	the length of the	13
121	the difference between the	13
122	the design of a	13
123	results are shown in	13
124	is worth noting that	13
125	is presented in the	13
126	is determined by the	13
127	is defined by the	13
128	is a part of	13
129	be seen that the	13
130	be considered as a	13
131	authors would like to	13
132	and as a result	13
133	This is due to	13
134	It is worth noting	13
135	In this paper the	13
136	As depicted in Fig.	13
137	the shape of the	12
138	the method of images	12
139	the impact of the	12
140	the development of the	12
141	that it is possible	12
142	presented in the paper	12
143	presented in Table I.	12

No	lexical bundle	frequency
144	of this paper is	12
145	is related to the	12
146	is presented in Figure	12
147	in order to minimize	12
148	due to the fact	12
149	can not be used	12
150	can be described by	12
151	are presented in the	12
152	an increase in the	12
153	The main advantage of	12
154	The block diagram of	12
155	The authors would like	12
156	The architecture of the	12
157	It can be observed	12
158	the use of a	11
159	the evaluation of the	11
160	the description of the	11
161	the behavior of the	11
162	the amplitude of the	11
163	such a way that	11
164	on the performance of	11
165	is performed in the	11
166	is not suitable for	11
167	is defined as the	11
168	is a function of	11
169	are connected to the	11
170	an increase of the	11
171	In this work we	11
172	the structure of the	10
173	the properties of the	10
174	the parameters of the	10
175	the measurement of the	10
176	presented in the Fig.	10
177	part of the system	10
178	paper presents the design	10
179	on the number of	10
180	of the proposed method	10

No	lexical bundle	frequency
181	of the order of	10
182	is the same as	10
183	is the most important	10
184	is applied to the	10
185	in the previous section	10
186	in the presence of	10
187	in terms of the	10
188	in relation to the	10
189	in order to provide	10
190	in a way that	10
191	in Table I. The	10
192	can be approximated by	10
193	can be achieved by	10
194	based on the moduli	10
195	as a way of	10
196	as a part of	10
197	are based on the	10
198	The value of the	10
199	The main goal of	10
200	In order to obtain	10
201	In order to calculate	10
202	In case of the	10
203	At the same time	10

ŁÓDŹ STUDIES IN LANGUAGE

Vol. 1 Barbara Lewandowska-Tomaszczyk / Patrick James Melia (eds.): PALC'99: Practical Applications in Language Corpora. Papers from the International Conference at the University of Łódź, 15-18 April 1999. 2000.

Vol. 2 Lou Burnard / Tony McEnery (eds.): Rethinking Language Pedagogy from a Corpus Perspective. Papers from the Third International Conference on Teaching and Language Corpora. 2000.

Vol. 3 Barbara Lewandowska-Tomaszczyk / John Osborne / Frits Schulte: Foreign Language Teaching and Information and Communication Technology. 2001.

Vol. 4 Piotr Cap: Explorations in Political Discourse. Methodological and Critical Perspectives. 2002.

Vol. 5 Ewa Waniek-Klimczak / Patrick James Melia (eds.): Accents and Speech in Teaching English Phonetics and Phonology. EFL perspective. 2002.

Vol. 6 Barbara Lewandowska-Tomaszczyk / Kamila Turewicz (eds.): Cognitive Linguistics Today. 2002.

Vol. 7 Barbara Lewandowska-Tomaszczyk (ed.): PALC 2001: Practical Applications in Language Corpora. 2003.

Vol. 8 Corpus Linguistics by the Lune. A Festschrift for Geoffrey Leech. Edited by Andrew Wilson, Paul Rayson and Tony McEnery. 2003.

Vol. 9 Barbara Lewandowska-Tomaszczyk (ed.): Practical Applications in Language and Computers. PALC 2003. 2004.

Vol. 10 Imagery in Language. Festschrift in Honour of Professor Ronald W. Langacker. Edited by Barbara Lewandowska-Tomaszczyk and Alina Kwiatkowska. 2004.

Vol. 11 Seana Coulson / Barbara Lewandowska-Tomaszczyk (eds.): The Literal and Nonliteral in Language and Thought. 2005.

Vol. 12 Piotr Cap (ed.): Pragmatics Today. 2005.

Vol. 13 Jacek Waliński / Krzysztof Kredens / Stanisław Goźdź-Roszkowski (eds.): Corpora and ICT in Language Studies. PALC 2005. 2007.

Vol. 14 Krzysztof Kosecki (ed.): Perspectives on Metonymy. Proceedings of the International Conference "Perspectives on Metonymy", held in Łódź, Poland, May 6-7, 2005. 2007.

Vol. 15 Barbara Lewandowska-Tomaszczyk / Tomasz Płudowski / Dolores Valencia Tanno (eds.): The Media and International Communication. 2007.

Vol. 16 Krzysztof Kredens / Stanisław Goźdź-Roszkowski (eds.): Language and the Law: International Outlooks. 2007.

Vol. 17 Barbara Lewandowska-Tomaszczyk (ed.): Corpus Linguistics, Computer Tools, and Applications – State of the Art. PALC 2007. 2008.

Vol. 18 Barbara Lewandowska-Tomaszczyk / Katarzyna Dziwirek (eds.): Studies in Cognitive Corpus Linguistics. 2009.

Vol. 19 Barbara Lewandowska-Tomaszczyk / Marcel Thelen (eds.): Meaning in Translation. 2010.

Vol. 20 Łukasz Bogucki / Krzysztof Kredens (eds.): Perspectives on Audiovisual Translation. 2010.

Vol. 21 Piotr Stalmaszczyk (ed.): Turning Points in the Philosophy of Language and Linguistics. 2011.

Vol. 22 Stanisław Goźdź-Roszkowski: Patterns of Linguistic Variation in American Legal English. A Corpus-Based Study. 2011.

Vol. 23 Kamila Ciepiela (ed.): Identity through a Language Lens. 2011.

Vol. 24 Stanisław Goźdź-Roszkowski (ed.): Explorations across Languages and Corpora. PALC 2009. 2011.

Vol. 25 Krzysztof Kosecki / Janusz Badio (eds.): Cognitive Processes in Language. 2012.

Vol. 26 Alina Kwiatkowska (ed.): Texts and Minds. Papers in Cognitive Poetics and Rhetoric. 2012.

Vol. 27 Paul A. Wilson (ed.): Dynamicity in Emotion Concepts. 2012.

Vol. 28 Piotr Pęzik (ed.): Corpus Data across Languages and Disciplines. 2012.

Vol. 29 Mikołaj Deckert: Meaning in Subtitling. Toward a Contrastive Cognitive Semantic Model. 2013.

Vol. 30 Łukasz Bogucki: Areas and Methods of Audiovisual Translation Research. 3rd Revised Edition. 2019.

Vol. 31 Janusz Badio / Kamila Ciepiela (eds.): Language, Action, Interaction. 2013.

Vol. 32 Barbara Lewandowska-Tomaszczyk / Krzysztof Kosecki (eds.): Time and Temporality in Language and Human Experience. 2014.

Vol. 33 Iwona Witczak-Plisiecka (ed.): Cognitive and Pragmatic Aspects of Speech Actions. 2014.

Vol. 34 Małgorzata Anna Kamińska: A History of the *Concise Oxford Dictionary*. 2014.

Vol. 35 Łukasz Bogucki / Mikołaj Deckert (eds.): Accessing Audiovisual Translation. 2015.

Vol. 36 Joanna Jabłońska-Hood: A Conceptual Blending Theory of Humour. Selected British Comedy Productions in Focus. 2015.

Vol. 37 Krzysztof Kosecki / Janusz Badio (eds.): Empirical Methods in Language Studies. 2015.

Vol. 38 Katarzyna Stadnik: Chaucer's Choices. Through the looking-glass of medieval imagery. 2015.

Vol. 39 Paulina Pietrzak / Mikołaj Deckert (eds.): Constructing Translation Competence. 2015.

Vol. 40 Małgorzata Fabiszak / Karolina Krawczak / Katarzyna Rokoszewska (eds.): Categorization in Discourse and Grammar. 2016.

Vol. 41 Marcel Thelen / Gys-Walt van Egdom / Dirk Verbeeck / Łukasz Bogucki / Barbara Lewandowska-Tomaszczyk (eds.): Translation and Meaning. New Series, Vol. 1. 2016.

Vol. 42 Łukasz Bogucki / Barbara Lewandowska-Tomaszczyk / Marcel Thelen (eds.): Translation and Meaning. New Series, Vol. 2, Pt. 1. 2016.

Vol. 43 Łukasz Bogucki / Barbara Lewandowska-Tomaszczyk / Marcel Thelen (eds.): Translation and Meaning. New Series, Vol. 2, Pt. 2. 2016.

Vol. 44 Przemysław Łozowski / Katarzyna Stadnik (eds.): Visions and Revisions. Studies in Theoretical and Applied Linguistics. 2016.

Vol. 45 Marek Kuźniak / Bożena Rozwadowska / Michał Szawerna (eds.): From Motion to Emotion. Aspects of Physical and Cultural Embodiment in Language. 2016.

Vol. 46 Anna Rędzioch-Korkuz: Opera Surtitling as a Special Case of Audiovisual Translation. Towards a Semiotic and Translation Based Framework for Opera Surtitling. 2016.

Vol. 47 Mateusz Sajna: Video Game Translation and Cognitive Semantics. 2016.

Vol. 48 Kamila Ciepiela (ed.): Identity in Communicative Contexts. 2016.

Vol. 49 Mikołaj Nkollo: The Entrenchment of the 'unus alterum' Pattern. Four Essays on Latin and Old Romance Reciprocal Constructions. 2016.

Vol. 50 Paweł Rydzewski: Backness Distinction in Phonology. A Polish Perspective on the Phonemic Status of *y*. 2016.

Vol. 51 Piotr Pęzik / Jacek Tadeusz Waliński (eds.): Language, Corpora and Cognition. 2017.

Vol. 52 Janusz Badio (ed.): Events and Narratives in Language. 2016.

Vol. 53 Mikołaj Deckert (ed.): Audiovisual Translation - Research and Use. 2017. 2nd Expanded Edition 2019.

Vol. 54 Michał Szawerna: Metaphoricity of Conventionalized Diegetic Images in Comics. A Study in Multimodal Cognitive Linguistics. 2017.

Vol. 55 Artur Gałkowski / Monika Kopytowska (eds.): Current Perspectives in Semiotics. Signs, Signification, and Communication. 2018.

Vol. 56 Artur Gałkowski / Monika Kopytowska (eds.): Current Perspectives in Semiotics. Text, Genres, and Representations. 2018.

Vol. 57 Łukasz Bogucki / Piotr Cap (eds.): Exploration in Language and Linguistics. For Professor Piotr Stalmaszczyk on the Occasion of His 60th Birthday. 2018.

Vol. 58 Michał Kornacki: Computer-assisted Translation (CAT) Tools in the Translator Training Process. 2018.

Vol. 59 Marcin Walczyński / Piotr Czajka / Michał Szawerna (eds.): On the Verge between Language and Translation. 2018.

Vol. 60 Łukasz Bogucki / Paulina Pietrzak / Michał Kornacki (eds.): Understanding Translator Education. 2018.

Vol. 61 Marcin Walczyński: Psycho-Affective Factors in Consecutive Interpreting. 2019.

Vol. 62 Kamila Ciepiela (ed.): Language, Identity and Community. 2019.

Vol. 63 Olga Łabendowicz: Audiovisual Translation in Poland. Changing Audiences. 2019.

Vol. 64 Enrique Bernárdez / Joanna Jabłońska-Hood / Katarzyna Stadnik (eds.): Cognition in context. New insights into language, culture and the mind. 2019.

Vol. 65 Montse Corrius / Eva Espasa / Patrick Zabalbeascoa (eds.): Translating Audiovisuals in a Kaleidoscope of Languages. 2019.

Vol. 66 Barbara Lewandowska-Tomaszczyk / Valeria Monello / Marco Venuti (eds.): Language, Heart, and Mind. Studies at the intersection of emotion and cogni-tion. 2020.

Vol. 67 Marta Chodkiewicz: Understanding the Development of Translation Competence. 2020.

Vol. 68 Urszula Paradowska: Developing Information Competence in Translator-Training. 2021.

Vol. 69 Luca Valleriani: Upper-class English in Natural and Audiovisual Dialogue. 2021.

Vol. 70 Michał Kornacki and Gary Massey (eds.): Contextuality in Translation and Interpreting. Selected Papers from the Łódź-ZHAW Duo Colloquium on Translation and Meaning 2020–2021. 2022.

Vol. 71 Monika Kopytowska / Artur Gałkowski / Massimo Leone (eds.): Thought-Sign-Symbol. Cross-Cultural Representations of Religion. 2022.

Vol. 72 Bartosz Pietrzak: The Concept of Honor in the Language of Early Arabic Poetry. A Cultural Linguistic Study. 2022.

Vol. 73 Aleksandra Beata Makowska: Terminology and Phraseology in Research Papers in the Domains of New Technologies. 2024.

www.peterlang.com

www.ingramcontent.com/pod-product-compliance
Ingram Content Group UK Ltd.
Pitfield, Milton Keynes, MK11 3LW, UK
UKHW041823031026
15587UKWH00002B/522

9 783631 87320